W9-AIA-126

FIRE WITHIN

THOMAS DUBAY, S.M.

FIRE WITHIN

St. Teresa of Avila,
St. John of the Cross,
and the Gospel—on Prayer

IGNATIUS PRESS   SAN FRANCISCO

Cover art by Gary Hoff
Cover by Roxanne Mei Lum

With ecclesiastical approval
©1989 Ignatius Press, San Francisco
ISBN 0-89870-263-1
Library of Congress catalogue number 89-83653
Printed in the United States of America

CONTENTS

ACKNOWLEDGMENTS

I wish to acknowledge gratefully the use of a number of editions of the primary sources, that is, the writings of the two saints and the contemporary witnesses to their lives. For the latter I am indebted to the Carmel of Flemington, New Jersey, for excerpts taken from their private printing of the *Depositions of the Processes of St. Teresa of Jesus,* translated by Elvira Sarmiento and a Carmelite of Grand Rapids, Michigan, published by the Carmel of Flemington in 1969. For most of St. Teresa's works, major and minor, I have used the translations of E. Allison Peers, some published by one firm, others by another. For *The Way of Perfection* and the *Interior Castle* I have cited from the Image edition of Doubleday and Company (Garden City, New York, 1964 and 1961, respectively). For her *Book of Foundations* and almost all of her minor works (*Constitutions, Visitation, Maxims, Answer to a Spiritual Challenge, Judgment, Thoughts and Maxims*) use has been made of volume 3 of *The New Ark Library* (London and New York: Sheed and Ward, 1963). References to the saint's letters come from *The Letters of St. Teresa of Jesus,* two volumes translated and edited by E. Allison Peers (London: Sheed and Ward, 1951). Her autobiography, *The Life, Spiritual Testimonies* and *Soliloquies* are from *The Collected Works of St. Teresa,* volume 1, translated by Kieran Kavanaugh and Otilio Rodriguez (copyright 1976 by Washington Province of Discalced Carmelites. ICS Publications, 2131 Lincoln Road NE, Washington, D.C. 20002). All citations from St. John of the Cross are from *The Collected Works of St. John of the Cross,* translated by Kieran Kavanaugh and Otilio Rodriguez (copyright 1979 by Washington Province of Discalced Carmelites. ICS Publications, 2131 Lincoln Road NE, Washington, D.C. 20002).

In the case of St. Teresa I have added references to the Kavanaugh-Rodriguez edition (volumes 2 and 3) to the Peers sources given in footnotes throughout this volume for the convenience of those readers who may wish to compare translations.

A special expression of gratitude is due to Sister Joseph Marie of the Trinity, H.T. In the quiet of her hermitage she spent long hours in putting at the service of author and reader alike her previous journalistic experience as she enhanced the text with her expert editorial improvements. She likewise spent many more hours in preparing the final typescript for the publisher.

The Author

CHAPTER ONE

A QUESTION OF RELEVANCE

The Son, radiant Image of the Father's glory, proclaimed that He had come to cast a fire upon the earth and that He longed for it to burst into blaze. It was in the form of fiery tongues that the Holy Spirit of Pentecost descended upon a timorous group of men and women. Their minds and hearts having been enkindled with a burning love and ardent zeal, those who received the Spirit sparked the astonishing transformation of an unbelieving and corrupt civilization into a community of faith and love.

In our day the divine fire has not been extinguished. The consuming conflagration has not been contained. The proven incapacity of committees and clubs, speeches and surveys, electronics and entertainment profoundly and permanently to change vast numbers of people for the better has to be conceded. As the experience of the centuries attests, true transformations in the world and in the Church continue to come about only through the interventions of men and women on fire — that is, through saints. The evidence is overwhelming. It is also widely ignored, for it contains an otherworldly wisdom that this world does not welcome. For some, taking the evidence seriously presents a snag, since it implies striving for this same kind of transformation within oneself as a starting point for improving the world. Indeed, at this very moment, deep and lasting changes in the Church are being brought about by a faithful few who are burning interiorly as a consequence of the deep prayer given by the Holy Spirit, who renews the face of the earth in ways other than our own. These quiet, humble, unassuming individuals seldom write position papers, and they are not likely to appear on controversial television talk shows or to attract front-page headlines. They are not identified with any "ism", and they care nothing for a life of luxury or notoriety. They do not achieve popular acclaim by opposing ecclesial leadership and rejecting received doctrine. Rather, they are like the saints have always been. The burning ones are the unflickering light of the world, the savory salt of the earth, the lively leaven in the mass.

Thus, contemplative husbands and wives are examples of holiness to their children not unlike a Hedwig or a Thomas More. Prayerful clergy serve to inspire parishioners through soul-stirring homilies, sound guidance in the confessional and comforting concern in times of need. Teachers who are aflame ignite their students by their contagious enthusiasm as well as by the attractiveness of the truth they proclaim. Nurses close to God have a healing influence on both soul and body. In the home, in the marketplace, in the cloister, the love steadily radiating from these simple ones permeates and invigorates the world around us. It is unmistakable evidence of God living in and among us, a clear manifestation to our world that the Incarnation has taken place.[1] Common folk instinctively grasp this, while it easily escapes the more sophisticated, who often fail to comprehend what transcends the tangible order of meetings and strategies and publicity campaigns.

Not long ago a layman engaged me in conversation after the Sunday liturgy, his face beaming with joy. "Father, I've never heard that before", he enthused. He was referring to a theme that should be commonplace in homilies. What was this happy discovery, this good news he had never heard before? For the most part, it was two remarks, one of a first-century man, the other of a sixteenth-century woman, interwoven with about fifteen minutes of commentary.

If this had been the only time I had met with this sort of reaction to this particular message, the incident probably would not have lingered in my mind. But as I regularly travel about in retreat and lecture work, it is usual for me to encounter individuals, lay and religious alike, who are yearning for the same message. Nonetheless, I hear repeatedly that this momentous message rarely receives mention and is never explained.

What is it that so many are hungering to hear? Who were the first-century man and the sixteenth-century woman? What did they say, and to whom did they say it? Was it of enduring value, or was it merely a fad, no more than a fanciful notion? What is the explanation for the enthusiasm it continues to evoke? The extensive answer to these questions constitutes the content of this book. In brief, the homily dealt with the universal call to holiness and to a deep prayer life. The man was Paul of Tarsus, and the woman was Teresa of Avila. St. Paul told his hearers, laymen and laywomen for the most part, that they should aspire to be "filled with the utter fullness of God".[2] St. Teresa, expressly writing of generous married people seriously living their Gospel obligations, forthrightly said that there is no reason why people in the world should not attain to the very highest mansions of prayer growth, to the transforming union.

Admittedly the idea is an attractive one, so attractive that many people assume that it is not something that can be realized in their own lives. Could lofty contemplation actually be meant for all men and women in all vocations? We shall consider at length the answer that St. John of the Cross and St. Teresa of Avila give to this question, and we shall see that for anyone who looks carefully at all the evidence (not just one or two isolated texts), it is completely clear that their response is resoundingly affirmative. What is even more compelling is that the contemporary Church, in her liturgy, in Vatican II and in the new canon law repeatedly takes it for granted that "contemplation", "mystical treasures", an "abundance of contemplation", "the experience of divine things" and "an assiduous union with God in prayer" are meant for each and every person in the Church.[3] In the official liturgy the Church places on the lips of all the faithful the petition that we would be "fed with her [Teresa's] heavenly teaching" and that all of us would "imitate John [of the Cross] always".[4] These two saints have been declared Doctors of the universal Church precisely for what they have to say about contemplative prayer and the way to reach it. Universal teachers are of course universal, intended for all classes and conditions. Teresa and John present the Church's mind about mystical prayer, about the deep things of God, about a complete love immersion in Him. They are addressing any and all who desire a serious prayer life and aspire to live the Gospel with the totality characteristic of the saints.

It is sometimes held to be proof against the universal call to contemplation that in the case of some saints we lack external evidence of advanced infused prayer. This argument lacks substance for two reasons. The first reason is that a saint is characteristically inclined to avoid drawing attention to outstanding favors from God, and especially to keep hidden what has transpired in the innermost recesses of the heart in the most intimate of all relationships. Louis Bouyer, in support of the universal call, observes that Jacques and Raïssa Maritain have "pointed out quite rightly that this mystical development of every Christian life carried to holiness will be more or less conscious according to the innate tendency and capacities of the subject for reflex consciousness of what is going on within him. Thus saints who at first sight do not seem to be mystics actually live a mystical life without talking about it."[5]

The second reason that the argument fails is that its premise is simply false: there is external evidence in every saint of lofty infused prayer, namely, heroic virtue. Such remarkable virtue cannot be hidden, at least not entirely. As we shall explain in its proper place, it is the gradual growth toward the heights of transforming union and nothing less that produces an accompanying heroic holiness. Both Teresa and John hold strongly that sanctity blossoms along with the development of infused contemplation. There is a mutual causality. Without the second passive night that proximately purifies one for the perfect sanctity of the seventh mansions, there cannot be the holiness that the Church canonizes in her saints.

Because we are all without exception called to the heights of holiness, this volume is emphatically intended, also without exception, for all men and women in every way of life. When later we examine the inner reasons why this must be so, it shall become clear why our two saints are accurate in their assessment and fully in accord both with Scripture and the mind of the Church.

Hedonism has never begotten happiness, and our disillusioned contemporaries are learning this lesson with a vengeance. While the pleasure seekers often enough make a shallow show of their self-satisfaction for the media and thus foster a false impression among the young, those who do let down their defenses admit the emptiness of lives lived without transcendent ideals and hopes. This phenomenon is common not only in Europe and the Americas but also in any materialistic society. One social critic writing from Australia describes the now middle-aged "baby-boomers" as the me generation who center their attention and energies on self-development and self-gratification. He cites Manning Clark, a historian, who considers that "they are probably the first generation who don't believe in anything at all. Previous generations have held firm beliefs, whether they were religious beliefs or just the hope of better things from humanity, but this generation are nihilists." Not surprisingly, they have found that their egocentrism has yielded only a vast inner void: "The greed and titillation culture has proved empty and hollow."[6]

Even though it almost goes without saying, perhaps the obvious should be emphasized: a philosophy that produces nothingness has issued from nothingness, that is, from no intellectual principles rooted in reality. "From their fruits you shall know them." This volume deals with a "philosophy" that produces not only contentment but also a perduring, unspeakable joy even on earth, a foretaste of eternal joy. This claim is verifiable in experience for anyone willing to pay the price of pursuing it. There will be those, of course, who will read in these words a sheer utopianism or an incredibly naïve enthusiasm born of ignorance of the real world. Yet facts are facts, and one cannot fly in their face except at great loss to oneself. Disregard for life's ultimate realities, life's most enriching experiences as epitomized by the saints, is runaway escapism. For reasons less than noble some people choose to reject, perhaps angrily, always selfishly, what is incompatible with their chosen life-style.

No one may contest the testimony of Ss. Teresa and John unless he has himself been where this woman and this man have been (and where others who follow their teaching also arrive). These two Carmelites have been to the summit of the mountain: they know what it is like and how to get there. Unlike oriental gurus who promise much but produce at best an apersonal state of awareness, or at worst immoral chaos, these two saints point to nothing but what the Gospel already promises: "A joy so glorious that it cannot be described" . . . a delight that is complete . . . such that "hearts will be full of joy" that no one can take away.[7]

A book on advanced prayer is a book on advanced joy. It is a love story, a book about being loved, and loving, totally. It is a book on holiness, the heights of holiness to which the Gospel invites everyone.

Still, we must face the fact that there are people who think the message is too good to be true. Strange as it may seem, among these people are not a few contemporary priests and nuns. It is regrettable, but understandable, that there are those who reject it out of ignorance, men and women who may know of our two saints only from hearsay, not close contact. Not infrequently, among these are religious who were told in their early formative years that Ss. Teresa and John "are not for you" and who could not find these saints' works in the convent library, for they were erroneously judged as dangerous. Others, very likely, have heard stray bits about the *nada* doctrine and supposed it was only one spirituality among others that one could take or leave with impunity. Invariably these are people who have so tenuous a grasp of the New Testament that they would be astonished to learn that these two Carmelites say nothing significant that is not already in the Gospels and the canonical Letters of Paul and Peter, James and John. It is one of the tasks of this volume to show this last point to be true.

But how do we face the further fact of people who have read the sanjuanist and teresian works and who either misunderstand the message or forthrightly reject it? Few if any of these are serious scholars, but they do include some nuns, friars and priests. It may be useful to listen to their objections and respond briefly to them before proceeding further.

Perhaps the most frequent objection bears on the *nada* doctrine, the drastic detachment taught by both Teresa and John but especially emphasized by the latter. Death to one's senses and desires is unhealthy if not impossible, it is said, and we understand better today that we can find God not in negation but in affirmation, joy and celebration. Mortification, penance and self-denial are considered to be of the old school, whereas an emphasis on delight and jubilation is more appealing nowadays.

The full response to this objection may be found positively explained in our chapter on freedom, for thorough understanding is the best answer to partial views. A few short comments will suffice for now. People who argue against detachment and self-denial are perhaps unaware that they are simultaneously rejecting the same teaching found in the New Testament. Jesus lays it down that to be his disciple, anyone and everyone must "renounce *all* that he possesses", not just part or most of it.[8] In Titus 2:12 we read that "what we have to do is give up *everything* that does not lead to God". John and Teresa ask not a whit more . . . or less. Texts like these could be multiplied. We must further note that in our human, finite condition, every choice necessarily entails negations. If I spend money for one thing, I cannot spend it on something else. No man can love two women with his whole heart. No one can serve God and mammon. No one can attain an ecstatic joy in God without giving up paltry, self-centered pleasures in things less than God. People who reject Gospel detachment cannot have clearly thought it through. Like the adolescent who sees little value in Dante or Shakespeare or Michelangelo because comic strips have captured his fancy, the adult who discounts evangelical detachment cannot have experienced the sublime infused love found in advanced prayer. One can only wonder if this individual has ever tasted even a morsel of it. Can he know what St. Paul meant when he spoke of rejoicing in the Lord *always*[9] or "having nothing, possessing all things"?[10] Does this person believe what Jesus himself taught, namely, that it is a hard road and a narrow gate that lead to life and that there is no other way to happiness on earth?[11]

Reflecting on it, one readily notices that the reinterpretations and rejections of St. John of the Cross (and thus of the Gospel) are inherently implausible even on the merely natural level. If a single one of the substitute teachings advocated greater self-denial or more heroic sacrifices, the proposals would be less obviously self-serving and slightly more persuasive. This same implausibility appears in the current dilutions of principled sexual morality. Not only are the dissenting foundations in consequentialism and proportionalism intellectually bankrupt (one may recall, among others, the devastating and unanswered critiques of John Finnis and Germain Grisez), but the unfailing widening of the gate and easing of the road renders this approach suspect from the start. So also the persisting lack of understanding and appreciation in certain circles for our two saints has in our day reached the point of pathology. These are hard words, yes, but they are not directed toward people of goodwill who wish to acquire a better understanding but need help to do so. It is for these especially that this volume is intended. Rather, I refer to those who have had ample opportunity to study, to see, if they will, that the Gospel demands remain eternally valid and, despite this, tout contrary teachings. Indeed, the unpopular path of cross-to-resurrection traveled by all the saints is the sole way to life.

A rejection of the *nada* doctrine is a failure to see that the dark night of faith

> is in no sense a nothingness; it reflects the radiance of the invisible stars of love. It is itself the fluidity that is in itself already the glory of God, so that it is only a question of time, of patient, expectant vision, before this obscure glory is transformed into a manifest, self-glorifying splendour.[12]

There is another segment of individuals who have dabbled in Christian and oriental mysticisms and consider that they are more or less indistinguishable. An expert will not, of course, make this astonishing mistake, but others notice similarities (for example, an asceticism, an imageless awareness, a reaching out for the transcendent), while they fail to recognize vast gulfs between the two. Buddhist "contemplation" is impersonal, not a love matter at all, whereas that represented by Teresa and John is preeminently a profound personal love union with God. The Buddhist writer neither affirms nor denies God; he simply has nothing to say about communing with the supreme Being.[13] There are other major differences between the two mysticisms, but we may be content here to note that the differences between personal and nonpersonal, between theism and agnosticism, are vast. They are neither minor nor a mere matter of taste. The same must be said of Hinduism. While this latter system is theistic, not agnostic as is Buddhism, yet the contemplation of its adherents is far removed from Christic communion. "In Hinduism," remarks Louis Bouyer, "as in many other Far-Eastern spiritualities more or less closely related to it, like Chinese Taoism, the spiritual man tends toward an absorption of his proper personality in a deity which is itself impersonal."[14] While John and Teresa insist on the incomparable closeness of divine-human union in the seventh mansions, they likewise insist, as do all authentic Christian mystics, that God and the individual remain unambiguously two distinct beings: the one is not absorbed and lost in the Other. Speaking of the Hindu mystic, Sankara, Bouyer notes that "whatever the personalist expressions that Sankara used, he tended toward nothing other, in the final analysis, than an absorption or a reabsorption of himself in a great whole that was no one . . . and in spite of the images of fusion, or loss of self, or extinction of the 'I'."[15] People who confuse the mysticism of Paul, Augustine, the Gregorys, Teresa and John with what oriental writers discuss have only a surface-level grasp of their subject.

Equally inept are psychological explanations of the teresian mansions. One will hear it said that the phenomena of the stages of prayer described by St. Teresa are purely psychological experiences, or one will find that attempts are made to explain these stages according to Carl Jung. The best response to these preposterous ideas is experience, the experience of advanced contemplation. Anyone who knows the reality from the inside, that is, in more than an academic manner, can only smile at the naïveté of the proponents of such theories. But even those who lack experience can detect the basic inadequacy of naturalistic explanations by weighing everything Teresa and John say. We may select one example out of a dozen possible ones: the progressive growth in holiness that is part and parcel of infused prayer and its developments cannot be accounted for on any natural basis. Only one who has not studied the transforming union closely and carefully would even begin to think of equating the burning sanctity found in it with either pagan examples of virtue or the goodness possible through active prayer. The reader may test for himself whether what we describe in the course of this volume bears any natural explanation.

Does infused contemplation occur with any frequency today? Some think not. These people range from one extreme that maintains that prayer in solitude is a waste, that we get to God only through dealing with our neighbor, to another extreme that admits that mystical prayer is the ideal, but it just does not happen much in our day. Other prayer forms have largely replaced it. Once again the complete answer to both of these views and the variations that lie between them is the entire picture as sketched within this volume. However, given the nature of these allegations, it may be useful for me to add a few observations derived from three decades of giving retreats and renewal lectures combined with the considerable number of spiritual direction encounters this work entails.

One of the many things I have learned is that advanced infused prayer is well and thriving among those who live the Gospel with entire generosity. This has always been the case through the centuries, and it is the case today. Retreat masters and others who say they seldom meet advanced contemplation in the people they deal with can speak for themselves. I cannot vouch for those they serve. However, I likewise may speak from my own experience: among both active and cloistered religious I meet infused prayer frequently, and I find that Teresa and John remain the best guides we have to the mystical experiences that continue to flourish among our saintly laymen, sisters, brothers and priests. If others do not find what I find, several questions might be asked.

Are the people to whom they speak wholeheartedly living Gospel humility, poverty, obedience and commitment to the Church in the way that saints live these virtues? If not, they will not, of course, find much infused prayer. Do these retreat masters teach these virtues? If not, they should not expect advanced contemplation in their listeners. Without humility, detachment and sound doctrine there is no deep communion with the Lord. There could not be, for quality of prayer correlates with quality of life, that is, of evangelical life, not a naturalistic substitute. Do these spiritual directors understand advanced prayer well enough in both its delicate beginnings and its profound growth to recognize it when they do meet it? Do they by the example of their lives and their teaching inspire others to approach them about matters of deepening prayer? One needs little imagination to understand that people will not discuss a matter as intimate as their communion with God if they sense that the retreat master is tinged with worldly views or does not give proper priority to prayer.

A second thing I have learned is what St. Teresa herself learned regarding the sanctity and prayer of her companions in the early years of the reform: they were saintly women, and most of them had lofty infused prayer. That combination, holiness of life and radiant contemplation, is no mere coincidence. So it is today: men and women in any vocation who live the revealed word as Thomas More (married man), John Vianney (diocesan priest) and Catherine of Siena (consecrated virgin) lived it do enjoy a profound intimacy with the Lord they serve so completely and untiringly. Life-style and prayer grow or diminish together. If people today or in any age lack mystical prayer, it is not because it has been tried and found lacking. It is the Gospel that has not been tried.

More disturbing than isolated aberrations is the widespread indifference to contemplation in the formation and education of priests and other clergy. Despite the fact that Jesus Himself declared in the Martha-Mary episode that drinking undividedly of the Lord is the "one thing", the overriding necessity in any human life and of greater importance than activity,[16] the academic training of our clergy bears almost exclusively on work. Despite the fact that the apostles themselves considered their duty to be prayer first of all, and then proclaiming the word,[17] seminaries rarely, if indeed ever, direct serious course attention to equipping the students to lead the faithful to drink deeply, to taste and see how good the Lord is[18] and to do the same themselves. Despite the fact that Vatican II laid it down that for all men and women "action is subordinated to contemplation",[19] rare is the seminary that pays much attention to the latter, to the "one thing". The results of this enormous vacuum (which seems to worry almost no one in officialdom — the Popes are notable exceptions: they do worry about it) are predictable and obvious. Everywhere I meet sincere people who are hungering for something deeper than what they hear in the Sunday homily. Over and over men and women tell me that they never hear of contemplation in their parish churches and rarely in retreats. In the latter they may hear on occasion a few passing references to the subject, but nothing adequate. Repeatedly I am told that competent spiritual direction for growth in prayer is simply not available. It is no wonder that some of these people turn to faddish gurus, occidental and oriental.

This volume does not have a polemic purpose. But if it does propose a thesis, I would have to insist that it derives from no preconceived idea I set out to prove but from one that gradually emerged after some years of immersion in the writings of our two saints. The thesis is that the teachings of Teresa and John are nothing more or less than the integral Gospel. I can think of nothing significant in their works that cannot be found in Scripture as understood and explained according to the mind of the Church and the best of exegesis, past and present. If this statement appears to be an exaggeration, I merely invite the reader to proceed. A superficial acquaintance with either the inspired word or with our saints is not enough. The more one delves into all three, the more one finds a remarkable identity of message. Each one illumines the other two.

I am well aware of those who dip a bit into St. John of the Cross, promptly put him aside as "too much" and then declare that they prefer either "the simple Gospel" or some other saint or else a popular contemporary writer. These people likely enough feel that they have "really tried John" and that there are other viable choices of spirituality that dispense with a detachment emphasis. While there are surely diverse spiritualities in the great Tradition of the Church, no valid approach can or does depart in the least from evangelical teaching. What is so terribly shallow in this view is that those who hold it apparently do not realize that all saints concur exactly with what John and Teresa teach about sacrifice and detachment. They are unaware that John is, as Pius XI remarked, "pure Gospel". If the reader wishes a rapid confirmation of this simple truth, he may turn to Chapter 8, which deals with the *nada* doctrine.

Because men and women of heroic virtue are fully responsive to the Holy Spirit, they are the best exegetes of the divine word inspired by the same Spirit. One has only to compare the biblical commentaries of Augustine or Bernard to the often jejune explanations of mere technicians. The latter may excel in philology or archeology, they may summarize a variety of opinions offered through the ages and in our own day as to what this or that text means, but they are no match for the personal depth and wisdom found in the patristic commentaries and in the concrete lives of the saints, whether these latter were scholars or not. In fact, as I was writing these lines I referred to several contemporary exegetes for their insights into four texts we shall touch upon in the next few paragraphs. These passages deal with our deep interpersonal immersion in God, indeed, with our transformation into the trinitarian life. I found no sufficient explanation of a single text. One exegete made no comment whatsoever on Ephesians 3:19, even though he was prolix about its preceding context—a remarkable omission. The impression this gives is that while he and the others show some facility with factual details, they are at a loss and strangely silent in matters pertaining to deep communion with God.

"I have come to cast fire upon the earth, and how I would that it were already blazing."[20] How perfectly this captures the contents of this book. The radiant Image of the Father's glory[21] has come to light a fire in us, a burning love, a consuming yearning. There is nothing lukewarm about the God of revelation. Always radical and total, never does He reduce what He expects of us to fractions. Our communion with Him is to become a blazing fire, a perpetual ecstasy. These strong words will sound strange and exaggerated only to those who have not tasted that the Lord is good. They may have studied and read, but they have not drunk deeply.

Reflecting like mirrors the very brilliance of the Lord, we are even in this life to be "transformed from one glory to another into the very image that we reflect—this is the work of the Lord who is Spirit".[22] This text, too, is an excellent summation of much of this present work, namely, the gradual but inevitable transformation of a generous person that accompanies parallel growth in depth of communion with the indwelling Trinity. They who think that fullness of contemplation is meant to be confined to an elite few do not understand the contents of Sacred Scripture. Nor do they understand the great patristic commentators (e.g., St. Gregory of Nyssa in the fourth century) who join with John and Teresa in writing of this transformation.

"Eye has not seen, ear has not heard, nor has it dawned upon our human imagination what things God has prepared for those who love him."[23] This pauline statement, astonishing however one understands it, refers not only to our final destiny in beatific vision and risen body but also to the unspeakable, indeed unimaginable, gifts God has in store on earth for totally generous lovers. Once again, without the teaching of saints like Teresa and John we would be at a loss to suggest what Paul actually had in mind. This, no doubt, is why the mere biblical technician can say so little about ideas like this one. It is only in the perspective of what the mystics say of the culmination of contemplation on earth that we come to see in concrete terms what the apostle had in mind.

In another equally astounding text Paul, himself a mystic, writes that as we grow in the love of Christ that surpasses all knowledge we are to be "filled with the utter fullness of God".[24] Scripture commentator Max Zerwick finds this to be "a thought of bewildering magnitude".[25] No doubt. The thought cannot be exaggerated. That I, of myself a puny nothing, am to be filled *utterly* with boundless beauty, power, joy and love staggers the imagination. Zerwick is surely correct, but it is interesting to note that he goes on to remark that "there is much in this section which remains obscure. In these last verses, Paul soars off on a lofty flight which leaves us far, far behind, bewildered and astonished."[26] Yes. Precisely because we ordinary people are far, far behind, bewildered and astonished, we need reliable guides like Ss. Teresa and John, who can familiarize us with the path to the spiritual summit and help us discover how we too can become disposed for the inflowing of divine fullness, the fire within.

CHAPTER TWO

THE WOMAN AND THE MAN

Genuine prayer, liturgical or contemplative, does not happen in a vacuum. Depth of communion with the indwelling Trinity occurs only in a person intent on living the Gospel totally, one who is humble and patient, temperate and obedient, pure and kind, free of selfish clingings. It is not accidental that our very best explanations of contemplative prayer have their origin in a woman and a man of marvelous sanctity. To appreciate this assertion one would have to read the depositions for the canonization processes together with other current accounts of Ss. Teresa of Avila and John of the Cross. We cannot, of course, detail in a single chapter the external happenings of their lives, but we do wish to present a personality sketch of each saint, and that for two reasons.

We have already noted in passing that saints are the best exegetes we have of Scripture. They not only lived the revealed word well; they also have lived it heroically well. Both the biblical word and their lives are inspired by the one Holy Spirit. While scriptural commentators often contradict one another in their explanations (and as logic points out, in a contradiction one of the two parties must be mistaken), saints do not contradict one another in the ways in which they concretize the Gospel. True enough, each is unique, and all together they present a multifaceted and complementary diversity in their various life situations. St. Thomas More lived Gospel poverty as a husband and a father, in a manner different from that of St. Francis of Assisi or St. Robert Bellarmine. This kind of complementarity enriches, whereas the contradictory type is damaging to the mistaken party, for error puts one out of touch with a given reality.

The lives and traits of Teresa and John tell us far more about contemplative prayer than many of us imagine. We tend to think that their messages about communion with God are confined to their written words. Not so. Their lives and their writings are mutual commentaries. We understand John's (and Teresa's) teaching about detachment not only from studying his explanations but also from seeing how he applied the doctrine in his own circumstances. We derive a great deal of light about the practicalities of growing through the advanced mansions of prayer not only by studying *Interior Castle* but also by know-

ing well the woman who lived the message before she put it down
on paper. Her experiences illustrate her words. Some people, for example, consider that lofty contemplation renders a person impractical
regarding the affairs of this world or unconcerned about the ordinary
problems of life, but even a cursory knowledge of Teresa's activities
and her letters will rapidly disabuse one of that misconception. Others
imagine that detachment is a dark, dreary, joyless, forbidding enterprise, but if they study flesh-and-blood saints, they find that, on the
contrary, selfless people are actually the happiest. They learn concretely
in these men and women the truth of Jesus' teaching that the hard road
and the narrow gate lead to life, while the easy, broad road leads to
disaster.[1]

Our second motive for beginning with character sketches is that when
later we discuss what "eye has not seen nor ear heard",[2] we will have
to recall the kind of man and woman we are dealing with. Their hearts
soar heavenward, but their feet are firmly planted on earth. There are
some people whose grasp of reality is so tenuous or whose imagination is so overactive that when they speak of transcendent experiences,
we are not likely to take them seriously. But when these experiences
are narrated by intelligent, well-balanced, realistic individuals who
know human nature and its illusions from the inside out, we have no
sensible choice but to examine the evidence with sober care and an
open mind. Later we are going to deal with incredibly beautiful experiences of God, and it will be important to know something about
the traits and temperaments of the woman and the man who tell us
where they have been and how we may get there.

While the saints are citizens of their times—what else could they
be?—they have a knack for transcending the myopias and smallnesses
of the concrete circumstances in which all of us live. They are always
up to date because their vision and love are rooted in eternity. Despite
the trivialities of time and place, they love their fellowmen far more
than the worldly possibly could, because they are immersed in the
Origin who makes lovable any loveableness anywhere.

ST. TERESA OF JESUS

By all accounts St. Teresa, the foundress from Avila, was a woman
extraordinarily gifted, both naturally and supernaturally. In her were
combined physical beauty, especially in her youth, and a charm of personality that neither illness nor age diminished. All witnesses seemed
to agree that she was the type of woman no one can adequately describe

in a few pages. She was one of those rare personalities who combine qualities that seem to exclude one another and are seldom found together in one individual. She loved tenderly and affectionately, yet would brook no nonsense from anyone. She possessed both a strong self-image and an astonishing humility. A born leader, she was yet completely obedient to her superiors. She could be a windmill of activity at one time and at another be lost in mystical contemplation. Though she was highly intelligent and amazingly efficient, she gravitated toward simple, humble men and women.

Yet Teresa had her faults, for saints are not born out of the blue. They are weighed down with the same weak human nature we all have, and they experience the same temptations. The difference is that they say a complete Yes to the healing grace God offers to everyone, whereas most of us say "maybe", or "somewhat", or "wait a while . . . not yet". Teenager Teresa was proud, concerned about what she later called points of honor. At least once she covered up her ignorance with fellow novices. As a youngster at home she had a quick temper and fell into "terrible rages". Beautiful as she was, the young girl was much concerned with pleasure and feminine finery. She tells us that she loved to be liked, for she was admired wherever she went. On this trait she later commented with a typical example that she "could be bribed with a sardine". She was given to subterfuge but had a "horror for lies". She loved to talk, even if about God, and she did too much of it in her youth and even as a young nun in the lax convent she first entered. Of all her early sins, this waste of time through excessive chatting was the one she most regretted in later life, if we may judge from the number of references she made to it in her writings.

Because there is a crucial connection in the divine plan between advanced prayer and generous suffering, we may not omit to mention the extraordinary continuity and number of physical illnesses that beset Teresa from about the age of twenty until her death at sixty-seven. While most writers dealing with the teresian account of contemplation may see no particular significance in the saint's sicknesses, spiritual direction over the years has taught this observer that there is a close correlation between suffering well and growth in prayer depth. Of itself, of course, suffering improves no one, for a person can become bitter in his woes. But trials borne with love and in union with the crucified Beloved make one grow by leaps and bounds. I have noticed this connection over and over through the years. Students of contemplation must attend to what cannot be coincidental, namely, that this woman who reached the heights of contemplative prayer also descended to the inner abyss of pain. From her early twenties Teresa was in daily discomfort, sometimes in agony.[3] She suffered from fevers, tinnitus and a serious heart condition. So grave were some of her afflictions that she "always nearly lost consciousness" and sometimes completely lost it.[4] Early in her autobiography she tells us that her heart pains were so severe that she felt she was near death: "For sometimes it seemed that sharp teeth were biting into me . . . because of nausea I wasn't able to eat anything." Teresa was so shriveled and wasted away from a daily purge prescribed for her that she considered her nerves to be shrinking, and she said this caused "unbearable pains". All hope was given up for her life, because in addition to her heart problem she was also tubercular. This last diagnosis did not bother Teresa much because the "bitter torment" of her other problems had already drained and exhausted her. She added that the latter "were like one continuous entity throughout my whole body".[5] A little further on she noted that she was "almost never, in my opinion, without many pains, and sometimes very severe ones, especially in the heart".[6] In a letter to Don Antonio Gaytan she observed that "I was going to say I am well, because, when I have nothing the matter beyond my usual ailments, that is good health for me."[7] From a mere factual point of view one must marvel at what this woman accomplished in her supremely busy life and how it was that she lived as long as she did, for while she lacked the skilled medical treatment of our century, she by no means pampered her body.

Eyewitness accounts agree that throughout her life, from her early teens to mature age, Teresa of Avila had a remarkable impact on people. Though she made no effort to achieve notoriety, as a young woman she became a celebrity. At the Incarnation convent, the important people of Avila who frequented the parlors (apparently as a pastime and for spiritual edification) considered this nun the number-one attraction because of her charm and intelligence and holy conversation. When later during her travels she began to speak at rest stops on the road, the men who cared for the carts and the animals stopped their swearing and quarreling because they preferred hearing about God from her to indulging in their customary pastimes.[8] Her persuasive force was such that she transformed an everyday Catholic, none other than her own father,[9] into a mystic. One can only be amazed that, in a century hardly known for feminism, a nun could have exercised so strong an influence over men. She was authorized by Rubeo, the master general of the Carmelite Order, to found reformed houses of men, and she gave the discalced habit to St. John of the Cross. She was spiritual director to her married brother Lorenzo, who not surprisingly became a mystic himself, and to at least one bishop. Men had so great a trust in her person and her judgment that they would give her large sums of money to use as she saw fit. About this she confided to Lorenzo that "people have such a blind confidence in me—I don't know how they can do such things".[10]

In undertaking to describe and analyze the personality of Teresa, I must give a forewarning: here is a woman who does not easily fit into usual categories. While she surely did have traits in common with other women and men, her incomparable blending of these traits distinguished her. Even so sober a literary critic as E. Allison Peers observes that

> her character has countless delicate shades which baffle every effort of the investigator who seeks to classify and define them. Even were we entirely to disregard the part played by the supernatural in St. Teresa's life and personality, there is such inexhaustible wealth in them for the student of psychology that he finds the immortal Foundress one of the most interesting individuals who have ever lived.[11]

While physical beauty is hardly the most significant of human qualities, it is a gift of God and so should be noted even when it occurs in a saint. Serious witnesses and scholars seem agreed that Teresa was a highly attractive woman. Luis de Leon, a contemporary, remarked that anyone who came into close contact with her would "have his head turned". Marcelle Auclair observes that the word *beautiful* hardly does her justice, for her charm was irresistible.[12] She speaks of this girl as "maddeningly beautiful". We read that her features were of extraordinary loveliness; that she had curly chestnut hair, three dimples near her mouth and lovely hands; and that she was "well built" and graceful in carriage. Maria de San José said of the saint that "perfect in every way, she had an indefinable something in addition".[13] And so the descriptions go. It should be mentioned, however, that while physical comeliness must have left her as the years passed by, the magnetism of her personality did not. Throughout her life and even in the course of her severe illnesses, Teresa remained joyous, enthusiastic, buoyant, humorous and fervent.

> At the time when she began her great foundations Teresa was fifty-two. Religious life had in no way stifled that which had made her life in the world such a brilliant success: she was still beautiful, gay, lively, more eloquent than ever and endowed with a charm which it was useless to try and resist. In her, one experience did not efface a previous one, each merely added something to her amazing personality without taking away or destroying anything of it.[14]

At times the Lord Teresa loved so much chose to add a supernatural touch to all this. Witnesses in the process of canonization remark that on occasion her face would become visibly radiant. Isabel of the Cross testified: "Whenever she ceased praying owing to a few words she would utter and to a beautiful colour in her face and to such a strange manner so different from her usual self . . . it was obvious what great favours Our Lord had granted to her."[15] Anne of St. Bartholomew spoke of Teresa's face "shining resplendently" on two occasions, and Isabel of St. Dominic several times saw the saint's "resplendent face" as she wrote her books.[16] Likewise, witnesses who had seen Teresa's body after her death report on its incorrupt beauty years and even centuries later. We cite one contemporary, Julian of Avila, who knew the saint from many personal contacts. In the processes he testified that

> she also bore witness with her marvelous body for fourteen years. It is now fourteen years since she died and her body is still intact and incorrupt. This fact does not need to be proved—if anyone disbelieves eye witnesses, let them go and see for themselves in Alba where her body is still kept intact.[17]

St. Teresa also possessed a keen mind. Though we cannot appeal to psychological testing to discover the intelligence quotient of historical figures, we can in other ways establish their intellectual acumen. We know, for example, that a love for serious reading correlates with intelligence, and we find in the canonization processes and in the saint's own avowals that she was very fond of reading.[18] Keen minds are also highly creative and fruitful, while the dull are rarely burdened with a new idea. Genius that he was, St. Thomas Aquinas could keep several secretaries busy while he dictated to them on several subjects at one time. When Teresa wrote, she too would experience a rush of ideas. On one occasion she says of herself, when reflecting on how much there is to be said about prayer: "I only wish I could write with both hands, so as not to forget one thing while I am saying another."[19] One may doubt that most writers have this problem. The saint's sharpness appears in her rapidity of thought and also in her many decisive and sound judgments occasioned by her new foundations. Jerome Gratian observed of her that "the Foundress had a horror of lies and her diplomacy was beyond reproach. I have never seen anyone more skilled in the art of disclosing nothing she wished to hide, yet without lying."[20] Only rapid and clear minds can do this, of course.

Though Teresa had no formal education and never took a course in theology, and even though she often touches upon theological questions in her writings, she was remarkably accurate both in her assumptions and in her statements. While there is no doubt that some of her insights came from divine enlightenments, her accuracy of expression must have been due both to her initial correct grasp of what the "learned men" had shared with her in conversations and to a much better than average retentive power. Anyone who has taught theology knows how rare is the student who understands exactly what was said in class lectures and is able to explain it with proper qualifications and nuances in a later examination. We are told that the saint liked to speak with professional scholars and that she had no problem in holding her own in discussions concerning their own fields of specialization. One prominent one, a Doctor Manso, declared that he "would rather argue with all the theologians in Spain than with this nun who knew no Latin" — and Latin was the gateway to advanced studies in those days.[21] Teresa's fruitful mind and sharp insight are made apparent also in the abundance of images and examples that flowed effortlessly from her pen. In a rough count I have found that she used approximately four hundred different images and illustrations to explain her thoughts, and some of these were used many times over in differing contexts. Skilled teachers know that to use a wide variety of examples with accuracy of application requires sharp powers of observation and keen insight into both terms of the comparison.

Even though St. Teresa's robust psychological health is apparent in almost everything one finds out about her,[22] the no-nonsense approach she brought to human relations together with her warmly affectionate nature especially underline her thorough normalcy. Some people possess one of these traits, while others are gifted with the other, but rare is the individual who is so well balanced that both are blended together. Teresa was that rare person. She called a spade a spade and made no bones about the matter. The foundress considered the vicaress of the Seville Carmel who was suggested as a candidate for the office of prioress to be "laughable and enough to ruin the community".[23] She was no shrinking violet in expressing her view of the friars who were persecuting the reform: "wolves" was her description of them.[24] Teresa's love for honesty appears in her refusing to tolerate pious exaggerations. Regarding a nun who wrote about the virtues of another, the saint remarked to Maria Bautista in a letter: "Do not entrust the work to Juliana, for the stuff and nonsense she wrote in her account of Beatriz de la Encarnacion was so full of exaggeration that it was intolerable."[25] Teresa minced no words about counterfeits of sanctity,[26] and she was hard-nosed in matters of business. To a lay spiritual son she wrote: "I cannot think where your eyes and Father Julian of Avila's can have been, that you wanted to buy such a place."[27] By no means hesitant to take on men in dispute, the foundress remarks to one of her nuns that "these Canons make me tired. . . . If my Father (Banez regarding an authorization) has power to give this . . . for pity's sake let him send it me soon, unless he would have me rotting in my grave first. If it were not for those miserable three thousand maravedis, we should be in the house by now."[28] We would expect that a woman of this cast of mind would be cold and unfeeling, something of an autocrat, one who cared little for the sensibilities of others and trampled them down when they got in her way. Not so in Teresa's case.

Our later chapter on friendship will bring out at length the depth, even the intimacy of St. Teresa's close relationships. We wish at the moment merely to suggest this aspect of her personality with a few examples. As normal women generally do, the saint loved children and was affectionate in her manner toward them. Regarding two girls, fourteen and sixteen years of age, who had received the habit from Teresa, she writes to the nuns at Soria: "Remember me very warmly to my little girls: I am glad to hear they are so well and bonny."[29] She comments on a teenaged convent boarder that "she is very pretty",[30] and of three girls who had entered the convent Peers tells us that "she uses diminutives untranslatably tender: 'Teresica, la mi Bela (Isabel), la mi Casilda, los mis angelitos'."[31] Her correspondence with adult friends, male and female alike, is sprinkled with expressions of warm affection. To a laywoman she writes: "I should like to go on and on—I don't know how I can bear to go so far away from one to whom I owe so much and whom I love so dearly."[32] To Francisco de Salcedo, a saintly layman, she observes "how much your letters cheer me. . . . May God grant you to live until I die, and then I shall ask Our Lord to take you quickly, so that I may not be parted from you in Heaven."[33] An extraordinary prayer, indeed! She writes to one of her favorite nuns: "I assure you I very much appreciate what you say about feeling lonely without me. . . . Believe me, I have a great affection for you. . . . You will not say I am not writing you plenty of letters. See that you write me plenty, too, for I love hearing from you."[34] In another letter to the same nun she teases her: "My brother's affection for you is remarkable and it has infected me as well."[35]

Anyone who studies this daughter of Avila soon learns that she was possessed of tremendous willpower. Auclair calls her determination the keyword of her spiritual life. Not only did Teresa use the word repeatedly in her writings; we find the reality lived in her from childhood to deathbed. As a little girl she had heard that martyrs went immediately to heaven and that the Moors were putting Christians to death. Unlike other children, who were content to play with their toys, she put two and two together and came up with a decided conclusion. Since Moors mean martyrs, and martyrs mean instant heaven, she got hold of her brother, and together they ran off to find the Moors and get themselves a rapid ticket to paradise. Happily for us, their uncle intercepted them on the way.

As a normal teenager, the young Teresa felt the pull of the world as it reacted against her growing conviction that God wanted her in a convent. "Although my will did not completely incline to being a nun," she said, "I saw that the religious life was the best and safest state, and so little by little I decided to force myself to accept it."[36] This decision, made by sheer force of will aided by grace, the saint never regretted, for she later remarked as a mature nun how she had enjoyed an immense and continual joy in convent life. Yet when she reflected on her early struggle, she could observe that "when I recall this, there is no task that could be presented to me, no matter how hard, that I would hesitate to undertake. For I have already experienced in many ways that if I strive at the outset with determination to do it, even in this life His Majesty pays the soul in such ways that only he who has this joy understands it."[37] Though few of us are open to this lesson, Teresa was. When she was sure that "His Majesty" wanted a particular course of action, nothing could stop her, nothing except obedience to her superiors. Nonetheless, she, like all the saints, labored with the same weak human nature that the rest of us bear along, but the saints differ from us in that they trust in God to give them what they lack, and they are determined to use what He offers. "My nature sometimes rebels", admits Teresa, "when there are difficult things to be done, but my determination to suffer for this great God never wavers, so I ask Him not to pay any heed to these feelings of weakness, but to command me to do what He pleases, and, with His help, I shall not fail to do it."[38]

Although St. Teresa possessed a highly gifted and entirely unique personality, evidence abounds that she was a well-rounded, well-adjusted member of the human race. This normalcy already appeared in childhood, for she had a passionate love for tales of war and glory and chivalry. We read that she was "wilder than all her brothers put together"[39] and fearless in horseback riding. Even as a youngster she was vibrantly vital: she did what she did with a reckless abandon. While she was at first opposed to the idea of becoming a nun, when she did finally decide in the affirmative, it was with her "all-or-nothing" disposition. Teresa of Avila did not operate by fractions. When she spoke or wrote it was with an entire, even if unconscious candor. When she expressed her gratitude to Doña Catalina Hurtado for a small gift, she added what most of us would only think but not say: "The butter was delicious, as I should have expected it to be, coming from you, and as everything is that you send me. I shall accept it in the hope that, when you have any more nice butter, you will remember me again, for it does me a lot of good."[40] The saint could make a social blunder in misaddressing a noble lady, but she passes it off with an amusement that was shared by her addressee.[41] She is humanly touched by the presence of a sole Dominican friar at a huge civic and religious celebration welcoming the nuns to their new foundation in Villaneuva de la Jara, for she appreciated what Banez of that Order had done for her. "The Franciscans were also there", she noted, "as well as a Dominican friar who happened to be in the place, and, although he was the only one, I was very pleased to see that habit there."[42] Teresa suffered from the extremes of cold and heat, and she comments upon the weather in her typically colorful language. She writes in one letter of spending the summer in "this fire" at Seville, and she tells Gratian in another that "the climate is killing the prioress at Toledo".[43]

Because the purpose of this volume suggests a limit on our discussion of Teresa's natural gifts, we will merely touch briefly on a few more of her traits that the interested reader may wish to bear in mind in any further study of this remarkable woman and her writings. She possessed a keen shrewdness both in appraising the idiosyncracies and the foibles of human beings and in carrying off business deals to the advantage of her new foundations. The saint is well known for a sense of humor born of her charming candor and original way of seeing things. She was a down-to-earth person who entertained no illusions or fancy frills either in her thinking or in her actions. Teresa was a born leader who saw no problem in disagreeing with men, in giving spiritual direction (when sought of her) to a bishop and in negotiating with officialdom, secular or religious. Even though she considered women as given to an excess of emotion and imagination and as less educated than men (through no fault of their own), she assumes that they are often superior to men in judgment, and she openly asserts that many more women than men receive advanced "favors" from God.[44] There seems to have been no trace of racial prejudice in her, if we may judge from her seeing no problem at all in accepting two black girls into her novitiate.[45] The foundress must have had a great natural love for cleanliness, for the depositions repeat over and over how she was at pains to scrub and clean in the convents. Gifted with a natural optimism, Teresa had a native sense for the richness, beauty and mystery of creation and especially of the human person. She mused in *Interior Castle* not only on the splendor of the soul but also on the "many secrets" an all-wise Creator has hidden in the marvels of visible creation generally: "I believe", she wrote, "that in every little thing created by God there is more than we realize, even in so small a thing as a tiny ant."[46] Lacking our powerful microscopes and telescopes, the saint could not have known the extent to which science now shows her to have been right, but the basic reality did not escape her.

While what we have said thus far of St. Teresa's natural gifts is important for an adequate understanding of her and her teaching, without a grasp of her direct relationship with the triune God of revelation, we simply do not know this woman as she was. The saint was profoundly affected and enlightened by a whole stream of undoubtedly authentic and deep encounters with the Lord Himself. No one who takes the trouble to study what she has to say about these matters and at the same time recalls the highly intelligent and no-nonsense person we are dealing with will be inclined to question the reality of what she narrates. It has authenticity and actuality written all over it.

Deep as these experiences of God were, they did not occur suddenly. The young nun was not struck as by thunderbolts out of the blue. Already at the age of twenty Teresa was attempting to give herself to God seriously, and she enjoyed the prayer of quiet and sometimes that of union (both will be explained later), but there was still a great deal of struggle and "determination" ahead of her. What we aim to do at this point is neither to describe at length the saint's prayer life nor to explain her concept of immersion in God at prayer. We wish to offer some samplings only of her advanced "favors", as she would call them, so that we might understand better this gifted woman and the message she has for the modern world.

St. Teresa was given absorptions in God so deep that she would be almost beside herself with amazement and delight, not knowing what really she was saying to Him. Her soul at these times was so transported that she did not "notice the difference there is between it and God", a remark that reminds one of St. Paul speaking of the person clinging to the Lord as being of one spirit with Him.[47] At another time Teresa would be struck by "a mighty impulse", which would come without her understanding the reason for it:

It seemed my soul wanted to leave my body because it didn't fit there nor could it wait for so great a good. The impulse was so extreme I couldn't help myself, and it was, in my opinion, different from previous impulses; nor did my soul know what had happened, nor what it wanted, so stirred up was it. Although I was seated, I tried to lean against the wall because my natural power was completely gone. . . . The glory of this rapture was extraordinary. I remained for the rest of Pentecost so stupefied and stunned I didn't know what to do with myself, or how I had the capacity for so great a favor and gift. I neither heard nor saw, so to speak, but experienced wonderful interior joy. I noted from that day the greatest improvement in myself brought about by a more sublime love of God and much stronger virtues.[48]

These encounters with the Trinity indwelling were so impressive that Teresa felt unable to describe the least of them. She would be given inner enlightenments, "secrets", that would leave her marveling but unable to explain. The best she could do would be to say that next to this infused light "the sun's brilliance seems to be something very blurred". Along with this knowledge God bestowed "a delight so sublime as to be indescribable, for all the senses rejoice to such a high degree and in such sweetness that the delight cannot be exaggerated — so it's better not to say any more".[49] On one occasion, while the saint was reflecting on her unworthiness, her soul "began to grow more enkindled", she said, "and there came upon me a spiritual rapture that I don't know how to describe. It seemed I was carried into and filled with that majesty I at other times understood. Within this majesty I was given knowledge of a truth that is the fulfillment of all truths. I don't know how to explain this", she added, "because I didn't see anything."[50] At another time Teresa experienced what she calls a flight of the spirit in which her soul seemed to be transported with great speed and with a power that could not be resisted. Not surprisingly, her initial reaction to this divine impact was fear, and she tells the nuns that great courage is needed in the recipient. To illustrate her impression of the divine might, the saint used two images, one of a giant picking up a straw, the other of a small ship being lifted up by a huge wave: the soul is utterly unable to resist.[51]

As a final sample, we will cite what theologians now term an extraordinary phenomenon, Teresa's transfixion by an angel. What we have described thus far are all "ordinary" developments of infused prayer. The saint tells us that many times angels have appeared to her, though usually not in bodily form. The occasion we cite here was not an intellectual vision.

> This time, though, the Lord desired that I see the vision in the following way: the angel was not large but small; he was very beautiful, and his face was so aflame that he seemed to be one of those very sublime angels that appear to be all afire. They must belong to those they call the cherubim, for they didn't tell me their names. But I see clearly that in heaven there is so much difference between some angels and others and between these latter and still others that I wouldn't know how to explain it. I saw in his hands a large golden dart and at the end of the iron tip there appeared to be a little fire. It seemed to me this angel plunged the dart several times into my heart and that it reached deep within me. When he drew it out, I thought he was carrying off with him the deepest part of me; and he left me all on fire with great love of God.

Teresa then described the extraordinary pain of this transfixion and yet the equally extraordinary delight that it brought to her. The pain was not of the body but of the spirit, even though the latter redounds and flows over into the bodily senses. The saint added that "the loving exchange that takes place between the soul and God is so sweet that I beg Him in His goodness to give a taste of this love to anyone who thinks I am lying".[52] During the days that this experience lingered Teresa went about, she remarks, as though stupefied: "I desired neither to see nor to speak, but to clasp my suffering close to me, for to me it was greater glory than all creation."[53]

We would expect that these ordinary and extraordinary encounters with the Lord she so loved would leave in St. Teresa indelible impressions, and so they did. We read in the processes for her canonization that they likewise produced results visible to the eye. Maria de San José tells us that once when a priest spoke to the foundress about loving God, she fell into ecstasy and her face began to glow.[54] Maria Bautista deposed regarding these ecstasies that "on those occasions her face became so radiant, beautiful and devout that one who saw it could never forget it".[55] At times these encounters with the divine so deeply moved Teresa even on the physical level that she would have to do something externally (for example, attend to business matters) to be able to cope with the prayerful absorption.[56] However, the more important results were interior. It was from her experiences of the transcendence, beauty and power of God that the saint most of all learned that finite reality is precisely that, limited, and next to God is nothing at all. She had so deeply drunk of purest delight, beauty and love that to return to ordinary life, good as it is in itself, was a pain to her.

> O my delight, Lord of all created things and my God! How long must I wait to see You? What remedy do You provide for one who finds so little on earth that might give some rest apart from You? O long life! O painful life! O life that is not lived! Oh, what lonely solitude; how incurable! Well, when, Lord, when? How long? What shall I do, my God, what shall I do?[57]

It is the saints who know what being in love is all about. Earthly love pales by comparison.

Our earlier thumbnail sketch of the kind of woman Teresa was makes it apparent that these meetings with God have no natural explanation. Only divine intervention can account both for what Teresa describes and for the effects it left in her. There are no equivalents in the natural order.

We find in these meetings with "His Majesty" an explanation of how and why St. Teresa viewed her sins with such horror. Tepid, lukewarm

people consider this hatred for sin, even venial sin, as being a senti-
ment overblown by the saints, but that is because they know so little
about what being in love is like. Mediocrity has little contact with infinite purity, goodness and love. In an effort to explain herself, the saint
compares the Divinity to a very clear diamond, "much greater than
all the world", and she pictures her sins as visible in this infinitely
beautiful jewel:

> It was a frightening experience for me to see in so short a time so many
> things joined together in this diamond, and it is most saddening, each
> time I recall, to see appearing in that pure brilliance things as ugly as
> were my sins. It happens whenever I recall this, I fail to know how I
> can bear it; as a result I am then left with such shame that I don't think
> I know where to hide.[58]

She goes on to marvel at people who commit "very indecent and ugly
sins", and to say how they merit hell even through one mortal sin
"because one cannot understand how dreadfully serious it is to commit sin before such awesome Majesty".[59] This woman has met God.

Because prayer happens in a context, not in a vacuum, we come to
an indispensable aspect of any serious contemplative life: How completely, how unselfishly is the Gospel being lived? We must look briefly
at St. Teresa's heroic virtue. Though this chapter may not seem to some
as having much relevance to prayer, we must insist that it has everything
to do with it, everything on the human level of cooperation with the
divine initiatives.

Heroic sanctity is no ordinary goodness; it is a miracle of holiness
impossible to unaided human nature. It is so rare that there is one
Church alone that dares to examine in an extended process and under
sworn testimonies certain of her children, that they may be proposed
to all the faithful as models of what living a Christ life is concretely
like in the various states of life. It obviously lies beyond the scope of
this book to explain at length how God chose to transform a naturally
gifted woman into the saint whose writings we study in these pages
along with another miracle of holiness, St. John of the Cross. I shall
here simply make a few remarks that may entice the reader to explore
Auclair's biography of Teresa and Teresa's own writings.

St. Teresa's humility was no mere attractive modesty and self-efface-
ment. One might think that her lofty prayer experiences would have
been so many handles for pride. Quite the contrary—she considered
that they were so many reasons for looking upon herself as wicked,
for in her eyes she repaid God poorly for all he gave her. She so wished
others to know her limitations and faults that she rejoiced at the com-

ing of a severe and legalistic priest-visitor, and she conceived a special love for him because of his ruthless correction of her "faults": "This Father Visitor gives me new life," she remarks, "and I do not believe he will have illusions about me, as everyone else has, for God is being pleased to show him how wretched I am, and he is catching me out in imperfections the whole time. This comforts me very much and I see to it that he is fully aware of them."[60] So rare is this degree of humility that one can live an entire lifetime and not encounter a single case of it. Regarding a woman of prayer and penance who came to visit her, Teresa remarks that "she was so far ahead of me in serving the Lord that I was ashamed to stand in her presence", and she says of the nuns with whom she lived in her first reformed convent that "this house was a paradise of delight for Him. . . . I live in their company very, very much ashamed."[61] She was of the opinion that she deserved to be persecuted, and she welcomed even untrue accusations against herself.[62] Foundress though she was, Teresa must have been known widely for choosing to do menial tasks, for that trait comes up more than once in the depositions of her process.[63]

In the very nature of things there is an intimate connection between humility and obedience, and while I am omitting in this sketch many of St. Teresa's heroic virtues, I feel that the latter should be joined to the former. To appreciate both of these virtues in her, we need to recall that she was anything but a timid, passive individual. Diffident people often do not find it difficult to acquiesce to another's decisions either because they are reluctant to assume responsibility for important decisions or because they fear failure and criticism. But as we have noted, Teresa was of an entirely different cast of mind: she was full of ideas and abounding in initiative and determination. Criticism bothered her not in the least. Being a born leader, she must have found submitting to another's will naturally irksome. Yet her obedience was legendary. We cannot here detail the many examples of the prompt, joyful carrying out of difficult directions that she must have found extremely painful to her buoyant determination. What she taught, she lived. One of the nuns deposed that

> she was so obedient that she not only obeyed her superiors and confessors in everything but also when one of us, her subjects, asked her to do something even if it were not very sensible she would do it. Afterward we regretted it saying: "Heavens, Mother, seeing that it was not sensible yet your Reverence did it." She used to say: "It is less important to make a mistake of that sort than to fail to obey for love of God so long as it was not against His will."[64]

Perhaps the most trying and long lasting of the precepts the saint received was the series of directives requiring her to write her major works. She was not bashful in letting her strong distaste for writing be known on more than one occasion:

> Why do they want me to write things? Let learned men, who have studied, do the writing; I am a stupid creature and don't know what I am saying. There are more than enough books written on prayer already. For the love of God, let me get on with my spinning and go to choir and do my religious duties like the other sisters. I am not meant for writing; I have neither the health nor the wits for it.[65]

An interesting self-assessment coming from perhaps the most widely read author in the Spanish tongue. Yet despite this deeply engrained dislike for the task, Teresa did what she was told with marvelous humility and purity of intention.

> May His Majesty always keep your Reverence in His hands and make you so great a saint that with your spirit and light you may illumine this miserable woman who has little humility and is very bold in having dared to undertake the task of writing things so sublime. May it please the Lord that I did not err in doing so since my intention and desire was to do what was right and to obey, and that through me He might receive some praise, which is what I have been beseeching Him for many years. Since I do not have the deeds that praise Him, I have dared to recount this dissipated life of mine, although I haven't spent any more care or time on this account than was necessary to put it in writing and record as clearly and truthfully as I could what has taken place in me.[66]

A fit conclusion to one of the greatest autobiographies of all times.

Although there is no doubt that St. Teresa received authentic communications from her Lord, she would never subordinate mediated obedience to immediate; that is, never would she prefer her inner enlightenment to the obedience she owed to human superiors. Her integrity, so entirely rooted in the Gospel,[67] is a stinging rebuke to illuminists of all times who are convinced that they have a privileged inner light from the Holy Spirit, convinced that they know better than does the Church sent by Jesus Himself to teach in His name. Though the Lord would give Teresa directions in a vision, she would not carry them out until they were approved by her confessor. Even more, if the confessor's judgment went contrary to what the saint's vision had indicated, she would unhesitatingly obey the former. This policy the Lord Himself approved.[68]

While saints do not cut corners, they do keep things in balance. Lest we leave the impression that St. Teresa's determination was only a natural gift, we need here to notice, even if briefly, that her thoroughgoing ardor was supernaturally elevated to a new level. With no hesitation and no rationalizing, Teresa threw herself into whatever she saw God wanted of her. Even while speaking of her "wickedness" she could yet avow that "I can remember no occasion . . . when . . . He did not grant me grace . . . to fling myself into whatever I believed to be most truly conducive to His service, however difficult it might be."[69] She would, she said, rather "be cut in pieces" than commit a single venial sin.[70] There was nothing fractional about her approach to God. In the teresian consciousness, transformed by grace, self-seeking and corner cutting were simply foreign: they did not enter the picture. She could aver regarding the numberless details attendant upon her many foundations that "never in any respect have I done, or would I do, anything which I believed in the least degree contrary to the Lord's will, according to the advice of my confessors. . . . Indeed, so far as I remember, it has never occurred to my mind to act otherwise."[71] Teresa was so intent on utter conformity to the divine good pleasure that, not content with simply avoiding any sin, no matter how tiny, she also decided always to carry out what she perceived as the more perfect course of action.[72]

In their totality of pursuit, saints have the happy but rare gift of combining in their persons qualities that seem to be opposed to one another. Fanatics may have one natural virtue to an eminent degree, but they lack its balancing opposite. Mediocre people have no outstanding qualities, and so there is nothing to balance. The activist may think himself the cutting edge of the future, but if he is not a mystic, he is frightfully narrow — and part of the narrowness is that he may not possess even a small suspicion of his myopia. St. Teresa was magnanimous: she saw and lived the whole picture. On the one hand she did an amazing amount of work both in the monastery and on the road, and yet on the other hand she loved long periods of prayerful solitude. Rare indeed is the man or woman who, as Vatican II put it, is "*eager* to act and yet *devoted* to contemplation".[73] Teresa was wholeheartedly both. She likewise combined a tender love for her family and yet would not waste time in idle talk with them. She could say as her father neared death that "it seemed my soul was being wrenched from me, for I loved him dearly".[74] She so loved him and the others in her family that she would not lead them into the guilt of idle chatter for which we shall give account on judgment day[75] — which is to say that she really loved her relatives as very few people do. Her balance was likewise evident in her ability to combine a great deal of asceticism and penance in her

personal life with a willing and appreciative reception of comfort from
dear friends. To Gratian she wrote that "I was thinking what a comfort it would be to me if my daughter Maria de San José were here:
she writes so well, and she is so clever and gay, that she could do
something to lighten my burdens."[76] During her many travels Teresa
saw to it that her companions on the road would combine times of
silent prayer in the covered carts with periods of healthy fun and conversation. Seldom does one meet an individual who is unashamedly
ascetic and yet warmly appreciative of human comfort, who can enliven
a conversation with wit and joy and then can turn to a long solitude
of deep prayer afterward. For most of us it is at best a question of one
or the other, not both. A saint is indeed a rare work of divine art.[77]

We may do well to cast a glance at St. Teresa sitting at her desk.
The odds that a girl born into the sixteenth century anywhere in the
world would become the most widely read author in a widespread
modern language were not high. But much more than odds were operating in Teresa's case. She had no training in the literary craft, and she
entertained a hearty dislike for it. Though Teresa felt inept, she nonetheless possessed the strong intellectual traits we have already noted.
Yet her immediate circumstances did not help. She had no library to
consult, and she was usually pressed for time. Repeatedly she was interrupted as she wrote.[78] Of set purpose she did not preorganize and
plan what she was going to say.

> I shall also write of other things, according as the Lord reveals them
> to me and as they come into my mind; since I do not know what I am
> going to say I cannot set it down in suitable order; and I think it is bet-
> ter for me not to do so, for it is quite unsuitable that I should be writing
> in this way at all.[79]

The saint felt no need to put an idea in its proper place, that is, within
the framework of a previously prepared outline. She wrote as thoughts
occurred to her.[80] For this reason readers must be careful not to assume
they know Teresa's entire mind on a particular subject because they
have read one paragraph or one page in one work or letter. Careless
writers, for example, speak confidently about her thought on the universal call to contemplation because they have read chapter 17 of *The Way
to Perfection*. They seem blissfully unaware of thirty to forty texts that
run flatly counter to their interpretation of that chapter. Others read
two or three negative remarks of the saint about pampering the body
and fail to realize that in other places she comes out strongly for the
proper care of one's health.

St. Teresa wrote with intensity both because she was forever short of time and because she was a woman burning with the divine fire. Maria del Nacimiento observed that when the foundress was writing *Interior Castle* (usually after receiving the Eucharist), "she was very radiant and wrote with great rapidity, and as a rule she was so absorbed in her work that even if we made a noise she would never stop, or so much as say that we were disturbing her".[81] A corollary of this intensity and lack of time was Teresa's habit of not rereading or correcting what she had written. At the end of her autobiography she explained herself to the priest who had ordered her to write it:

> I did what your Reverence commanded me and enlarged upon the material. I did this on the condition that you do what you promised by tearing up what appears to you to be bad. I hadn't finished reading it after the writing was done when you sent for it. It could be that some of the things are poorly explained and others put down twice, for I had so little time I couldn't read over what I wrote.[82]

Teresa wrote in solitude, but she was not alone. From eyewitness accounts it is clear that she was often in direct, deep prayer communion with "His Majesty", for it was often from Him that she received what she communicated. While we need not and ought not to bypass natural explanations for her "heavenly teaching" (as the liturgy puts it in the original Latin text for her feast day on October 15), we ought not either to fail to appreciate what she herself tells us:

> The little time at my disposal is little help to me and so His Majesty must come to my aid. I have to follow the community life and have many other duties since I am in a house which is just beginning, as will be seen afterward. As a result, I write without the time and calm for it, and bit by bit. I should like to have time, because when the Lord gives the spirit, things are put down with ease and in a much better way. Putting them down then is like copying a model you have before your eyes. . . . It seems to me most advantageous to have this experience while I am writing, because I see clearly that it is not I who say what I write; for neither do I plan it with the intellect nor do I know afterward how I managed to say it.[83]

That St. Teresa of Avila was a woman of the Church par excellence is so well known that we need not dwell upon it here. She founded her reformed monasteries precisely to support the "learned men" as they defended the Church, and to offer her nuns and herself to be love within the heart of the Mystical Body. In each of her major works she submits her message entirely to the judgment of "the Holy Roman Catholic Church", and she protests that "through God's goodness, I am, and shall always be, as I always have been, subject to her".[84] She declared herself not only in the most complete accord with magisterial teaching but also ready to die over and over "for the least ceremony of the Church". Thoroughly Catholic in mind and heart, Teresa loved the Church in her everyday life: sermons, holy water, blessings, liturgy. On her deathbed the saint did not forget to thank God that he had made her a "daughter of the Roman Catholic Church and allowed her to die within it".[85] She possessed in a striking manner the mark of authenticity proclaimed by St. Augustine and repeated by Vatican II: "A man possesses the Holy Spirit to the extent of his love for Christ's Church."[86]

ST. JOHN OF THE CROSS

When we compare the amount of information available about the person of St. John of the Cross with what we have for many other saints, such as Teresa and John Vianney, we may say that we know both more and less. Concerning biographical data, concrete facts, historical happenings, we know less about the former than we do about the latter. From the extensive eyewitness accounts given for the canonization processes for the Curé of Ars and for Teresa of Jesus, we know a great deal about their daily activities and about how they appeared in the eyes of others. The latter also tells us much about herself in her autobiography, her *Book of Foundations* and the many letters that have survived. St. John of the Cross said nothing about his activities in his major works, and a mere handful of his letters have come down to us. However, we do know from other parties enough of his manner and deeds to form an accurate picture of his personality.

Yet in some ways we know much more about John than about other saints and other famous men and women. What we know so extremely well about him is what is most important about anyone: his deepest self. And because his inner life was so immensely rich, there is far more to know than what we find in the ordinary heroes and heroines of history. Though this saint seldom used the personal pronoun *I* in his writing, he is of course constantly revealing his inner depths. In this John is incomparable. There are few men or women in history who have combined in their persons the loftiest sublimity of love experiences with an extraordinary talent for describing them.

While we have already noted that a man's life activities and written words are mutual commentaries, we must add that this truth is especially pertinent to St. John of the Cross. His teaching is the unvarnished Gospel, neither more nor less, and to understand it rightly with neither exaggeration nor diminution we need to see in his manner and deeds how he himself applied it to the concrete circumstances of the daily round. His mode of life is likewise a silent but eloquent testimony of what is indispensable for deep prayer to be given and received.

What kind of man was this saint who is so seldom well understood? We may say that he was serene, plain, simple . . . fearless of enemies but gentle toward everyone . . . intelligent and logical . . . outspoken but soft spoken . . . powerfully resolute and completely honest . . . moderate but by no means mediocre . . . uncompromising with principles but compassionate with human failings . . . poetically brilliant but no weaver of euphemisms . . . hard on himself but tender with others.

John so loved nature that Peers called it his dominant interest on the natural plane. He enjoyed going outdoors and praying immediately from the book of creation lying before his eyes. It is said of him that he would be found in his cell with elbows on the windowsill, gazing, in absorbed prayer, upon the flowers during the day or the stars at night. That nature sparked a burning love for God in this man is shown likewise by the inspired imagery we find in his works.[87] That the saint also enjoyed a keen appreciation for music appears, for example, in the verse, "silent music, sounding solitude", of *Spiritual Canticle*.

People who know St. John of the Cross only superficially may consider his spirituality to be predominantly negative. That there is a prominent sacrificial element is true, just as there is in the Gospel. But what is not sufficiently understood is that in both John and the Gospel the negative is never sought for itself, and that the positive overwhelmingly predominates. That this is so we will consider in its proper place, but it may be well to note here that this man had an exceptionally affirmative, optimistic vision of both the human person and the divine plan. Even his *nada* doctrine was entirely aimed at reaching an enthralling immersion in God. The sanjuanist optimism can be seen, for example, in his portrayal of all creation as a resplendent bride given by the Father to the Son: "I will hold her in My arms and she will burn with Your love, and with eternal delight she will exalt Your goodness. . . . By these words the world was created, a palace for the bride."[88] It would be difficult to find in all of literature a more jubilant, a more positively ecstatic outlook on creation and the human person within it. The critics of John seem not to read this far or else not to absorb what he says. Optimism is found everywhere in the saint's writings, even in the most stark sections on detachment and self-denial. Always he invites the reader to an entire enthrallment, an abiding joy beyond imagining.

St. John of the Cross did not seem to excel in speaking to large groups of people with the effectiveness of a John Chrysostom or a Francis of

Assisi, but he did have a powerful gift for relating to individuals and small groups in informal chats. Peers tells us that while he could easily be missed and passed over in a crowd, "once seen and spoken to alone, [he] could never be forgotten".[89] This charism, together with his uncommon grasp of the interior life, readily explains his popularity as a spiritual director. He was much sought after in this capacity by all sorts of people: laymen and laywomen, nuns, university students and their professors. His insights into Scripture were so well known and appreciated that professors at the university in Baeza consulted him to learn of these "new" explanations of the biblical word.

On the natural level it appears that John's greatest talent was his poetic genius. The Spanish scholars I have met and read are agreed that he is probably the greatest poet in the Spanish language. Kavanaugh and Rodriguez write that the saint is known as "the loftiest poet of Spain", not because of volumes upon volumes of verse but because of a mere handful of ten to twelve compositions. They add that "these compositions, however, display such variety that it can almost be affirmed that each of them represents a completely distinct poetic vision and technique, a singular accomplishment in Spanish literature".[90] E. Allison Peers considers John "a supremely skillful artist endowed in the highest measure with natural ability". Commenting upon the poetic perfection of *Spiritual Canticle,* this critic observes that

> either his stanzas were kneaded, pulled to pieces and refashioned again and again in the cell of his mind —"polished and repolished ceaselessly" as the French preceptionist has it—or he was possessed of the most marvelously intuitive poetic faculty imaginable and developed what the Catalan Maragall was later to call the art of the "living word" (*paraula viva*) to an extent heretofore unknown.[91]

Peers notes the saint's extraordinary achievement of attaining to "the very highest rank of European poets" by a tiny output of a little over fifty stanzas. That this friar knew what love is all about can be witnessed even from the secular world, for he is considered "a poet's poet, whom in these days of a Spanish lyrical renaissance, contemporary singers revere as perhaps no other".[92] Citations, some even more superlative, could be multiplied, but we shall add only that the saint's literary genius was not confined to his poetry:

> St. John of the Cross is also a poet in his prose, and the very abundance of his talent in this respect throws into sharper relief the austerity of his doctrine. The sum total of his merits as a writer of prose, of which its poetical quality is of course only one, constitutes a very remarkable achievement. . . . [Up to John's time] there had, in fact, been very little

mystical prose at all, and that little had mainly been concerned with one aspect of mystical experience — the Prayer of Quiet. St. John of the Cross had therefore to invent phrases in order to express ideas which previously had had no outlet in Spanish.[93]

It surely had to be a singular work of divine providence that God would prepare as the prince of mystics a man who not only experienced abundantly the very highest gifts of prayer but also was endowed in the natural order with matchless literary talent and poetic power to express worthily, that is, beyond the inadequacy of prose, the raison d'être of being human, an intimate immersion in the indwelling Trinity.

However, as is the case with any man or woman, the most important thing about St. John of the Cross was not what he did but what he was. Sheer sanctity was his paramount trait. This man was on fire, utterly absorbed in God. He experienced ecstatic prayer even though he said almost nothing about the subject (because "Madre Teresa" had already so well said all that needed to be said about it), and he reached the transforming union while still a young man. The saint was capable of an absorption during meals such that he could not recall what he had eaten — much like St. Thomas Aquinas, who provided his own anesthetic for bleeding by the simple procedure of going into contemplative prayer.

As we would expect, John's transformation into the divine (understood, of course, in a nonpantheistic sense) showed itself in his active caring for others. The dire poverty of the nuns at the Incarnation convent while he was their confessor so touched his heart that he went out to beg alms for them, and he made a point of seeking delicacies for the ill. When his own friars were sick, the saint gave them exquisite care. If one of them had no appetite, John would suggest kinds of food he might like and then procure them immediately. He would rise at night to check on the welfare of an ill confrere even when another friar had volunteered or been appointed to watch at the bedside. We know that he had a special love for the nuns at Beas, and he showed it at least once by walking several miles out of the way to visit them. This affection appears likewise in letters addressed to them. In one he remarks how they will know from his coming visit that he has by no means forgotten them, and he refers to "the beautiful steps you are making in Christ, whose brides are His delight and crown".[94] Further on he speaks to them as "my beloved daughters in Christ",[95] and in another he assures them that their letter to him was a great comfort.[96] In still another he strives to lighten the burden of pain in one of these Beas nuns: "Do not think, daughter in Christ, that I have ceased to grieve for you in your trials and for the others who share in them."[97]

The depth of John's love for his fellowmen can perhaps be best seen in two incidents the outside world would not have noticed at all. We understand those incidents adequately only when we recall the saint's uncompromising teaching on and practice of detachment from every single selfish desire. He had an extraordinary love for Francisco, his blood brother who was himself a mystic and remarkably holy. The saint called Francisco his most loved treasure in the world. When this brother once visited John and had decided to leave after two or three days, John told him not to be in so much of a hurry and to remain on for a few more days.[98] The other incident illustrates both the saint's fondness for St. Teresa and his insistence that no self-centered egoism is to be permitted in any event, even if another saint is the object of it. I refer to John's finally deciding to destroy the letters from her that he had saved. It is easy to imagine the terrible pull in his sensitive heart. On the one hand he knew the goodness resulting for both parties from a friendship entirely immersed in God. He knew, too, that he and Teresa loved each other dearly and purely. But he also knew that there could be danger, not in their case of any obvious sin, but of slight, imperceptible clingings that could result from retaining a packet of letters. Peers' comment is interesting:

> I have always thought, for example, when rereading the letters in which St. Teresa refers to St. John of the Cross and trying to realize what the two must have been to each other, that few things he did in his life can have been harder than the burning of a bundle of her letters to him — probably all he had ever had from her.[99]

In tracing out the traits of this saint, we may not omit a few words about a characteristic that we would hardly expect in a man so widely known both in name and in teaching for devotion to the Cross. I refer to John's gentleness. Serene, calm, at peace in his own personal life even under harsh, cruel persecution, John did not retaliate, did not deal brusquely, rudely or severely with others. He was clement, indulgent, benign and forgiving. Unwittingly he gave us a portrait of his own manner when he sketched out his counsels on how all of us are to behave under duress. "A soul enkindled with love is a gentle, meek, humble, and patient soul", he observed. "A soul that is hard because of its self-love grows harder."[100] People deeply in love with God invariably grow in a habit of amiable and compassionate responses to those whom God Himself loves. "Keep spiritually tranquil in a loving attentiveness to God," advised John, "and when it is necessary to speak, let it be with the same calm and peace."[101] Virile and brave though he was, the saint showed this same humane compassion for others in the very imagery he chose in his writings:

It should be known, then, that God nurtures and caresses the soul, after it has been resolutely converted to His service, like a loving mother who warms her child with the heat of her bosom, nurses it with good milk and tender food, and carries and caresses it in her arms.[102]

Chrisogono tells us that a young woman wishing to go to confession but knowing John's reputation for an austere life approached him with a fear bordering on panic. She drew from the saint the observation that a confessor who is holy ought not to frighten people. Disclaiming holiness in himself, he nonetheless went on to remark that "the holier the confessor, the gentler he is, and the less he is scandalized at other people's faults, because he understands man's weak condition better".[103]

Perhaps the surest mark of sanctity is the bearing of piercing suffering with much love, first for God and secondly for those inflicting the pain. It is easy for most of us to appear humble, patient, modest and loving when the sun shines, when others commend us, when we succeed, when we are healthy, when the way is clear of obstacles. What man or woman really is shines forth under contradiction, failure, illness. Any biography will make plain that John lived throughout his life the title he bore and the doctrine he taught. One example must suffice. While he was imprisoned for the second time by the calced friars, he was verbally abused and whipped on two occasions. He lived in a cell that was six feet by ten, with boards on the floor as his bed. There was no window, only a two-inch opening at the top of the wall facing the corridor. It was so cold during the winter that the skin on his toes came off from frostbite. His food was bread, water and sardines. He was administered the periodic "circular discipline", so called because each of the eighty members of the community took turns in lashing his bare back. He bore through life the scars of this brutal punishment. During and after these nine months of dark solitude and torture, John uttered not a single complaint and bore no resentment toward his captors.[104] One could see the image of the Crucified in him.

But the saint's affliction and agonies suffered at the hands of others did not satisfy his thirst to imitate the Master in his Passion. It is worthy of notice that while John says almost nothing in his writings about external penances, he practiced a great deal of them in his personal life. While he was prior at El Calvario monastery, he was first among the friars to set to menial tasks such as washing dishes. As prior of Los Martires he chose the narrowest and poorest cell in the monastery as his dwelling. He slept on "handfulls of rosemary twigs interwoven with vine shoots" and later used bare boards as his bed.[105] John wore a penitential chain so tightly around his waist that when it was later pulled away during an illness, the links were found to be embedded in his flesh.[106] Because the saint loved music so much and because during his final illness he was suffering intensely, a layman, Pedro de San José, thought he might soothe John's discomfort by bringing in some musicians. The response of gentle John was typical both of his kindliness and of his love for the Cross:

> Brother, I am most grateful for the kindness you wished to do me; I appreciate it very highly; but, if God has given me the great sufferings I am enduring, why wish to soothe and lessen them by music? For the love of Our Lord, thank those gentlemen for the kindness they had wished to do me: I look upon it as having been done. Pay them, and send them away, for I wish to endure without any relief the gracious gifts which God sends me in order that, thanks to them, I may the better merit.[107]

The reader who wishes to develop a deeper appreciation for this remarkable man may consult the three books on John referred to in the footnotes to this chapter. We may for now be content with the judgment of our other saint. Teresa puts the whole matter in a nutshell in brief excerpts from two of her letters. Of Friar Juan de la Cruz she writes that "he is a divine, heavenly man. . . . You would never believe how lonely I feel without him. . . . He is indeed the father of my soul."[108] "People look upon him as a saint, which, in my opinion he is and has been all his life."[109]

It is no wonder that these two contemporaries have joined to leave in the Church a doctrine on prayer and life unmatched in the twenty centuries of the Christian era. We now enter upon the humbling task of attempting to summarize and explain their teaching in one volume.

CHAPTER THREE

THE EXPERIENCE OF GOD

One can hardly imagine either St. John of the Cross or St. Teresa of Jesus beginning a work on prayer with the systematic question "What is the experience of God?" They knew it so deeply from their own prayer that they took it for granted. Yet this query is a favorite contemporary starting point, even if we who love to talk about experiences are usually unable to say what they are in a prayer context. In my own study of the literature on contemplation, I have found it frustrating more than once to come upon an article with the words *experience of God* in the title, and then, upon reading, to find that there is little or nothing dealing with this subject. The title may have been merely an attention-getting device. In any event, while contemporary writers are not much help in telling us what it means to come into contact with the living God, our two Carmelite saints, having met him in profound and authentic encounter, do have a great deal of light to cast on our inquiry. But first a few introductory comments may be of use.

EXPERIENCE IN GENERAL

We cannot, of course, offer a logical definition of experience via genus and specific difference. Like existence and being, experience is so basic that it falls into no ready category. We can, however, work inductively, and by noting common elements in our meetings with reality, we can give a descriptive definition. We may distinguish five of these elements: contact, awareness, cognition, affectivity and passivity.

When we listen to the music of Beethoven or smell the fragrance of a rose, we must somehow be in touch with the orchestra and the flower via sound waves and odor particles. But contact is not enough, for two pebbles on the beach that touch each other have no experience. A second element, a living awareness, is also necessary. If a person has lost consciousness completely, he does not experience the world. Third, there must be cognition, sense and/or intellectual. A field of wheat does not feel the sun and breeze, but a hunter and a rabbit do. Fourth, there is the element of affectivity, that is, pleasantness or painfulness, dullness or excitement, sweetness or sourness, smoothness or roughness. These and other affectivities are found in all sorts of varieties and intensities and mixtures. It is usually affectivity that predominates in our perceived contacts with the world and other people. When we listen to exquisite music or gaze at a breathtaking panorama, we may or may not be immediately inclined to philosophical reflection, but,we do thrill in delight. The more sublime the experience, the more lofty the thrill. Finally, there is the element of passivity: reality does something to us when we experience it. We receive from the other, from the sun or the flower or the orchestra.

We may say, therefore, that experience is an awareness caused by contact with an objective other, and in this contact affectivity predominates. We need to notice, too, that experiences change us for better or for worse. Damaging encounters (a blow or a gunshot wound or an accidental fall) diminish us, at least physically and sometimes psychically. Positive happenings improve and enrich us: we are "musified" by Bach, "rosified" by gazing on a rose, energized by food. We are put into a knowing contact with reality by conversation, reading and study.

THE EXPERIENCE OF GOD

When faced with the question of coming into a living contact with God, many people take one of two extreme positions. At one end of the spectrum are those who reject out of hand the idea of experiencing God, or who at least regard the proposition with excessive suspicion and distrust. They have an inbuilt prejudice against the idea, or they entertain a strong distrust that is not overcome by contrary evidence. At the other end of the spectrum are those who so exalt the idea that they uncritically accept almost any alleged communication as being of divine origin. They speak facilely of "listening to the Spirit" and attribute to God thoughts and desires whose sole origin is themselves. As is often the case in human life, the truth of the matter lies between these extremes.

Scripture and the official Church take for granted that personal contacts with the God of revelation do occur, and indeed ought to occur. The psalms speak of our tasting and drinking deeply of the Lord and of our being radiant with joy in relating to Him. Jesus declares that we know the Spirit from His very indwelling presence, and St. Paul admonishes his people to rejoice in the Lord always.[1] Vatican II spoke of all the faithful tasting fully of the paschal mysteries and burning with love during liturgical celebrations. Our chief ways of growing in the understanding of revelation, noted the council, are contemplation and the experience of divine realities. Religious engaged in active apostolates are to be "thoroughly enriched with the treasures of mysticism".[2] Solid historical studies show that through the centuries we have the universal testimony of the saints and other holy men and women that mystical experiences are common among those who are close to their Lord and do His will faithfully.

A careful study of our two saints makes it abundantly clear that authentic meetings with God can be distinguished from merely imagined ones. The former have characteristics completely absent from the latter. For example, divine "touches", in sanjuanist terminology, can occur independently of natural antecedents. They can be sudden in occurrence and quite removed from what the person was thinking about at the moment. Genuine contacts with the divine can be so indelibly impressed that they are never forgotten, even in the minute details of accompanying circumstances. It is important to note that authentic meetings with God produce personal goodness, even a heroic goodness that is far beyond human capacity. From their fruits you will know them, says the Lord Himself. Mere emotions have none of these traits, nor those that shall be apparent as we go along in these pages.

What is the experience of God? Perhaps it is well first to point out that we are not speaking here of extraordinary phenomena such as visions, words and revelations. These will be discussed in a later chapter. Moreover, contact with God is not immediately perceptible to the senses: nothing bodily or material is felt, seen or heard. This is contrary to what almost everyone naturally assumes, namely, that emotions run high in a meeting with the Lord. There may be an emotional dimension, but if there is, it is secondary and derivative. The contact itself is of the spiritual order, an order beyond sense phenomena.[3]

Nor do we mean to include here a reaching to God through a reasoning process, either by way of intellectually based proofs of His existence or through immediate inferences from a striking sunset or the innocent eyes of a baby. In an extended sense these can be called meetings with God, but at the moment we envision more. We are concerned with contacts not through created reality but by immediate effects directly produced in us by the Lord Himself and beyond the natural order.

We ask, therefore: What are these immediate effects that can be called contacts with the living God? In their beginnings they are delicate, wordless and imageless awarenesses of the divine. These perceptions are received, that is, not produced by our thought processes. Ordinarily God does not commence His self-communication as though by sudden and splendid bolts out of the blue. Rather, He operates gently and gradually, just as He does in nature. Niagara Falls begins with the imperceptible evaporation of oceans and rivers and lakes, and oak trees get their start from acorns, which develop imperceptibly over the years.

St. John of the Cross has a wide variety of expressions to describe initial contacts with God in prayer: loving light . . . dark, secret wisdom . . . thirst of love . . . inflow of God into the soul . . . serene, loving contemplation . . . enkindling and burning of love . . . general, spiritual, purifying knowledge . . . dark fire of contemplation. We should notice that there is no question of concepts or reasonings or images. One finds that a loving attention to God is simply present without the recipient's activity or effort. Often it takes the form of a given or infused desire for God. It is not a loving attention or yearning that results from a reasoning process. Because this communion is a gift, it is called infused.

St. Teresa, understandably enough, has her own ways of speaking of these initial encounters in advanced prayer. In the "supernatural recollection" of her fourth mansions, people are given what we may call a being-drawn-to-God, a quiet leaving of worldly things, a desire for solitude with Him, "a call so gentle that even they can hardly recognize it".[4] They are at times "within the castle before they have begun to think of God at all".[5] As one grows, God leads the soul "into a state of absorption", and He gives an understanding of divine things unattainable by human reasonings.[6] The Lord gives an awareness "which holds its attention and makes it marvel".[7] It is a quiet attention that the recipient cannot attain by his own efforts.

This teresian "recollection" seems similar to or identical with the sanjuanist delicate infusions, infusions so gentle at first that they may be hardly noticed and very easily snuffed out by clumsy efforts at active meditation. We shall explain St. Teresa's teaching on the growth of this initial experience more thoroughly in our later discussion of her seven mansions.

ADVANCED EXPERIENCES

As one grows in prayer, these gentle beginnings slowly develop in both intensity and duration. The desires become ardent yearnings and burning thirstings for God. Delightful times are intermingled with periods of emptiness. Knowledge of the divine is deepened, as is the love. Though the meetings with God occur on the spiritual level, that is, beyond the senses, they can and often enough do overflow into the felt level of the emotions. "Sometimes", says John, "the unction of the

Holy Spirit overflows into the body and all the sensory substance, all the members and bones and marrow rejoice, not in so slight a fashion as is customary, but with the feeling of great delight and glory, even in the outermost joints of the hands and feet. The body experiences so much glory in that of the soul that in its own way it magnifies God."[8]

This overflow is quite to be expected in deep experiences of the indwelling Trinity, for the human person is one living being, not, as Descartes thought, a soul inhabiting and driving a body. We are so one that the interinfluence between spiritual and material elements is unavoidable. Contemporary medicine is convinced that the state of mind can have an impact on bodily health — so also in contact with the living God: the transcendental touch, though profoundly felt in the core of one's being, easily carries over into the physical dimension also.

Closely related to contemplative contacts with God are sudden conversion experiences, which we read of in lives of some of the saints and occasionally find among our own contemporaries. I am not at the moment thinking of the charismatic "baptisms of the Spirit" that have been so frequently mentioned in recent years. These latter may be authentic meetings with the divine, or they may be little more than well-intentioned emotional responses to the psychological effects of group prayer. Rather, I have in mind experiences that have no natural explanations either for what happens at the time of conversion or for the solidity of the moral goodness that enduringly flows from it. These interventions from on high can occur in the form of a vision (St. Paul), a voice (St. Augustine in the garden), a sudden burning love (Mary Magdalen) or an unexpected, brilliant inner light (André Frossard in our own day). Theologians today would speak of the first two types as "extraordinary", that is, as outside the usual processes of grace life, and of the last two as "ordinary", that is, as within the scope of God's usual dealing in salvation history. Anyone who has done extensive spiritual direction has probably met a number of completely normal men and women (and sometimes even small children) who have been suddenly swept off their feet by an unspeakable inner flooding of light and/or love and/or delight whose origin can be nothing other than God Himself. Thomas of Celano tells how the worldly and mediocre Francis Bernardone was suddenly transformed into the burning and heavenly minded Poverello. After a party one evening and in the midst of his pleasure-loving friends, he was precipitously "inundated with such a torrent of love, submerged in such sweetness, that he stood there motionless, neither seeing nor hearing anything. They might have cut him to pieces, he said later, and he would not have moved." Everyone who has read a life of St. Francis of Assisi knows what happened as a result

of this encounter. Thomas adds that "he tried hard to conceal from
everyone the change that had been wrought in him; but he nonetheless
lost all taste for business".[9]

These conversion encounters with the divine can be transformations
from atheism to theism, from hatred to love, from mediocrity to totality.
We considered an example of the last when we spoke in Chapter 2
of St. Teresa's awesome experiences of God. They changed her from
an ordinary pious nun into the moral marvel we know her to have
been.

Beginning with the mystics of Scripture and continuing to our own
day, those who meet God profoundly are of one mind in declaring
that the divine gifts are ineffable, literally unspeakable. This they remark
over and over. In the prologue of his lofty *Living Flame of Love*, St.
John of the Cross wishes the reader to understand that "everything
I say is as far from the reality as is a painting from the living object
represented", and further on, in stanza 2, he pauses to observe that

> the delicateness of delight felt in this contact is inexpressible. I would
> desire not to speak of it so as to avoid giving the impression that it is
> no more than what I describe. There is no way to catch in words the
> sublime things of God which happen in these souls. The appropriate
> language for the person receiving these favors is that he understand them,
> experience them within himself, enjoy them, and be silent.[10]

St. Teresa is of like mind. She speaks of experiences so delicate, subtle
and deep that she can find no comparison that suffices to explain her
mind.[11] These spiritual happenings are beyond and unlike anything
we can see or grasp here below.[12] There are, says the saint, encounters
with God such that the devil cannot possibly counterfeit them, nor
can one's imagination create them.[13] Some are so indelibly imprinted
in the center of one's being that they can neither be described nor
forgotten.[14]

If a person has only a skimpy understanding of how God communicates Himself to the person who loves much, he would probably
assume that contacts with God are, like emotions of joy, rather uniform,
that they may vary in intensity but in little else. Spiritual direction of
individuals advanced in prayer continually furnishes me with fresh surprises: there are always new ways of divine Self-giving that I have not
previously met. There are, to be sure, general patterns and thrusts of
prayer growth through which everyone passes — we are discussing them
in this volume. But within these similarities there abound a great variety
and many fluctuations in the divine manifestations. We have already
noted that at the beginnings of infused contemplation the prayer given

can be so gentle and delicate that it may go unnoticed by one who lacks instruction. Further on there will be infusions of a burning love, but with no increase of "particular knowledge" (as John puts it); that is, a person finds himself loving much but with no new understanding of who or what. Or the experience can be the reverse: much light and understanding but little perception of new love.[15] There can be a delightful inebriation that lasts for differing lengths of time, even as long as a day or two, and not always with the same degree of intensity.[16] The exhilaration can be so intense that it could cause death. Says John, "nature would be torn apart" were God not to impart strength.[17]

So various are these contacts with God indwelling that the saint typically describes "the most that God communicates to the soul at (a given) time. Yet, he cautions, "it must not be thought that He communicates to all those who reach this state everything declared in these two stanzas, or that He does so in the same manner and measure of knowledge and feeling. To some souls He gives more and to others less, to some in one way and to others in another."[18]

A skilled teacher illustrates ideas with examples, and the clearer the examples, the more effective the teaching. To explain an oak tree to people living in the middle of the Sahara desert, a professor of botany would need more than a picture of a ten-inch sapling. So also, to understand adequately what experiences of God are like, we need to notice more than the beginnings of infused prayer. We shall therefore say something of advanced "touches" and "wounds of love".

TOUCHES

A mystical touch is a deep, intimate contact-union-experience of God in one of His attributes such as power, light, goodness, beauty, or joy. It is not only a contact but also a union, and not only a union but also an experience. John speaks of touches as "wholly divine and sovereign", for the "substance of God" is in a union-contact with the "substance of the soul". Although this touch is not the beatific life of heaven, it is what the saint calls a tasting of eternal life: "The soul tastes here all the things of God, since God communicates to it fortitude, wisdom, love, beauty, grace and goodness, etc. Because God is all these things, a person enjoys them in only one touch of God."[19] This contact brings incomparable delight, for in the touch God is sublimely perceived in one of His attributes. "As often as this experience occurs, it remains fixed in the soul. Since this communion is pure contemplation, the soul clearly understands that it is ineffable."[20] These touches are not messages or flashes of inner lightning, and they are not clear vision as in glory. But they are contacts with the very Divinity, and they effect a union with God. There is, says John, "no experience similar or comparable" to them.[21] The delights they engender "more than compensate for all the trials suffered in life, even though innumerable", and at times God produces them when the person is not in the least thinking of such matters.[22] While touches can reverberate mightily in the body, they are not always felt so forcefully. Actually, they are often weak, and "yet no matter how weak they may be, one of these divine touches is worth more to the soul than numberless other thoughts and ideas about God's creatures and works".[23] It goes without saying that these sovereign contacts with Divinity immeasurably surpass the sublimest of earthly experiences, whether of taste, music, drugs, sight or sexual union. They are so deeply impressed that they cannot be forgotten. They produce the transforming goodness of heroic virtue.

In the beginnings of infused prayer, more commonly one experiences a burning of love within the will rather than a light of understanding in the intellect.[24] This common trait of touches makes it clear that they are not derived from our reasonings and meditations. Touches purify, strengthen and quiet a person, and they make the inner life more stable. They prepare the recipient to receive permanently the divine union of espousal and eventually the transforming union itself.[25] Since John is convinced that everyone is called to this summit, he does not tire in showing how all the divine initiatives are aimed at preparing us to reach it.

WOUNDS OF LOVE

There is a close relationship between what we have just considered and what mystics call wounds of love. St. John points out how love-touches deeply pierce one's inner center like fiery darts. They thus bring an immense torment and yearning to see God face to face in final vision. They cause, he says, a dying with love.[26] We may, therefore, ask: Just what are these wounds? The saint describes them as "flames of tender touches" and "tender flares of delicate love".[27] There are many ways and varying degrees in which God cauterizes, sears the soul with love. Explaining one of these ways, John observes that while a person is inflamed with love for God "it will feel that a seraphim is assailing it by means of an arrow or dart which is all afire with love. . . . In this cauterization, when the soul is transpierced with that dart, the flame gushes forth, vehemently and with a sudden ascent. . . . The soul feels the wound with unsurpassable delight." The recipient feels this wound "as though it were a sharp point in the substance of the spirit, in the heart of the pierced soul", and it seems as though it possesses "seas of loving fire within it. . . . It seems to it that the entire universe is a sea of love in which it is engulfed, for, conscious of the living point or center of love within itself, it is unable to catch sight of the boundaries of this love."[28] All of this may strike the uninitiated as a wild exaggeration or a mere pious effusion, but this conclusion would be drawn out of human narrowness. Jesus himself said that he came to cast fire on the earth, and he vehemently wished that it were blazing already.[29] Therefore, John is in good company when he says that "the soul is converted into the immense fire of love which emanates from that enkindled point at the heart of the spirit".[30] Experiences of God are far, far more than anything we can fabricate for ourselves.

These touches of fiery love spark and enflame longings for the beatific vision itself. The person's complaint is not because of the wound but because God does not "slay her completely" by death, so that she can be healed by what she terms "the delight and glory of your sweet presence" in final glory. This individual can be almost beside herself in this pining for vision, and she looks in vain for a solution to her painful yearnings. The solution to this best of problems is unlike any other type of healing. Ordinary burns are cured by medication quite the opposite of fire, "whereas the wound effected by the cautery of love is incurable through medicine; for the very cautery that causes it, cures it, and by curing it, causes it. As often as the cautery of love touches the wound of love, it causes a deeper wound of love, and thus the more it wounds, the more it cures and heals. The more wounded the lover, the healthier he is."[31]

The experiences of God found in ecstatic prayer, the espousals and the transforming union itself, we shall deal with in St. Teresa's final mansions. We have seen sufficiently in these few sketches that when God gives someone the unspeakable experience of Himself in contemplative immersion, He leaves no stone unturned. Indeed, eye has not seen nor ear heard what God has in store for those who place no limits on their self-gift. Earth is prelude to heaven, time to eternity.

CHAPTER FOUR

CREATION AND MEDITATION

While Jesus and Paul, Teresa and John invite us to be fully immersed in the triune life, we immediately recognize that a serious prayer life does not begin with fullness. It commences humbly with small steps. Oak trees emerge from acorns, and scholars first learn the alphabet. While God is supremely free to give in a divine manner when and how He chooses, He ordinarily prepares the soul through the human mode of meditation upon His works of creation and redemption.

Neither John nor Teresa is known for detailed discussions of meditative prayer. What may not be well known is that they did not only consider the subject; they also treated it as important, indeed indispensable, for most neophytes. Nonetheless, they did not say much about the matter, and with good reason, since not much needs to be said. Some spiritual directors and writers make the tragic mistake of representing active methodologies and esoteric techniques to be the sum total of what is to be explained and done in one's communing with God. For our two saints meditation is only the introduction, the initiation into what should become a profound contemplative communion with the indwelling Trinity: we begin to pray in a human way and slowly are led by the Lord Himself into a divine way. While it is true that the latter needs far more explanation than the former, we may neglect neither. We turn our attention, therefore, to the sanjuanist approach to discursive meditation. The teresian account of the beginnings we shall cover in our review of the early mansions of *Interior Castle*.

For John creation was vividly sacramental. He saw in it so many signs of the hidden Beloved, and it sparked in his soul a burning response. The finite powerfully led him to the infinite. We read in his life how he loved to rest his elbows on the windowsill of his cell at night and to survey the stars, absorbed all the while in the Creator of the nocturnal jewels. During the day he turned his glance upon a flower with the same ecstatic result. As we point out elsewhere, it was precisely because St. John of the Cross, like St. Francis of Assisi, was so purified of selfish clingings to things that he could find in them a delight far outstripping what the worldling experiences.

> O woods and thickets
> Planted by the hand of my Beloved!
> O green meadow,
> Coated, bright, with flowers,
> Tell me, has He passed by you?[1]

Because creation shouts the Creator to the attentive heart, the man or
woman who sets out on a serious pursuit of God uses the finite order
as a stepping-stone to the infinite. "She begins", says John, "to walk
along the way of the knowledge and consideration of creatures . . . by
considering His greatness and excellence manifested" in them.[2] The
saint then goes on to describe the vast diversity and variety and numbers
of plants and animals, and he concludes that "only the hand of God,
her Beloved", could create such grandeur. He explicitly speaks of the
"beautiful stars and other heavenly planets" together with the beauty
of angels and saintly souls.[3] In bestowing all this splendor on the visible universe God leaves "some trace of Who He is", and this in turn
should enkindle love in the faithful soul who gazes with seeking and
receptive eyes.[4] Yet, good as all this is, these created realities are among
the lesser works of God:

> Pouring out a thousand graces,
> He passed these groves in haste;
> And having looked at them,
> With His image alone,
> Clothed them in beauty.[5]

Resplendent and fascinating as are the meadows and the forest, the lakes
and the seas, the sun and the stars, the flora and the birds, men and
angels, yet they "are the lesser works of God, because He made them
as though in passing", in haste. Though He clothes the world with
"beauty and gladness" by His mere gaze, much more attention does
He give to the Incarnation and the mysteries of the Faith, and thus
they enjoy a far greater loveliness.[6]

> Ah, who has the power to heal me?
> Now wholly surrender Yourself!
> Do not send me
> Any more messengers,
> They cannot tell me what I must hear.[7]

John sees created splendor as normally enkindling a great love in
the human person, a love that is soon thirsting for a far greater vision
of and immersion into the divine beauty than finite reality can possibly
trigger. Discursive meditation, then, is to lead one rapidly to so pene-

trating a yearning for the Beloved's presence that nothing short of Him can cure her grief. Nothing worldly satisfies one who has tasted the divine: "Any other communication further increases and awakens her appetite, like the crumbs given to a famished man."[8] Created messengers are no longer adequate. The knowledge of God they bring is "remote". Lofty John portrays the growing soul to be thirsting now for nothing less than some direct contact with the Fountain: "You have revealed Yourself to me as through fissures in a rock; now may You give me that revelation more clearly." Through the beauties of creation God has communicated "as if joking with me; now may You truly grant me a communication of Yourself by Yourself".[9] Good as meditation is, the holy person will find that finite beauty is only a messenger. An intermediary is no longer enough: "May You, then, be both the messenger and message."[10]

> All who are free
> Tell me a thousand graceful things of You;
> All wound me more
> And leave me dying
> Of, ah, I-don't-know-what behind their stammering.[11]

St. John of the Cross is incomparable. While ordinary spiritual writers go on and on in their descriptions of meditative methodologies, oriental and occidental, discursive and centering, this saint so on fire with love cannot hold himself back from jumping almost immediately into the I-don't-know-what of lofty mystical communion. And he is right, of course: people who live the Gospel as saints do, that is, without compromise and corner cutting, do soon find the infused flame being given to them. God does not delay. When we are disposed, He gives immediately and openhandedly. Through angelic inspirations and the truths of Scripture, the soul comes to a "dying of love . . . due to an admirable immensity these creatures (angels and men) disclose to her". Yet the communication is not complete, even if indescribable.[12] Wounded by a progressing love, the person "lives by dying until love, in killing her, makes her live the life of love, transforming her in love". This death is brought about by "a touch of supreme knowledge of the divinity", one that passes quickly and leaves the recipient "dying of love".[13] Whatever else one may say about this treatment of meditative prayer and its intended consequences, I know of no other that matches this optimism and confidence that God will give everything just as soon as we give up everything.

It would be a mistake, however, to give the reader the impression that St. John of the Cross says nothing about the nitty-gritty of meditative procedures. I shall merely summarize his thought, for the double reason that in our day we already have an overload of emphasis on methods of prayer and that the saint says nothing really new about procedures as such. We may, therefore, be content in noting simply that he does describe meditation[14] and that he considers it necessary for most beginners, even if it is only a remote means for union with God.[15]

One of the benefits deriving from discursive prayer is that through the delight it affords it draws the beginner away from "sensual things", and the world thus loses some of its appeal. Incipient progress occurs.[16] We are, says John, to see creation and meditation only as means to the end and to use them as such. The saint likens discursive reflections to the Church's use of paintings and statues to excite devotion in the faithful:

> We are not asserting, as they [iconoclasts] do, that there be no images or veneration of them; we are explaining . . . how souls should use the painted image in such a way that they do not suffer an impediment in their movement toward the living image, and how they should pay no more attention to images than is required for advancing to what is spiritual. . . . But when a person uses and dwells upon the means more than he ought, his excessive use of them becomes as much an impediment as anything else.[17]

We are to allow ourselves "to soar when God bestows the favor".[18] Because "considerations, forms and concepts" are unproportioned to the goal, they must eventually be left behind. Thus people "err greatly", says John, if they do not after due time give up methods when God begins to give a superior communion.[19]

FAITH AND FINITUDES

The eventual disappearance of images, concepts and reasoning as vehicles for communing with God is not merely a chronological occurrence that we await and then adapt to when it happens. In the nature of things, intimate relating to the divine demands a new dimension, an infused communion that transcends the created order. Finite realities are not adequate and proximate means to the infinite. There exists no proportion between them. Jumping higher and higher is no way to try to reach the moon. There is no proportion between human muscle power and leaving the planet. Something entirely new, rocket power, must be introduced if the latter is to be achieved.

To appreciate what John is saying as he insists upon the insufficiency of the created order to bring us to the Uncreated, we must first grasp something of the utter otherness, the transcendence of God. He is not only beyond all things; He is boundlessly beyond them. Created realities are, as one of the councils puts it, more unlike God than like Him.[20] Because no one gets anywhere without a means fit to the destination, so faith is radically necessary to reach the inner life of the Trinity. The saint appeals to the philosophical axiom that all means must be proportioned to their ends. If a person wants to get to a particular city, he must take a road that leads to it. If a log is to burn, heat must be applied to it. The wood must be made like to the fire so that it may eventually ignite. "If the intellect, then, is to reach union with God in this life, insofar as is possible, it must take that means which bears a proximate resemblance to God and unites with Him."[21] That which bears this near similitude to God is the virtue of faith. While created things bear a trace of the divine, none of them unites proximately with Him or has an essential correspondence to Him. The distance between creation and its Author is endless, and it is faith alone on earth that can bridge the gap.[22]

Because discursive meditation proceeds by means of images and concepts, themselves of the created order, it cannot effect union with God—there is no proportion:

> That the two extremes, the soul and the divine wisdom, may be united, they will have to come to accord by means of a certain likeness. As a result the soul must also be pure and simple, unlimited and unattached to any particular knowledge, and unmodified by the boundaries of form, species, and image. Since God is unincluded in any image, form, or particular knowledge, the soul in order to be united with Him should not be limited by any particular form or knowledge.[23]

FAITH IN JOHN'S TEACHING

The reader will notice in the excerpt we have just cited that union with God is effected by likeness: we must be made like unto God if we are to become one with Him (meaning a nonpantheistic oneness, of course). Because created things, good as they are, lie at an infinite distance from the divine and are more dissimilar than similar to God, they cannot bring us into union with Him. In Karol Wojtyla's doctoral dissertation on the subject of faith according to St. John of the Cross, the point is made that "the concept of 'likeness' . . . is the nucleus of the theology of union".[24] Since the finite realm is more unlike the infinite than like it, created reality cannot effect an "essential likeness". But since faith essentially "resembles" God, it can effect a basic "agreement". By means of faith God is present to the intellect as the known is to the knower, but this presence is in darkness and obscurity, not in vision and light.

Faith is an obscure quality, habit, empowerment in the soul that enables us to assent to the divine word and cling to God's revealing Himself.[25] John always considers faith as vivified by love, never as a mere intellectual assent devoid of charity. His concept of faith is a loving knowing, a knowing loving. We should recall that Scripture presents our final consummation, our eternal enthrallment in the Trinity as a knowing, a vision, a contemplation. We shall be like Him because we shall see Him just as He is.[26] We see now darkly as in a mirror, but then we shall see clearly; we shall know just as we are known.[27] Eternal life is to know the Father and His Son.[28] St. John of the Cross, in complete accord with traditional theology, relates faith to vision: both unite the intellect to God, faith darkly *de non visis* (concerning invisible reality), vision perfectly *de Deo viso* (concerning God seen). This dark, loving knowledge (it is not the "faith alone" of Luther) is to this life what the beatific vision is to the next.[29] Faith goes out "beyond every natural and rational boundary . . . and penetrates the deep things of God".[30] It "contains and hides the image and beauty of her [the soul's] Beloved".[31]

Faith comes through hearing, as St. Paul puts it,[32] and its object bears no proportion to the senses.[33] The more it darkens and blinds the natural knowing capacities of the human person, the more it enlightens and opens into the inner trinitarian beauty.[34] This is what the Christian mystic means when he says that we reach God through unknowing: we penetrate into the divine by a divine gift, not through an oriental process or set of techniques. We enter into God through no human means, no methods, no ideas. We must pass "beyond everything to unknowing. . . . A person who reaches this state no longer has any modes or methods, still less is he — nor can he be — attached to them."[35] This perception of the divine is poles apart from Zen satori, a brief, impersonal insight produced entirely by human technique. "Passing beyond all that is naturally and spiritually intelligible or comprehensible," says John, "a person ought to desire with all his might to attain what in this life is unknowable and unimaginable", that is, the Father, the Son and the Spirit, the divine Fire of love and light.[36] Meditation is a method, yes, but it leads to a prayer beyond all methods. It leads into the profound center of the Trinity.

St. John of the Cross draws the conclusion from all this that only faith is the secure guide to God, and that, therefore, one who abandons this guide for another is heading toward delay at best, disaster at worst.

> Insofar as he is capable, a person must void himself of all, so that, however many supernatural communications he receives, he will continually live as though denuded of them and in darkness. Like a blind man he must lean on dark faith, accept it for his guide and light, and rest on nothing of what he understands, tastes, feels or imagines. . . . For however impressive may be one's knowledge or feeling of God, that knowledge or feeling will have no resemblance to God and amount to very little.[37]

This we should recall when further on we study John's insistence that we set aside special communications from God and live rather according to the word of Christ and the teaching of His Church. The saint offers no comfort at all to illuminists and others who are persuaded that they know better than the Church, which the Lord Himself commissioned to teach in His name. Both John and Teresa repeatedly insist that the mystic must live a profound faith life, a life rooted in the word of God as it is proclaimed in the community He established. Along with St. Paul and the rest of the New Testament writers, the Carmelites make no room for dissent: even if an angel from heaven should declare something contrary to what the Church proclaims, he is to be anathema, says Paul.[38] John is exactly of the same mind: we can easily be mistaken about what we think is from heaven, but we cannot be mistaken about the Faith proclaimed by the Church, for it rests on the revealed word of Christ Himself.

For St. John of the Cross each of the theological virtues empties in order to fill. Faith frees the intellect of merely human ways of knowing, which are as different from the divine as heaven is above the earth.[39] Hope empties the memory of passing allurements that we might seek eternal enthrallment. Charity unburdens our will and heart of false and fleeting loves that we might cling unimpededly to true and lasting Beauty and experience the complete fulfillment found only in the divine embrace. These three virtues free us of the ephemeral that we may be transformed into the eternal.[40] As we outgrow the multiplicities of meditation, we enter into the darkness of an infused, simple communion that is to culminate in the enthrallment of clear vision in risen body.

CHAPTER FIVE

WHAT IS CONTEMPLATION?

For many sincere people the term *contemplation* is either frightening or mysterious or esoteric, or possibly all three. It conjures up in some cases an image of the plump Buddha with his eyes closed, or a monk set apart from the multitudes of ordinary men and women. It is not commonly considered to be an activity meant for plumbers as well as Poor Clares, for the married as well as for religious, for young and old. Over the years I have gradually come to the conclusion that one reason so many people assume that contemplation is reserved for a select few is that they imagine it to be what it is not. They presume that this type of prayer could not be for them because in a vague sort of way they consider it to be something other than it is. They equate it with oriental states of consciousness or with extraordinary phenomena such as divine messages and visions. Being active and busy and little inclined to any lingering reflection, natural or supernatural, they do not take seriously, as meant for them personally, the mystical expressions sprinkled freely throughout Scripture and liturgical worship. They embrace an unconscious minimalism and thus implicitly adopt a two-tier concept of holiness incompatible with the universal call to holiness so emphasized by Vatican II.

We do not in this volume deal with oriental mysticisms, that is, with Buddhist contemplation or with the Hindu transcendental meditation. These are states of impersonal awareness, not a love communion with God. In saying this I am making no judgment as to what the individual oriental does or does not attain in such exercises. We may hope that, through the workings of grace, contact with the living God may result. Rather, I am referring to theoretical explanations of Zen contemplation, which is explicitly agnostic apropos of God, and transcendental meditation, which at least for Western beginners is presented merely as a state of neutral awareness.

Christic contemplation is nothing less than a deep love communion with the triune God. By depth here we mean a knowing loving that we cannot produce but only receive. It is not merely a mentally expressed "I love You". It is a wordless awareness and love that we of ourselves cannot initiate or prolong. The beginnings of this contemplation are brief and frequently interrupted by distractions. The reality is so unimposing that one who lacks instruction can fail to appreciate what exactly is taking place. Initial infused prayer is so ordinary and unspectacular in the early stages that many fail to recognize it for what it is. Yet with generous people, that is, with those who try to live the whole Gospel wholeheartedly and who engage in an earnest prayer life, it is common.

ST. TERESA'S CONCEPT OF CONTEMPLATION

One need not be a theologian to understand St. Teresa's treatment of growing prayer. She is charming, simple and profound. For her, contemplation is an experienced, mutual presence, "an intimate sharing between friends", a being alone with the God Who loves us.[1] Hence, this prayer is a mutual presence of two in love, and in this case the Beloved dwells within. Actually, it is an interindwelling, a mutually experienced indwelling. She relates about herself how "a feeling of the presence of God would come upon me unexpectedly so that I could in no way doubt He was within me or I totally immersed in Him".[2] This experienced presence can be so strong that it removes all doubt of the indwelling mystery being lived in one's center.

The saint is in sound theological company, for we have this same idea in 1 John 4:16: God is love, and the person who loves abides in God, and God abides in him. For Teresa this indwelling presence is the focal point of prayer: wherever God is, there is heaven, a fullness of glory. We are to find Him deep within ourselves, just as Augustine did. We need no wings, only a place of silence where we can be alone and center our gaze on the Guests within.[3] We should note that this kind of entering within is just the opposite of introspection, for we are turning away from an egocentrism and turning toward the supreme Other.[4]

We are aware of the divine presence through the effects the Lord produces within us: faith, love, good resolutions. Indeed, we tenderly experience these effects, at least at times.[5] This teaching of Teresa is common among theologians such as St. Thomas and St. Bernard: God ordinarily reveals His indwelling presence not through visions but by prompting virtuous actions within us. Bernard uses the image of a boiling pot: as long as the fire burns under it, the water bubbles with life. So also, if a person is full of good works, bubbling with faith, hope and love, together with the moral virtues that flow from them, it is certain that the divine Fire is burning within.

This experience of the divine presence involves nothing extraordinary.

It is not a vision; nothing is seen or heard. Like other mystics, Teresa and John both use sense imagery such as fragrance and warmth in order to convey the idea that there is a factual experience, but they do not mean to imply that the senses or the emotions have a direct part in contemplation. A deep experience of God can overflow into our emotional life, but in its essence it is literally non-sensed. The new knowing and loving of God are a spiritual reality, not a tangible one.

Repeatedly, Teresa insists that contemplative prayer is divinely produced. She calls this prayer even in its delicate beginnings "supernatural", meaning by this term what we now intend with the word infused, that is, poured in by God. Entering into the prayer of quiet or that of union whenever she wanted it "was out of the question".[6] The fire of ecstatic prayer is so completely a divine, unmerited gift that she plays "no part in obtaining even a spark of it".[7] The divine infusion can be so strong, says the saint, that even when she would try to distract herself from it, the Lord would surround her in delight and glory: "The more I strove to distract myself, the more the Lord enveloped me in that sweetness and glory, which seemed to surround me so completely that there was no place to escape — and that was true."[8] This divine inflow can come unexpectedly with no human preparation: "Often when a person is quite unprepared for such a thing, and is not even thinking of God, he is awakened by His Majesty, as though by a rushing comet or a thunderclap. Although no sound is heard, the soul is very well aware that it has been called by God."[9] The sudden, unforewarned infusion can be likened to being caught on fire without perceiving what caused the igniting.[10]

Even though contemplation is utterly divinely given and humanly received, and as a consequence we can do nothing to force God to grant it, yet we can and must prepare ourselves for the gift.[11] God gives only to the extent that we efficaciously desire, that is, not merely wish something to happen but take concrete means to fit ourselves to receive it. "In reality," notes Teresa, "the soul in that state [of union] does no more than the wax when a seal is impressed upon it — that is, it is soft — and it does not even soften itself so as to be prepared; it merely remains quiet and consenting."[12]

Advancing communion with God does not happen in isolation from the rest of life. One's whole behavior pattern is being transformed as the prayer deepens. So true is this that if humility, patience, temperance, chastity and love for neighbor are not growing, neither is prayer growing. Hence, contemplation is not simply a pious occupation in the chapel or in some other solitude. Its effects are so necessarily seen in all the prosaic details of daily life that if growth in the virtues is lacking, so is the contemplation. St. Teresa speaks of an early attachment she could not break by her own efforts. Her confessor himself saw that he could not demand its surrender at that moment. It was only later, in a deep prayer experience, that she was given the strength: "In an instant He gave me the freedom that I with all the efforts of many years could not attain by myself."[13] This intrinsic connection between prayer depth and quality of life can be seen not only in exterior actions but also in interior aspirations. There is a great difference between good desires flowing from our own reflections and those that result from a divine prayer impulse. The former can be mainly if not exclusively a kind of intellectual velleity, a wishing things were thus and so, whereas the latter are informed and driven by an ardent love. We could call them love yearnings of great vehemence.[14]

I would imagine that many people assume that contemplation is all of one type—homogeneous. Indeed, they may think it quite boring in its sameness. They could not be more mistaken. A mere cursory reading of Teresa and John will soon dissipate the idea. In all types of infused prayer there are degrees of intensity, more and less, ebb and flow. There are dry, dark yearnings; slow and gentle enkindlings of love; ecstatic absorptions and delights; experiences of refreshment, peace, pain, light and insights. Being in love with God is never boring.[15] This rich variety and these degrees of intensity we shall consider at greater length when we discuss the stages of contemplative prayer growth in our next chapter.

ST. JOHN'S FORMULATIONS

Masterly works of art do not fit easily into human categories, and the slowly developing and deepening immersion into God is the supreme work of divine art that occurs on our planet. It cannot be surprising, therefore, that an adequate description of this immersion is not easy to come by. However, none of the attempts to delineate what infused contemplation is excels the works of St. John of the Cross. This prince of mystics is so imbued with the reality of what communing with God means that no concise definition can completely capture his experience and reflect his thinking. We can, however, help ourselves along by systematizing the various elements that make up infused prayer as we find them flowing effortlessly from the saint's pen.

The reader would be mistaken were he to conclude from this effort to systematize that contemplation is a highly involved and complex matter. Because it could not be more simple, the very simplicity is part of the problem of explanation. Material things, even humanly made artifacts, are comparatively easy to describe, because they have size, shape, color, consistency. But because we are dealing with an immaterial reality, all the more do we need the genius of John to supplement that of Teresa and thus open to us still more fully the subject of this volume. The elements that we now sketch should not be understood as though they were distinct or discrete experiences. They are, rather, aspects of one rich reality, each of which is necessarily mingled with all the others. A person well advanced in prayer will readily recognize these elements in their primal unity. The less advanced will need more or less patience as they move beyond an initial verbal understanding to a more profound grasp flowing out of their own prayer development. This is one reason, among others, why rereadings of Teresa and John characteristically yield new and richer insights: we grow in our understanding as we grow in our living of what we try to grasp.

Unintelligible peace

The beginnings of infused contemplation can well be described in terms of a peace that cannot be dissected or analyzed. It is a "calm and repose of interior quietude", a kind of "refreshment", a remaining "in that unintelligible peace". John calls it "that loving, substantial quietude where nothing is understood particularly and in which they like to rest". It is a "serene, limpid light".[16] The peace, refreshment, quiet here envisioned is not what we can sometimes achieve by an active effort to still ourselves, nor is it simply the result of a natural absence of conflict or worry. It is a new experience, one that is due to no oriental techniques or occidental methods. At the beginnings it is delicate and hardly perceptible, even though it is real. One is being led into a perceived contact with God indwelling.

A new loving of God

Like this undifferentiated, general peace, a delicate but deepening love for God is also received. John calls it a "secret and peaceful and loving inflow of God". At first it comes bit by bit and will be punctured with distractions (which obviously come from us), but as one grows, this love gets progressively stronger and deeper: "This divine, loving fire of contemplation . . . this burning of love . . . the fire and wound of this forceful love . . . this very fire of love" are typical sanjuanist expressions. The infusion from God grows to a point that the person is "dying with love of Him". One who has not experienced advanced prayer may, upon reading expressions like these, tend to write them

off as pious effusions and unreal exaggerations, but anyone who has
grown knows differently. No one is in love as the mystic is in love.

Delight and emptiness

We are mingling here two traits that could easily be separated, because
really they are separated. They are joined under one caption here to
bring out and indeed to underline a trait of advancing prayer that is
usually hard for people to accept as standard—namely, that infused
communion fluctuates and varies a great deal even from one moment
to another, surely from one day to another. We somehow assume that
contemplation should sail smoothly along in undistracted, uninterrupted
delight in God. It will be such in the final enthrallment of beatific vision, but here on earth we should expect a great deal of ebb and flow:
empty feelings mingled with occasional periods of delight, sometimes
delicate (especially in the early stages), sometimes dynamic (in advancing developments). Hence, we find St. John of the Cross writing of
"the sweet and delightful life of love with God . . . and very serene,
loving contemplation and spiritual delight . . . that delightful and wondrous vision". A person, he notes, "will be aware of the delight of love,
without particular knowledge of what he loves". This love, we need
to be reminded, is not of the senses; it is spiritual. And it is not the
result of reading and thinking; it is given from on high.

   In contrast, at other times the love is perceived not as pleasant but
as a painful yearning for what one seems not to have. Because painful,
it is often perceived as no love at all, and yet it may be deeper and
better than the pleasurable variety of prayer. The saint speaks of these
dry times frequently and in diverse ways: "The thirst of love . . . a living
thirst . . . [the] urgent longing of love". Once again we point out that
these empty-feeling yearnings are not nothing. They definitely are a
communion with God, a given and received communion. Consequently,
they are excellent prayer, even when lasting for weeks or months or
years on end.

A new, dark knowing

We consider next the element in infused prayer that is the most difficult
for many people to grasp. We are so accustomed to our ordinary human
way of knowing through images, ideas and concepts that imageless,
nonconceptual knowledge not only is foreign but also may seem like
no knowing at all. An example may help. Most of us know reasonably
well what genuine love is, even if we do not always achieve it, and
yet the essence of what we know cannot be expressed in an image or
concept: it is dark knowledge, that is, idealess knowing. Because God

can be enclosed in no finite representation whatsoever, our growing perception of Him will have to be dark, that is, beyond any ordinary human mode. Thus St. John of the Cross will call it "a secret inflow of God", secret, that is, to our usual clear, specific knowings. He follows an early patristic formulation (Dionysius) when he terms it a "ray of darkness . . . a bright ray of His secret wisdom . . . a divine and dark spiritual light . . . a wisdom so simple, general and spiritual", that is, a knowing far beyond all limited, finite details and concreteness. These paradoxes are crowned by a supreme one, "knowing by unknowing". To grow in a deep encounter with God as He truly is in Himself, unconstrained by the limited concepts we tend to have of Him, we must relinquish familiar ways of knowing. We must "unknow" in order properly to perceive Him, that is, in a manner beyond finite categories.

A loving knowing

Infused contemplation is by no means a dry or sterile intellectualism, a platonic gazing upon abstract essences. Nor is it an oriental, impersonal awareness. Rather, it is a "loving awareness of God . . . a loving contemplation . . . a loving wisdom . . . a loving light and wisdom". Indeed, it becomes "a fire of loving wisdom". When we put these traits together, a yearning or delightful loving with a cognitive contact touching the divine, we have, as John so well puts it, an inflow of God Himself. Contemplation is a deepening self-communication of the Trinity, a self-communication that we are given to experience.

A received divine communication

Though we have said it already, the point must be made explicitly and with some development: the prayer of which we are speaking can in no way be originated, intensified or prolonged by anything we can do. It is divinely given in its entirety. This is the literal meaning of infused, a word stemming from the Latin *infudere, infusum,* to pour in, that which is poured in. John therefore writes of a "tranquil reception of this loving inflow . . . the touch of burning in the will . . . the touch of understanding in the intellect . . . an inflaming of love". These expressions make it clear that the prayer is not a result of our efforts, our reading, imagining or reasoning. It is not of human origin.

An inflow of God

Because the Lord makes us aware of His presence in our deep center through the effects that He produces there, we may say that in these effects of a new knowing-loving-delighting-yearning He Himself is flowing into us and thereby transforming us from glory to glory into His likeness. Hence, our saint seems especially fond of speaking of this prayer as "a secret inflow of God into the soul . . . the divine inflow". Here we have the core of the economy of salvation: salvation effected by union; transformative participation in the divine nature; a beginning in faith of what shall be completed in vision; an eternal enthrallment in Father, Son and Spirit; purest Beauty, Joy and Love.

Initial delicacy

However, we ought not to imagine that the beginnings of infused prayer here in pilgrimage are ecstatic absorptions, thrilling delights. On the contrary, they are so gentle and unobtrusive at the outset that unless one is well instructed, they may go unnoticed. Says John, "It is noteworthy that this general knowledge is at times so recondite and delicate (especially when purer, simpler, and more perfect), spiritual, and interior that the soul does not perceive or feel it, even though occupied with it." Indeed, he goes on to state that "the purer, simpler, and more perfect the general knowledge is, the darker it seems to be and the less the intellect perceives". This infused light can shine so purely and simply that "it is imperceptible" to the person receiving it.

Transformative of life

Unlike a human word, the divine locution does what it says. The biblical *dabar* refers to an active, powerful, doing word, not simply to an intellectual construct. So also the contemplation given by the Holy Spirit burns faults away and produces virtues. The growth is usually imperceptible from one day to another, but growth necessarily follows if the prayer is genuine. Jesus' axiom applies here as well as elsewhere: "From their fruits you will know them."[17] The surest sign of genuine prayer is the steady deepening of faith, hope, love, humility, patience, purity and all the other virtues. St. John of the Cross speaks of the purifying fire of contemplation, of "a dark, loving spiritual fire", that increases all other goodnesses because it is itself increasing love. The love-giving Spirit brings with Himself all virtues: "Love, joy, peace, patience, kindness, goodness, trustfulness, gentleness and self-control."[18] We ought not, therefore, to envision contemplation as though it were divorced from the rest of life. We pray in solitude, yes, but we return to our brothers and sisters with something rich to share, a far deeper, more loving, more giving self. It is noncontemplative people who fall short of living a full human life.

Although St. John of the Cross is not given to offering complete definitions in single statements, we do have two sentences that summarize well his concept of contemplation. When a generous individual can no longer meditate discursively, "he should learn to remain in God's presence with a loving attention and a tranquil intellect", even though this seems like idleness to him. Soon he will find little by little that a "divine calm and peace with a wondrous, sublime knowledge of God, enveloped in divine love, will be infused into his soul".[19]

BIBLICAL FORMULATIONS

One of the most extravagant errors of recent decades among religious men and women is the idea that contemplation is a monastic enterprise, good in itself but the exclusive domain of the cloister. Otherwise intelligent people have argued that because contemplation is a matter for monks and nuns alone, religious in the active apostolates should not even include references to it in their rules, much less expect to experience it in their own prayer life. And, of course, even less so are laymen and laywomen to be bothering their heads about it. Apparently they have not considered that the real question is not whether contemplation is an occupation proper to secluded life but whether it is a Gospel reality and thus meant for all men and women in every vocation.

While it is true that the Scriptures do not speak of contemplation in terms that Plato or Aristotle used, it is decidedly untrue that the inspired word did not know and recommend the reality. A deep communion with God (and our Christic contemplation is nothing other than a love communion of increasing depth) is found repeatedly in the pages of both the Old and the New Testaments. The evidence so abounds that we shall here present only a representative sampling of it. Anyone who has read widely in the mystics knows well that these greatest of our contemplatives found endless nourishment for their advanced prayer in the inspired word.

Unworded prayer

We may commence our sketch of contemplation in Scripture by noting that biblical men and women were well aware that there is a prayer that surpasses mere vocalization. The psalmist's heart and flesh sing for very joy to the living God,[20] and he wishes at times simply to be still and know that the Lord is God indeed.[21] While Jesus warns us not to babble with many words as the pagans do when they pray,[22] He Himself spends whole nights absorbed in the Father—it is unlikely that He spent ten to twelve hours uttering words.[23] There is, therefore, a nonverbalized kind of prayer, a prayer that is quiet, still, inner and deep, a prayer very much like our above descriptions from Teresa and John.

Experience of God

So routine did the ancient Hebrews consider a vibrant experience of Yahweh that their expressions for knowing Him did not mean merely the intellectual grasp that our current concept of knowing implies. A man "knew" his wife in sexual intercourse; that is, he experienced her deeply in becoming one flesh with her. The Hebrew knew God intellectually, of course, but his contact was not via sterile concepts. The psalmist invites everyone to taste and drink deeply, to experience for themselves how good the Lord is.[24] They who look to Him encounter Him intimately and become radiant with joy.[25] This is not merely vocal prayer or discursive reflection; it is a profound communion that puts one in touch with the living Lord. St. Peter shares this experiential thrill when he tells his new Christians that though they have not seen the risen Jesus, they have a joy in Him so great that it cannot be described.[26] St. Paul wants nothing other than knowing, that is, experiencing Christ and the power of His Resurrection together with a sharing in His Passion and death.[27] Mystic Paul likewise admonishes his disciples that they are to imitate him as he imitates Christ.[28] Once again we find in the inspired word the very same reality spoken of by our two Carmelite saints.

Contemplative light/knowing

Biblical men knew remarkably well, in their own fashion, what we now call the connatural, nonconceptual element in Christic contemplation. The psalmist declares that the "one thing", the overriding necessity of all human life, is "to gaze on the beauty of the Lord" in His temple,[29] that we are to keep our eyes always on the Lord, an astonishing idea when one ponders what it says and does not dilute its radicality.[30] Indeed, if we keep Yahweh always before our eyes, nothing can shake us.[31] So strongly does the holy person cling to God that he looks to no one else either in heaven or on earth.[32] He is content to pause a while and imbibe the idea that God is indeed God.[33] So crucial is this deep knowledge of the Lord that contemplation is said to be the very reward of living a virtuous life: upright men will gaze upon His face, that is, will live in His presence.[34] Centered as they are on God, prayerful people spend the whole night in vigil as they ponder the divine name,[35] and they find that as the Lord's word unfolds it gives them the light that the simple understand.[36] In the new dispensation the Mother of the Lord is presented as the model of pondering the word in one's heart,[37] and the other Mary sitting on the floor undividedly drinking the incarnate Word is the very picture of what contemplation means.[38] St. Paul prayed for the Colossians that God would give them a perfect wisdom and spiritual understanding, that they might possess the fullest knowledge of His will.[39] Both the Old and the New Testaments, therefore, clearly describe the lofty knowing elements we now associate with infused contemplation both in its initial stages and in its advanced developments. That we are not reading an alien idea into Scripture can readily be seen by a simple comparison of the formulations of Teresa and John with the biblical expressions: simple gazing on the divine beauty . . . continual keeping of one's attention on the Lord . . . looking to no one else . . . pausing and resting in the sacred presence . . . awareness of him through the night . . . light-giving pondering . . . perfect wisdom, spiritual understanding, fullest knowledge. Our two saints simply accentuate, elucidate and illustrate what we already have in the divine word.

Infused love

The greatest of all the commandments is before all else a prayer commandment. To have one's whole heart, soul and mind filled to overflowing with the love of God is to be filled with the highest prayer. The core and essence of the transforming union are nothing other than a complete identification with God in love.[40] When one walks lovesick for God, as St. John of the Cross puts it, he is at the heights of prayer life, and he is fulfilling the greatest commandment to perfection. This spiritual marriage of the soul with God is celebrated in the whole book of the Song of Songs,[41] and it is no wonder that mystics for the last twenty centuries have gravitated to the Song of Songs to explain mystical contemplation. This love, says St. Paul, is poured into our hearts by the Holy Spirit Who is given to us.[42] Love poured out is, of course, infused love — the two words mean the same thing. The psalmist who declares that he delights in nothing else on earth but his Lord further proclaims that his flesh and his heart are pining with love, that his joy is to be near God.[43] So advanced a love could not be anything but the burning infusions of which Teresa and John commonly speak.

Deep delight and peace

The reader will recall that both in St. Teresa's description of the prayer of quiet and in St. John's brief characterization of advancing infused prayer, there was a frequent emphasis on the dimension of a divinely bestowed delight, one that is not the result of discursive meditation. Scripture, too, commonly speaks of the same delight in God, a delight that surpasses emotion—even though an emotional resonance may accompany the essential spiritual joy. The psalmist shouts that his heart exults and his soul rejoices in God, Who is before him always. Nothing can unsettle this singer to the Lord, and he knows that he will have unbounded joy in the divine presence, everlasting pleasures at his right hand.[44] St. Paul admonishes the Philippians to rejoice in the Lord always and to experience a peace that is beyond all understanding.[45] The infusion of divinely given strength, says Paul, comes from God's own glorious power, and it enables us to endure anything joyfully.[46] All this is exactly what the mystics say of their experiences at prayer.

Dry desire, ardent yearning

Not all contemplative prayer is sheer delight. Anyone who has seriously pursued a prayer life and the Gospel life-style that is a prerequisite for it to flourish knows well enough that in the contemplative nights so vividly described by St. John of the Cross one must encounter a vast inner void. A dry, empty-feeling yearning is also part and parcel of this pilgrim enterprise. Scripture likewise knows of it and often returns to the theme of an arid but earnest desire. From the depths of the wilderness the psalmist cries out to Yahweh that he is pining and thirsting for Him, that his flesh is longing as a parched desert, lifeless and waterless; he longs to gaze upon his Lord and to experience His power and glory, a perfect and appealing description of what it is like to have grown in prayer to this point of a strong yearning for God.[47] The longest of the psalms returns to this refrain in expressions that will touch any person who has entered the nights explained by St. John of the Cross: with my whole heart I seek you . . . I am overcome with incessant longing . . . I am worn out waiting for you to save me . . . I open my mouth panting for you . . . I long for you, my savior.[48] Isaiah expresses it well as he prays to his Lord: "At night my soul longs for you and my spirit in me seeks for you."[49] Biblical writers were well aware of the phenomena we now describe as a dark fire of purifying contemplation.

Absorption in God

One might summarize these biblical descriptions of advanced prayer by considering them as complementary aspects of an immersion in God, an absorption in the Beloved. For the saint of the old dispensation as for the saint of the new, the heart of the human enterprise is nothing other than a being filled with the divine, a being transformed into God Himself, a participation in the divine nature.[50] Mary is portrayed by Luke as a woman whose primary and typical occupation is pondering the word in her heart.[51] For Jesus the Father is like a powerful magnet to which He is continually drawn, and so He habitually goes off for long periods of protracted absorption in the Father, even throughout whole nights.[52] The infant Church immediately after the Ascension of her Lord groups herself around His Mother and spends so much time absorbed in God that Luke terms the prayer continual.[53] Not surprisingly, they are soon filled with the Holy Spirit.[54] The absorption is so satisfying that the psalmist says of it that he delights in nothing else, and St. Paul considers all else to be rubbish.[55]

Overflowing filling

Immersion in God entails a being filled with Him, a divine inflowing. Biblical men knew well enough that this self-communication of God is the sole destiny of men. The psalmist took it for granted that Yahweh lovingly gives him life,[56] and he declared that everyone is to feast on the bounty of the divine house and to see light in the divine light.[57] St. Paul's prayer for the Ephesians was that they know the fullness of God's love[58] and nothing less.

It is clear, therefore, that what we now call infused contemplation and mystical prayer was so well known in biblical times that it was taken for granted. Teresa and John, together with Augustine and Gregory of Nyssa long before them, invented nothing new. They have simply expressed in their own ways and with rich elucidations what we have long had in the deposit of revelation.

A CONTEMPORARY FORMULATION

Despite the fact that both Scripture and our saints are clear in their descriptions of what a deep communion with God actually is, it may be helpful to cast the whole matter into contemporary language and at the same time to add some supplementary observations. Infused contemplation is the normal, ordinary development of discursive prayer. The former gradually and gently replaces the latter when reasoned thought has run its course as a method of communing with the Lord. Infused prayer is given, not produced. Unlike oriental states of awareness, our prayer is a love communion that the divine Beloved Himself gives when we are ready for it. Hence, we may say that our contemplation is a divinely originated, general, nonconceptual, loving awareness of God. At times this is a delightful, loving attention, at times a dry, purifying desire, at other times a strong thirsting for Him. In the beginnings it is usually delicate and brief, but as it develops it becomes burning, powerful, absorbing, prolonged. Always it is transformative of the person. If all goes well, it eventually culminates in the transforming union itself.

The details of this growth in depth we shall consider when we deal with St. Teresa's seven mansions in our next chapter. For now it may be sufficient to note several traits that are common to all infused contemplation.

1. There is an experience of God's presence either after the manner of a peaceful, general, loving attention or of a dry reaching out for Him.

2. One experiences a great deal of fluctuation in the intensity of this communion and in the diverse manners in which God makes Himself felt and known.

3. In advancing contemplation God gradually and slowly "captures" the inner faculties. He first occupies the will and then the imagination and the intellect. This is why in the beginnings of infused prayer distractions are common: only the will is taken over. Later on, during deep absorptions and ecstatic prayer, these distractions cease. This capturing is termed the *ligature* by some writers.

4. Infused prayer is produced *modo divino,* in the divine manner, whereas discursive meditation was *modo humano,* in the human manner.

5. The contemplation itself is dark, that is, without images or concepts. God, Who is endlessly beyond all finite ideas and formulations, is now known in a superior way surpassing all our reasonings and thoughts. This prayer is neither vision nor locution nor feeling.

6. The prayer cannot be "figured out" or understood. Trying to dissect or analyze it by clear, concise ideas or concepts not only issues in frustration but also indicates a lack of understanding of what contemplation is.

7. There is in Christic contemplation a gradual lengthening of the time span during which the infusion lasts. In the beginnings the awareness is very brief and is punctured by frequent distractions, but as the years go by, and if one's living of the Gospel keeps pace, what God gives increases not only in intensity but also in duration. Even so, the principle of fluctuation mentioned in number 2 above is still operative.

8. While the beginnings of infused prayer appear utterly normal and cause no apprehension, later strong prayer gifts can trigger fear as a first reaction. It is not the beauty of the gift that begets the fear, but

unfamiliarity with it. One wonders what it is and whence it comes. Once assured that its origin is divine, the recipient loses his initial fear.

9. Deepening communion with the indwelling Trinity brings with it a steadily progressive growth in holiness: humility, love, patience, purity, fortitude and all the virtues. So necessary is this trait that a gradual increase in day-to-day Gospel living is an indispensable sign of the genuineness of any prayer: "From their fruits you will know them."

CHAPTER SIX

THE TERESIAN MANSIONS

Living things grow in visible creation. Acorns develop into oak trees, tadpoles into frogs, babies into adult men and women. We are so convinced that living things slowly mature to a fullness of life that if we were to notice that a three-foot sapling suddenly stopped growing, we would immediately and without any need for reasoning about it conclude that something had gone wrong. We use the severe word *retardation* to express a failure in the learning process of a child, for we expect a youngster to develop mentally along with his chronological age. An adult who can communicate only on the level of a six-year-old is definitely abnormal.

Many of us do not at all understand to be applicable on the supernatural level what we fully grasp on the natural level. We are not alarmed about truncated spiritual development. Yet Jesus said that He came not only that we might have life but also that we might have it abundantly,[1] and St. Paul insisted that we are to live so intensely that we are to be filled with the utter fullness of God, nothing less.[2] Unfortunately, many baptized persons depart this life without ever realizing that they were destined to a deep communion with God. Vocal prayer was all they knew, for it was all they were taught. This chapter deals with much of what the Church has in mind when she has us pray on the feast of St. Teresa that all of us be "filled with her heavenly teaching".[3] The saint's *Interior Castle* is not only her most mature work; it is also the all-time classic on the question of the development of prayer from its incipient beginnings to its mature fullness in the transforming union. While exploring the plan and content of this classic, we shall supplement and enrich our account with Teresa's other works as well.

WHY STUDY STAGES?

One of the most common mistakes made by some spiritual directors is to dismiss as irrelevant the question of where a directee is in prayer development. The indifference and at times active hostility toward the question is expressed in several ways: "Don't be introspective during prayer; forget about 'where you are' . . . if you are thinking about your prayer, then you are not praying . . . just practice the method I have given you, and don't concern yourself with anything else . . . prayer is not a study period." The assumptions behind these reactions cannot stand careful scrutiny. They are actually naïve. Before we consider St. Teresa's insistence that we should know where we are and the many reasons for her position, it may be well to answer the objections briefly lest they be an obstacle to our appreciation of her overall teaching.

No doubt we should not be introspective during prayer. It is precisely the person who does understand the various developments and how they differ from one another who needs no least inner examination. Knowing the stages of which Teresa speaks, we automatically know where we are, and we need little or no self-scrutiny to find out. Understanding these developments, we likewise know how to respond to our present mode of praying, and thus we avoid the inner turmoil found in the individual who has unreal expectations of what prayer should be like. If a man drives a thousand miles from one city to another, he should know where the destination is and how he is to get there. If he has no idea of the way, he will be filled with anxiety all along the trip. If he knows the way well, he spends little or no time reflecting on it. So it is with prayer. The person who understands Teresa's seven main mansions needs little or no conjecturing on how to proceed at any given stage of growth.

The first of the saint's reasons for describing "the end of the battle" is that we need to know our destination. People in her day as well as in ours suppose that drinking deeply from the "heavenly source" is not for them, and Teresa sets out to describe this prayer destiny so that they may correct their mistaken notion.[4]

The second reason is support and encouragement along the way: when we understand how prayer grows and that it entails sacrifices and difficulties, we will not be surprised by them and not be downhearted in the weariness we are bound to meet.[5] In our chapter on the passive purifications we hope to make it plain that a great deal of anxiety is the usual reaction of people who enter the two nights of sense and spirit and who do not understand the normalcy of their experiences.

Teresa's third reason is bound up with the first two: we should be able to recognize when we have reached the place for "drinking at the spring", lest we lose the "blessings" of this lofty communion.[6] Those who do not recognize the normal delicate beginnings of infused prayer are almost certain to impede the gift through a misguided attachment to their discursive methods. Spiritual direction over the years has repeatedly impressed upon me how extensive is the damage done in well-meaning souls who do not understand what is happening in their communion with the Lord.

The saint's fourth reason is that we should know how to operate at the different stages of growth, for one prays differently according to the stage one's prayer has reached. This is why she insists on explaining advanced prayer to beginners:

> I should like to explain this experience because we are dealing with beginners; and when the Lord begins to grant these favors, the soul itself doesn't understand them nor does it know what to do with itself. For if the Lord leads it along the path of fear, as He did me, it is a great trial if there is no one to understand it. To see itself described brings it intense joy, and then it sees clearly the path it is walking on. It is a great good to know what one must do in order to advance in *any* of these stages.[7]

Not only does the saint see no danger of introspection; she also takes it for granted that knowing where is on the path of prayer is normal.

Teresa's fifth reason for knowing these stages of development is that a traveler on a long, arduous journey is encouraged to see that he is making progress and coming nearer to the destination. So also in the life of prayer "it is most important that you should realize you are making progress".[8]

The saint's final explanation stems from her own reaction to new gifts she had received from God. The striking "favors" usually triggered fear in her, the fear of deception. Because the illuminists of her day made St. Teresa sensitive to the dangers of illusion, she wanted her readers to be prepared for genuine gifts and to know how they differ from self-deceptions or demonic intrusions.[9]

I might add two more motives for a careful study of the sevenfold development of contemplation. To comprehend the early stages of living things, it is useful to have knowledge of their mature states. One appreciates fully an acorn or a baby only after becoming well acquainted with the completely grown oak tree and the human adult. We do not grasp even discursive meditation and its implications until we see that it is a setting out on a path that leads to transformation of life and the spiritual marriage. We appreciate the prayers of quiet and union adequately only when we see that they are incipient stages of the seventh mansions.

Further, glimpsing the splendor of contemplative fulfillment is a strong spur toward making all the sacrifices entailed in reaching it. To have seen the beauty of a gigantic waterfall in a photograph provides a strong incentive to keep climbing over rough terrain in an effort to reach the reality. If we are to carry our cross every day,[10] if we are to enter through the narrow gate and walk the rough road,[11] we will be encouraged by discovering something of what eye has not seen nor ear heard, of what does not even dawn on us, namely, what God has prepared for those who love Him.[12] Knowing the way, therefore, and especially the lofty destination of the life of prayer, spurs us to continue onward without wearying and to make persevering effort to live the life that is its condition.

VOCAL PRAYER

Though official liturgical worship and the recitation of private prayer formulas are not conceived to be mansions in the teresian concept of communing with God, the saint by no means considers them unimportant or on the periphery of life. St. Teresa sees what we call vocal prayer not only as noble in itself but also as an occasion for what she calls "perfect contemplation". She tells her nuns that "while you are repeating the Paternoster or some other vocal prayer, it is quite possible for the Lord to grant you perfect contemplation".[13] Experience of prayerful men and women today bears out the correctness of the saint's remark. We are likewise reminded of the statement of Vatican II to the effect that the faithful are to "taste to the full" the mysteries they celebrate in the liturgy, and that within the Eucharist they are to be led into "the compelling love of Christ" and to be "set afire".[14] As we have remarked elsewhere in this volume, words like these can be understood only in the context of the universal call to the very heights of contemplation. St. Teresa sees liturgical worship as the council did, that is, as leading to and incorporating the loftiest infused prayer.

It need scarcely be noted that Teresa does not consider the mere rattling off of words as vocal prayer. For her, reciting prayers without attention to God is not prayer at all: "If a person does not think Whom he is addressing, and what he is asking for, and who it is that is asking and of Whom he is asking it, I do not consider that he is praying at all even though he be constantly moving his lips."[15] It follows logically enough that one vocal prayer, even so little as one petition of the Our Father, if well said, is better than many recited thoughtlessly or hurriedly.[16] Because any genuine prayer necessarily includes a strong inner element as its most important factor, we may say that for Teresa vocal prayer is actually verbalized mental prayer and thus poles apart from rote recitation.

If one objects that the teresian ideal here is extremely difficult to realize in practice, indeed, almost impossible for ordinary distracted human beings, the answer is a frank admission: yes, so it is. But the saint does not leave her readers without a remedy. She offers suggestions for the improvement of vocal prayer, and if we follow her leads, we can reach the point where we are led into infused contemplation. The first recommendation St. Teresa proposes is what she would style active recollection. By this she means that anyone who is serious about a prayer life must work hard and perseveringly to gather himself together, to still the wanderings of his mind and the restlessness of his heart. He does not simply kneel or sit down and hope something will happen. When she comes to specifics, Teresa is anything but ethereal. One begins with self-examination and the sign of the Cross. Then she (the saint is speaking directly to her nuns but indirectly to everyone) seeks out a companion, and of course the companion will be none other than the Teacher of all prayer: "Imagine that this Lord Himself is at your side and see how lovingly and how humbly He is teaching you."[17] She explains that she is not asking the nuns to work at elaborate meditations "but only to look at Him. . . . He is only waiting for us to look at Him. . . . If you want Him you will find Him."[18] We may picture the Lord in any of His mysteries, but Teresa prefers some scene of the Passion. She is so concrete that she goes on to advise her nuns to "get an image or picture of this Lord — one that you like — not to wear around your neck and never look at but to use regularly whenever you talk to Him, and He will tell you what to say".[19] A modern reader might find this approach artless or lacking in sophistication, but he does so at his own loss. St. Teresa knew human nature as few do, and she knew well that we need concrete beginnings. Even more important, she realized how to apply to the question of prayer the profound theological principle of the Incarnation: "No one goes to the Father except by me."[20]

The saint rooted both vocal and mental prayer in the trinitarian indwelling mystery. We do not address God as though He were located on a distant quasar. She lays great importance on learning to find the Lord where He revealed Himself to be for the person who loves: in the deepest center of one's being. Focusing on the indwelling presence, says Teresa, is for wandering minds "one of the best ways of concentrating the mind" in prayer.[21] She promises great things to those who do so:

> Those who are able to shut themselves up in this way within this little Heaven of the soul, wherein dwells the Maker of Heaven and earth, and who have formed the habit of looking at nothing and staying in no place which will distract these outward senses, may be sure that they are walking on an excellent road, and will come without fail to drink of the water of the fountain, for they will journey a long way in a short time.[22]

St. Teresa was not bashful with "His Majesty". She herself was intimate and affectionate at prayer. She allowed her feelings to show, and she advised the same to others: "Speak with Him as with a Father, a Brother, a Lord and a Spouse—and sometimes in one way and sometimes in another."[23] She tells her nuns plainly that since by their vows they are espoused to Him and He to them, they should ask Him to treat them as His brides.[24]

Vocal prayer is not to be thought of as cut off from infused contemplation. Rather, the one is to blend into the other. When we have withdrawn the senses from all outer things, when once we are purified of our self-centered clingings, "when no hindrance comes to it from outside, the soul remains alone with its God and is thoroughly prepared to become enkindled".[25]

ST. TERESA'S GROWTH IMAGES

Skillful teachers illustrate their ideas and principles, for they know that the human mind, being spirit in body, instinctively gravitates toward grasping concepts in images. Scripture abounds with examples taken from everyday life: birds, lilies, sun, moon, rocks, pastures, mountains. The master Teacher followed and improved upon this practice in his unforgettable parables. Although St. Teresa never spent an hour in a teacher's college, she knew that so ethereal a subject as contemplation requires graphic illustrations if one is to help people comprehend and appreciate it. Her favorite growth images were flowing water and inner castle. The saint uses water to represent the giftness of advanced prayer together with its progressive ease of effort. She distinguishes four ways of obtaining this favor. The garden of the soul, she says, can be watered in several manners. The first, drawing the water up from a well by use of a bucket, entails a great deal of human effort. The second way, cranking a water wheel and having the water run through an aqueduct, involves less exertion and yields more water. The third entails far less effort, for in it the water enters the garden as by an effluence from river or stream. The fourth and final way is the best of all: as by a gentle but abundant rainfall the Lord himself waters the garden, and the soul does not work at all.[26] With this imagery the saint is obviously explaining how prayer grows beyond the more laborious activities of discursive meditation to a less active effort and more simple communing, until finally reaching the effortless contemplation of the transforming union.

As much as St. Teresa was attracted to water as a symbol of how God gives growth in prayer, she used more extensively an inner castle as the vehicle of explanation, a vehicle given her by the Lord Himself. Like many another writer faced with an empty sheet of paper without having the least idea of what to put down on it, she felt at the outset of composing her *Interior Castle* that she had nothing to say and had no inkling as to how to carry out the charge laid upon her: to explain in writing the development of prayer. Unlike most other authors, Teresa had recourse to prayer in her dilemma. As she sought aid as to how to begin, she found herself thinking "of the soul as if it were a castle made of a single diamond or of a very clear crystal, in which there are many rooms, just as in Heaven there are many mansions".[27] In the center of the crystal castle, the soul, is the Sun. As we grow in prayer we draw closer to this divine Sun and are transformed into Him — nonpantheistically, of course. Living in the soul's center, the Sun gives it all its splendor and beauty, and the human temple "is as capable of enjoying Him as is the crystal of reflecting the sun".[28] The saint is careful to explain the precise way in which the reader is to understand the image and its application:

> You must not imagine these mansions as arranged in a row, one behind another, but fix your attention on the centre, the room or palace occupied by the King. Think of a palmito, which has many outer rinds surrounding the savoury part within, all of which must be taken away before the center can be eaten. Just so around this central room are many more, as there also are above it. In speaking of the soul we must always think of it as spacious, ample and lofty; and this can be done without the least exaggeration, for the soul's capacity is much greater than we can realize, and this Sun Which is in the palace, reaches every part of it.[29]

Among the depositions of the processes for St. Teresa's canonization, Fray Deigo de Yepes, confessor and member of her traveling party, gives an account of how she received the idea of this approach to prayer growth from God Himself.

> She was asked to write a treatise on prayer as she knew it from her own experience. On the eve of Holy Trinity when she was wondering what theme to take for her treatise, God gave it to her by showing her a very beautiful globe of crystal like a castle with seven concentric dwellings. The seventh which was in the centre was the King of Glory in great splendour who lit up and adorned all the dwellings as far as the outer ring. The nearer the centre the greater the light. This light did not shine beyond the outer ring.[30]

We should recall that the final contemplation of the beatific vision in the risen body is presented at the close of the New Testament as the fulfillment of the indwelling presence. The living God, says the book of Revelation, shall make His home among His people. They will dwell in the holy city Jerusalem coming down from God: "It had all the radiant glory of God and glittered like some precious jewel of crystal-clear diamond." This final temple in glory needs neither sun nor moon for light, for it is lit with the radiant glory of God, and the Lamb is the lighted torch for it.[31] The God of Teresa's private revelation chose the same image for her that He had already selected for His public revelation.

While the seven mansions provide an apt vehicle for explaining the development of contemplative prayer, we ought not to imagine them as pigeonholes and the developments as discrete jumps from one stage to another. Living things grow gradually, and communion with God, being the supreme of all living realities, likewise matures imperceptibly. Just as a teacher of developmental psychology cannot make the subject clear except by distinguishing one stage from another, so we cannot explain prayer growth without speaking of diverse degrees of progression. Yet the process is so gradual that we must describe it as a continuity. The multiplicities of discursive meditation naturally and normally and without any concentrated effort become less and less multiple and more and more simple. As we explain in its own place, the transition from discursive meditation to the beginnings of infused contemplation is likewise a gradual process. And in the last four mansions there is a decided blending of one mansion into the next. The experience of absorption in the fifth mansions can have some of the traits of the sixth's ecstatic prayer,[32] and the sixth and seventh can be fused because they have somewhat similar traits: "There is no closed door", says St. Teresa, "to separate the one from the other", even though the latter does have characteristics not found in the former.[33]

FIRST MANSIONS (FIRST WATER)

Spiritual writers since the sixteenth century have so gladly embraced Teresa's sevenfold schema for the development of prayer that it has become classic, but not all have dealt with the first three mansions as she did. I do not say that their treatments lack basis in reality but only that what they say is largely not what she says. We moderns tend to identify the first mansions with discursive meditation, the second with affective-discursive prayer, and the third with an active simple prayer. We then agree that the last four mansions are concerned with the developments of infused contemplation. The saint, on the other hand, says little about prayer in the first three mansions and says a great deal about the impediments caused by sins and attachments. We shall follow Teresa's teaching not only because she is a principal subject of this book but also because she has very good reason for proceeding as she does. Yet because the moderns are not entirely wrong in their additions to her mansions, I shall incorporate into these first mansions what the saint says about active, discursive prayer. This incorporation is not foreign to her mind, and it at the same time makes a helpful connection with our contemporaries.

St. Teresa's starting point is the absolutely basic condition for a serious prayer life: an earnest, continuing effort to rid oneself of sins, imperfections and attachments. If we may judge from the current superabundance of articles, books and lectures on contemplation, most of our contemporaries seem to assume that to engage successfully in meditative prayer one needs most of all to find the right methods, techniques and processes. Not so Teresa. She knows better. Christic communion cannot be produced by techniques, because it is above all a love matter before it is anything else—and precisely because interpersonal intimacy is its heart, it is suffocated, even killed, by selfishness in any form. Hence, in writing of the first three mansions, the saint wisely spends much time explaining how the beginner, even though in the state of grace, can and must emerge from a whole web of more or less petty faults.

First of all, we may allow St. Teresa to describe just what kind of people she has in mind. On the plus side she is speaking of men and women who want to avoid offending God and who "may perform good works". Yet they are, at this early stage, still absorbed in worldly matters and pleasures, and they are "puffed up with worldly honours and ambitions". Because they are free from serious sin, the King does dwell in their castle, but they have only a tenuous relationship with Him, and they scarcely see His light, so submerged are they in things of the world.[34] Perhaps the saint was not conscious of it when she penned this analysis, but she is in exact agreement with the thought of her Master. When He came to explain why people who listen to His word (and thus have some goodness in them) do not mature in their response to it, He laid the cause in their being smothered by the cares and riches and pleasures of life.[35] *Interior Castle* is a book on the maturing process we find both in prayer and in the rest of life, for the two cannot be separated. Neither Jesus nor Teresa explains spiritual retardation as resulting from a lack of techniques or methods. In almost identical terms they lay the blame on the free-will choice of worldliness in its sundry forms.

What, then, is the beginner to do? Most people cannot leave the world in a bodily sense, but every follower of Christ who is serious about genuine growth must leave the spirit of the world. Everyone, says Teresa, who wishes to go on to the second mansions

will be well advised, as far as his state of life permits, to try to put aside
all unnecessary affairs and business. For those who hope to reach the
principal Mansion, this is so important that unless they begin in this
way I do not believe they will ever be able to get there.[36]

The New Testament has already admonished us that we must not love
this passing world or anything that is in it, for the love of the Father
cannot exist in the person who loves the world, the sensual body, the
lustful eye, pride in possessions.[37] God's grace has taught us "that what
we have to do is to give up everything that does not lead to God, and
all our worldly ambitions".[38] The main business of the beginner, therefore, is to make a determined turnabout from preoccupation with this
worldly world to a life centered in the Trinity. The struggle will be
long and at times arduous, but there is no other way to accomplish
the ascent of the mountain and reach the rewarding outcome that awaits
one at the summit.

We direct our attention now to some of what St. Teresa says about
the methods of discursive meditation. While, in her mind, procedures
in prayer are clearly secondary, they do have their proper place for
beginners. She valued thoughtful reflection, and she herself had a keen
sense of the marvels of nature. Even though she did not enjoy our advantage of microscopes to penetrate into the magnificent microworld,
animate and inanimate, she found in a worm or a bee matter for meditating "upon the wonders and the wisdom of our God. What, then, would
it be if we knew the properties of everything?" she asks. "It will be
a great help to us if we occupy ourselves in thinking of these wonderful things and rejoice in being the brides of so wise and powerful a
King."[39]

Yet splendid as nature is, it is not sufficient. The mysteries of the
supernatural order are still more fruitful sources of meditative prayer,
and in the presentation of these mysteries nothing can surpass the
Gospels. "I have always been fond of the words of the Gospels", she
notes, "and have found more recollection in them than in the most carefully planned books — especially books of which the authors were not
fully approved, and which I never wanted to read."[40]

The careful student of St. Teresa will notice that her procedural advice
for beginners in prayer is extremely simple: there are no complicated
steps and substeps. What she insists upon is utterly basic and indispensable: in whatever degree of prayer one is in, it is love, not reasoning,
that is primary. She makes this very point in one of her most frequently
cited statements: "If you would progress a long way on this road and
ascend to the Mansions of your desire, the important thing is not to
think much, but to love much."[41] She offers the same advice to a layman

to whom she writes: "You must not tire yourself by trying to think a great deal, nor worry about meditation . . . keep occupying yourself all the time with the praise of the Lord."[42]

SECOND MANSIONS

We may clarify what St. Teresa has to say about the second mansions by grouping her thoughts under the two categories of traits and advice.[43] First, the traits—what are these people like who have made some progress but are as yet still far from their destination? They are still engaged in worldly pastimes, half giving them up and half clinging to them. They see imperfectly, and they act imperfectly, but nonetheless some growth has occurred. God is calling them ceaselessly, and they are able to hear Him now. In the first mansions they were both deaf and dumb, notes Teresa, but now the message is beginning to get through. Yet these people are not able to do the divine bidding immediately, for they are weak and irresolute. God's appeals to them come in several ways: conversations with good people . . . sermons and homilies . . . good reading . . . sickness and other trials . . . divine light during prayer itself.

The man or woman in the second mansions is a battleground where the conflict between the world and the divine call is being waged. There is a tug-of-war going on, and the individual experiences the two opposing pulls. The world's tug is experienced in several ways: earthly pleasures remain attractive, and they appear as though almost eternal. The soul finds it hard to give up esteem in the world and a selfish clinging to family and friends. It unreasonably fears doing penances to which it now feels called, and it vacillates, says Teresa, as to whether to return to the first mansions or to strive bravely on. In the opposite direction God's tug is likewise felt in diverse manners: reason itself shows the person how mistaken the world's message is and why it is mistaken. Significant growth has now taken place and has instilled a conviction that only in God is one's surety. Thus the will is inclined to love Him and to press on to leave worldliness with all of its falsehoods.

Given this conflict between the human and the divine, it is not surprising that the person in the second mansions is still a child in the practice of humility, obedience, love and patience. In her charming manner the saint observes that the virtues are "young", that they "have not yet learned to walk—in fact, they have only just been born". Hence, if prayer is to grow in depth, Gospel living must be perfected—the first cannot happen without the second.

What, then, is the program for those in the second mansions?[44] St.

Teresa's first bit of advice concerns companionship: the soul should avoid a close association with "evil" and mediocre people and make it a point to mix with the good, that is, not only with those in the early mansions but also with those who have advanced into the mansions "nearer the center", where the King is. To be in close touch with these latter is a great help, for they tend to bring others to higher things along with themselves. Second, there is need to "embrace the Cross" along with the suffering Lord. Resignation is not enough; there must be a generous, willed welcome to hardships and dryness in prayer. Third, there is the typical teresian insistence on daily fidelity to the divine will: "All that the beginner in prayer has to do . . . is to labour and be resolute and prepare himself with all possible diligence to bring his will into conformity with the will of God." The more one does this, the more "he will receive of the Lord". In the divine will "our entire welfare is to be found". In saying this the saint is, of course, reflecting the teaching of Jesus Himself: it is not those who merely proclaim "Lord, Lord" who enter the kingdom but those who do the Father's will.[45] Fourth, when one falls, there is no reason to lose heart but rather to continue making serious efforts toward progressing. People in the second mansions surely do fall, and if they repent and persevere in their efforts, God will bring good even out of the failures. St. Paul himself, noting that he was not yet perfect, forgot what was behind and pressed on; indeed, he raced toward the finish.[46] Finally, adds Teresa, people in the second mansions need to exercise fidelity to prayer. We cannot enter heaven without first entering our own souls, getting to know ourselves better, reflecting on the divine goodness and our need for mercy: "The door by which we can enter this castle is prayer." There is no other, for Jesus is Himself the door.[47]

THIRD MANSIONS

All the way through her seven mansions St. Teresa is thinking of laymen and laywomen as well as of religious and clerics, but it is interesting nonetheless that when she begins to describe people who have come as far as the third mansions, she expressly illustrates their advancement with examples from lay life, and she notes that "there are many such souls in the world" who reach the stage she is now considering.[48] These men and women of tender conscience are careful not to offend God: "They avoid committing even venial sins; they love doing penance; they spend hours in recollection; they use their time well; they practice works of charity toward their neighbours; and they are very careful

in their speech and dress and in the government of their household
if they have one."[49] Once again the saint says little about prayer life
as such but a great deal about doing the will of the Father. She remarks
that in the first three mansions human nature is an oppressive burden
on the spirit, "like a great load of earth". She adds that it shall be otherwise in the following mansions.[50] Anyone who has labored faithfully
in the first stages of prayer knows how true this is, for it is only later,
with the reception of infused prayer, that inner freedom becomes pronounced. Then one does more easily and joyously what ought to be
done and omits what ought to be omitted. However, while one at this
stage sometimes receives a few glimpses of the delights later to be had
in prayer, for the most part he finds few spiritual joys.[51]

How long may one expect to remain in mansions one through three
before beginning to enter those of infused contemplation? St. Teresa's
answer to this question may appear to be in conflict with the clear view
of St. John of the Cross that sincere people given to prayer "very soon"
enter the first night of sense, a night brought about by the beginnings
of infused contemplation. St. Teresa does not speak strongly on this
point, but she clearly inclines to the view that ordinarily people remain for a long time in the first three mansions. Writing at the beginning of chapter 1 of the fourth mansions, she remarks that

> it seems that, in order to reach these Mansions, one must have lived for
> a long time in the others; as a rule one must have been in those which
> we have just described, but there is no infallible rule about it, as you
> must often have heard, for the Lord gives when He wills and as He wills
> and to whom He wills, and, as the gifts are His own, this is doing no
> injustice to anyone.[52]

There may be an actual conflict of view beween Teresa and John
only if we suppose that his first dark purification is the same as her
first prayer of recollection and that of quiet. It seems to me, however,
that while these three types of initial infused prayer are closely related,
they are not identical. If this be true, there is no real contradiction in
the teaching of the two saints.

How does one pray in the third mansions? Consistently with her
whole approach, Teresa says very little about this question, because
the prayer is *modo humano,* still somewhat discursive. She does say that
an active focusing on the indwelling presence is the best way to prepare
for (notice that she does not say produce) the prayer of quiet,[53] but
this advice applies to the first two mansions as well. Contemporary
writers would answer the question by speaking of simplifying one's
active efforts and/or by using the approach of centering prayer.

FOURTH MANSIONS (SECOND WATER)

At this point in her classic on the development of prayer St. Teresa begins to speak at length and in great detail about the inner experiences of infused contemplation. The first three mansions take up about 30 percent of her text, and in these sections, as we have already remarked, she says relatively little about discursive meditation. The last four mansions take up about 70 percent of the text, and they are almost entirely about prayer in its infused developments. These simple facts are significant for our grasping the saint's mind about increasingly intimate communion with the indwelling Trinity.

One of the reasons Teresa gives for writing expansively about the fourth mansions is that "the greatest number of souls" enter these beginnings of infused prayer. Another reason is that it is at this stage of development that "the natural is united with the supernatural" and a great deal of harm can be done.[54] We have at this time of prayer development the mingling between the human and the divine modes of praying, and hence a good number of problems can and do arise. People do not commonly know how to effect the transition from the one to the other. It may be useful for us to summarize in contemporary terminology what we are now going to consider. Infused contemplation is a divinely given, general, nonconceptual, loving awareness of God. There are no images, no concepts, no ideas, no visions. Sometimes this awareness of God takes the form of a loving attention, sometimes of a dry desire, sometimes of a strong thirsting. None of these experiences is the result of reading or reasoning—they are given, received. The infusion is serene, purifying. It can be delicate and brief, or in advanced stages burning, powerful, absorbing, prolonged. Always it is transformative of the person, usually imperceptibly and gradually but on occasion obviously and suddenly.

St. Teresa uses her water image to distinguish actively produced, discursive prayer from this infused type. It is the difference between a person's filling a basin through human effort by drawing the water and transporting it through "numerous conduits" from a long distance and a basin receiving water because it rests in the very Source, that is, in God, the ever-flowing fountain. In this second case the rising of the water is quiet and peaceful; one does not know where it comes from or how it arises.[55] As the person grows into this new, infused prayer, God progressively takes over the will and then the intellect and imagination: He occupies and absorbs them by what He gives. St. Teresa calls this the suspension of the faculties; that is, they are relieved of the ordinary human necessity of working at thoughts, ideas and affections. It is not we who decide when this change shall take place; it is God Who gives the new communion, and thus it is He Who takes the initiative. Hence it would be foolish for a person to decide "I like this idea of infused prayer; I'll begin it tomorrow". Says the saint:

> The intellect ceases to work because God suspends it, as I shall explain afterwards if I know how and He gives me His help to do so. Taking it upon oneself to stop and suspend thought is what I mean should not be done; nor should we cease to work with the intellect, because otherwise we would be left like cold simpletons and be doing neither one thing nor the other. When the Lord suspends the intellect and causes it to stop, He Himself gives it that which holds its attention and makes it marvel; and without reflection it understands more in the space of a creed than we can understand with all our earthly diligence in many years. Trying to keep the soul's faculties busy and thinking you can make them be quiet is foolish.[56]

Later writers call this suspension of the faculties ligature, that is, a binding of our wills and intellects by God. This does not mean anything violent, of course, but simply a divinely bestowed absorption in knowing and loving and seeking.

In these fourth mansions St. Teresa distinguishes two kinds of infused prayer, the initial "recollection" and the prayer of quiet. Before the latter is given, almost always one will experience recollection, an infused and gentle awareness given by God and not produced by human effort. One is, as it were, gathered together in God and desires solitude to be with Him. The senses and external things slowly lose their hold upon the person. Here the Lord calls "with a call so gentle that even they can hardly recognize it", says Teresa, and these people "are sometimes in the castle before they have begun to think about God at all".[57] Hence, for the saint the beginnings of infused prayer occur in the fourth mansions before the prayer of quiet. A person, she notes, is "almost invariably" introduced to contemplative prayer in this manner. This being drawn to be alone with the Alone is not the result of a reasoned-out conclusion, as was the case with discursive meditation. Teresa calls this a "supernatural" recollection to bring out the idea that it is God Who is now drawing one from things of earth to Himself. The beginner needs to be well instructed, or he is likely to miss what is given at this point, so gentle and delicate is it. There is no absorption in God; rather, the inner person is serenely drawn to be occupied with Him.

This recollection seems similar to or identical with the initial delicate infusions mentioned by St. John of the Cross, infusions so brief and gentle that they may be hardly noticed by the recipient. Being such,

they can easily be stifled by unwise efforts to pray actively. Teresa notes
that in this prayer of recollection it is not necessary to abandon meditation completely, for the infusion is not continual by any means.[58] What
we say elsewhere about the transition from active to infused prayer
is applicable at this point.

The saint says a great deal more about the prayer of quiet properly
so called than she says about the initial recollection. In *Testimony* 59
she terms the former the prayer of "interior quiet and peace".[59] In *Way*
she defines it as a state of prayer "which is a quiet, deep and peaceful
happiness in the will", and yet one does not understand what it is.[60]
Teresa is here pointing out that this experience of delight in God is
far different from earthly pleasures, and yet it is unlike anything ex-
pressible in images or ideas.

Key to St. Teresa's explanation of the fourth mansions is the occupation of the will with God. At the moment when this prayer is given,
the soul is captive, she remarks, and is not free to love anything but
God.[61]

> The soul is so satisfied with God that as long as the recollection lasts,
> the quiet and calm are not lost since the will is united with God even
> though the two faculties are distracted; in fact, little by little the will
> brings the intellect and the memory back to recollection. Even though
> the will may not be totally absorbed, it is so well occupied, without
> knowing how, that no matter what efforts the other two faculties make,
> they cannot take away its contentment and joy.[62]

The saint seems to be making the point that during the prayer of quiet
some distractions are entirely possible, for while the memory and intellect may be somewhat stilled, they are not "completely lost", that
is, absorbed in God.[63] The person senses that he is close to the Lord
and knows Him better, but with no clear ideas. The quiet is felt in
differing degrees at different times. It may last for a long while, even
for a day or two.[64] It follows, then, that one can enjoy this interior
awareness even though engaged in exterior activities that require the
attention of the mind: "At such times they serve the Lord in both these
ways at once; the will, while in contemplation, is working without
knowing how it does so; the other two faculties are serving Him as
Martha did. Thus Martha and Mary work together."[65] The prayer itself,
therefore, is very easy when compared with the effort involved in
discursive meditation, and even if it lasts a long time, it does not weary
the recipient.[66] Because it is infused, this prayer can be neither originated
nor prolonged by our efforts or desire, and it can bring to one's intimate depths a great delight, a delight that can spill over into the body

on the emotional level.[67] Tears may accompany this contemplation, but if they do, they are, says Teresa, "gentle and without distress".[68]

Perhaps we should note in passing that these fourth mansions have nothing to do with the caricature of mysticism, the heretical doctrine called quietism taught by Miguel de Molinos in the seventeenth century. Quietism was a series of exaggerations: there was to be no human activity at all in prayer . . . no consolations . . . no yearnings for happiness . . . no petitionary prayer and no examination of conscience. Perfection was conceived as a love of God that excluded any concern for one's own salvation. Objectively sinful actions were conceived to be compatible with the state of contemplation. Quietism promoted a gross inertness in a spiritual void.

St. Teresa never divorces prayer from life. We have called attention to her insistence in the first three mansions on daily fidelity as a condition for prayer growth in any stage of development. In mansions four through seven she emphasizes also the transformative results of infused prayer as it brings about increasing fidelity to the demands of the Gospel. In the prayer of quiet "the virtues grow incomparably better than in the previous degree of prayer" . . . the person begins to lose the craving for worldly things . . . God gives a strong desire to grow in prayer and the resolve not to abandon it no matter what trials may arise . . . all servile fear disappears . . . one's love for God has much less self-interest . . . a need for prayerful solitude makes itself felt[69] . . . a "dilation" or inner freedom of soul brings about less constraint in serving God . . . an oppressive fear of hell disappears, and a firm confidence of eventual fruition of the Lord takes its place . . . a more lively faith begets a desire for penance and a diminution of fear of suffering . . . now knowing God much better, the person comes to realize more vividly his own misery . . . having tasted divine delight, he now sees earthly things as "mere refuse" . . . having grown so much in all the virtues, this person will infallibly continue to grow in them unless he returns to deliberate mediocrity and neglect.[70] To the uninitiated this description may sound too good to be true, but to those who have reached the fourth mansions Teresa's comments are seen to be completely correct. We should note that this growth is not chiefly the result of discursive deliberations together with an active plan of action. Imperceptibly and often with no explicit thoughts about the matter, one finds in oneself greater humility and patience and love and detachment and all else. Infused contemplation is indeed transformative of the person. St. Paul presents this same idea in his own manner. Love is poured out into our hearts by the Holy Spirit Who is given to us,[71] and it is this very love that brings along with it all sorts of inner goodness:

patience, kindness, humility, tolerance, trust, hope, endurance of whatever may come.[72] In another letter Paul tells us that the indwelling Spirit brings love, joy, peace, patience, kindness, goodness, trustfulness, gentleness and self-control.[73] For both St. Teresa and St. Paul intimacy with the indwelling God can do nothing other than issue in personal sanctity.

How does one operate in the prayer of quiet?[74] Because advancing prayer is so different from what has gone before, what we need to learn from our two Carmelites is how we are to avoid placing obstacles before the deepening divine action. The first bit of advice may well come as a surprise: we must learn receptivity. Infused contemplation cannot be acquired, initiated, intensified or prolonged, and yet despite our knowing this in theory, we tend to act as though we can more or less control it. We know likewise that God does not force Himself on the unwilling, but we are not as aware of the actuality that we can receive only what He chooses to give and when and how He chooses to give it. We constantly presume that we know what ought to be happening in our prayer life. In our consumerist-productionist societies there is a tendency to take for granted that we are in control of making happen whatever we want to have happen and of determining how it will come about. This expectation results in resistance to the receptivity required for prayer. Speaking of this prayer of quiet, St. Teresa observes that people "are tempted to imagine that they can prolong it and they may even try not to breathe. This is ridiculous: we can no more control this prayer than we can make the day break, or stop night from falling; it is supernatural (infused) and something we cannot acquire."[75] Because we are especially inclined to cling to the delight of it, she notes not only that this is impossible but also that the effort to cling is itself self-defeating:

> This prayer, then, is a little spark of the Lord's true love which He begins to enkindle in the soul; and He desires that the soul grow in the understanding of what this love accompanied by delight is. For anyone who has experience, it is impossible not to understand soon that this little spark cannot be acquired. Yet, this nature of ours is so eager for delights that it tries everything; but it is quickly left cold because however much it may desire to light the fire and obtain this delight, it doesn't seem to be doing anything else than throwing water on it and killing it.[76]

Learning to be receptive is not only difficult to do; it is difficult to teach. Teresa therefore uses the image of a baby nursing at its mother's breast. As the mother gives her breast and her milk without the baby's thought or effort, so the person at this prayer simply loves; there is no need to make efforts to understand or reflect on what is happening. "The soul should realize that it is in His company, and should merely drink the milk which His Majesty puts into its mouth and enjoy its sweetness. . . . It is not His will that the soul should try to understand how it is enjoying it, or what it is enjoying: it should lose all thought of itself."[77]

We have already noted that St. Teresa's prayer of quiet is far removed from its caricature, quietism. The dissimilarity between the two becomes still more clear when we ask of her what kind of activity is appropriate and what is not. She answers by insisting that attempts to force the mind to be empty do more harm than good. The Buddhist has methods for voiding the mind, but we are not Buddhists. We are not producing a neutral state of awareness; we are receiving light and love from God, and there is a vast difference between a sterile, impersonal awareness and a living, lightsome loving. When God wants our mind to cease operating in its ordinary human manner, He gives a delicate but loving luminosity in such manner that all we have to do is receive. Prayer grows, at His initiative, from our human manner to the divine manner.[78] When we notice the infused quiet, we leave aside discursive reasoning, but this does not mean that there is to be in the future no activity of the mind at all. "If we are not quite sure that the King has heard us, or sees us," says Teresa, "we must not stay where we are like ninnies, for there still remains a great deal for the soul to do when it has stilled the understanding; if it did nothing more it would experience much greater aridity and the imagination would grow more restless because of the effort caused it by cessation from thought."[79] When God wishes us to give up our human mode of praying, He illumines in His mode and leads us into an absorption in Himself. Teresa puts the matter well when she asserts that since God gave us our minds to be used in their own manner, "they must be allowed to perform their office until God gives them a better one".[80] She refers to this mingling of some activity with receptivity when she adds that "at this stage one doesn't have to renounce completely discursive mental prayer or the use of some words, or even vocal prayers if there should be the desire or ability; if the quiet is great, it is difficult to speak without a good deal of effort".[81]

While there is some room for activity in the fourth mansions, it is neither frenetic nor unduly multiplied. The saint advises the person here to be gentle and simple:

> The most we should do is occasionally, and quite simply, to utter a single word, like a person giving a little puff to a candle, when he sees it has

almost gone out, so as to make it burn again; though, if it were fully alight, I suppose the only result of blowing it would be to put it out. I think the puff should be a gentle one because, if we begin to tax our brains by making up long speeches, the will may become active again.[82]

Centering prayer is not new. Teresa is careful not to suggest it for all stages of the spiritual life, and she insists that, whatever activity is called for during the prayer in the fourth mansions, one should proceed "gently and noiselessly":

> What I call noise is running about with the intellect looking for many words and reflections so as to give thanks for this gift and piling up one's sins and faults in order to see that the gift is unmerited. Everything is motion. . . . The will calmly and wisely must understand that one does not deal well with God by force and that our efforts are like the careless use of large pieces of wood which smother this little spark.[83]

The excessive multiplication of vocal prayers (even aside from times of mental prayer) can likewise impede growth. There are people who get into a set habit of adding litany upon litany, devotion upon devotion, to the point where they leave little or no time for God to give what he wants to give. They do not understand contemplation, and they think that unless they are vocalizing, they are not praying.[84] We have already noted that St. Teresa sees no dichotomy between the celebration of the Liturgy of the Hours and other vocal prayers on the one hand and infused contemplation on the other. As a matter of fact, according to her, vocal prayer should easily lead into infused prayer. In her experience of guiding others she finds this to be a common happening: "I know", she says, "there are many persons who while praying vocally, as has already been mentioned, are raised by God to sublime contemplation (without their striving for anything or understanding how)."[85] After this remark the saint goes on to narrate the well-known story of the distressed nun who came to Teresa thinking that she was unable to do anything but recite vocal prayers. This nun was badly bothered by distractions during her prayer time, and so she would spend two or three hours reciting the Our Father several times and a few other vocal prayers in an effort to keep her mind focused on God. Upon asking the nun a few questions, Teresa learned that while this nun was reciting the Our Father, "she was experiencing pure contemplation, and the Lord was raising her to be with Him in union". Her mode of life also made it plain that "she was receiving great favours" from God in her prayer.[86]

It does not follow, however, that vocal prayer can never be an impediment to infused contemplation. There are people who fail to recognize the presence of the delicate beginnings of the new peace and love and light. Thinking that nothing is happening, they proceed to recite vocal prayers or mental words that do nothing but snuff out what God is giving. I am not speaking of vocal prayers that we are obliged to recite (for example, the liturgy of the Hours for priests and religious) but of time devoted to mental prayer. Referring to those who make up their own vocal prayer obligations, St. Teresa notes that "they are so fond of speaking and reciting many vocal prayers very quickly, like one who wants to get a job done, since they oblige themselves to recite these every day, that even though, as I say, the Lord places His Kingdom in their hands, they do not receive it. But with their vocal prayers they think they are doing better, and they distract themselves from the prayer of quiet."[87]

Distractions occur, of course, within the fourth mansions, for the infusion is often faint and fragile. In her typically vigorous style the saint refers to the mind as being wild as a madman "wandering off after the most ridiculous things in the world". Her remedy is simple: pay no attention to it, for one may well "laugh at it and treat it as the silly thing it is, and remain in her state of quiet".[88]

St. Teresa touches upon three conditions for continued growth when one reaches the fourth mansions. The first is never to give up the habitual practice of prayer, for one is doomed if he does. To illustrate her point she returns to the image of the child at the breast. Just as the baby who has just begun "to suck the breast" is sure to die "if it be taken from its mother", so, for anyone who gives up prayer, "unless he does so for some very exceptional reason, or unless he returns to it quickly, he will go from bad to worse".[89]

The second condition is further detachment "from everything". One might think that active purification is confined to the first three mansions. Not so, says Teresa. If there is no lessening of selfish clingings, there is no growth in prayer. God brings one thus far as a pledge of great things He has in store, but if He sees the person "return to earth", He refrains from showing him the secrets of His kingdom. "This is why", she sadly observes, "spiritual people are not much more numerous."[90] Her analysis of the problem is identical with Jesus' explanation of spiritual retardation: we do not mature, He said, because we are smothered by the cares and riches and pleasures of life.[91] This is why St. Paul exhorts the Colossians to rise to a new life, to seek the things above, not the things on earth.[92] There must be a complete renouncing of all self-centeredness, "all that we possess", if we hope to be total disciples.[93]

The third condition for continuing growth is the seeking of greater solitude — without, of course, neglecting work or community. Teresa

sees solitude as giving the Lord the opportunity to do His work
in us as well as our being readied for communion with Him.[94] In
this, too, she is advocating nothing other than what Jesus Himself
repeatedly did: going out to be alone in prayer with the Father for
long stretches of time early in the morning or all through the night.[95]
There is a built-in proclivity in advancing prayer to seek solitude with
the Beloved.

FIFTH MANSIONS (THIRD WATER)

We have been noticing throughout St. Teresa's mansions that infused
prayer slowly develops through progressing stages, a subsequent growth
being usually nothing more than an intensification of the previous one.
On occasion, of course, God can and does give new graces, sometimes
surprising, even frightening new experiences (frightening because the
recipient does not know whence they come). Nonetheless, each mansion is a gradual development of the previous one. So it is with the
fifth mansions, called also by the saint union or full union. It is here,
too, that the person is introduced into the spiritual betrothal.

The divine invasion occurring in the fourth mansions now grows
to the point where all of one's inner energies are in union with the
Trinity's indwelling: "The faculties are almost totally united with God
but not so absorbed as not to function . . . [they] have only the ability
to be occupied completely with God."[96] We should notice the adverbs
totally and *completely,* for in these fifth mansions the indwelling Guests
quite entirely take over one's inner life. This is why in full union distractions cease during the time of absorption, that is, for five, ten or fifteen
minutes at a time. Not only is the will taken up in God, as was the
case in the fourth mansions, but so also are the imagination, memory
and intellect.[97]

As we might expect, full union absorbs the soul in a deep delight,
a delight in which a person is almost beside himself:

> The consolation, the sweetness, and the delight are incomparably greater
> than that experienced in the previous prayer. . . . This prayer is a glorious
> foolishness, a heavenly madness. . . . Often I had been as though bewil-
> dered and inebriated in this love. . . . The soul would desire to cry out
> praises, and it is beside itself . . . it cannot bear so much joy . . . it would
> want to be all tongues so as to praise the Lord.[98]

The saints know what it is like to be in love, a love immeasurably
beyond what worldlings label as love. The delight is intense because

the love is intense. Teresa is a woman so keenly in love with her Lord that she must proclaim:

> My King, I beseech You, that all to whom I speak become mad from Your love. . . . This soul would now want to see itself free—eating kills it; sleeping distresses it . . . nothing other than You can give it pleasure any longer . . . and I would desire to see no other persons than those who are sick with this sickness I now have.

Needless to say, a person so intensely taken with her Beloved is completely forgetful of herself. She is entirely absorbed in Him Who is now everything to her.[99] We find here further evidence of the reciprocal interinfluence of deepening prayer and detachment from self-centeredness. Just as the latter frees one for progressively greater love, precisely as one is less and less cluttered by finite things, so as one grows in love, one effortlessly grows in the inner liberty of other-centeredness.

The saint points out that during the prayer of full union one understands nothing of the favor being received—unlike the seventh mansions, where one does understand something of the favor. She notes that the person is made blind and dumb, as Paul was at his conversion.[100] In this prayer of union of all the faculties "the intellect is as though in awe; the will loves more than it understands, but it doesn't understand in a describable way whether it loves or what it does; there is no memory at all, in my opinion, nor thought; nor even during that time are the senses awake, for they are as though lost, that the soul might be more occupied in what it enjoys."[101] We notice here in the saint's remark about the senses not being "awake" a blending into ecstatic prayer where this trait will be pronounced: the fifth mansions mingle into the sixth.

As we have indicated above, the length of this absorption in God is comparatively brief, never as long as a half hour.[102] What this prayer lacks in duration it makes up for not only in intensity but also in the certainty of the divine presence. St. Teresa finds herself unable to explain the how of it, but she does perceive that the certitude is such that it can be produced only by God's indwelling. The experience is indelible and cannot be forgotten. People who receive this absorption will remember years later the exact time and circumstances in which it occurred. The saint lays it down that if this certitude is not present, the experience was not a union of the whole soul with God.[103]

Although, as we have noted above, this union is akin to rapture and

even is a type of it, yet there is a difference, namely, that "the rapture
lasts longer and is felt more exteriorly, for your breathing diminishes
in such a way that you are unable to speak or open your eyes. Although
this diminishing of these bodily powers occurs in union, it takes place
in this prayer with greater force."[104] Teresa touches on this same point
in her autobiography when she notes that "rapture produces much
stronger effects and causes many other phenomena. Union seems the
same at the beginning, in the middle, and at the end; and it takes place
in the interior of the soul." Rapture produces its effects both interiorly
and exteriorly, since it is a union of a still higher degree.[105] Not surprisingly, the saint points out that the prayer of union is of a tender
and marital type, though it far transcends that of earthly marriage. It
may, she says, be likened to a courtship, but one with "nothing that
is not spiritual". To explain this last point Teresa remarks that "corporeal union is quite another thing and the spiritual joys and consolations given by the Lord are a thousand leagues removed from those
experienced in marriage. It is all a union of love with love, and its opera-
tions are entirely pure, and so delicate and gentle that there is no way
of describing them."[106]

We need not discuss at length the results of this prayer of full union,
for they are intensifications and developments of the already wonderful effects of the prayer of quiet in mansions four. Yet it may be well
to note that the person here continues to be "transformed from one
glory to another".[107] In this profound absorption one emerges with
a consuming desire to praise God and to die a thousand deaths for His
sake. There are likewise vehement yearnings for penance and solitude
together with keen longings that everyone would come to know this
God of unspeakable bounty. This person, having tasted so deeply of
the very best, understandably is satisfied now with nothing this world
has to offer, sets no store by what can be seen or touched and finds
no rest in anything finite. He experiences what Scripture talks about
in saying that we are "strangers and nomads on earth" and that we are
to long for a better homeland, the heavenly dwelling.[108] This pilgrim
experience does not mean a loss of peace, for this individual enjoys
a profound calm. Even severe trials now emerge from so sublime a
source that they themselves bring serenity and contentment. Yet at the
same time this person feels acutely that he cannot serve God well
enough, and he is pained that there are so few men and women in the
world who care much about the Lord and so many who offend Him
freely and often. This grief is infused and not simply the result of our
meditations. It reaches so deeply into one's being that it "seems to tear
it to pieces and grind it to powder".[109]

SIXTH MANSIONS (FOURTH WATER)

One might easily conclude that there could be no further growth in prayer depth after reaching the absorption and incipient ecstasy of the fifth mansions. Yet there is more, inestimably more. In these sixth mansions a number of different advanced experiences of God occur, all of them deepenings of the immersion we have been discussing. Ecstasy, rapture, transport, flight of the spirit are basically the same experience, though with accidental differences we shall explain below. Likewise, in these mansions we find the wounds of love, the spiritual betrothal and levitation.

We may begin with ecstasy, rapture. As we listen to St. Teresa explain in her expert manner this phenomenon, we need to keep in mind that we are dealing with infused contemplation, divinely given knowing and loving of God. We are not concerned with merely human experiences such as those brought about by sexual union or chemical stimulation or frenzied trance. One who confuses these latter with contemplative ecstasy does not understand the latter, even if he knows something of the former.

In ecstatic prayer one's inner life of knowing and loving is so intensely increased that the sense perception of the outer world is proportionately lessened, even to the point of disappearance. What Teresa calls the "bodily energies", that is, seeing, hearing and touching, lessen and fade away. This lessening of the operation of the external senses is sometimes gradual, at other times sudden. The saint speaks of these "powers" being lost at once and rapidly. One can scarcely move the hands; the eyes close (or if one can keep them open, almost nothing is seen); one cannot speak or form words because there is no strength for it. We may listen to the saint herself:

> Now let us return to raptures and speak of what is more common in them. I say that often, it seemed to me, the body was left so light that all its weight was gone, and sometimes this feeling reached such a point that I almost didn't know how to put my feet on the ground. Now when the body is in rapture it is as though dead, frequently being unable to do anything of itself. It remains in the position it was when seized by the rapture, whether standing or sitting, or whether with the hands opened or closed. Although once in a while the senses fail (sometimes it happened to me that they failed completely), this occurs rarely and for only a short time. But ordinarily the soul is disoriented. Even though it can't do anything of itself with regard to exterior things, it doesn't fail to understand and hear as though it were listening to something coming from far off. I do not say that it hears and understands when it is

at the height of the rapture (I say "height" to refer to the times when the faculties are lost to other things because of their intense union with God), for then, in my opinion, it neither sees, nor hears, nor feels.[110]

It would be a mistake to conclude from this description that the person in ecstatic prayer is inert or living in a marginal manner. Quite the contrary is the case. Inner life and vitality and energy are increased, so intensely increased that they take over one's consciousness. This is supreme living. There is an experience of deep union with God. One's "will is fully occupied with Him",[111] "fully awake to the things of God . . . completely absorbed".[112] Ecstatic experiences of the indwelling Trinity are often if not always indelible: "These meetings with the Spouse remain so deeply engraven in the memory that I think it is impossible for the soul to forget them until it is enjoying them for ever."[113]

Complete ecstasy, that is, suspension of all the faculties, is very short, for the intellect and the memory soon return. But then they are absorbed again with the will.[114] A person can spend several hours in this type of fluctuating prayer. The saint speaks of a rapture she had for two hours, and it seemed to be a short time.[115] In her autobiography she explains how she experienced these fluctuations in ecstatic prayer:

> Your Reverence will ask how it is that the rapture sometimes lasts so many hours and occurs so often. What happens in my case, as I said in speaking of the previous prayer, is that the rapture is experienced at intervals. The soul is often absorbed or, to put it better, the Lord absorbs it in Himself suspending all the faculties for a while and then, afterward, holding only the will suspended. It seems to me that the activity of these other two faculties is like that of the little pointer on the sundial that never stops. But when the Sun of Justice wants to, He makes the faculties stop. This suspension of the two faculties, I say, is brief.[116]

The "other two faculties", of course, are intellect and memory. These are not continuously absorbed, whereas the will may be absorbed for a considerable length of time.

Can one successfully resist falling into this ecstatic union with the Trinity? Usually not. Teresa remarks that the enrapturing immersion was so forceful that many times when she wanted to resist and used all her energy to do so, especially when she was in a public place, or even when alone and wanting to avoid deception, she was only marginally successful. "At times", she writes, "I was able to accomplish something, but with great loss of energy, as when someone fights with a giant and afterward is worn out. At other times it was impossible for me to resist."[117] In her *Book of Foundations* she is a little more absolute: "If it is a genuine rapture we ourselves are powerless, whatever our efforts at resistance."[118]

As to frequency of occurrence, St. Teresa declares that raptures occur often, even continually, since they are readily triggered by the mere thought of God or the mention of His name. Souls in the sixth mansions are so obviously head over heels in love, a love of which the world has no cognizance or experience, that they live on the summit, so to speak. Using the image of a butterfly, Teresa remarks that "her love is so full of tenderness that any occasion whatever which serves to increase the strength of this fire causes the soul to take flight; and thus in this Mansion raptures occur continually."[119]

We might suppose that once a person reaches this growth in prayer, there would never again occur periods of dryness and emptiness. Not so. We are not yet in the transforming union. In a letter to her brother Lorenzo Teresa remarks that it is useless to try to resist raptures and impossible to conceal them. She then adds that "latterly I have been going about almost as if I were drunk. . . . Previously, for nearly a week, I had been in such a state that I could hardly think a single good thought, so severely was I suffering from aridity."[120] This drastic change from inebriatingly delightful immersion in Beauty to dry emptiness surprises only those who do not understand the fluctuations of infused prayer short of the seventh mansions. And even at the summit there are ebb and flow in the intensity of communion.

What is the cause of ecstatic prayer? From all we have considered thus far, one can easily conclude that there is no natural explanation for it. We see this, for example, in the fact that Teresa often experienced her raptures while she was engaged in business matters. "It often happens to me", she writes, "that this recollection and elevation of the spirit comes upon me so suddenly I cannot resist; and in a moment I receive the effects and benefits that it carries in its wake. This recollection occurs without my desiring to reflect on the things of God and while I am dealing with other things and thinking that even if I tried to practice prayer I wouldn't be able to because of great dryness, intensified by bodily pains."[121] It is also true, however, that her ecstasies could occur while she was already in the prayer of quiet.[122]

The cause of ecstatic love is, of course, God Himself. We have here one of the many differences between this experience and lesser ones in the natural order. St. Teresa observes of one of her raptures that it seemed to have lasted only for a short time and yet had actually been of considerable duration. "I was amazed", she added, "when the clock struck and I found I had been in that rapture and glory for two hours. It seems that this fire comes from above, from God's true love: for however much I may desire and seek and strive after it, I play no part in obtaining even a spark of it."[123] One's joy in God is so profound that it simply suspends the normal operation of the inner and outer senses.[124] Mystics speak of this experience as a sober inebriation: one remains with the use of reason and thus is "sober" but at the same time is quite overcome with delight after drinking deeply of the divine. The aftereffect of having tasted this potent cup of God's goodness is something akin to reeling from drunkenness without having any of the demeaning defects of that disagreeable state.[125]

St. Teresa distinguishes several phenomena that occur in the sixth mansions: ecstasy, rapture, transport, flight of the spirit, impulses, wounding, the betrothal and sometimes levitation. Some moderns would probably term the last "extraordinary", that is, beyond the normal, usual workings of the grace life. Even if we look upon levitation in this manner, the other experiences are all normal developments of a deepening communion with the Trinity. The first four of this listing differ only accidentally, and it will not therefore be necessary to dwell upon them at length. In *Interior Castle* the saint mentions transport as synonymous with flight of the spirit,[126] and rapture is the same as ecstasy. We need consequently to distinguish rapture from transport. The former comes upon one, says Teresa, gradually, whereas transport comes swiftly. In a sudden transport

> the soul really seems to have left the body; on the other hand, it is clear that the person is not dead, though for a few moments he cannot even himself be sure if the soul is in the body or no. He feels as if he has been in another world . . . and has been shown a fresh light there, so much unlike any to be found in this life that, if he had been imagining it, and similar things, all his life long, it would have been impossible for him to obtain any idea of them. . . . It is a fact that, as quickly as a bullet leaves a gun when the trigger is pulled, there begins within the soul a flight (I know no other name to give it) which, though no sound is made, is so clearly a movement that it cannot possibly be due to fancy. . . . Great things are revealed to it.[127]

What is an impulse? The saint defines it as a desire, frequent and even habitual, that comes upon the soul suddenly and without any preceding prayer. It involves a keen remembrance that one is separated from God (that is, in this life one does not see Him face to face), a remembrance so powerful and experienced with such impact that instantaneously the soul seems beside itself. Nothing in this world can comfort or console the person in this state, and it "dies with the longing to die" that it might be immersed in the Trinity through facial vision. From time to time God gives this individual a secret and ineffable knowledge of Himself that she might see what she lacks here on earth. So keen and absorbing is this experience that Teresa thinks one would not feel bodily torments were they inflicted. Yet the person is in possession of her senses and can speak and see, even though she cannot walk "because the forceful blow of love prostrates it [the soul]".[128] We need hardly add that as a result of these powerful impulses, there is a great growth in the recipient and "an extremely tender desire to serve God, along with tearful wishes to leave this exile".[129]

Another type of prayer given in these sixth mansions is the wounding. In this experience, infused as are all the others, "it seems as though an arrow is thrust into the heart, or into the soul itself. Thus the wound causes a severe pain", but it is a wondrously delightful pain. So felicitous is it that the recipient would like it never to leave. The suffering is entirely spiritual and has no connection with the senses or the physical body. It lies in the interior depths of the spirit. These wounds of love at other times arise from the inner core of the soul. They are longings "indescribably alive and refined".[130] In her *Interior Castle* St. Teresa amplifies her thought:

> While the soul is in this condition, and interiorly burning, it often happens that a mere fleeting thought of some kind (there is no way of telling whence it comes, or how) or some remark which the soul hears about death's long tarrying, deals it, as it were, a blow, or, as one might say, wounds it with an arrow of fire. I do not mean that there actually is such an arrow; but, whatever it is, it obviously could not have come from our own nature. . . . It passes as quickly as a flash of lightning and leaves everything in our nature that is earthly reduced to powder. . . . It instantaneously enchains the faculties. . . . All I say falls short of the truth, which is indescribable. It is an enrapturing of the senses and faculties. . . . The soul burns so fiercely . . . I do not believe it would feel anything if it were cut into little pieces. . . . She is parched with thirst [for God]. . . . It is well that great things should cost a great deal, especially if the soul can be purified by suffering and enabled to enter the seventh mansions.[131]

There is, of course, no cure for these wounds of longing love but death itself and the sight of the Trinity in the beatific vision.[132]

One might easily conclude from the sublimity of these divine self-communications that nothing more is possible in the life of prayer, but this would be measuring infinity by our finitudes. We are not yet at the consummation of transforming love, the spiritual marriage, the complete union in which the soul is "oned" with God (as *The Cloud of Unknowing* puts it). This final wedded state is, however, now coming close, for in these sixth mansions the betrothal occurs.

St. Teresa does not say much about the betrothal, but she notes that it occurs in the sixth mansions.[133] It is true that she also says that during rapture the soul becomes a bride,[134] but she probably means only in the sense of engagement, because when she comes to deal with the spiritual marriage she distinguishes it from the betrothal.[135] In the former God and the soul are so united that they cannot be separated anymore, whereas in the latter they are frequently separated in one's conscious experience.[136] This difference is clearly seen when the saint explains the spiritual marriage in the seventh mansions.

The final phenomenon Teresa describes as occurring in the sixth mansions is levitation. This happening is closely allied with the transport of the soul, for it sometimes happens that God takes the body along as well. When this first occurred with the saint, she was greatly frightened, for the Christian levitation is by no means self-induced or merely imagined. She did not expect it, and she did not know what to make of it at first.

> When one sees one's body so elevated from the ground that even though the spirit carries it along after itself, and does so very gently if one does not resist, one's feelings are not lost. At least I was conscious in such a way that I could understand I was being elevated. There is revealed a majesty about the One who can do this that makes a person's hair stand on end, and there remains a strong fear of offending so awesome a God. Yet such fear is accompanied by a very great love for Him.[137]

What we have been noticing throughout the development of infused contemplation is true also in these sixth mansions: namely, the person continues to advance in God-centeredness and in living the specifics of the Gospel message. In rapture one's will is left "completely absorbed", and one's mind can be entirely transported for a day or even for several days. Ecstatic prayer causes no physical harm and actually improves one's health. The whole person is rejuvenated:

> Frequently the body is made healthy and stronger—for it was really sick and full of great sufferings—because something wonderful is given to it in that prayer. The Lord sometimes desires, as I say, that the body enjoy it since the body is now obedient to what the soul desires. After the soul returns to itself—if the rapture has been intense—it goes about for a day or two, or even three, with the faculties absorbed or as though stupified; it seems to be outside itself.[138]

After prayer of such intensity, understandably enough, there are no attachments to anything created, no pleasure seeking in worldly things. One who so completely has the best feels no attraction or need for the least. As a matter of fact, life on earth, surrounded as it is with dull trifles, becomes a great burden.[139] The soul's situation is much like that of a man madly in love with the woman of his dreams. He finds burdensome, even frustrating, the mundane daily duties that keep him from her. The soul in the sixth mansions is this man (woman) in love: its consciousness and speech are completely centered on the Beloved. There are ardent and permanent desires to be used in any way for the promotion of the divine kingdom. There are experiences of opposite drives to solitude with the Lord in prayer and to plunging into the world to proclaim Him far and wide.[140] And all of this growth is accompanied with genuine humility, for in this lofty prayer the soul sees clearly not only major defects but also even tiny specks of dust, no matter how small, "because the sun is very bright". In this mansion "true humility is gained so that the soul doesn't care at all about saying good things of itself, nor that others say them. . . . All the good it possesses is directed to God."[141]

Surprising though it may seem, as the person continues to advance in prayer, raptures cease. Father Julian of Avila, apparently sharing the common expectation that ecstatic prayer should gradually become both more extended in time and more intense in absorption, one day asked the saint why her raptures had ceased. The account in his deposition in the canonization process is charming:

> One day when we were traveling and discussing many things I said to her: "Mother, how is it that your Reverence used to be in rapture very frequently, yet it is a long time since I saw you in ecstasy?" For it was sufficient for the Mother to see a well painted picture to be carried away and reach great heights of prayer. She replied to this: that it was true that she no longer had any ecstasies but that the prayer she had now was greater than the prayer she used to have in her raptures. The reason for this was that at the beginning all that God gave her to perceive and understand, as they were supernatural, were strange to her and caused her great amazement, and this amazement resulted in her being carried away and unconscious in the excessive pleasure that her soul experienced within her. Now, as she was more experienced, she enjoyed it more and it made less noise, because she was more used to the great experiences God gave her.[142]

SEVENTH MANSIONS

This final thought of the saint leads us to the culmination of contemplation on earth, the transforming union. Though this consummation is itself susceptible to growth—on pilgrimage we should never cease advancing—there remains after the seventh mansions only the beatific vision. But the word *only* is a gross understatement, for the final immersion in the Trinity seen face to face is an unspeakable enthrallment, the most burning of loves, the ultimate glorification. We shall be transfigured into a likeness of Father, Son and Holy Spirit through participating without end in their purest light, love, joy.

St. Teresa teaches that the person is brought into the seventh mansions by an intellectual vision of the Blessed Trinity:

> First of all the spirit becomes enkindled and is illumined, as it were, by a cloud of the greatest brightness. It sees these three Persons, individually, and yet, by a wonderful kind of knowledge which is given to it, the soul realizes that most certainly and truly all these three Persons are one Substance and one Power and one Knowledge and one God alone; so that what we hold by faith the soul may be said here to grasp by sight, although nothing is seen by the eyes, either of the body or of the soul, for it is no ordinary vision.[143]

St. John of the Cross does not mention a trinitarian vision as the point of entry into the transforming union, but neither does he deny it. In his approach he is less concerned to explain how things occur in sequence and precisely when they occur. St. Teresa notes that all visions received at this stage of the spiritual life are very different from the others she has previously mentioned, but she does not elaborate on her statement.[144] We find here another example of how the saint makes no line of demarcation between what we today call ordinary and extraordinary phenomena in the spiritual life. We term all contemplation ordinary, and visions extraordinary, but the two Carmelites can mention both experiences in the same breath and with no concern about the distinction (although elsewhere they do say that we should desire the highest contemplation but not visions).

Even though we discuss at considerable length in Chapter 10 the teaching of St. John of the Cross on the transforming union, and granted that he cannot be surpassed in the thoroughness and beauty of his exposition, I think it well to summarize St. Teresa's approach to this same culmination of prayer. We cannot know it too well, for the more fully we are exposed to its splendor, the more likely it is that we will not hesitate to pay the price indispensable for reaching this summit.

This full union, the spiritual marriage, is utterly of the spirit. It is a "secret union" that takes place in one's deepest soul center, and it begins with Jesus appearing through an intellectual vision in this center "just as He appeared to the Apostles" after the Resurrection through closed doors. This instantaneous communication of God is so sublime a favor and causes such delight that Teresa cannot think of any comparison worthy of it. The two, God incarnate and this ordinary human person, are now inseparably united. Previous prayer gifts, lofty though they be, are passing, but in this wedded union "the soul remains all the time in that centre with its God". The saint is so taken with the splendor of this union that she immediately proceeds to give examples in an effort to communicate what she found. It is like the rain falling into a river or a pond; the waters thus joined cannot afterward be separated or divided. Or it is as beams of light entering a room through two windows: once their brightness has blended together within the room, they are inseparably one light.[145] She recalls immediately the remark of St. Paul that "he who is joined to the Lord is one spirit with him".[146] Deep streams of life and love flow from this Lord, so that "Christ is now its life".[147] These experiences of Him are deep and lightsome and often vehement.[148]

The reader should remember in reading Teresa and John that they are not suggesting that every person receives every gift they mention at a particular stage of growth. This is true of the seventh mansions: "You must not take it, sisters," says Teresa, "that the effects which I have described as occurring in these souls are invariably present all the time; it is for this reason that, whenever I have remembered to do so, I have referred to them as being present 'habitually'."[149]

We have already noted that an experienced oneness with the indwelling Lord becomes permanent in the transforming union. St. Teresa's descriptions of this continuing awareness are similar to those of St. John of the Cross. She expresses her mind in several ways: "The soul is almost continuously near His Majesty . . . the presence of the three Persons is so impossible to doubt . . . this presence is almost continual . . . the three Persons are very habitually present in my soul . . . she feels within herself this Divine companionship."[150] At other times Teresa uses still stronger language and says that the presence is not merely "almost continual" but is also uninterrupted: "The soul is always aware that it is experiencing this companionship . . . the essential part of her soul seemed never to move from that dwelling place . . . they have become like two who cannot be separated from one another."[151]

These absolute statements may appear to be contradicted by an earlier remark that Teresa does not "think it possible for the Spirit of the Lord to remain in a soul continuously in this way [permanent absorption] during our life of exile".[152] Yet there is no actual contradiction, because a close examination indicates clearly enough that the saint is speaking of two related but different realities. On the one hand the continuous presence is perceived on a deep level, "the essential part", whereas the interrupted experience is on what she and John call the "faculty" level. To cast their distinction into contemporary terminology, we might say that in the transforming union the person perceives in his profound center a peaceful, gentle awareness that the Trinity is continually present. On a more surface level he experiences bursts of light and/or love, enkindlings and absorptions, but these are intermittent. This is what Teresa means when she remarks that permanent absorptions are not possible in this life of pilgrimage. Yet the calm, gentle, unwavering awareness is possible and does occur permanently in the transforming union.

From this trait of the seventh mansions there follow what we may call dual awareness and operation. A person is able to attend to the indwelling Trinity and yet carry on the ordinary business of daily life. The saint explains her own experience of this dual operation in a quaint manner. Speaking of herself in the third person and noting that her profound center never moved from the indwelling Three, she remarks that "in a sense she felt that her soul was divided; and when she was going through great trials, shortly after God had granted her this favour, she complained of her soul, just as Martha complained of Mary. Sometimes she would say that it was doing nothing but enjoying itself in that quietness, while she herself was left with all her trials and occupations so that she could not keep it company."[153] Teresa describes this dual activity in a clearer manner as it can sometimes occur in the fifth mansions but in a less perfect way. The person can be both Martha and Mary in such a way that

> it is as though engaged in both the active and contemplative life together. It tends to works of charity and to business affairs that have to do with its state in life and to reading, although it isn't master of itself completely. And it understands clearly that the best part of the soul is somewhere else. It's as though we were speaking to someone at our side and from the other side another person were speaking to us; we wouldn't be fully attentive to either the one or the other.[154]

In this final development of prayer we find the relative perfection of Christian life that the Gospel lays upon us as both privilege and precept: we are to love the Lord our God with our whole heart, soul and mind, nothing less. We are to be perfect as the heavenly Father is perfect and to be completely one.[155] While growth is always possible in our pilgrim state, the person in the transforming union has indeed been transformed from one glory to another into the image that he reflects.[156] A relative perfection is now reached. St. Teresa does not omit sketching what this means. Of this picture we will supply only a few summarizing lines. The soul is living a new life, the new creation of which St. Paul speaks. Its life is not only improved; it is new. There is a complete self-forgetfulness, an entire seeking after God for whom she would gladly lay down her life. While she does not neglect to sleep and eat, these are as nothing to her. The desire for the will of God to be done is extreme. Persecution itself brings great interior joy with no enmity toward those who ill-treat her. This person is no more afraid of death than she would be of a gentle rapture. She experiences no aridities and inner trials and no fear that this sublime prayer may be counterfeited by the devil. Indeed, there is an unwavering certitude that it comes from God and no other. "He and the soul alone have fruition of each other in the deepest silence." So deep and perfect is this enjoyment that there are no more raptures, save very occasionally. It is here that God gives the soul the kiss for which the bride in the Song of Songs besought Him. And "sometimes the many favours they [people in the seventh mansions] receive leave them overwhelmed, and afraid lest they be like an overladen ship sinking to the bottom of the sea".[157] This being overwhelmed with joy and goodness was, of course, apparent to those who knew St. Teresa at all well. In his deposition at the canonization process Julian of Avila remarked that this woman "enjoyed God so much that what did not pertain to God tasted bitter to her. . . . Thus we saw how to the Mother trials were a rest and what was reposeful to others in the world she found trying. For instance what worldly people mostly shun, viz. poverty, she sought. What they avoid in persecutions she enjoyed."[158]

The peace and repose of the seventh mansions are inner, not necessarily outer. One can suffer intensely from human sins and ignorance and ineptitudes, but there remains down deep in the soul a great calm.[159] On the sense and emotional levels there may be little or no peace, but in the center of the soul, as the saint explains, there are stability and serenity. Teresa finds it difficult to explain how this can happen, and so she resorts to examples. "A king is living in his palace," she remarks, "many wars are waged in his kingdom and many other distressing things happen there, but he remains where he is despite them all. . . . Our whole body may be in pain, yet if our head is sound the fact that the body is in pain will not cause it to ache as well." These comparisons are so inept, she adds, that they make her smile. Yet she knows no others.[160]

One of the rare differences between the two Carmelite Doctors occurs at this point. St. John of the Cross held that a person in the transforming union is confirmed in grace. St. Teresa insists that even in these seventh mansions one is not sure of his salvation or free from the danger of backsliding. She considers it certain that even if this state of prayer has lasted for years, one ought not to think himself safe from falling away.[161]

PURE GOSPEL

If this book has a main thesis, it is that the teachings of Ss. Teresa and
John are nothing other than the Christic message proclaimed in the
New Testament. Neither more nor less. Anyone who considers them
to be merely the best representatives of the Carmelite tradition, that
is, one spirituality among others, simply does not understand the two
saints and/or the New Testament. We may close this discussion of the
teresian mansions with a few brief samples showing how the Gospels
and inspired letters, provided they are taken with neither exaggeration nor dilution, proclaim the very same transformation of prayer and
person that we have just studied in St. Teresa. The chief difficulty in
seeing this point is, perhaps, that many people unwittingly water down
Scripture as they read it. They fail to notice or attend to the uncompromising totality that we read on every page, the same wholeness
we find in the lives of the saints. We lesser ones tend to be so enmeshed
in the mediocrity of our worldly world that we fail to be affected much
or moved by the divine message.

Do the sacred pages have anything resembling the seven mansions
to describe a progressive development in prayer and in transformation of life? If the question means a precisely delineated sevenfold
description all in one account, the obvious answer is negative. If,
however, it refers to the substance of Teresa's account, the response
must be affirmative. We do find in the New Testament both the active
growth in the virtues and the detachment that she insists upon in her
first three mansions. We likewise find the main stages of prayer, all
the way from vocal beginnings through a transforming consummation.

We have already noted that St. Teresa says little about approaches
to prayer in the first three mansions of her *Interior Castle*. And even
though she does speak elsewhere of discursive methods and recommends their use for many beginners, she insists far more often on the
basic necessity of obedience, fraternal charity, humility and detachment as conditions for anyone who wishes to live a serious prayer life.
This, too, is Scripture's insistence. For the sacred writers, anyone who
desires to belong to the Lord, to be a faithful disciple, to grow in intimacy with Him must lay the foundations in these same virtues. Christianity is no oriental exercise in which "contemplation" is the result
of techniques. It is a love communion with the supreme Beloved and
not a mere impersonal, neutral awareness of reality and of oneself at
the center of it. Because this supreme Beloved demands goodness as
a condition for intimacy, Scripture insists, just as St. Teresa does, that
we begin by practicing the ordinary virtues with extraordinary fidelity

and entirety. We are to walk along a hard road and enter the narrow gate that leads to life.[162] We carry our cross every day.[163] We obey our leaders in the Church, for when we listen to them, we listen to Jesus, and if we reject them, we reject Him and His Father.[164] For the same reason, we obey our superiors and do as they tell us.[165] We love our neighbors as ourselves, indeed, as Jesus Himself loves them.[166] We give them food and drink and clothing,[167] and we forgive them as readily as God forgives us.[168] We are gentle, loving and cordial,[169] and we keep close guard over our tongues, for they can do tremendous damage to community.[170] We are to be completely one, with a shared vision rooted in sound doctrine.[171] We are to take the last places in the assembly and to consider others better than ourselves, knowing that indeed we are sinners much in need of the divine mercy.[172] The greatest among us is to be as the least,[173] even to the washing of our brothers' and sisters' feet.[174]

Anyone aspiring to intimacy with God must learn to detach his heart from things not God. Indeed, he must renounce all that he possesses, in some sense, at least in the clingings of his heart.[175] He gets rid of everything that does not lead him to God,[176] or, to put the same idea positively, whatever he eats or drinks, whatsoever else he does, he does it all for the glory of God.[177] In Luke 8:14, when Jesus explains why ordinarily good people do not reach maturity (and the transforming union is maturity), He points the finger at the smothering effects of attachments: these people are, He says, choked by their possessions, their cares and the pleasures of life. All of this is exactly what St. Teresa points out in her first three mansions. Without taking these steps, there is no question of maturity, no growth to the fullness to which all are called.

We need not dwell on the obvious point that biblical men and women knew of vocal prayer: the psalter is full of it. That they knew also of what we now call discursive meditation is clear from references to meditating on the law of the Lord day and night,[178] reciting it also by day and by night.[179] But does Scripture speak of what we now term infused prayer? Yes, and in many ways — always, of course, using concepts and thought patterns appropriate to the writer's day. "Gazing on the beauty of the Lord"[180] is a perfect definition of contemplation as we Christians understand and live it. Keeping the eyes of our mind always on God[181] is a trait of advanced prayer, a gift that the Lord Himself gives to those growing in intimacy with Him. Biblical men and women experienced a meeting with God that made them radiant with joy,[182] and they tasted His very goodness.[183] This is mystical language. They knew how to sit quietly before Him and simply enjoy

His being.[184] St. Luke presents the Mother of Jesus as a contemplative woman par excellence: he styles her twice in one chapter as one who ponders the word in her heart.[185] The same evangelist sketches in a single verse a perfect picture of a contemplative, one who drinks deeply of divine wisdom with undivided attention: "[Martha] had a sister who seated herself at the Lord's feet and listened to his word."[186] One could not paint a better concrete picture of what a contemplative looks like.

All the elements of advanced infused prayer are taken for granted by the biblical writers. In communion with the Lord, they have their *fill* of His *prime* gifts . . . He gives them to drink from His delightful torrent (not just a trickle) . . . in His fountain of light they see light.[187] So deep is the divine infusion that their very hearts and flesh sing for joy.[188] The greatest of all the commandments is a total love, of heart, mind and soul.[189] To take total love seriously is to see that it is a love that is found only in the transforming union. In this union one literally does "live through love in his presence".[190] In this culmination of contemplative prayer there are a praising of Him "always and everywhere"[191] and a being "filled with the utter fullness of God".[192] We would be at a loss to explain these texts if we knew nothing of the transforming union. St. Paul speaks of knowledge, love and perception that "never stops growing".[193] We could not ask for a better one-sentence description of the sevenfold growth explained by St. Teresa. For the apostle the indwelling Spirit is He Who transforms us from one glory to another into the very image that we reflect.[194] It is not a surprise, therefore, that it has not "even dawned on our minds what things God has prepared for those who love him".[195] In this text St. Paul is speaking of this life as well as of eternal life, and no human experience can correspond to it except the culmination of contemplative communion with the divine indwelling Trinity. Ss. Teresa and John are indeed pure Gospel.

CHAPTER SEVEN

CONDITIONS FOR GROWTH: ST. TERESA

Anyone who studies carefully our two masters of contemplation and then turns to lesser luminaries, the popular writers and speakers of our day, will find a number of important differences in outlook and approach — yes, even in teaching. One of these divergences becomes apparent in this present chapter on the conditions necessary for a prayer life to deepen. We find here one of the concretizations of the Isaian statement that God's thoughts are not our thoughts, and His ways not our ways.[1] It is likewise a predictable consequence of getting one's ideas about prayer from the atmosphere of the day rather than from the purity of the biblical word and the people who live that word best, the saints.

Living, as we do, in a consumerist age that looks to technology to solve most of its problems, we will, unless immersed in a serious prayer life ourselves, assume as obvious that prayer is mainly something produced in a human manner. This is partially true of beginning discursive meditation, but the trouble begins when the assumption is uncritically extended to all mental prayer. That it is so extended is made clear when one reads books and articles on the subject of contemplation, or if one simply reads advertisements to see what is being sold. The literary and audio markets are replete with techniques and methodologies, oriental and occidental: methods, ways, mantras, centering, ashrams, gurus, koan exercises, yoga techniques, discursive procedures. These are presented and promoted in streams of articles, tapes, books, workshops and courses. While some of this is good for some people at some times, the extension of it to most people at most times is more than misleading. Extended indiscriminately, it becomes a dead end and more than a dead end. It blocks real prayer growth.

What we find in Ss. Teresa and John and in Scripture is a very different message. Though I shall detail this statement as we go along, we may note at the moment that the inspired pages have, as far as I can find, not a single sentence that speaks of methodology as a means to deep communion with the God of revelation. Contemporaries rarely recognize this obvious fact, which is in itself indicative of inattention to Scripture and the lives of those who do in fact enjoy profound contemplative prayer. One can only wonder if some current writers actually know what infused prayer is.

In any event, Ss. John and Teresa do know, and their prescriptions for growth are as different from the techniques and productionist approaches as the heavens are from the earth. In this chapter we shall study St. Teresa alone and point out how her teaching is firmly rooted in the biblical word as well as in the experience of prayerful men and women of every age.

BASIC TERESIAN PRINCIPLES FOR GROWTH

While St. Teresa was well acquainted with methods of meditation and wished her young nuns to be instructed in them,[2] she emphatically insisted that the primary need for beginners is not to find the ideal method but to do God's will from moment to moment throughout the day—which is probably the last thing the beginner thinks is primary. Her thought is strong and unambiguous: "The whole aim of any person who is beginning prayer—and don't forget this, because it is very important—should be that he work and prepare himself with determination and every effort to bring his will into conformity with God's will." She then adds that "it is the person who lives in more perfect conformity who will receive more from the Lord and be more advanced on this road [of prayer]".[3] It does not seem to occur to the saint when she is discussing the primary condition for growth at any stage of development to say a word about techniques or methods. Rather, when she is asked why she insists on practicing the virtues when she had been requested to explain contemplation, she replies that meditation and contemplation are two different realities: that the latter simply cannot be had unless one is serious about living the Gospel generously. "I say that had you asked about meditation I could have spoken about it and counseled all to practice it. . . . But contemplation is something else. . . . This King doesn't give Himself but to those who give themselves entirely to Him."[4]

A second basic teresian principle is that growth in prayer does not depend on a person's immediate situation. We tend to suppose that if only we could find an ideal community, be it marital or religious or clerical, if only we could locate in another setting, if only we had a different superior or set of associates, if only we had more money (or less), we would skyrocket in prayer. Not so, says the foundress, for "the time is always propitious for God to grant His great favours to those who truly serve Him".[5]

St. Teresa's third principle is an outgrowth of the first. Conformity to the divine will does not mean merely that we fulfill commandments but also that we generously go beyond what is strictly required. A man in love happily fulfills obligations, yes (and this, too, is an act of love), but he is eager to do much more: he gives the beloved everything and anything that will please her and that lies in his power to give. The saint puts the matter in axiomatic form: "Everything we gain comes from what we give."[6] Noting that attaining the divine riches is possible for everyone, provided each gives what he has, she adds that "if you are to gain this, He would have you keep back nothing; whether it be little or much, He will have it all for Himself, and according to what you know yourself to have given, the favours He will grant you will be small or great".[7] Indeed, this complete, unstinting generosity is so crucial for prayer growth that Teresa lays it down in the very next sentence that "there is no better test than this of whether or no our prayer attains to union".[8]

The fourth fundamental is purification. Though she does not go into the thoroughgoing details of John's *Ascent,* Teresa is as insistent as he that there is no prayer development unless it be accompanied by purification from faults. Given what a love communion with utter Purity demands, one could not conceive the matter to be otherwise: only the pure can commune deeply with the all-pure One. Obvious as this is to the saint, the lesser of us have difficulty in understanding that we have many defects that need to be rooted out. Some people are so blind to the pauline "illusory desires" that when a trial strikes them, they complain to God, "what have I done to deserve this?" — the implication being that they have done nothing, that they are innocent of a great deal of inner disorder lurking in their minds and hearts. Even after she had been purified a great deal and was receiving "sublime contemplation" from her Lord, St. Teresa still saw an abundance of imperfections in herself: "How I fail, how I fail, how I fail — and I could say it a thousand times — to get rid of everything for You! . . . How many imperfections I see in myself! What laxity in serving You! Indeed I think sometimes I would like to be without consciousness in order not to know so much evil about myself."[9]

In working actively at rooting out what is amiss, we are to be guided by the principles of revelation, not by a naturalistic common sense. There are people, says Teresa, who desire penance that they may serve God the better, but they are overly careful about not injuring their health. "You need never fear that they will kill themselves . . . their love is not yet ardent enough to overwhelm their reason." Going on "at a snail's pace . . . we shall never get to the end of the road. . . . So for the love of the Lord, let us make a real effort."[10] While we know from other texts that the saint does not counsel imprudent penances, she has no time for pampering of oneself, either. It is, after all, a hard road and a narrow gate that lead to life.[11]

Like St. John of the Cross, St. Teresa cannot insist enough on our sixth principle: God gives prayer growth precisely according to our degree of readiness for it. He forces no one. According as we are more or less receptive, He bestows more or less depth of communion. In the same manner, five hundred people in a parish church all hear the same sound waves during the homily, but they profit from it exactly as they are or are not disposed for the message. Jesus taught the same truth in his parable of the sower: from the word of God some hearers yield nothing at all, while others yield thirty or sixty or a hundred-fold.[12] A receptive readiness for infused prayer is far, far more important than any number of methods or techniques, occidental or oriental. Teresa marvels at the greatness of God, Who shows his power in giving courage to an ant (meaning herself). "Since we are never determined, but full of human prudence and a thousand fears," she says, "You, consequently, my God, do not do your marvelous and great works. Who is more fond than You of giving . . . when there is someone open to receive?"[13] That is the core of the matter of prayer growth: "When there is someone open to receive" — easy to say, arduous to do. It is true that Teresa also says elsewhere that God gives His gifts "in proportion to the love which He bears us". At the same time, she is careful to tie this in with the degree of generosity He finds: "He gives in accordance with the courage which He sees that each of us has and the love we bear to His Majesty."[14] Noting that the Lord leaves "nothing undone for those who love Him", she immediately adds that "in the measure He sees that they receive Him, so He gives and is given".[15] Consequently, it follows from this principle that progress in prayer life is not measured chronologically by the number of years one has lived in religious life or has practiced meditation. Growth is determined first of all by readiness and generosity. When these are present in a high degree, the Lord gives much in a short time. We wrongly suppose that

> we must measure our progress by the years in which we have practiced prayer and, it even seems, put a measure on Him who gives His gifts without any measure, when He so desires. He can give more to one in half a year than to another in many years! This is something I have seen so clearly in many persons that I'm amazed how we can even stop to consider it.[16]

Teresa's seventh principle is frightening: retrogression in prayer is possible. Just like an acorn growing into an oak tree can at any point fall into decline, disease and even death, so a person who has begun well in the life of prayer can come to a point of laxity that begets stagnation and possibly even death. The saint notes that those in the third mansions are so lacking in proved strength, so close yet to the first mansions, that they can only too easily slip back into the mediocrity of the bare beginnings. When they meet trials and sufferings, they readily feel new desires to return to worldly compensations and pleasures.[17] Even those who have grown to the lofty prayer of the fifth mansions can fall from their "very high degree of spirituality", and if they do, it most likely will not be the result of gross sins but of petty selfishnesses. Experience bears out Teresa's view: advanced people can only too easily indulge their petty preferences, always, of course, under the appearance of good.[18] From what I have observed in this type of regression, I would think that the trivial selfishnesses often center on interpersonal relations: coldness, insensitivity or oversensitivity, insistence on one's views and ways, unwillingness to be wronged (apparently or actually), dominating of conversations, vanity regarding position or accomplishments, refusal to be admonished or corrected by either peers or superiors. Just as we are adept at rationalizing sins on the sense level, so are we on this level. People advanced in prayer need to be especially alert to the subtle attractions to mediocrity that still lie before them. The devil, says Teresa, is cunning with them, and he does not try to get them with obvious sins. Prayer, she feels, is the best way to detect these allurements.[19]

The dangers of retrogression do not appear out of the blue like a flash of lightning. God gives the prayerful person "a thousand inner warnings" of the danger.[20] The saint does not specify what these warnings are, but we may suggest a few of them: loss of peace at prayer . . . pricks of conscience at small omissions and clingings . . . minor returns to worldliness such as undue time spent on mass-media entertainment and slight excesses in regard to clothing and food . . . corner-cutting in conformance to regulations . . . idle chatter.

The eighth principle underlying conditions for growth in communing with God is that there is a correlation between virtue and prayer. This means, of course, that the earnest practice of virtue (humility, temperance, patience, love of neighbor and the like) directly causes a deepening prayer, and at the same time, as prayer develops, so does one find it much easier to be humble, temperate, patient and loving. In *Book of Foundations* St. Teresa speaks of a remarkably holy nun and of how humble, joyful, docile, uncomplaining, amiable and happy in suffering she was. No one could ever find a fault in her that could be mentioned in the chapter meetings. When the saint comes to explain the extraordinary demeanor, she says that "this was because her mind was ever dwelling upon eternity . . . her life was one perpetual prayer".[21] Anyone who experiences being in love will readily understand how depth of love communion transforms style of life, and conversely, how style of life deepens (or damages) love communion.

The final fundamental teresian principle for prayer development is her key personality trait: determination. Weak wishes were foreign to her cast of mind, and to none of us in any field of endeavor does lack of determination bring excellence. Psychological and educational studies have shown that top performance in scholastics and athletics is due far more to motivation and determination than to native talent. Though this may contradict our assumptions, the evidence is clear. And so it is here: sublime prayer life is not due to a superiority of one's human nature—we are all weak and wounded. On the human level it is due to dedication, to the hard and persevering decision to live like saints live, that is, with no corner cutting. The reader is invited to notice, and indeed encouraged to ponder, the italicized words in the following passage, where St. Teresa speaks to those who wish to embark on a life of serious prayer:

> It is most important—all-important, indeed—that they should begin well by making an *earnest* and *most determined* resolve not to halt until they reach their goal, *whatever may come, whatever may happen* to them, *however hard* they may have to labour, whoever may complain of them, whether they reach their goal *or die on the road* or have no heart to confront the trials which they meet, *whether the very world dissolves before them*.[22]

Faintheartedness was not one of the saint's traits, and it may not be a trait of anyone who embarks on a contemplative life with the all-holy God.

These teresian principles for growth are identical with what we find in the New Testament. Jesus expressed it perfectly in one verse of His parable of the sower and the seed. There are many who hear His word, but as they live day by day, they are choked by things good in themselves but damaging when clung to selfishly. These people fail to reach maturity not because they lack methodology but because of the "cares, riches and pleasures of life".[23] Twice in the final book of Scripture does the Lord severely reprimand the mediocre. Their initial eagerness evaporated, and the inspired writer is told to say that he has "failed to notice anything in the way [they] live that [his] God could possibly call perfect". A single word spells out the solution: "Repent".[24] Toward the end of the same chapter another group of the lukewarm, who are neither hot nor cold, hear the frightening message that they are to be vomited out of the mouth of the Amen, the Lord Himself.[25] They and we are never to be Yes and No, but always Yes, after the pattern of Jesus Himself. Like St. Paul we are to be driven by love for Him.[26] When this happens, prayer happens.

HUMILITY

We are now prepared to examine the specific conditions St. Teresa especially insisted upon as absolutely requisite for a growing prayer life. We may speak of a teresian triad of indispensables: love for neighbor, detachment from all that is not God and a genuine humility.[27] Consistently in all her major works and throughout her life the saint stressed the fundamental importance of humility, which she considered "the principal virtue which must be practised by those who pray".[28] It is God's policy in our life of contemplation to do literally what Jesus said He does, namely, to exalt the lowly and thus to grant a deepening communion only after humiliation. "What I have come to understand", remarks Teresa, "is that this whole groundwork of prayer is based on humility and that the more a soul lowers itself in prayer the more God raises it up. I don't recall His ever having granted me one of the very notable favors of which I shall speak later if not at a time when I was brought to nothing at the sight of my wretchedness."[29] This same teaching we find in her most mature work, the very treatise on the development of prayer. Writing on the seventh mansions in a context dealing with our being the slaves of God and suffering for Him, the saint remarks that unless we so live, we ought not to expect to make great progress in prayer: "The foundation of this whole edifice, as I have said, is humility."[30] Hence, the beginner at prayer will do far better to look to the question of pride in its manifold manifestations than to entertain grandiose ideas about jumping into advanced stages through processes and methods and techniques. "Nothing matters more than humility", says this woman who has been to the heights. "And so I repeat that it is a very good thing — excellent, indeed — to begin by entering the room where humility is acquired rather than by flying off to the other rooms."[31]

Not any concept of humility, however, will do. Prayer is intertwined with reality, for it is a communion with the supreme Reality, and thus unadulterated truth, not a caricature, is necessary. St. Teresa was a woman who joined strength to femininity and intelligence. She flatly stated that she did not want nuns in her convents who were mentally dull, people who "are good at talking and bad at understanding".[32] Nor did she view humility as implying timidity, weakness or mere passivity. Though she did not hold herself up as an example, she wanted her nuns to be magnanimous and bold, just as she was. People who do not love much, she noted, are weak minded and cowardly; they "are filled with a thousand fears and scruples arising from human prudence". His Majesty works "marvels and wonders" for the magnanimous, and so she desired that her sisters be strong, confident and courageous.[33]

The saint did not deny her gifts. Rather, she saw them as reasons for greater humility and considering others better than herself. To the vain individual this appears an odd way of thinking, but it is rooted in simple reality. She does not consider herself better than others because God gives her lofty prayer and divine enlightenments. Rather, her conclusion is that she is worse, since she profits so little from what she receives. The virtues of her companions and other people often stem from fewer divine favors, and so they merit more. She concluded that God has led her by the path denied to others because they are strong and do not need these helps, whereas she is "weak and wretched".[34]

We need to follow the saint still further. Positive benefits accrue to people who openly admit the gifts they have received through no merit of their own. For one thing, if we acknowledge the gift and the Giver, we are prompted to love Him. For another, knowing that we are rich from Him and yet poor in ourselves, our humility is real. We are not intimidated in spirit, thinking that we are not capable of great blessings — what we today call a weak self-image. Thus, when God does choose to give advanced favors, we are not beset with foundless fears of vainglory.[35] Likewise, the person who is genuinely humble, that is, who recognizes the gifts received, is much more likely to be magnanimous and generous in sharing. "How can anyone benefit and share his gifts lavishly", asks the saint, "if he doesn't understand that he is rich? In my opinion, it is impossible because of our nature for someone who doesn't know he is favored by God to have enthusiasm for great things."[36]

As to the vanity of living in other people's minds, Teresa openly admitted that in her early life she was "very fond of being liked". But as she later grew in age and grace, what others thought of her mattered to her hardly a trifle. Being liked actually became wearisome to her except in the two cases of her spiritual directors and those whom she hoped to bring closer to God. "I desire that the former like me so they might bear with me and that the latter do so that they might be more inclined to believe what I tell them about the vanity of everything."[37] But for the rest it mattered to her not at all what other people thought or said of her. She was a free woman, free to be both joyous in living and deep in prayer.

Scripture teaches this relationship between humility and depth in God in a number of ways. Psalm 25:9 has it that Yahweh guides and instructs the humble in His way, whereas He looks upon the proud from afar. Peter lays it down that God refuses the proud and gives His grace to the humble,[38] and of course without grace there can be no prayer at all, let alone advanced prayer. As a matter of fact, the Master Himself has determined that unless we be converted and become as little children, there is no question of being in His kingdom. Still more pointedly, He declares that the more one possesses a childlike humility, the greater he is.[39] This translates easily into the statement so like the thought of St. Teresa, that the more childlike one's humility, the greater is his depth of prayer. Indeed, it is the Father's policy, for "it pleases him", to give His light and love to the little ones and to leave the conceited alone.[40]

The humility that is the foundation of any serious prayer life is not merely an intellectual acknowledgment of one's actual position in the human and divine order of things. Like all else in the spiritual life it must be reduced to practice. Teresa sprinkles through her writings a number of examples of how this condition for prayer is to be concretized in daily life. We are to try to be and to act as the least of all in our milieu, that is, to please and to serve not ourselves but our companions. Indeed, we are to consider ourselves happy and privileged "in serving the servants of the Lord".[41] This service is to include a joyous pliability, that is, a glad willingness to bend to the preferences of others when no principle will be violated: "Always do what those in your community bid you, if it is not contrary to obedience."[42]

One of the acid tests of humility and thus also of prayer growth is obedience to human superiors. Proclaiming that one is "listening to the Spirit" rather than to the visible representatives Jesus has appointed in His Church can conveniently camouflage what is really a refusal to obey. It is surprising how otherwise intelligent people can convince themselves that they are listening to the Spirit when it is obvious to others that they are doing nothing other than baptizing their own personal insights and inclinations. The New Testament is far more realistic when it gives as a criterion of listening to the Lord the very obedience given to His representatives: "He who hears you, hears me; and he who rejects you, rejects me."[43] Egocentrism is of course at the root of the refusal to obey human superiors and teachers in the Church: it is often the I-know-better syndrome: I know better than those whom "the Holy Spirit has made overseers to feed the Church of God".[44] This arrogance kills prayer at its root.

On this connection between prayer growth and obedience St. Teresa's mind is one with what we find in Scripture: "There is no path which leads more quickly to the highest perfection than that of obedience. . . . Obedience brings us the sooner to that happy state and is the best means of attaining it."[45] The saint cites the very text we have just quoted, Luke 10:16, and in her explanation of why obedience to human superiors is so important, she notes that by submitting our wills to the Lord's in this way He makes us master of ourselves, and thus "the fire of His love may come down from Heaven".[46]

St. Teresa penetrates deeply as she exposes the poisonous effect of pride, which withers a vibrant prayer life. Though her terminology may not be so familiar in our day, we can appreciate her castigating the "points-of-honor" type of vanity. No doubt she was reflecting her early love for Spanish tales of chivalry as she noticed that our felt need to be superior to others is found not only in the worldly spheres of athletics, fashions, film, business and politics but also in the quiet atmosphere of the cloister. The points of honor may be trivialities, but that does not prevent their chilling effects on prayer. Concern for rank in community or hurt at being slighted or overlooked can be "wretched niceties" sufficient to make one laugh or cry.[47] The vanity may be tiny in itself, but no matter how "small the point of honor may be, the concern for it is like that of sound coming from an organ when the timing or measure is off; all the music becomes dissonant. This concern is something that does damage to the soul in all areas, but in this path of prayer it is a pestilence."[48] Anyone who wants seriously to attain union with God must follow Jesus in the humiliations of His Passion and crucifixion: if we do not, "it's not possible to reach this union, for we aren't taking the same road".[49]

A further aspect of humility as an indispensable condition for growth in prayer is our reactions to praise and blame. Because St. Teresa can never forget the incarnate Word, for her His being despised in his Passion and death provides a pattern for our development. She finds that human blame is more secure than human praise, and she considers the latter in her case as a "torment". Because Jesus was hated and abused and reviled, and because the saints did not advance except through being despised, we cannot expect to advance unless we follow in their footsteps. As a matter of fact, the soul is freed and it reigns when it is persecuted.[50] Each of us should say that he deserves to be wronged by others and to suffer from them. "At this moment", says the saint, "I see that I am so guilty in Thy sight that everything I might have to suffer would fall short of my deserts, though anyone not knowing, as Thou knowest, what I am, would think I was being wronged."[51] One who entertains this view finds it far easier to forgive others and thus finds also that a number of obstacles to prayer growth are consequently removed.

Most people would consider that excusing oneself under blame, especially unjust blame, has little to do with prayer life. A naturalistic ethic would assume that a person may without any fault defend himself as long as his defense is fair and honest and nonabusive toward the accuser. Not so St. Teresa. While there are occasions when it is right to explain oneself, they are in her view comparatively rare. Because the saint could say of herself that "I never seem unable to find a reason for thinking I am being virtuous when I make excuses for myself ",[52] she considers that she does not have the humility to know when it is fitting to explain herself and her actions. It is better, then, usually to abstain from self-justification under accusation except when failing to explain will cause either offense or scandal.[53] So important does Teresa consider this advice that she devotes several pages to offering her reasons. The first is the silence of Jesus in his Passion. He was supremely guiltless and yet did not open his mouth in self-defense. Even if we understood none of the other reasons, this one would be sufficient. Connected with this fact is another: imitating the Lord in his humiliations requires neither bodily strength nor the aid of anyone but God. This penance will not harm one's health as excessively corporal ones may do. A third reason is that silence under accusation can be practiced in small matters, and it accustoms one to "gain great victories" in other important affairs. Fourth, we are all so full of faults for which we are not blamed that "we can never be blamed unjustly". In other words, we have criticism coming to us, and when we receive it well, we make reparation for other sins as well. A fifth benefit stems from the good example silence gives to the accuser and to others, especially when they find out eventually that we were not guilty. "Such an experience", observes the saint, "uplifts the soul more than ten sermons." St. Teresa finds a sixth reason in the example of Jesus, Who twice defended a woman who was unjustly accused. Often people will do the same in our behalf. "His Majesty, then, will put it into somebody's mind to defend you; if He does not, it will be because there is no need." Last, and directly pertinent to growth in prayer, the person who usually remains silent under criticism gains a great freedom from concern and worry about other people's opinions. No longer living as a slave to others' minds, such a person more easily soars into the divine mind.[54]

DETACHMENT: A NOTE

Inner freedom from selfish clingings is so basic a condition for growth to maturity that an entire chapter in this book has been devoted to the subject. Thus we shall not deal here with St. Teresa's insistence upon it, for her thought has been incorporated into the even more extensive treatment of St. John of the Cross.

SOLITUDE

While all of God's people are called to a profound communion with Him, few receive the divine beckoning to the solitary life of a hermit. This present volume surely includes these favored souls among its intended audience. But solitude here broadly refers to a need common to all human persons in all ways of life. What we have in mind is poles apart from isolation. The latter is an unhealthy withdrawal from human society, a turning in on oneself that is only too often a trait of neurosis. Solitude, in contrast, is a healthy turning toward one's beloved. Anyone in love seeks to be alone with the dear one at frequent and prolonged intervals, but people in love likewise take a wider interest in the rest of humanity. Even a hermit seeks solitude for the sake of absorption in God but shuns self-centered isolation. Only those properly embrace the eremitical life who can live successfully with others and who have to a considerable extent matured in their communion with God.

The monasteries founded by St. Teresa blended a close communal life with an atmosphere of silence, conducive to being alone with the Alone. Vivacious and outgoing by nature, she fell so deeply in love with "His Majesty" that she was convinced that for those who love Him, solitude is the atmosphere in which they live and breathe. The solitude she envisioned was no empty, lifeless void; it was, on the contrary, alive with expansive love. Just as a fish lifted out of the water is in a dying condition and can be revivified only by being returned to its natural milieu, so we humans need to be immersed in the atmosphere proper to us, the divine milieu.[55] We can make sense of the saints only by recalling continuously that they are men and women entirely in love. Bearing this in mind, we find completely logical Teresa's remark, "I often reflect, my Lord, that if there is something in life by which I can endure being separated from You, it is solitude."[56]

However, she did not view solitude as needful for herself only but as necessary for anyone who wishes to lead a serious prayer life. Those individuals who are completely absorbed and immersed in business, possessions and concerns of prestige (she is speaking of men and women free of obviously sinful pursuits and passions) simply cannot make progress in prayer unless they free themselves as much as duties of state permit. "Everyone", she states, "who wishes to enter the second Mansions, will be well advised, as far as his state of life permits, to try to put aside all unnecessary affairs and business. For those who hope to reach the principal Mansion [the transforming union, which Teresa took for granted is everyone's destiny], this is so important that unless they begin in this way I do not believe they will ever be able to get there."[57] If the saint's admonition seems impractical for laypeople, they need to reflect on Jesus' saying much the same thing: the world is suffocated by the cares and riches and pleasures of life, and so it does not mature.[58] Advanced prayer is mature prayer, and it is impossible unless we free ourselves from being smothered (this is the very verb the Lord uses) by finite realities sought for themselves.

If the reader recoils at the thought of much solitude and at the unappealing prospects of fitting it into a crowded schedule, St. Teresa is an understanding mentor. She adverts to our needing to learn to like and to appreciate being alone with God, and she is mindful that we need to get used to it, that it does not come easily at the outset.[59] Determination is therefore in order to see to it that first things do come first, that we are prepared to provide the suitable time and place for growth to happen.

Silence and solitude do not refer only to the lessening of decibels. A person, notes Teresa, cannot understand the indwelling mystery and fully realize Who is present within until he closes his eyes to the vanities of this world.[60] Were she in our midst at the end of the twentieth century, the saint would no doubt specify that this means a drastic reduction in our exposure to the mass media, especially the electronic media of television, radio and film. If we spill out and drain our psychic energies by the endless multiplicities of images and sounds, many of them garish and deafening, we just cannot retain the inner stamina for prayer. When we realize that the average home in our society, according to a recent survey, has its television set turned on for seven hours and ten minutes per day, we may not be shocked at what Teresa considers the amount of time everyone should give daily to prayerful solitude:

> I do now know, my Creator, why it is that everyone does not strive to reach You through this special friendship, and why those who are wicked, who are not conformed to Your will, do not, in order that You make them good, allow You to be with them at least two hours each day, even though they may not be with You, but with a thousand disturbances from worldly cares and thoughts, as was the case with me.[61]

The saint suggests that even distracted presence to the divine presence is bound to transform one from sin to virtue and eventually from common goodness to heroic sanctity.

But ample time and a suitable place for prayer are not enough. We must also learn to carry out St. Paul's admonition to the Thessalonians: "Live quietly and mind your own business."[62] St. John of the Cross considered this idea so important that when he wrote a three-page work on how to reach perfection in short order, he made it the first of four counsels:

> You should live in the monastery as though no one else were in it. And thus you should never, by word or by thought, meddle in things that happen in the community, nor with individuals in it, desiring not to notice their good or bad qualities or their conduct. And in order to preserve your tranquillity of soul, even if the whole world crumbles, you should not desire to advert to this or interfere.[63]

What is the connection between minding our own affairs and growth in prayer? One reason for the advice is that serious people are likely to be agitated and even shocked at all sorts of things that occur through the typical day. Their inner peace is unsettled, and prayer is hindered. Another reason is that those who meddle in other people's concerns are likely to make mistakes in their judgments and even to offer misguiding advice. Thus, says Teresa, we ought to let God take care of His own.[64] She observes likewise that pain is often enough caused to the one in whose business we are meddling,[65] but the most pointed reason is that people who are minding others' affairs are not minding their own. If our mind is free enough to notice what others are doing, it is free enough to carry out what Scripture repeatedly tells us, namely, to keep our eyes always on the Lord, to sing to Him in our hearts always and everywhere.[66] The saint considers distress over the sins and failings of others in everyday life as a demonic temptation. The devil puts it into people's heads that their meddling really arises from a desire that God be not offended and be better served. They usually focus on the petty faults of which the world is full. A pervasive concern disturbs peace. All the while meddlers consider that they are being virtuous in their preoccupations. Teresa's conclusion is that "the safe path for the soul that practices prayer will be not to bother about anything or anyone and to pay attention to itself and to pleasing God".[67]

Closely allied to mental meddling is idle talk. These two go hand in hand, not only as companion traits but also as obstructions to a contemplative spirit. The harms of useless chatter St. Teresa knew from her own early experience. Both as a young woman and as a mature religious, she was noted for her intelligent, witty, charming conversation. Citizens of Avila loved to seek out this beautiful young nun in the parlor of the Incarnation convent because they enjoyed listening to her speak about God and the spiritual life. This chatting seemed to be similar to our contemporary substitute, television talk shows. In her later years, however, the saint saw how much time she had frittered away, even though much of the conversation was on solid subjects. The mature Teresa did not tire of repeating how unfaithful to God she had been: she had not been attending to Him. She found this trait one of the obvious signs of religious laxity.

Oh, tremendous evil! Tremendous evil of religious — I am not speaking now more of women than of men — where religious life is not observed, where in a monastery there are two paths (one of virtue and religious life, the other of a lack of religious life) and almost all walk in like manner; rather, in place of like manner I should say evil manner. For on account of our sins the greater number take the more imperfect path. True religious life is practiced so little that the friar or nun who is indeed about to follow wholeheartedly his call must fear those of his own house more than all the devils. . . . I don't know why we are amazed that there are so many evils in the Church since those who are to be the models from which all might copy the virtues are so obscurely fashioned that the spirit of the saints of the past has abandoned the religious communities.[68]

One does not need a great deal of creativity to imagine what Teresa would say about the current hours per day spent on television by both laity and religious. She would have seen this habit as a prominent reason why while many of us talk about contemplation and read books about it, so few actually make significant progress. Waste of time and prayer depth are incompatible.

Mindful of Jesus' warning that we shall give an account on judgment day of every idle word we speak,[69] St. Teresa is concrete in how we should handle the problem. If in a chat "no effort is being made to make the conversation a fruitful one, they should bring it to a quick conclusion, as was said. It is very important that those who visit us leave with some benefit, and not after having wasted time, and that we benefit too."[70] While the saint in this context is speaking to her nuns, and while it is true that people in the world face great problems in trying to relate to others in this fashion, it does remain that her advice needs to be taken seriously by anyone who takes Jesus' dictum seriously. The one implies the other. Speaking of friends and relatives who visit (or, we might add today, telephone), Teresa remarks that "if these persons are not the kind who find their satisfaction in speaking about the things of God, they should be seen seldom, and the visit kept short".[71]

SUFFERING AND GROWTH IN PRAYER

Saints have a knack for penetrating into the depths of Scripture that are denied to the mere technician. The latter may know Aramaic and Greek, archeology and philology, history sacred and profane, but if he lacks the deep drinking of the Spirit Who inspired the biblical writings, he remains an outsider and an amateur. He is like the psychologist who has a doctorate but has never been in love. He knows the words but not the realities. The saints grasp the revealed message because they are filled with the same Holy Spirit that gives both the message and its meaning. Our two Carmelites knew both from the inspired word and from personal experience that there is a close linkage between suffering with love and growing into the depths of the Trinity. Just as Jesus Himself had to suffer and thus enter into His glory,[72] and just as we must die with Him if we are to rise with Him,[73] so must anyone who hopes to reach a lofty prayer gladly embrace the daily crosses that are sure to come.

St. Teresa uses one of her favorite images to explain how sufferings, both from within and from without, prepare a person for reaching the advanced prayer of union: "If the soil is well cultivated by trials, persecutions, criticisms, and illnesses — for few there must be who reach this state without them — and if it is softened by living in great detachment from self-interest, the water soaks it to the extent that it is almost never dry."[74] We should notice the words *to the extent*. There is a direct correlation between what and how one suffers and the depths of one's growth. The "how" transfigures a mere passive undergoing into a newness of life, the new creation. We ought not to view the relationship as extrinsic, that is, as though suffering is a ticket that admits to prayer but without inner causality. On the contrary, suffering borne with much love and in union with Christ crucified purifies and renews. For Teresa carrying the cross is a gift that has the power to transform us into a divine likeness and to effect our union with God.[75] John remarks that we ought to see those with whom we live as so many chisels whom God uses to chip away our defects and make of us a beauteous creation.[76] Contemplation cannot be separated from the Incarnation and redemption, from a co-living of the paschal mystery with the crucified, risen One. Zen contemplation and Hindu meditation can be produced by techniques, but Christian communion is entirely a love matter wrapped up with the Cross. Any spouse worthy of the name wants to share in the lot of her beloved, and Jesus' lot was one of being insulted, whipped, mocked, nailed to cross beams.[77] This sort of worthy suffering with the Beloved has, says Teresa, a transforming power, a power that effects a union between Creator and creature.[78]

Unfortunately, however, what we are calling worthy suffering is not common, and this is a principal reason why advanced prayer is not common, even though everyone is called to it. We have pious desires for a generalized carrying of the cross, but when the time comes, our desires dissolve like mist before the morning sun. Contrary to all the evidence, many of us assume that our progress in prayer will be furthered if only we find the right procedures, occidental or oriental, some method of meditation or centering. We treat contemplation as the result of performing an exercise and forget that it is infused by God who gives His communion only to the extent that we are conformed to His Son.

St. Teresa speaks of several principles regarding the trials that God sends to contemplatives. They are often severe, indeed, intolerable, and of such a kind that they could not be borne were God not to give also special consolations. Because the Lord chastises those whom He loves, the more He loves prayerful people and the higher He wishes to raise them, the greater will be the hardships they must endure. In my own work of spiritual direction I have seen this truth exemplified over and over again. I cannot recall a single case in which a directee has reached a lofty infused prayer without having suffered much and well. It is true, of course, that God gives help commensurate to the sufferings He sends or permits. Teresa wrote to Jerome Gratian that "after all, His Majesty will give you help proportionate to your trials; and so, as you are suffering great trials, you will enjoy great favors too". St. Paul was of the same mind: "You will have in you", he wrote to the Colossians, "the strength, based on his own glorious power, never to give in, but to bear anything joyfully."[79] Teresa summarized the matter succinctly in one sentence: "Love is the measure of our ability to bear crosses."[80]

OVERALL CONDITION: LOVE-GENEROSITY

Contemplation is no ivory-tower matter. Job's remark that life is a warfare can be literally applied to prayer, for it also implies a battle, even if it is, in itself, a blissful rest and fulfillment. When Jesus comes to explain why people listen to His word but do not mature as a result, He does not explain that they have not found the right techniques or the right guru or the right book or the right workshop. The problem is that their slovenly living of the message smothers maturation: "As for the part that fell into thorns, this is people who have heard, but as they go on their way they are choked by the worries and riches and pleasures of life and do not reach maturity."[81] St. John of the Cross repeatedly explains a lack of growth by underlining our reluctance and even refusals to undergo the purification necessary. So prominent is this truth in the sanjuanist writings that we have devoted Chapters 8 and 9 to it. Here we shall discuss the teresian analysis.

For the foundress, growth must happen in the midst of a life lived on a battlefield. The man or woman who aspires to lofty contemplation ordinarily lives in a community of one kind or another, with all its demands for kindness, patience, humility, forgiveness and obedience. One does not satisfy conditions for prayer "by getting alone in corners".[82] While the saint emphasizes the need for prayerful solitude and "frequent inward recourse to our God", she also lays it down that "it is not length of time spent in prayer that brings the soul benefit: when we spend our time in good works, it is a great help to us and a better and quicker preparation for the enkindling of our love than many hours of meditation".[83] When God sees us strong in this battle of life, He fulfills His will in us and raises us high.[84] Speaking of her own personal experience with the need for generosity as a condition for thriving prayer, she remarks that "since His Majesty was not waiting for anything other than some preparedness in me, the spiritual graces went on increasing in the manner I shall tell. It is not a customary thing for the Lord to give them save to those with greater purity of conscience."[85] Teresa, of course, attained to a remarkable degree of purity of soul, and for this reason she attained to the summit of prayer itself. Despite her profound humility, she could say of herself that she would rather die a thousand deaths than offend God knowingly. She not only avoided deliberate sin, even tiny sin, but she also determined to do always the more perfect thing.[86] She likewise admonished the nuns that they were to omit nothing at all in the divine service.[87]

We cannot emphasize too much this generosity as the fundamental condition for a deep prayer life. Petty selfishnesses and trivial self-indulgences stifle interpersonal intimacy. Married couples know only too well that deliberate selfishness dampens a deepening relationship, and if there is no sincere repentance, intimacy is doomed. Marital intercourse is still possible, but it is no longer fully what God intends it to be—husband and wife likewise know something is amiss. Divorce is often the direct result of unrepented selfishness on one or both sides. Tepidity in prayer is a consequence of preferring oneself to the Beloved. Love cools, understanding is darkened and the will is weakened.[88] Contemplation collapses.

St. Teresa singles out brotherly/sisterly love as a prime example of an area in which a lack of generosity kills growth. She states plainly that "if you find you are lacking in this virtue, you have not yet attained union".[89] Though her communities are houses of prayer before they are anything else, the saint reserves some of the strongest language in all her writings to express her horror that a lack of sisterly love could occur in them. She says that her blood runs cold as she speaks of a nun's being angry with another because of some hasty word, or of a nun's harboring a grudge, or of some party strife. A nun who will not love her sister is a Judas in the house, and the prioress must put a stop to the matter at the very outset. Regarding the community member who is causing trouble, Teresa declares, "Drive away this plague; cut off the branches as well as you can; and, if that is not sufficient, pull up the roots. . . . God deliver us from a convent into which it enters: I would rather our convent caught fire and we were all burned alive."[90] In any vocation it is "brutish" not to love the members of one's own household.[91] Though the saint's hard language may strike a modern ear as extreme, we need to bear in mind that loving one's neighbor is bound up with eternal salvation or damnation. The stakes cannot be higher, and anyone who believes in eternity cannot consistently think otherwise. Prayer is primary, but it cannot be severed from fraternal love. The Lord Himself has made it clear that if we are on the way to the altar for worship and recall that we have offended the brother, we are to turn in our tracks and make peace with the brother, and only after this return to the prayer.[92]

A NOTE

The perceptive reader will readily recognize that the teresian analysis of conditions for growing in prayer are not what we commonly read in current discussions of contemplation. Humility, detachment, solitude, suffering, obedience and generosity are not only often bypassed but also sometimes looked upon with a degree of disdain. These virtues are considered to be "negative" and hardly worthy of serious consideration by people who "have come of age". The chronological snobbery implicit in this attitude of supposed superiority over our ancestors does not merit attention, but it may be useful to point out that men and women who lack these virtues are never known for their depth of prayer. Those who reject Teresa's teaching are of course rejecting the New Testament together with the experience of the ages. The saint is herself an eloquent witness to the solidity of her doctrine. At age fifty-two she was still beautiful, cheerful, charming and eloquent. Prayer and the virtues she extols diminished nothing in her but her early faults; they enhanced her beauty all the more. Marcelle Auclair is able to say that at this later period "religious life had in no way stifled that which had made her life in the world such a brilliant success: she was still beautiful, gay, lively, more eloquent than ever and endowed with a charm which it was useless to try and resist. In her, one experience did not efface a previous one, each merely added something to her amazing personality without taking away or destroying anything of it."[93]

CHAPTER EIGHT

THE FREEDOM OF DETACHMENT

Only the free can love, and only the completely free can love unreservedly. Obvious as this is upon a moment's reflection, the idea is perhaps the least understood of everything Ss. John of the Cross and Teresa of Jesus have written. Many people interested in the Gospel are confident they know what these two saints mean by detachment, but their evident misjudgments are typically a tangle of inattention and misinterpretation. To anyone who has loved purely and deeply, the saints' teaching is both tremendous and transparent, once it is understood. But the problem is not only that few of us love in the manner of the saints but also that we tend not to read them carefully, if we read them at all.

A discussion of five facets of detachment can perhaps put the matter into proper perspective. The first is what detachment is not. Many think that strong attractions to persons or things are attachments, or that the feeling of pleasure in seeing, hearing, tasting or possessing and using things is attachment to them. The second misunderstanding bears on what attachment does mean. Not infrequently, people have difficulty distinguishing that this is a question of will, not of feelings. Third, most do not grasp the *why* of detachment. If not thought to be positively unnatural and inhuman, the whole idea is at least fuzzy and the reaction therefore unfavorable. Fourth, the large majority even of priests and religious seem to consider that the sanjuanist doctrine of *nada* is peculiar to John and that one is at liberty to take it or leave it — usually the latter. It comes as a surprise to these people to learn that all the saints teach just as John and Teresa do. Last, almost no one realizes that this teaching is found explicitly in the New Testament, and without the least dilution. Otherwise sincere men and women innocently reject *The Ascent of Mount Carmel* and unwittingly contradict themselves by asserting, "I prefer the plain Gospel." This naïveté is proof positive that they do not know the Gospel in this matter. This strange phenomenon is not necessarily or entirely their fault, for it is a rare teacher who is brave enough to explain thoroughly what Jesus and Paul and John and Peter and Luke say about renouncing everything, about poverty of fact, about the rejection of superfluities, about minding the things of heaven, not those of earth. These are highly unpopular subjects, for as the Lord Himself put it, few there are who will take the hard road and the narrow gate that lead to life.[1] Popular or unpopular, welcome or unwelcome, we must here proclaim the undiluted message in season and out of season.[2]

TERMINOLOGY

A basic problem in understanding the negative element in the Gospel is the words that are used to speak about it. St. John's terms and the contemporary English translations of them sometimes contribute to misunderstanding, and it is not always the fault of the reader. We do well, therefore, to begin with a brief glossary.

1. *Desires.* Repeatedly the saint speaks of our need to eliminate desires from our lives — which, of course, immediately strikes one as a sheer impossibility. No one can so much as take a glass of water without desiring it. As we shall see below, what John means is inordinate and self-centered desires. Even when he does not repeatedly use these modifying adjectives, this is what he has in mind.

2. *Appetites.* This frequently occurring term is even less felicitous than the first, but once again the saint means voluntary disordered seekings. Appetite comes from the Latin *appetere* and *appetitum,* to seek and the thing sought. It does not refer to hunger for food. For all practical purposes, desire and appetite mean the same in the writings of St. John of the Cross: willed seeking of finite things in and for themselves rather than seeking them in God, their true Source and Purpose.

3. *Affection for . . . satisfaction in . . . fixing on . . . attachment to . . . gratification in.* Each of these expressions refers to the act of desiring or centering on something created for its own sake. The saint is by no means suggesting that we should be cold or indifferent toward others or find no delight in anything. As we shall note further on, we are to find delight in everything but to cling to it in nothing. John himself loved others dearly, as did Teresa, and he enjoyed music and stars and nature immensely. For him they were nothing but pure mirrors of the divine — which, of course, is exactly what everything is meant to be.

4. *Fixing on . . . feeding on . . . being bound to.* These verbs in sanjuanist usage refer to the same sort of willed clinging that the other terms designate. We fix on something or are bound to it when we pursue it apart from God and for its own sake.

WHAT ATTACHMENT IS NOT

Before we examine St. John's own explanations, we may be helped by expressing in our own language what he does not mean when he refers to obstacles to divine union. First of all, attachment is not the experiencing of pleasure in things, not even keen, intense pleasure. The complete avoidance of pleasure is neither possible nor advisable in human life. If one is hungry enough, a dry crust of bread is delicious. If one is tired enough, lying on a hard board is a blessed relief. And who can possibly avoid enjoying the breathtaking beauty of roses and sunsets and human loveliness? There is no doubt that the pleasures of the five senses easily lead to a selfish clinging to them for their own sakes, but nonetheless, the pleasures themselves are not blameworthy. God made them, and they are good.

Nor is possessing or using things an attachment to them. Once again, we cannot avoid possession and usage entirely in the daily conduct of our lives. Even if I have a vow of poverty and thus own neither pen nor typewriter, they are nonetheless reserved for my use, and I cannot do my duty without them. True enough, I may selfishly cling to an efficient machine, but the mere use of it is not of itself an obstacle to seeking God wholeheartedly.

Nor is being attracted, even mightily attracted, to a beautiful object or person an unhealthy attachment. As a matter of fact, we should be drawn to the splendors of creation, for that is a compliment to the supreme Artist. Saints were and are strongly attracted to the glories of the divine handiwork and especially to holy men and women, the pinnacles of visible creation. Anyone who has read lives of the saints knows well how deeply they appreciated the "marvels of the Lord" and how profoundly they loved their friends, especially their saintly friends.

WHAT ATTACHMENT IS

Before we come to a concise definition of attachment that no serious theist could find objectionable, we must examine John's expressions of the matter. Otherwise the reader may be tempted to think that we are reading our own thoughts into the saint's writings and imposing our own concept instead of presenting his precise thinking on the topic. Though he touches on this subject frequently throughout his works, we shall be content with two texts, for they say most of what needs to be noted. At the beginning of the *Ascent* St. John of the Cross alarms the reader by declaring that we are to deprive ourselves of the "gratification of the appetite in all things". He spells this out by saying in no uncertain terms that this means giving up desires for the delights of hearing, seeing, smelling, tasting and touching. This complete surrender of desires leaves one living in "darkness and a void".[3] No one will contest this last remark.

Yet one badly distorts John by not reading the saint carefully and by forgetting the definition of terms we have considered. John is simply observing that if anyone is serious about loving God totally, he must willingly entertain no self-centered pursuit of finite things sought for themselves, that is, devoid of honest direction to God, our sole end and purpose. St. Paul makes exactly the same point when he tells the Corinthians that whatever they eat or drink, or whatever else they do, they are to do all for the glory of God. Whatever does mean whatever, and all does mean all. St. John of the Cross simply adds a detailed amen to the pauline doctrine.

A little further on he notes what we all know, namely, that "it is true that the sensory perceptions of hearing, sight, smell, taste, and touch are unavoidable".[4] Thus he is not speaking of some absolute prohibition or abstention. He goes on to observe that though King David was manifestly a wealthy man, he was poor in spirit "because his will was not fixed on riches; and he thereby lived as though really poor".[5] That we are interpreting the saint according to his actual mind is clear in the following paragraph:

> Hence, we call this nakedness a night for the soul. For we are not discussing the mere lack of things; this lack will not divest the soul, if it craves for all these objects. We are dealing with the denudation of the soul's appetites and gratifications; this is what leaves it free and empty of all things, even though it possesses them. Since the things of the world cannot enter the soul, they are not in themselves an encumbrance or harm to it; rather, it is the will and appetite dwelling within it that causes the damage.[6]

People misconstrue St. John of the Cross when they forget passages like this one. He teaches simply what any consistent theist must hold and what Scripture itself plainly says. He develops this thought when he explicitly states that he is speaking of voluntary desires and not "natural ones", for the latter are "little or no hindrance" to advanced prayer as long as the will does not intervene with a selfish clinging. By natural desires the saint has in mind, for example, a felt need for water when we are thirsty, for food when hungry, for rest when fatigued. There is no necessary disorder in experiencing these needs. He notes again that to eradicate these natural inclinations and "to mortify them entirely is impossible in this life".[7]

Especially damaging to normal development are what John calls "habitual appetites", that is, repeated and willed clingings to things less than God for their own sakes. An occasional slip must be avoided as much as possible, but it does not do nearly the harm that a fully willed habitual practice does.[8]

Since the saint makes it clear both in what we have said and in the references in footnote 8 that he is speaking only of voluntary and inordinate desires, we may ask when a desire becomes inordinate and therefore harmful. I would offer three clear signs. The first is that the activity or thing is diverted from the purpose God intends for it. If I use my intellect and speech capacities to tell a lie, I am directing these gifts away from their social purposes of interhuman communication (informing, recreating, loving, asking) to my personal ends of blocking communication, or of selfishly covering up my faulty action, or of trying to gain an unjust advantage over another. This diversion of speech makes it clear that I am clinging selfishly and egocentrically to a number of unworthy ends. I am decidedly attached in the pejorative sense of the term.

The second sign is excess in use. As soon as we go too far in eating, drinking, recreating, speaking or working, we show that there is something disordered in our activity. We cannot honestly direct to the glory of God[9] what is in excess of what He wills. Hence, a person who buys more clothes than needed is attached to clothing. One who overeats is clinging selfishly to food. The individual who watches more television or travels more extensively than needful is proven to be an inconsistent theist. This person wants things for himself in a competition with the Lord of all.

The third sign of attachment is making means into ends. We have one sole purpose in life: the ultimate, enthralling vision of the Trinity in glory, in our risen body. Everything else is meant in the divine plan to bring us and others to this final embrace with Beauty and Love. When therefore we speak idly, that is, for no good purpose, just for its own sake, we have made speaking into a little idol. As soon as honesty requires us to admit that this eating or that travel, this television viewing or that purchase is not directly or indirectly aimed at Father, Son and Spirit, we have made ourselves into an idol. We are clearly clinging to something created for our own self-centered sake. We cannot be entirely in love with God.

These reflections, then, lead us to three brief definitions. An attachment is a willed seeking of something finite for its own sake. It is an unreal pursuit, an illusory desire. Nothing exists except for the sake of God who made all things for Himself. Any other use is a distortion.

THE WHYS OF DETACHMENT

To a considerable extent our definitions themselves explain why a human person endowed with common sense will flee egocentrism, but more yet must be said. This question of inner freedom can be dealt with both negatively and positively in terms of the harms of attachments and the benefits of detachment. While the thought of St. John of the Cross is thoroughly positive in its orientation to consummate love, it is both negative and positive in spelling out the details. We will follow his pattern of treating the subject, but it may be well to preface this account with his fundamental outlook.

Throughout his writings the saint continually has in the back of his mind the transforming union. Even when he is discussing the rudiments of prayer or detachment, he is thinking of bringing the reader to "union"—and union for John means the final, perfect union. To think of an incomplete union with divine Beauty is foreign to the sanjuanist mind. The human person is destined to this complete oneness of likeness with God, a oneness effected through total love that transforms the human partner into divine splendor: "From one glory to another as we are transformed into the image that we reflect", as St. Paul puts it.[10] This union of likeness effected by perfect love can happen only when everything unlike and unconformed to God is cast out, for otherwise the entire image cannot be received into the soul. Therefore, says John, we must become purified of anything ungodly with no admixture of imperfection. In a similar manner, the more a pane of glass is free of anything not pure glass, the more it can be transformed into a ray of sunlight. Since we are destined to become God by participation in the divine nature,[11] we must be purified of anything and everything that is not God. Consequently, "perfect transformation is impossible without perfect purity".[12] St. John of the Cross is in complete agreement with New Testament John, who has already said that anyone who entertains the hope of the final vision of eternity must try to be as pure as Christ Himself.[13] There is no higher ideal than this.

St. John of the Cross details this basic rationale for detachment with an analysis of the specific harms that selfish clingings, even small inordinate ones, introduce into the soul's pursuit of the Lord. It is difficult to see how a theist who approaches this sanjuanist analysis without a preconceived bias against Gospel self-denial could have a significant problem accepting the saint's thought. What are these harms?

1. *The dimming of vision.* Even though the sixteenth century knew little of air pollution caused by the burning of fossil fuels, they did know of fog and the effect it produces on sunlight. St. John observes that the human intellect is befogged in its natural capacity and in receiving supernatural wisdom when it clings to finite things for their own sakes. This clouding of the mind by sin was well known to biblical writers as well, for we have the psalmist complaining that as his sins close in upon him he is unable to see.[14] As a punishment for his transgressions the light of his eyes has left him;[15] his vision is wasted as he laments his offenses.[16] St. Paul lays it down that the worldly individual not only does not grasp the things of the Spirit; he cannot grasp them.[17] So, says John, our unredeemed desires are like a cataract over the eyes, a truth that any experienced spiritual director can verify. People who are singlemindedly and wholeheartedly pursuing God immediately understand the finer points of evangelical perfection, while equally intelligent but worldly men and women simply cannot comprehend an identical explanation. This is one reason why five hundred people listening to a Sunday homily have such diverse reactions to it, ranging from an eager enthusiasm through bland indifference to hostile rejection. Even people who do want God to some extent often fail to see the damage to their supernatural vision that their petty clingings bring about. In this connection John remarks that

> the ignorance of some is extremely lamentable; they burden themselves with extraordinary penances and many other exercises, thinking these are sufficient for the attainment of union with the divine wisdom. But these practices are insufficient if a person does not diligently strive to deny his appetites. If these people would attempt to devote only a half of that energy to the renunciation of their desires, they would profit more in a month than in years with all these other exercises.[18]

We have here the fundamental reason why a Curé of Ars possesses far more divine light than a worldly cleric, or a Thomas More more than a self-centered layman. It is the pure of heart that see God, they and no others.[19]

2. *Sinful ramifications.* Seeking things for themselves rather than as means leading to God not surprisingly leads to all sorts of other aberrations. Just as good is diffusive of itself, so sin begets a progeny of evils. One might reflect on how, for example, an attachment to television or to clothing brings about any number of other faults, faults that St. John of the Cross enumerates: judging others badly . . . waste of

time . . . envy . . . avarice . . . vanity . . . fear of what should not be feared . . . a loss of taste for the Eucharist ("this bread of angels is disagreeable to the palate of anyone desirous of tasting the food of men") . . . forgetfulness of God . . . gossiping . . . neglect of work.[20] If the just man falls seven times a day, the sinner falls more times than can be enumerated. And to most of the falls he is probably blind.

3. *Impediments to prayer and awareness of God.* This result of attachments needs little explanation. Each of us is sinner enough to know well from experience that a selfish clinging focuses our attention on ourself and draws us away from the divine presence. It prevents us from preferring what is more pleasing to God instead of our own pleasure. Many, perhaps most, of the distractions we suffer in prayer are due to these disordered concerns and desires.

4. *An affront to God.* Just as atheists prove to be extremely inconsistent in their daily lives and thus fail to follow out what they profess to believe, so theists are inconsistent to the extent that they recede from sanctity. Given that God is endless Beauty and Joy and Love, seeking anything aside from Him and for its own sake is sheer nonsense. Preferring something finite to God is an insult to Him. "He who loves something together with God", says our saint, "undoubtedly makes little of God, for he weighs in the balance with God an object far distant from God."[21] It follows then that "love for God must never fail, nor be mixed with alien loves. . . . God allows nothing else to dwell together with Him."[22] The principle involved here is readily seen even on the human level. A husband who prefers his bowling to his wife insults her, and a wife who chooses her own vanity or comfort to her husband's well-being insults him. Immeasurably more demeaning is the preference for a finite frill to purest Love.

5. *Drying up joy.* Contrary to what the world thinks, attachments are killjoys. The worldly man and woman take it for granted that the more they can multiply experiences and accumulate possessions, the more they shall be filled with contentment. They so want to believe this that they will discount a constant stream of evidences to the contrary. Boredom at parties, hangovers after bouts of drinking, heartburn after overeating, aftereffects of drug abuse, emptiness after loveless sexual encounters and failure to find fulfillment in fine fashions or in expensive excursions make it abundantly clear that sense pleasures are not joy. No matter how intense they may be for the moment, they inevitably leave in their wake a vacuous disillusionment. Where one does find genuine joy is in the heart and on the lips of those who have generously given up all else to have Christ. In the fervent monastery that has not given in to compromise with the world, in the home where

father and mother love God before all else, and everything in Him, we still do find the shouts of joy of which Scripture speaks. Saints are experimental proofs that the world has things upside down. "The more a person rejoices over something outside God," notes St. John of the Cross, "the less intense will be his joy in God."[23] Worldlings may have their brief pleasures, but God "does not permit gladness to enter their hearts".[24] It would not be going too far to say that in proportion as one is stripped of all self-centered seeking, so the capacity for deep, calm, enduring delight is heightened. Not by accident did St. Paul admonish the Philippians to "rejoice *in the Lord* always".[25] Genuine joy, lasting joy, is impossible elsewhere.

6. *Diminishing the person.* Love places one on the level of the object loved, or as John puts it, attachments diminish the person, because love effects a likeness with the object loved. To make his point the saint uses a vivid biblical example: he who touches pitch is defiled by it. We might call this the argument from the "perfect and extremely beautiful image of God" that is the human person. So marvelous are men and women, says John, that their clinging to anything less diminishes them just as a diamond or a golden vessel is stained by admixture with anything less than itself. The person, therefore, must cling only to God and in this clinging be elevated, ennobled and beautified.[26]

7. *Blocking transformation.* All that St. John of the Cross has said thus far makes it easy to grasp how attachments prevent the final transformation into divine beauty. Until a person is purified of his clingings, "he will not be equipped to possess God, neither here below through the pure transformation of love, nor in heaven through the beatific vision".[27] Though John can extol the beauty of creation in his *Spiritual Canticle,* he insists that in comparison to the divine beauty the "grace and elegance of creatures [is] quite coarse and crude". Hence to cling to the latter makes one incapable of the infinite elegance of God.[28] A person attached to the finite is incapable of transformation into the infinite — as becomes even more clear in our chapter on the transforming union.

8. *Desires beget desires.* Unrest is the omnipresent accompaniment of earthly pursuits, and anyone who has lived a few years into adulthood and is therefore capable of a rudimentary reflection on the human situation knows well from experience that nothing fully satisfies. Soon after even peak experiences one begins to feel the inner gnawing emptiness. Using a down-to-earth example, we may call this phenomenon the peanut effect. Just as it is extremely difficult to eat one peanut and stop, so it is with anything we really like to do. Because spirit as spirit opens to the infinite, it can be satisfied and rested only in the infinite. All

else leaves it incomplete and desiring more. Desires, says St. John of
the Cross, beget desires. They whet the appetite as crumbs do the
famished person. Or, says the saint, they are like restless children always
whining after their mother, or like a starving individual who opens
his mouth to eat air.[29]

9. *Drain on psychic energy.* We all readily understand that our physical
energies are limited. Distance runners approach the state of collapse
at the end of a twenty-six-mile marathon. Most of us do not easily
grasp that our mental resources are also limited. This is why the individual who spills himself out in sense stimulations, who is engulfed
in the mass media, is never a person of deep prayer. Self-centered desires
"sap the strength needed for perseverance in the practice of virtue",
notes John, and "the more objects there are dividing an appetite, the
weaker becomes this appetite for each".[30] The saint multiplies examples
to illustrate why this happens: hot water loses its heat if left uncov-
ered . . . unwrapped aromatic spices eventually lose the pungency of
their scent . . . shoots burgeoning from a tree sap its strength and
decrease its fruitfulness.[31]

BENEFITS FROM DETACHMENT

Because we can explain inner freedom positively as well as negatively,
we can speak of the benefits of detachment as well as of the harms from
its opposite. Yet given John's thorough analysis of the latter, we need
not devote a great deal of attention to the former: the one approach
implies the other.

God, being most respectful of the freedom He has given to us, speaks
to our heart when it is uncluttered and silent. He does not interrupt
worldly conversations and pursuits. We hear Him, therefore, only to
the extent that we are disposed by inner stillness and undistracted by
selfish desires. He allows us to have exactly what we want. The detached
individual is saying by his life, "Speak, Lord, for your servant is listening."[32]

It is the pure heart that sees God,[33] the singleminded person who
seeks the things above, not those on earth.[34] This heart is sensitized
to the Holy Spirit, His enlightenments, movements and enkindlings.

The detached man enjoys a great freedom because he is no longer
enslaved to the opinions of his fellows. He need not fret about what
others think of him, his appearance, work and accomplishments. Prestige seeking is a slavery, and he is liberated from it: "He who is dominated by anything is a slave to it."[35] He who clings to nothing finite
for its own sake is as free as a bird in flight.

Finally, notes our saint, when the Beloved sees His beloved empty of all else, He cannot long stay away. So much does God love us that when He finds us open and ready, He cannot refrain from filling us to the extent that we are emptied. Just as nature abhors a vacuum, so does the Lord of supernature.

CHRIST, EXEMPLAR OF DETACHMENT

Sanjuanist thought is centered on the incarnate Word both in its goal and inspiration and in its detail and means. John's message is utterly foreign to the impersonal self-denial of the stoic or Buddhist. He means to be teaching nothing other than what Jesus both taught and lived. It was, after all, the eternal Son Who said that it is a narrow gate and a hard road that lead to life, and only a few find them.[36] It was He Who declared that unless we renounce *everything* we possess, we cannot be His disciples.[37] Indeed, we are to renounce our very selves, take up our cross and follow Him. To save our lives, we must lose them. Winning the whole world is supreme vanity, if it leads to losing one's soul.[38] The grain of wheat, therefore, must be cast into the earth and die, if it is to be fruitful for itself and for others.[39]

St. John of the Cross, who has sounded so deeply this teaching of Jesus, sadly remarks how few people understand it: "I think it is possible to affirm that the more necessary the doctrine the less it is practiced by spiritual persons. . . . They are of the opinion that any kind of withdrawal from the world or reformation of life suffices. . . . They think a denial of self in worldly matters is sufficient without an annihilation and purification of spiritual possessions."[40] They flee from dryness, distaste and sufferings as from death and thus "become, spiritually speaking, enemies of the cross of Christ".[41] They do not understand, and surely do not embrace, "the extent of the denial Our Lord wishes of us", a denial that "must be similar to a complete temporal, natural, and spiritual death".[42] Rather, they think that the road to God consists mainly in a multiplicity of methods and experiences, and so they go about in circles making little or no progress. Preferring delight and ease, they avoid a death patterned on that of Christ, and so they leave aside Him Who is "our model and light". John is much impressed by Jesus' life of sacrifice and His dying abandoned on the Cross, a self-denial by which He "accomplished the most marvelous work of His whole life, surpassing all the works and deeds and miracles that He had ever performed on earth or in heaven". The saint concludes from this widespread lack of understanding of detachment and denial that "from my observations Christ is to a great extent unknown by those

who consider themselves His friends".[43] Many people do not understand St. John of the Cross simply because they do not understand the
Gospel itself.

A PROGRAM FOR ACTION

We approach now the section in the sanjuanist corpus that has probably occasioned more misunderstanding than any other: What does one
do to attain inner freedom, that is, a perfect nudity of spirit? The first
norm is to imitate Christ, to bring one's life into conformity with His,
to behave in everything as He did.[44] The second is that, in order to
effect this imitation, we are to set aside any satisfaction of the senses
that is not purely for the honor and glory of Him who sought no other
food or drink but the will of the Father.[45] This means that we seek
to see, to hear, to experience created realities only in the service of God
and not for themselves. "If you cannot escape the experience of this
satisfaction, it will be sufficient to have no desire for it. . . . With such
vigilance you will gain a great deal in a short time."[46] John then presents
his famous maxims:

> Endeavor to be inclined always:
>   not to the easiest, but to the most difficult;
>   not to the most delightful, but to the harshest;
>   not to the most gratifying, but to the less pleasant;
>   . . . . '
>   not to the most, but to the least;
>   not to the highest and most precious, but to the lowest and
>   most despised . . .
>   and desire to enter for Christ into complete nudity, emptiness,
>   and poverty in everything in the world.[47]

There is no doubt that these lines are stark, and unfortunately they
have frightened many away from any further contact with St. John
of the Cross. Some flee simply because they prefer the world to God.
Others, sincere people, leave John aside because they lack instruction.
They do not realize that the *Ascent* does nothing more than detail what
we have in the New Testament: "What we have to do is give up everything that does not lead to God."[48] Everything does mean everything.
And God is God, after all. They likewise fail to notice what John really
says. He does not say that we must "choose always" what is most
difficult and harshest and lowest but that we be *inclined* always, that
is, all else being equal. Often in human life even the saint must choose

what is more pleasurable: to eat a dry crust of bread or drink tepid water is, if one is hungry or thirsty enough, more pleasing than not to eat or drink. For those who love God worshipping is more delightful (often, if not always) than not to worship. John's point is that out of love for Jesus Crucified and in cooperation with His redemption we prefer to suffer deprivation with Him when we may. The saint expressly remarks that, while we may not dilute this teaching (for it is the Gospel), we are also to use good judgment in its practice. "If", notes John, "you sincerely put [these maxims] into practice *with order and discretion,* you will discover in them great delight and consolation."[49]

The saint's next practical pointers involve a semantic problem for us moderns. We are, he says, to have a contempt for ourselves and to desire that others entertain the same view. We are likewise to think and to speak contemptuously of ourselves and to wish that all others do the same. On reading this we spontaneously wonder how possibly we may contemn ourselves when we are bound to love ourselves and one another. St. John knows this Gospel precept, of course, and he is the same man who elsewhere extols the beauty of the human person. This idea of self-contempt has a long history in Christian spirituality. It has early antecedents in the "despise-the-world" idea that has found its way into the liturgy itself. What to make of this? The words *despise* and *contempt* do not in this context refer to hatred, for hatred of what is good is sin pure and simple. Despise comes from the Latin *despicere,* which means literally to look away from, and the intent is that we are to look away from ourselves and from the world and turn our gaze on the Source of all goodness and beauty. In this sense a gourmet despises, looks away from a lowly hot dog, if he can dine on steak and lobster instead. Since nothing can compare to God, we are to turn away from all else, that is, seeking it for itself, and turn our seeking to the divine alone.

St. John of the Cross offers some additional verses as concrete guidelines for achieving this singleminded pursuit and thus climbing to the summit of the mountain:

> To reach satisfaction in all
> desire its possession in nothing.
> To come to possess all
> desire the possession of nothing.
> To arrive at being all
> desire to be nothing . . .
>
> For to go from all to the all
> you must deny yourself of all in all . . .

> In this nakedness the spirit finds
> its quietude and rest.[50]

These sayings are admittedly so stark that most people, reacting with aversion and alarm, see only the negative half of the message. Indeed, they miss entirely the more important positive half, which supplies the sense to the other portion. We have here an example of why so many do not understand St. John of the Cross: they do not read him as he is. We must first notice in this passage its utter positiveness: the saint wants us to delight *in everything,* to possess everything, to be everything. No worldling dares to present to us this kind of promise. We are called to reach a point where we delight in working and resting, speaking and keeping silence, seeing and hearing, suffering and rejoicing, failing and succeeding, living and dying. One cannot be more thoroughly optimistic. But there is only one way to this utter fulfillment, the way that Jesus said is hard and narrow. It leads to life, however, and it is the only road that does.

How do we reach this consummation, which "God has prepared for those who love him"?[51] It can happen only when our desires are completely purified of all selfish seekings and clingings. Hence, says John, we are to be cleansed of seeking finite pleasures for themselves, freed of a desire for possessions and fame and esteem. The pure of heart really do see God,[52] because, uncluttered by anything else, their hearts are open to be filled. The message, therefore, is the purification of desires: we are to give up everything that does not lead to God.[53] When egocentrism vanishes, we are filled with the supreme All.

Because there is a reciprocal causality between love for God and detachment from created things, anyone who is seeking the latter must grow in the former. Evangelical freedom is not a pagan negativism. Hence, St. John of the Cross would have us make detachment a positive love matter, a pursuance of the Beloved in everything: in eating, drinking, resting, working. He notes how Mary Magdalen was so intent upon Jesus after His death that she paid no attention even to the angels when she sought Him out.[54] Because a genuine Christian is a man or woman in love, it is the love that prompts an indifference to anything unrelated to the Beloved.

The program for action includes several items that can be briefly touched upon. The first is that attachments are to be nipped in the bud while they are still incipient and weak, that is, before they get a strong hold by habit. He who is faithful in small things is faithful in the greater,[55] and, "as the saying goes, 'once begun, half done'".[56] Second, factual frugality is an aid to inner freedom: "He who gives, and wants to give, the highest", says John to a prioress, "cannot fail to give the least. Be careful that you do not lack the desire to be poor and in want, for if you do, at that very hour devotion will fail you and you will gradually weaken in the practice of virtue."[57] The advice to Timothy is relevant here: we entered the world with nothing, and we shall leave it with nothing; we should be content with basic necessities.[58] Third, we are to divest our memories of all superfluous thoughts, rumors, news, tastes, fears, pleasures, remarks, sights and sounds "as though one were not in the world at all".[59] Fourth, we should notice that our aberrations are mutually strengthened or weakened. Our joys, fears, griefs and sorrows "are so brother-like that where one goes actually the others go virtually".[60] Fifth, we are to recall that while it may seem to us that we are losing out on something, we are actually gaining far more than we are giving up. To the worldly man this is nonsense, but, contrary to his own assumptions, he is incompetent to make a sound judgment. Only the person who has experienced both the pleasures of this world and of God can make a valid comparison. John knew the loftiest joys creation can offer: nature, music, friendship. St. Augustine knew these and sinful ones as well. Both saints agreed that these, compared to what the mystic finds in God, are "the smoke and air of this earth". In our experience of the beauties of creation we "must direct [our] heart to God in joy and gladness [because] God is Himself all these beauties and graces — eminently and infinitely".[61] Finally, says John, we need to approach the work of surrendering our clingings with solid determination. Velleity will not do. Words and pious prayers are not enough. Slothful, occasional efforts are insufficient. Unless we search we will not find. "Many desire that God cost them no more than words, and even these they say badly. . . . Yet, unless they go in search for God, they will not find Him, no matter how much they cry for Him."[62]

NORMS FOR SENSE PLEASURES

The life of the senses presents a special puzzle, a peculiar dilemma in the pursuit of God. On the one hand we cannot live a human life without eating, drinking, seeing, hearing and touching. On the other our fallenness makes us prone to indulge in sense experiences far beyond genuine need. How can we know when enough is enough, when our desires to see and hear and touch and taste are really directed to the glory of God and when they are not?[63] No easy question.

St. John of the Cross explicitly poses this problem, and he offers a clear answer to it. Because this text requires a careful reading, we shall set it down piece by piece and comment on it.

When the will, in becoming aware of the satisfaction afforded by the object of sight, hearing, or touch, does not stop with this joy but immediately elevates itself to God, rejoicing in Him who motivates and gives strength to its joy, it is doing something very good. The will, then, does not have to avoid such experiences when they produce this devotion and prayer, but it can profit by them, and even ought to for the sake of so holy an exercise. For there are souls who are greatly moved toward God by sensible objects.[64]

This passage makes it clear that St. John of the Cross is by no means opposed to the senses as such or to the pleasures they afford. But, and this is the acid test, sense delights may be deemed beneficial only when they immediately raise one to God. This any consistent theist must hold: all is to be directed to the Origin and Destiny of all. We are so immersed in our disordered selves that we assume that sense pleasures are their own end, that we were created for them, that we may pursue them aside from the very reason they exist: to plunge us into unending Beauty, Joy, Love and Truth. Hence, our sense life is properly oriented when it sparks prayer. Saintly people are indeed "greatly moved toward God" in what they see and hear and taste. But until we reach that degree of purification, we have to wage unrelenting war on our wayward pursuits of creation-centeredness. A creation-centered spirituality is an absurdity, a contradiction in terms. Yet there are, says the saint, many people who indulge in sense pleasures "under the pretext of prayer and devotion to God". They are regressing, not growing.

I should like to offer a norm for discerning when this gratification of the senses is beneficial and when not. Whenever a person, upon hearing music or other things, seeing agreeable objects, smelling sweet fragrances, or feeling the delight of certain tastes and delicate touches, immediately at the first movement directs his thought and the affection of his will to God, receiving more satisfaction in the thought of God than in the sensible object that caused it, and finds no gratification in the senses save for this motive, it is a sign that he is profiting by the senses and that the sensory part is a help to the spirit. The senses can then be used because the sensorial objects serve the purpose for which God created them: that He be more known and loved through them.[65]

St. John goes on to note that the person who experiences this "purely spiritual effect" does not cling to or desire the sense goods for themselves. A sign of this purity of use is found in the fact that when this person is presented with sense delights, he promptly passes on from them to God Himself. God is his genuine love, and he does not care for anything else. When on the contrary one finds that his will "pauses in and feeds upon" sense goods, he is "suffering harm from them and ought to turn from their use".[66] They are more a hindrance than a help.

St. Augustine captured this truth in his magnificent expression: "Too little does any man love You who loves something together with You, loving it not because of You." The saints know that unlimited Beauty calls for undivided love. They are consistent.

THE POSITIVE BEAUTY OF DETACHMENT

While the worldly minded dismiss the very idea of detachment, regarding it as repugnant, to the person in love with God it is appealing, attractive, desirable. Anyone deeply in love instinctively wants to give everything to the beloved, and anything that is an obstacle to union with the loved one is gladly surrendered. The worldling does not understand detachment because of a failure to understand selfless love. St. John of the Cross did understand it:

> He who is sick with love
> Whom God Himself has touched,
> Finds his tastes so changed
> That they fall away
> Like a fevered man's
> Who loathes any food he sees
> And desires I-don't-know-what
> Which is so gladly found.

> For when once the will
> Is touched by God Himself
> It cannot be satisfied
> Except by God;
> But since His Beauty is open
> To faith alone, the will
> Tastes Him in I-don't-know-what
> Which is so gladly found.

> Tell me, then, would you pity
> A man so in love,
> For he takes no delight
> In all of creation . . .

> I will never lose myself
> For that which the senses
> Can take in here,
> Nor for all the mind can hold,
> No matter how lofty,
> Nor for grace or beauty,
> But only for I-don't-know-what
> Which is so gladly found.[67]

The I-don't-know-what is one of the classical mystical expressions for the ineffability of a deep experience of God in advanced prayer. The saint is saying that he would never give up the beauties and delights of the visible world for anything created, but he would indeed gladly surrender them all for a deep immersion in God. One need not pity the man who gives up paltry delights for supreme Delight. It is the person who does not make this exchange who deserves pity.

Detachment, therefore, is simply a condition for the lofty gifts God wishes to grant anyone who is ready for them. John gives assurance that for each pleasure renounced with love for God we will receive a hundredfold in this life.[68] Further, the spiritual joy achieved in renouncing selfishly sought sense pleasures is "a hundred times greater".[69] One who has not grown into infused prayer will probably be incredulous and inclined to view statements like these as pious exaggerations, but it is to one's own loss to do so. The saints have been to the summit, and they speak from what they directly know. In addition to a far more joyous life in this world, detached persons are destined to an immense weight of eternal glory.[70] Detachment is consequently a purification process that enables one to blossom into being a divinely transformed human person.[71]

While delight in God is of course the crowning result of complete purification, a sublime joy in creation is also part of the package. Francis of Assisi found far more delight in the created order than the worldling does. This phenomenon we have explained in our chapter on the transforming union, and so we may simply note here a comment by C. S. Lewis: "All the beauty [in nature] withers when we try to make it an absolute. Put first things first and we get second things thrown in: put second things first and we lose both first and second things. We never get, say, even the sensual pleasure of food at its best when we are being greedy."[72]

OTHER SAINTS AND THE NEW TESTAMENT

One of the odd phenomena that may be noticed among those who dabble in the literature on the spiritual life but never apply themselves to more than surface study is the idea that the teaching of St. John of the Cross on detachment, the *nada* doctrine, is somehow uniquely his. If they happen to be disinclined to self-discipline they may well say, "His spirituality is not for me. I prefer the New Testament or others of the saints." They are unaware of the fact, patent to anyone who studies the Gospels and the saints with some thoroughness, that John's teaching is of one piece with the whole of Christian Tradition. One could write a volume showing how the contents of this chapter are found over and over again in Scripture, in patristic literature and in the teaching and lives of all the saints. John's distinction lies not in the content of his doctrine but in the scope and clarity and mystical depth with which he expounds it. To illustrate the universality of his teaching, we shall consider a few examples from patristic and hagiographical literature.

As St. Augustine comments on Jesus' admonition that we seek first the kingdom of God, he observes that we "cannot serve two masters. But a man does try to serve two masters if he seeks both the kingdom of God for the great good it is and also those other temporal things. He will not be able to keep his eye undivided and serve the Lord alone."[73] Earlier in the same work Augustine had said that we ought to place our heart and treasure "in the spiritual firmament — not in the heaven that is to pass away, but in that which abides forever".[74] The thought is, of course, identical with John's *nada*.

St. Raymond of Capua in his scrupulously exact life of St. Catherine of Siena tells us that

> the first and fundamental point she made was, that one who comes to the service of God, if he be truly intent on entering into union with God, must strip his heart of all sense-love — not merely love of any other person, but of any created thing whatever. He must strive towards God his Creator with his whole mind and his whole heart. For the heart, she always said, cannot be given over wholly to God, unless it first be set free from every other love.[75]

St. Francis of Assisi laid it down in his rule: "In that love which is God I entreat all my friars, ministers and subjects, to put away every attachment, all care and solicitude, and serve, love, honour, and adore our Lord and God with a pure heart and mind."[76] The saint likewise admonished his followers to the effect that "a man is really clean of heart when he has no time for the things of this world but is always searching for the things of heaven".[77] These two texts could have been written verbatim by St. John of the Cross.

St. Bonaventure, theologian that he was, explains that because "in God alone there is primordial and true delight . . . in all our delights we are led to seek this delight". God being supremely good, "nothing can be loved by a creature except out of a desire for it. Creatures, when they take the image and copy for the Truth, are deceived and in error."[78] The saint concludes in terms that anticipate our Carmelite: "Let us, then, die and enter into the darkness; let us impose silence upon our cares, our desires and our imaginings."[79] He describes St. Francis of

Assisi as a man "made totally insensible to earthly desires through his love of Christ".[80] What John taught, Francis lived—as indeed do all the saints.

St. Paul of the Cross, founder of the Passionists and devotee of John, was of the same mind. "As for food and clothing," he said, "I will always seek the worst and die to every desire and pleasure of the senses. . . . [Jesus] wants my affections to be pure, with no love for creatures or anything else." In language reminiscent of John he added that God "wants me to be free of desires . . . dead to every pleasing of myself. . . . I will always deprive myself of personal pleasure both in temporal and spiritual things."[81] One could not get more radical.

When St. John de Brebeuf wrote his instructions for young French missionaries coming to North America to work among the Indians, he left them under no illusions as to the radical self-denial and detachment they were to bring along:

> It is He alone and His Cross that should be sought in running after these people; for if you strive for anything else, you will gain naught but bodily and spiritual affliction. But having found Jesus Christ in His Cross, you have found the roses in the thorns, sweetness in bitterness, everything in nothing.[82]

DETACHMENT AND PRAYER IN ST. TERESA

Although the sanjuanist discussion of inner freedom leaves no stone unturned, we stand to profit from St. Teresa's treatment of the same subject. Not only does she enrich us with the value of her contribution, but we can benefit from the feminine and nontheological manner in which she presents her convictions. If one asks her, "What is detachment?" the simple, crystal-clear answer is "not paying attention to what doesn't bring us closer to God".[83] Or we hear that it consists in "never indulging our own will and desire, even in small things".[84] It would be difficult to put the matter more briefly or more accurately. And of course she is expressing exactly what we have in the New Testament: that we are to give up everything that does not lead to God,[85] that we are to offer everything we eat and drink and all else to the glory of God, not to our own self-centeredness.[86]

It is quite surely correct to say that Teresa derived much of her acute insight into our distortions of reality from her awesome experience of God and from the light with which He flooded her mind. She never tires of marveling at His mercy toward her who had been so imperfect in early life. Though by natural temperament the saint hated deceit, she refers to her faults as a lying use of reality.

> What power this Majesty appears to have since in so short a time He leaves such an abundant increase and things so marvelous impressed upon the soul! O my Grandeur and Majesty! What are You doing, my all-powerful Lord? Look upon whom You bestow such sovereign favors! Don't You recall that this soul has been an abyss of lies and a sea of vanities, and all through my own fault? For even though You gave me the natural temperament to abhor the lie, I myself in dealing with many things have lied. How do You bear it, my God?[87]

The saint is correct in seeing selfish clingings as so many deceptions, for things were not made for themselves but to lead us to the divine. They are merely means to an end, and we subvert them into goals, little gods. Egocentric desires are illusory; they are lies.

A sign of growth in inner freedom is the delight one begins to find in detachment.[88] No doubt a willingness to sacrifice and thus to suffer deprivations is a part of the process, but as one grows there will be a developing sense of freedom akin to what a person experiences when a great burden is lifted.

The eroding effects of egocentrism on contemplative prayer are explained by St. Teresa in her own way, but with a close similarity to the thought of St. John of the Cross. For one thing, clingings deprive a person of spiritual joy and calm, for delight in God cannot coexist with a seeking of pleasure in things not God.[89] The saint remarks how joy-filled her nuns are with all of their austerity, and she notes that some of them who left "a world of much vanity and ostentation" have been given by their Lord "a hundred joys for every one they left", and thus they cannot have enough of thanking Him for their vocation to the cloister.[90] She has known a few people who have lived upright lives and gained a certain mastery over worldliness, and yet when they are later tested, they have become so restless that they "drove me silly", as she puts it in her vivid expression.[91] In another typical teresian observation she asks bluntly, "If we fill the palace with vulgar people and all kinds of junk, how can the Lord and His Court occupy it?"[92]

Not only do clingings disturb and even destroy peace; they also imply a refusal of the gifts God wants to give: "Cupidity for life's consolations" squanders real treasures in God, notes Teresa.[93] In our own day we need to examine how much prayer and consequent personal enrichment and good to neighbor have been canceled out in favor of endless hours of television, empty amusements and idle chatter. The attached person has refused to make the great exchange and is trying unsuccessfully to serve God and mammon. The task is impossible; a choice must be made.

Like John, Teresa remarks about our limited psychic energies. Attachments drain away the strength we need to pursue God in an effective way. The saint tells how, as she was striving after purity of conscience and asking the Lord to aid her, she found that her "soul didn't have the strength to reach such perfection alone on account of some attachments that, though in themselves were not bad, were enough to spoil everything".[94] Anything that hinders perfection hinders prayer. If a person "is neglectful and sets her affection on anything other than Himself, she loses everything".[95] Indeed, people who have advanced to the prayer of quiet "must try to become more and more detached from everything, for otherwise they will only remain where they are".[96]

If we are detached, we do not sin. "If one has genuine detachment," observes Teresa, "it is, I think, impossible to offend the Lord. For in that case, in all one's conversations and intercourse with others, one never leaves Him, and in the same way His Majesty seems to be unwilling to withdraw from the soul."[97] This inner freedom brings with it a lordship over everything, for "he who cares nothing for the good things of the world has dominion over them all".[98] In this spirit St. Paul exults that "having nothing, [he] possesses all things".[99] One thereby becomes ablaze with burning love for God: "When no hindrance comes to it from outside, the soul remains alone with its God and is thoroughly prepared to become enkindled."[100]

Inner freedom prepares one for death in that it is a deliverance from all illusory desires that prompt the worldly person to imagine there is some kind of fundamental satisfaction here below. The completely liberated individual knows well that final fulfillment is found only in the beatific vision in risen body and thus welcomes the portal that leads proximately to it. "If only we were not bound to anything," declares Teresa, "if our satisfaction were not derived from any earthly thing, how the pain experienced from always living without Him and the desire to enjoy the true life would temper the fear of death."[101]

PROGRESS IN DETACHMENT

No one will claim that unlatching our wills from the strong hold of created realities is an easy job. Persistent effort is indispensable for anyone who wishes to grow in prayer. St. Teresa has two main items of advice for those determined to progress. The first is that we keep our thoughts constantly on the vanity of all things and fix them on eternity. This was St. Paul's idea when he said that he had no eyes for things that are visible but only for those that are invisible, for the former last only for a time, while the latter are eternal.[102] Keeping in mind the rapidity with which things of earth pass away, Teresa remarks, may seem a weak kind of help, but it does "have the effect of greatly fortifying the soul".[103] She notes that in regard to small things we need to be especially watchful, and as soon as we notice a fondness for them we are to turn our thoughts from them to their Creator.[104]

A second aid to the liberation process is a growing prayer life. Once again we have an interinfluence, a mutual causality. While detachment furthers prayer, so also prayer furthers detachment. In addition, notes the saint, growth in prayer gives us a realism about what is and what is not really important in life.

> If their recollection is genuine, the fact becomes very evident, for it produces certain effects which I do not know how to explain but which anyone will recognize who has experience of them. It is as if the soul were rising from play, for it sees that worldly things are nothing but toys; so in due course it rises above them, like a person entering a strong castle, in order that it may have nothing more to fear from its enemies. It withdraws the senses from all outward things and spurns them so completely that, without its understanding how, its eyes close and it cannot see them and the soul's spiritual sight becomes clear.[105]

Since we consider elsewhere in this volume the warm love for their families and companions in religious life that characterized both Teresa and John, we need not emphasize it here. What we do wish to point out, however, is what any consistent theist weaves into the horizontal dimension of life, namely, that whatever we do, we do it for the glory of God,[106] and whomever we love, we love in and for the supreme Love. Most adults leave their families when they enter upon their state in life. Separation is part of the human maturing process, and it is part of the process of growing in prayer. St. Teresa was able to combine a tender love for her family, especially for her parents, with a strong resolve not to waste time in idle gossip with relatives. Her nuns were not to refuse comfort to their parents when they needed comfort, and they were to do the same for their brothers and sisters.[107] Yet at the same time, since religious leave the world to follow the Lord singlemindedly, they may not take part in the recreations of their relatives or spend a great deal of time with them. They are to commend their families to God, but they should not look to them for temporal needs. Religious are to find the help they need in the midst of their communities, and especially they are to find everything in God.[108]

PLEASURES AND PASTIMES

Contemplation and self-indulgence do not mix. If the former is to be genuine, it requires the support of fasting, discipline and silence.[109] In her early years Teresa learned this lesson when she tried to combine a call from God and happiness in Him with a pursuit of the world:

> It seems I desired to harmonize these two contraries — so inimical to one another — such as are the spiritual life and sensory joys, pleasures, and pastimes. In prayer I was having a great trouble, for my spirit was not proceeding as lord but as slave. And so I was not able to shut myself within myself (which was my whole manner of procedure in prayer); instead, I shut within myself a thousand vanities.[110]

They who are contented with pleasures and pastimes are refusing to carry the cross with Jesus, for He and worldly things do not mix. We find the same message in the New Testament: we are not to love this passing world, for the love of the Father cannot be found in anyone who does love it. This is so because what the world offers — the sensual body, the lustful eye, pride in possessions — simply does not derive from the Father — and all this comes to an early end.[111] Hence, with some modification in the manner of practice, what St. Teresa teaches is meant for the married as well as for her nuns. The Gospel is written for everyone.

A person who observes life closely will agree with the saint that worldly pleasures are accompanied by trials and cares and annoyances: someone interferes with this television program . . . or rain curtails that game . . . or a visitor interrupts what I am doing . . . or sickness makes my amusements impossible. However, one who seeks delight in God alone finds peace and joy no matter what happens.[112] Thus the selfless individual finds the life of penance and solitude a delight, whereas the one who is "discontented is like one suffering from severe nausea" — genuine good causes him disgust.[113] It may be difficult for the lesser of us to understand or accept this sort of thing, but we ought to believe those who have been to the summit. Teresa cites with admiration a nun of extraordinary virtue who

> never sought her own pleausre, either by going into the garden or by means of anything else created; for it would be dreadful, she said, to seek relief from the pains which Our Lord was giving her; and so she never asked for anything but accepted whatever was given her. She used also to say that it would be a cross to her to find pleasure in anything but God. As a matter of fact, when I asked the nuns in her house about her, there was not one who had ever observed in her anything which seemed not to belong to a soul of great perfection.[114]

The saint is aware that this kind of virtue is not gained in a week and without long struggle, and yet if we are resolute and make the first break, much of the battle is won. "Once you are placed in so high a degree as to desire to commune in solitude with God and abandon the pastimes of the world, the most has been done."[115] Yet it is also true that few people receive support from others as they walk this hard road and enter through this narrow gate that lead to life.[116] Most by far prefer the easy road and the wide gate, as Jesus Himself noted. Moreover, says Teresa, it is the rare spiritual director who does not dilute in this area. She found herself that she could have made more rapid progress in her younger days if she had had a director who had not watered down the Gospel.

> Although in this matter of desires I have always had great ones, I strove for what I have mentioned (worldly vanities): both to practice prayer and to live for my own pleasures. I believe that if I might have had someone to make me fly, I would have turned the desires into deeds more quickly. But on account of our sins, so few and so rare are the spiritual masters who are not excessively discreet in these matters that I believe it is one of the main reasons why beginners do not advance more rapidly to high perfection.[117]

POVERTY AND PRAYER

Prayer and poverty are twins. They live or die together. By poverty we mean not destitution but frugality, evangelical, sharing frugality. Like all the saints, Teresa linked a sparing life-style with providence, for she wanted only those necessities that were given her as alms. She knew well enough that not all Christians are called to this degree of factual poverty, but she looked upon it as a "favor" given her by His Majesty. "And so I have a strong desire to be in a place where I live only on alms. It seems to me that when I'm in a place where I'm certain I shall not be lacking food and clothing, I don't fulfill as perfectly the vow, or the counsel of Christ, as when I'm where there will be no income and these things will be sometimes lacking." She added that "the blessings gained through true poverty . . . are many, and I wouldn't want to lose them".[118] A layperson may acquire more property if the opportunity comes to him, "but if he strives after it, and, on obtaining it, strives after more and more, however good his intention may be (and good it must be, because, as I have said, these are all virtuous people and given to prayer), he need not be afraid that he will ever ascend to the Mansions which are nearest the King".[119] The Master Himself had long ago made the same point: His word does not mature when it is smothered by the pleasures and cares and riches of life.[120] He astonished His disciples (and the rest of us) when He warned that it is easier for a camel to pass through the eye of a needle than for a rich man to enter the kingdom of heaven.[121] Money, says St. Teresa, is an impediment to prayer because it nearly always is linked with "honor". The world despises the poor, whereas anyone who desires honor never hates money. And in the saint's mind concern for honor is devastating for prayer.[122] The more bread we are given, the less we are fed from heaven.[123] It would be hard to put the matter more succinctly.

Throughout this chapter we have been tying in specific ideas with New Testament teaching. But here we concentrate on a few of the many scriptural passages that prove that the teaching of John and Teresa (and all the saints) emerges not from mere private opinion but from the inspired word.

We begin with the core. While the greatest of all the commandments is rightly put into a positive formulation, its affirmative universality necessarily requires a correlative negative universality. If we are to love someone completely, there can be no room for a competing love. A totality spirituality requires a total detachment condition, and so the Lord Himself laid it down that no one can be His disciple unless he renounce not merely most but all that he possesses.[124] We who have risen with Christ are to mind the things above, not the things on earth.[125] Whatever we do, eat, drink or anything else, all should be done not for our self-centered pleasure but for the glory of God.[126] St. Paul rejoices in having nothing, [127] and he insists that laymen and laywomen are, along with everyone else, to give up their "illusory desires" and be renewed by a "spiritual revolution".[128] St. Peter proclaims that to be "dominated by anything" at all is to be a slave to it.[129] St. John of the New Testament flatly states that we who entertain the hope of final vision must so work at a complete purification that our aim is to be "as pure as Christ" Himself.[130] St. Paul echoes this idea when he declares that in baptism we become so dead to this world that we are buried in the tomb with the crucified One.[131]

For the New Testament writers material goods are not to be sought for themselves. They are means only, not ends. This is why we give up all superfluities: coming into the world with nothing and leaving it with nothing, we are to be content with food and clothing.[132] God's grace has taught us "that what we have to do is to give up everything that does not lead to God".[133] This is a perfect, one-sentence summary of the whole of *The Ascent of Mount Carmel*.

There can be no doubt that this ascetical program requires no little sacrifice, but Jesus already said that any follower of His must renounce himself and take up his daily cross.[134] Without a doubt this is a hard road and a narrow gate, but it does lead to life, which is exactly the message of our two Carmelites and their fellow saints. Truth is indeed symphonic.

CHAPTER NINE

FIRE IN THE NIGHTS

One might understandably conclude from the radical purifications described in our last chapter that in order to be filled with God nothing more is necessary. But this assumption could arise only from an inadequate grasp of the boundless perfection of God on the one hand and the extent of our woundedness on the other. Until the Lord beams inwardly the searching light of advancing prayer and discloses this to us, we have little or no idea of the vast number of unredeemed clingings that still need to be burned away in us.

Since the transforming union is a union of likeness, St. John of the Cross insists along with Scripture that any least seeking of finite things aside from God is an impurity that prevents the complete union. This impurity is not limited to sexual impurity. It includes all willed seekings that are not for the glory of God, which, of course, is also for our own genuine good. Silver is good, but if it is mixed even in slight amounts with gold, the gold suffers an impurity in the sense meant here. Created things are good, indeed, very good, says Genesis, but they are not God. To pursue them for themselves is to make them idols, little gods. The little gods may be small, but they are in competition with the one and only Lord. He who worships finite divinities cannot be united with the one God. He must be thoroughly rid of what Paul calls "illusory desires".[1] Of ourselves we are incapable of this radical purification, a truth the serious person soon finds out from experience.

The sanjuanist explanation of purification is twofold: it envisions what we can do to be rid of our imperfections (the active night, the subject of our previous chapter) and what God must do by infused prayer to complete the work (the passive nights, the subject of this chapter). The passive nights are two: sense and spirit. *Passive* is not the best modern term to describe them, for it suggests inactivity, inertness. As we use the word here it means received. It is a purification effected by God through His gift of infused contemplation. The first of these received purifications concerns the sense level of the human person: the stripping of seeing, hearing, smelling, tasting and touching, until emptied of all their disordered seekings. In this emptying process these bodily senses are "accommodated to the spirit".[2] The second passive night concerns the purification of the intellect and the will, and at the same time it completes the reformation of the senses.³ It is much more painful than the first night, but it is also far more beneficial, fitting a person to be united in a perfect oneness with God.

It must be emphasized that the sanjuanist nights are contemplative experiences, not ordinary sufferings attendant on human life such as illness, depression, failures, contradictions and blame. These latter purify to some extent when they are accepted with love (if with bitterness, they make one worse, not better), but they are not what John is talking about.⁴ They may in some cases accompany the contemplative purification, but they are different and distinct. One of the most common mistakes spiritual directors and confessors tend to make is the easy diagnosis of ordinary sufferings as "dark nights". This mistake has, of course, unfortunate consequences for the directee.

Saint John of the Cross offers three reasons why he calls these received purifications night. The first is the point of departure in our journey to God: we must deprive ourselves of seeking finite things for themselves, and this is experienced as an emptying, a "night" for the senses. The second reason is the means or road to union with God: we travel by faith, by accepting and acting on His word rather than on our own perceptions. This, too, is perceived as a darkness to our merely human ways of thinking. The third reason is the point of arrival, God Himself, Who necessarily is dark to our limited minds. He Who is purest light is nonetheless a "hidden God"⁵ Who dwells in "light inaccessible".⁶ Paradoxically, He Who is endless light is beheld by our minds as darkness because He utterly transcends us. Hence on earth we must know Him darkly, as in an imperfect mirror.⁷

Why are the passive nights painful? This purification process is a cure of illness and therefore involves a cutting away, a removal of the roots of spiritual maladies, and a separation from the egocentrism that wounds us. The imperfectly redeemed person is so accustomed to disordered pursuits that when he gives them up and is divinely freed from them, he necessarily experiences pain in the process. The correction of a decayed tooth with no anesthetic is painful for a similar reason.⁸ St. John of the Cross likewise points out that the penetrating contemplative light at first strikes what is closest to us, and that is our faults and "miseries". What it discloses hardly gives cause for delight.⁹ Hence he speaks of contention and destruction resulting. Though God is purest delight, the beginner is not yet capable of experiencing Him as such: "The very fire of love which afterwards is united with the soul, glorifying it, is that which previously assails it by purging it, just as the fire that penetrates a log of wood is the same that first makes an assault upon it. . . . Because this flame is savory and sweet, and the will possesses a spiritual palate disturbed by the humors of inordinate affections, the flame is unpleasant and bitter to it."[10]

These received purifications of sense and spirit are not optional or peripheral in the spiritual life. John speaks of their necessity a number of times and in unmistakable terms. In a context in which he is discussing our proclivity to self-seeking in all sorts of ways, he goes on to comment:

> Until a soul is placed by God in the passive purgation of that dark night, which we shall soon explain, it cannot purify itself completely from these imperfections nor from the others. . . . No matter how much an individual does through his own efforts, he cannot actively purify himself enough to be disposed in the least degree for the divine union of the perfection of love. God must take over and purge him in that fire that is dark for him.[11]

The "dark fire" is infused contemplation, the only means of burning away the deep roots of our woundedness, roots we cannot actively reach and eradicate. As we have noted in the chapter on the universal call to infused prayer, we have here another reason why mystical prayer is for everyone, for everyone is called to perfection, a complete holiness free of all defects.

NIGHT OF SENSE

We are now prepared to investigate the first of these purifications and what it entails. Because we have already made the point, we shall assume here that we are dealing not with natural human sufferings but with divinely caused sanctification. In these beginnings of infused prayer God is communicating nothing less than Himself through a light and love that itself consumes our egocentrism. We do not, however, perceive this communication as light and love but as darkness and pain. This strange perception is due to our incapacity and opaqueness and unlikeness to the divine. In a similar manner a sick person regards delicious food as revolting. Hence, in this night one perceives the love he is receiving as dryness and emptiness, and he concludes that his prayer is going from bad to worse, even though he is trying to serve God well.[12]

The inner emptiness and absence of God are therefore only apparent. The situation is profoundly different from a real hollowness due to laxity and deliberate sin on the one hand or from a natural indisposition brought about by illness on the other.[13] The actual emptiness due to mediocrity or sickness can be corrected by a return to generosity or to good health, but the apparent void due to purification, being normal and beneficial, is found in the individual who is already wholeheartedly with God and basically healthy in body and mind.

People in the first night are typically worried and upset about their condition. Their distress, however, is not due primarily to the feelings of emptiness but to the fear that they have gone astray in their pursuit of God. They think their prayer is next to zero; they experience many distractions; they can no longer meditate; they feel lazy and as though wasting time. Added to this many find that their spiritual directors or confessors do not understand what they are talking about and may even make the blunder of diagnosing the problem as depression—which it certainly is not. They then make things still worse by offering bad advice.[14]

Other trials may accompany the dry, distracted prayer: temptations against purity or faith, blasphemous thoughts or scruples.[15] Because these are not the result of the purifying contemplation, they are not the night itself. It is understood, of course, that a person can easily be in the night with none of these temptations present or, in contrast, can be subject to them without being in the night.

When, one may ask, does this first purification occur in the course of the spiritual life? Is it common or rare? The answers St. John of the Cross gives to these questions are as accurate for our day as they were for his—as any experienced spiritual director can verify. God begins to give this new, dry, nondiscursive type of prayer with the results we have described very soon after a person begins to take the Gospel seriously, to live it generously and to give adequate time to mental prayer. "Not much time", says John, "ordinarily passes after the initial stages of their spiritual life before beginners start to enter this night of sense. And the majority of them do enter it, because it is common to see them suffer these aridities."[16] So it happens in our day: people in any state of life who are humble, patient, prayerful, chaste and obedient to due authority soon find in their daily mental prayer that they are led to drop discursive procedures and to enter into this type of dry prayer. Our communion with God grows as Gospel living grows.

However, we encounter at this juncture a sobering fact: comparatively few of those who reach the first night grow beyond it. Though everyone is called to the fullness of union, and though God brings us into this first purification precisely in order to lead us to the summit, He does not force anyone to pass beyond it. What is the problem? John's answer points plainly to the human level: our neglect and selfishness and/or bad spiritual direction. Even among spiritually earnest men and women only a few get beyond the first purification, because they do not persevere "in treading this narrow road that leads to life".[17] These are people who never bring themselves to give up worldly values entirely. They cut corners on time given to prayer; they engage in gossip, unkind and idle words; they live comfortably themselves and do not share much with the poor; they allow themselves minor disobediences as well as the more serious rejection of magisterial teaching; they indulge in worldly amusements and expensive tastes in dining, drinking, clothing and vacations. God allows us to have what we want, and if we want these things, we may have them. But together with them we will not have God in a deep communion. No one can serve God and mammon.

How do we know that we have entered upon the beginnings of infused prayer and are receiving the initial purifications that will prepare us, if we persevere, for still deeper communion? Before we consider the signs that St. John of the Cross identifies, it may be well to lay to rest a spiritual direction blunder that is not rarely made, namely, the confusing of a mental problem with the dark night. Too often people use John's terminology without knowing what he actually has in mind. Clarifying the sharp differences between a mental/emotional problem and the purifying nights can prepare us to understand the genuine signs better. We may arrange a few contrasting traits of each experience in two columns:

Mental/emotional problem	*Dark, purifying night*
1. Excessive introspection, self-concern, self-analysis. The person can scarcely get his mind off himself and his problem. Advice does little to remedy this trait, at least at first.	1. Little or no introspection once the condition is adequately explained. Little awareness of the problem aside from prayer time.
2. Unrealism. The depressed person's situation is not as dismal and hopeless as he considers it (when the problem is depression). The moral case is not as the scrupulous person thinks, nor one's worth as the person with a weak self-image supposes.	2. The pains of the dark night are objectively well founded: we are very imperfect, and we need exactly what is happening. The situation is as realistic as a laundry washing-machine operation and what it is doing for the soiled clothes.
3. Depression. The person with a mental problem often suffers from clinical depression more or less severe.	3. There is no depression at all. At work, play, meals, the person is as cheerful as at any other period in the spiritual life.

4. Many mental problems are difficult to heal; years of therapy may be needed, and even then progress may be only partial.

4. A competent explanation clears up the anxiety occasioned by the first night. Therapy is not needed in either night, even if the second must run its course — just as a washing machine must complete its cycles.

5. Chronic fatigue and/or insomnia often accompany the emotional disturbance.

5. No problem at all.

6. Fixing of attention on studying, reading or a lecture can be impossible.

6. Attention at prayer can be difficult and at times impossible, but there is no attention problem in the rest of life.

7. Mental/emotional problems do not *of themselves* promote virtue or increase depth of relationship with God.

7. The two nights do *of themselves* greatly increase love, humility, patience and the like, and they decidedly prepare one for deeper prayer.

It can happen that a person with some emotional problem may at the same time be going through contemplative purification, and it may be difficult in a given case to sort one out from the other. But all the same, the two phenomena are very different and distinct both in their causes and in their effects.

St. John of the Cross offers three main signs that one is in the first night of sense. We are not now discussing the transitional stage from discursive to infused prayer but rather the situation where one has quite completely left the former and is at least usually in the latter. The first sign is an absence of "satisfaction or consolation" in either things of heaven or of earth.[18] This cannot mean that a person feels no pleasure at all in created reality: a beautiful sunset, a cold drink on a hot day, joy in a dear friend. John must mean by "satisfaction and consolation" what we would refer to as lasting contentment, an ultimate meaningfulness. The worldling seeks to attain and may even think he does attain his fundamental reason for being in the created order. The person at this stage of prayer knows better. There is an awareness like that of St. Augustine, who found out by wide experience in sin that our hearts remain restless until they rest in their Creator. Hence an individual in the first night tends no longer to seek created things for themselves. Though he is not perfect, the process of his being emptied of selfish strivings is well under way. At the same time his prayer is dry and unsatisfying: he finds little or no delight in it. While it may be indeed bleak and painful, it is surely characterized by aridity and distraction.

The second sign is a concern for and a habitual turning to God, even though there may be little pleasurable taste for Him. We are dealing with a generous person who is considerably detached from earthly things and desires to give God everything. There is consequently a great difference between this apparent emptiness of purification and the actual emptiness of mediocrity. In the first case we find a habitual concern about giving God more, whereas in the second that thought seldom enters the mind as a serious intent.[19] We must insist that the void in the night of sense is only apparent, for the soul is actually being filled with a highly profitable infusion of light and love. But being yet very imperfect and unaware of hidden faults, one is not yet fitted to experience the delight this infusion brings that, later on, one will be enabled to perceive.

This dry contemplation is "secret and hidden from the very one who receives it [and] it imparts to the soul, together with the dryness and emptiness it produces in the senses, an inclination to remain alone and in quietude".[20] By this secret hiddenness the saint means that the infusion is so delicate that an uninstructed person will hardly notice it at all — it is so unlike his previous reasonings and felt affections. This inclination to remain alone is not to be confused with an extremely different antisocial isolation. In the latter case an emotional problem causes one to shun human society for unhealthy reasons. In the former case the desire for solitude is the robust, healthy, altruistic inclination to be with one's beloved, in this case the supreme Beloved. This propensity to be quiet in the divine presence is a result of the new, infused prayer. Blessed Elizabeth of the Trinity understood her being "alone with the Alone", the indwelling triune God, to be effected both by her active efforts and by the inner word, the contemplative fire given by the Spirit. She observed: "If my desires, my fears, my joys or my sorrows, if all the movements proceeding from these 'four passions' are not perfectly directed to God, I will not be solitary; there will be noise within me."[21] The quiet infused by the Holy Spirit calms and stills one's sense life by purifying it of its aberrations. As St. John of the Cross would put it, the soul, in its quiet, care-free solitude, is being given an interior nourishment. Though nothing seems to be happening, a great deal is going on, substantially more, actually, than was occurring in the bustle of discursive meditation.

It follows, then, that in this habitual turning to God sought in a holy solitude, the Master is slowly taking over the person's will. While the imagination and intellect are still free to roam distractedly through the universe, a divine invasion, entirely unforced, is taking place. It is not in our power to produce or prolong it but only to receive it and not interfere. When John says here that God is binding the faculties, he means that the Lord is giving them their Object in a new, divine manner, so that human efforts now become an obstacle.[22] The peace that ensues "is something spiritual and delicate, [and] its fruit is quiet, delicate, solitary, satisfying and peaceful, and far removed from all these other gratifications of beginners, which are very palpable and sensory".[23]

The third sign of the night of sense is the inability to meditate discursively.[24] We do not mean by this that the inability prevents discursive reasoning in spiritual reading or in other areas of daily life. Nor should we conceive it as entailing an ironclad inability to form one thought after another in prayer. This person can force a reasoning process, but it runs counter to one's bent. In prayer we ordinarily follow the gentle lead of the Spirit, and in these beginnings of infused contemplation His action tends to preclude our action. We are thus disinclined to meditate, and should we force ourselves to it, we would find little or no profit and would forfeit inner peace.

No definite duration can be ascribed to the passive purification of the senses, for length of time varies from person to person. At the very end of Book I of *Dark Night* (pp. 328–29), St. John of the Cross does mention three factors that determine how long the purification will last: (1) the greater or lesser amount of imperfection to be burned away, (2) the degree of love to which God wishes to raise the person and (3) the generosity with which one responds to the divine operation.

BENEFITS FROM THE NIGHT OF SENSE

We may recall that one of the reasons all of us are called to infused prayer is that we cannot be purified of our many defects, our "illusory desires",[25] without the experience of the two passive nights. Perhaps the best proof that something helpful has been going on in the arid contemplation we have been describing is the result that comes from it. Though the growth in virtue is imperceptible from day to day, over a long stretch of time it is unmistakable. After some years of this difficult prayer a person becomes aware of having acquired a more thorough, truer knowledge of himself . . . there is a keener appreciation of the grandeur and goodness of God . . . humility is deeper and more real . . . one consequently thinks more highly of others and actually considers them to be better than himself[26] . . . there is more readiness to learn from others and to obey them, even to obey those who are subjects . . . disordered desires have lost much of their strength . . . motivation is less self-centered and more directed to God . . . one is more gentle toward oneself, toward one's neighbor, indeed, toward the Lord Himself . . . a new freedom from the world, the flesh and the devil is enjoyed, for natural concupiscences are lessened . . . one's only real concern now is to serve God better.[27]

What is remarkable about this growth is not only that it occurs but also that these virtues were growing with comparatively little attention having been explicitly given to them. They have been produced by the divinely infused light and love. St. John of the Cross is thus correct in speaking of these "precious benefits" and in proclaiming of this night, "Ah, the sheer grace!—I went out unseen."[28]

COURSE OF ACTION

Repeatedly over the years and with almost no variations in substance, spiritual direction has impressed upon me that people interpret this stage of prayer development as though their inner world is caving in. They have little idea of what is going on and consequently fail to realize how beneficial it is. Even when they have read about the two nights, they usually do not see that this applies to themselves. They are so convinced that their prayer is abysmal that they assume the writer could not really be writing of them. Extreme discouragement is the typical result. Sometimes prayer is abandoned as impossible due to unrealistic expectations of what it ought uniformly to be like.

A man as experienced as St. John of the Cross could remark that "many individuals think they are not praying, when indeed their prayer is intense. Others place high value on their prayer, while it is little more than nonexistent."[29] If the reader does not see this statement as odd, I fear he has not seen the point at all. The saint's observation is much like saying that a person is sprinting energetically or eating voraciously and yet does not know he is running or eating. John is talking about people whose prayer is not simply satisfactory but intense, and yet they think they are not praying at all. In the first night of sense God is infusing an excellent contemplation, but the recipient quite completely misses what is happening. The principal reason for this mistake is unreal expectations of what purifying prayer ought to be.

As for John's remark about those who overestimate their prayer, this is not an instance of the night of sense. He has in mind people who

think that their strong feelings during meditation are indications of
advanced contemplation. Their expectations are also unreal, but in the
opposite direction.

If, then, we suppose that a person is realistic in his assessment of
this first purification, we may continue with several concrete suggestions as to what he ought and ought not to do. First of all, he should
not abbreviate prayer time or abandon the effort but should be patient
with this inner emptiness and refuse to be downcast about it. Second,
he is to "pay no attention to discursive meditation, since this is not
the time for it".[30] When one is fully into the first night, he is not in
a transitional stage and so has no need to attempt what he cannot do.
Rather, he should remain quiet with a simple attentiveness to God and
with no desire to taste or to feel divine things.[31] Third, this person
should put aside his concern that he is wasting time, that he could be
doing something more profitable. Divine artist that He is, God is
transforming the contemplative. The work ought not to be disturbed
by agitation and anxiety or otherwise impeded.[32]

NIGHT OF SPIRIT

Most people would tend to conclude from a careful reading of John's
painstakingly detailed account of active purification in the *Ascent* together with the first passive purification in the *Dark Night* that there
could hardly be any impediments left to hinder a most intimate union
with God. Yet those who come thus far and know themselves well
will readily agree with the saint that much work remains still to be
done. And most of it needs to be done by the Lord Himself. This final
task is the night of spirit.

By very definition the first purification, while greatly beneficial,
purges only the senses. It does not get down to the deepest roots of
our faults, not even of our sense faults. The divine fire has not yet seared
the spirit sufficiently. The first passive operation is like clipping the
tops of weeds—the roots remain. These roots are usually not perceived,
so deeply embedded are they. What these residual defects are the saint
suggests: a dullness of mind . . . lack of sensitivity to the Holy Spirit . . .
a distracted and inattentive inner life . . . "a lowly and natural" mode
of communion with God . . . a feeble and imperfect knowing of Him . . .
an ill-founded persuasion that one has visions and prophesies . . . rem-
nants of pride still surfacing, such as wanting to be seen in stances of
advanced prayer . . . an undue security in one's own spiritual experiences.[33]

It is hard to pinpoint exactly when the second purification, that of spirit, occurs. There are some indications, however. It does not begin immediately after the first night. Ordinarily the person spends "many years" in a patient growth in what St. John of the Cross calls the state of proficients. During this time the soul enjoys a new spiritual freedom and a serene, loving contemplation and delight in prayer. Yet because the entire purification has not been effected, "certain needs, aridities, darknesses, and conflicts are felt. These are sometimes far more intense than those of the past and are like omens or messengers of the coming night of spirit."[34] These omens, however, are short lived, though they can be very disturbing because of their intensity. After a short period of a day or two they usually disappear, and the person returns to the customary serene prayer. The night itself is a more protracted purification. Its cessation will occur before the transforming union, its purpose being to prepare for that complete oneness.

What does one experience in the second night?[35] Because the whole process of Christic prayer is a gradual transformation into a Godlikeness, it follows that in this intense period of purification the person is further divested of merely human ways in memory, imagination, intellect and will. Cozy feelings at prayer are gone, and one feels left high and dry, suspended between heaven and earth. There is now a deeper passage from the *modo humano* to the *modo divino,* from the human manner to the divine manner, and consequently the change brings a feeling of dislocation from what one is used to and comfortable with. All the while God is imparting Himself, but the person's residual impurity blocks a fuller reception of the divine self-gift. St. John of the Cross uses strong words to describe what the divine infusion of light and love does as it penetrates into the soul: "Assails . . . strikes . . . disentangles . . . dissolves . . . divests . . . chastizes . . . afflicts . . . purifies". He calls the whole process an "oppressive undoing". The person therefore feels spiritually unclean and wretched. There is an impression of being rejected and abandoned by God. It appears that the person will never be worthy again and that the lofty blessings already received will never return. One needs little imagination to grasp how extremely painful this is, for the soul vehemently wants God and nothing else. This feeling of the divine rejection is the deepest suffering in the second night. "Sometimes", says the saint, "this experience is so vivid that it seems to the soul that it sees hell and perdition open before it. These are the ones who go down into hell alive,[36] since their purgation on earth is similar to that of purgatory." John adds that the person who has gone through the second night is after death detained in purgatory only a short while or not at all.[37]

Individuals in this second night love God greatly, and they know that they do, but they find no relief in their knowledge. Rather, it causes still deeper suffering, because in loving God so much that they would willingly "give a thousand lives for Him", they cannot be persuaded that God loves them. Prayer, of course, seems impossible, and reassurances from the spiritual director are of little avail, for the sufferers feel that the director simply does not understand what they are going through. Indeed, there is no remedy for these trials until the Lord has finished with the entire purification.[38]

The hardships and deep pains of the second night vary in their intensity, and it is only at intervals that their full fury is felt.[39] Intervals of light and love also occur but with a continuing sense that something is yet missing.[40]

How long does the second night last? Just as was the case with the first purification, John does not here assign a quantity of time, not even a usual length. Rather, he observes that the duration will depend on what is needed to render the soul delicate, simple, refined and pure enough that the final transformation can take place. And this will be according to the degree of holiness to which God wishes to raise each person and also according to the amount of purification needed.[41]

The completion and cessation of this purification are not abrupt. Rather, there is a blending of the painful darkness into the love of union. This mingling would surprise only those who do not understand that the agony of the second night is effected by infused love and that the very summit of love is made possible by the purification itself. Hence, the saint is able to say that the soul "in the midst of these dark conflicts feels vividly and keenly that it is being wounded by a strong divine love, and it has a certain feeling and foretaste of God". This "impassioned and intense love . . . is now beginning to possess something of union with God".[42]

We need not say much about the effects of the second purification because they are clear: remaining imperfections are burned away by the divine fire or pulled up by their roots. The results are displayed in the heroic virtues of the transforming union, "profound blessings", as John calls them.[43] Distressing and agonizing as this night is, the person within it steadily advances in love. Even though this progress is not always perceived in the midst of the daily round, it afterward becomes obvious.[44] The saint had strong words for a directee of his who was much disturbed by her desolation and apparent abandonment in prayer. Even though it seemed to her that God was failing her, he insisted that "nothing is failing you, neither do you have to discuss anything. . . . He who desires nothing else than God walks not in darkness, however poor and dark he is in his own sight. . . . Do not worry, but rejoice! . . . You were never better off than now, because you were never so humble nor so submissive . . . nor did you serve God so purely and disinterestedly as now."[45]

ST. TERESA'S EQUIVALENTS OF THE DARK NIGHTS

Although Teresa seldom if ever used the expression "dark nights", she knew in her own experience the reality of dry, difficult, purifying prayer, and she wrote of it for the guidance of those who were to read her works. She differs from St. John of the Cross not in basic teaching but in the considerably less attention she gives to the problem[46] and in the fact that what she does say seems to be concerned mostly with the second night. Because she did not think or write according to John's categories, I shall not try to force her thought into his divisions. Rather, we shall consider her treatment just as it occurs in her works.

Even after she had attained to a lofty infused communion with God, what she called "perfect contemplation", she experienced times of darkness, distraction and a plain inability to pray. She knew at these times that her will was with God and that, therefore, not all was lost, but still she could scarcely produce a single devotional thought. During this experience of emptiness she remarked that "I can't even form in a fitting way a thought about God or of any good, or practice prayer, even though I'm in solitude; but I feel I know Him. I understand that it is the intellect and imagination that does me harm here, for the will is all right it seems to me and disposed toward every good."[47] She adds that she often undergoes this "scattering of the faculties", and she is aware that while it can be caused by her poor physical health, yet it is also due to human woundedness, original sin and personal sin. She observes that "my lack of physical health has much to do with it. I frequently recall the harm original sin did to us; this is the source, I think, of our being incapable of enjoying so much good in an integral way. And my own sins must be a cause; if I hadn't committed so many, I would be more integrated in good."[48] In this text the saint does not ascribe a purifying effect to the dark, dry knowing of God. To this extent she falls short of John's explicit statements, but she does reflect his teaching that it is our sins that often impede our "enjoying so much good".

A little before this section the saint describes a desolation at prayer that does not seem due to physical illness but to the terrifying purifications of the second night described by St. John of the Cross. Faith seems dead, though the virtue is not lost. The soul accepts what the Church holds, but the acceptance seems to be only words. The soul is so afflicted that it feels numb and knows God "almost as it does something it hears far in the distance". Love feels lukewarm, and there is no recalling of the former experiences of deep prayer that were received. "Going to prayer or remaining in solitude means nothing else but more anguish, for the torment it feels within itself, without knowing why, is unbearable. In my opinion the experience is a kind of copy of hell."[49] Reading, as a means of exciting some semblance of devotion, is of no use: four or five readings of the same paragraph yield nothing even by way of mere understanding.[50] St. Teresa, in this passage, sees the black night as beneficial and purifying, for she finds that after this type of crucifying prayer she receives "favors" in abundance, indeed, "great abundance": "I only think that the soul comes out of the crucible like gold, more refined and purified, so as to see the Lord within itself. So afterward these trials that seemed unbearable become small, and one wants to return to suffering if the Lord will be more served by it."[51]

In still another passage of her *Life* Teresa describes an infused and painful prayer that comes after ecstatic immersion. It is, she says, an experience of extreme desolation that we cannot produce but can only receive. Its intensity varies: sometimes it is more, sometimes less, though on occasion God will intersperse some of his "grandeurs". For the most part, however, he places the soul in an inner desert solitude far distant from all things on earth. Human words of comfort are of little or no avail because the solitude is infused and independent of what others may do or say. The inner pain is "delicate and penetrating", and it seems to Teresa "that the soul is crucified since no consolation comes to it from heaven, nor is it in heaven; neither does it desire any from earth, nor is it on earth. Receiving no help from either side, it is as though crucified between heaven and earth."[52] Yet she finds this "an arduous, delightful martyrdom", and the person is in good supernatural condition, seeking God alone. This type of desert and solitude is preferable to all the companionship the world has to offer. So pleasing and valuable is this torment that the soul desires this kind of prayer more than all the delightful favors it has previously received.[53] St. Teresa appeals to the Lord Himself as the source of her conviction that this extremely painful prayer is of greater benefit to her growth than all the other favors He had granted to her up to that point of her life: "The Lord told me not to fear and to esteem this gift more than all the others He had granted me. In this pain the soul is purified and fashioned or purged like gold in the crucible so that the enameled gifts might be placed there in a better way, and in this prayer it is purged of what otherwise it would have to be purged of in purgatory."[54] Although the saint does not use the terminology of St. John of the Cross, it is obvious that she is speaking of the purifying fire of his second night of spirit.

What does one do in this difficult but profitable purification? The saint advises us to do exactly what we are least inclined to do, that is, to be fully acceptive of this arduous, arid, trying pursuit of God. In her vigorous manner Teresa says that she is annoyed to observe how serious and pious theologians "make so much fuss that God doesn't give them devotion". She is annoyed not because she thinks devotion harmful or useless but because these individuals ought to know better, namely, that they need purification in prayer, and that if they need the consoling type of prayer God will give it to them. She considers their desire for feelings of devotion a fault and a lack of courage in making solid progress in the spiritual life.

It is the foundress' opinion that while many begin to lead a serious prayer life, few reach the end of the road, mainly because they want no hardships at prayer. Bereft of thoughts, "they cannot bear it", and so they get distressed about the matter, unaware that the dry contemplation is strengthening their will at the very time it leaves their intellect empty. Teresa is aware that she repeats the advice she gives here, but "even if I repeat it many times this doesn't matter — it is very important that no one be distressed or afflicted over dryness or noisy and distracting thoughts".[55]

Along with this calm acceptance of hardship, the saint advises a complete surrender to the fact that one cannot pray at this time as accustomed. Too much activity will tend to smother the dry love that actually is present: "For even though a soul breaks its head in arranging the wood and blowing on the fire, it seems that everything it does only smothers the fire more."[56]

PASSIVE PURIFICATIONS IN SCRIPTURE

There is no doubt that the God of revelation, being pure goodness and pure love, corrects and reproves His people not out of a desire to make them suffer but to right what is wrong, to heal those whom He loves. We read, therefore, that Yahweh corrects those He loves just as a father checks a well-loved son.[57] The Lord led His people in the wilderness for forty years in order to test and humble them,[58] and they were to learn from this ordeal that Yahweh their God was training them as a good father trains his child.[59] This Lord chastised Israel's enemies "ten thousand times harder" to teach His people to ponder His kindness to them and to "look for mercy".[60] The calamities that God visited upon His chosen ones were not meant to destroy them but to discipline and correct their aberrations, and thus they were a sign of His benevolence.[61] While the Lord punished other nations after their sins had come to full measure, He dealt differently with His own people and disciplined them before their sins came to a head. Thus He never forgets mercy, and he does not desert His own.[62] St. Paul told the Corinthians that when the Lord punished them it was for their good so that they would be healed and thus not be condemned with the world.[63]

The divine policy is clear. God sets straight in us what we cannot set aright ourselves. Moreover, the process is a purifying one. The prophet Malachi foretells that the Lord will suddenly enter His temple. No one will be able to resist the day of His coming, for He will be like the refiner's fire and the fuller's lye. He will sit refining and purifying the sons of Levi. He will purify them like gold and silver so that they make their offerings to Yahweh as those offerings are to be made.[64] There is here some sort of purification that is directly connected with worship and prayer being what they ought to be. Jesus tells us that in the Mystical Body (under the image of the vine and the branches) the Father prunes the good branches, those that are bearing fruit, so that they may bear still more.[65] St. Paul tells the Corinthians that the Spirit's indwelling transforms them from one glory to another as He brings about in them the very image of God—this, says Paul, is the work of the Spirit.[66] In these last three texts we should notice that (1) they all deal with a perfecting and purifying process, (2) the work is done by God and (3) it is meant to further the growth already in progress. These three traits are part and parcel of the purifications described by Ss. John of the Cross and Teresa of Jesus.

CHAPTER TEN

THE TRANSFORMING SUMMIT

When the theme is such a lofty one, human language can be stretched to its furthest expanse and yet rather poorly represent the wider-reaching reality. Even so, in writing of sublime realities, despite endeavoring to portray them precisely as they are, one risks appearing to indulge in mere hyperbole. Because of the dulling effects of the mass media and the gross exaggerations we find in advertising and political oratory, our contemporaries are understandably suspicious of inflated language and extravagant claims. Our problem in this chapter is that the teresian and sanjuanist descriptions of the culminating apex of contemplative communion with the indwelling Trinity press even poetic song to its outer boundaries—perhaps one should say its inner limits as well.

The two Carmelites were not the first to wrestle with this problem, and they will not be the last. St. Paul pushed his Greek to its furthest frontier when he attempted to explain to the Ephesians what a profound immersion in God is like. Referring to the love of Christ that surpasses all human knowing, the apostle longed for the recipients of his letter to be "filled with the utter fullness of God". This staggering statement is incapable of exaggeration. Yet he goes on to remark that God's working in us "can do infinitely more than we can ask or imagine".[1] Infinitely more! If anyone is tempted to think either that later mystics are overstating what occurs in the transforming union or that this summit is not for everyone, I would simply invite the doubter to stop, to reread Ephesians 3:19–20, and then to think about it seriously for five uninterrupted minutes.

From the outset it is well for us to recall that the whole of prayer development from the first to the last of St. Teresa's seven mansions is one continuous evolution from seed to blossom. The transforming union is in its basic essence neither vision nor revelation. It is communion come to maturity, a communion that brings along with it the culmination of a slow growth in holiness that has been taking place all through the development of infused prayer. At this summit the unforced divine invasion reaches its fullness; the knowing-loving-delighting fusion between God and man reaches its nonpantheistic consummation. This new creation[2] is found not only in prayerful solitude but

also in the multiplicities of daily life: there is in both action and contemplation a remarkable newness of goodness, strength, freedom and
delight.[3]

St. John's descriptive organization of prayer growth differs from the
sevenfold scheme of St. Teresa. While the two saints agree in all essen-
tials (except the confirmation in grace), they approach the issue of
development from two diverse points of view. We have studied Teresa's
treatment in Chapter 6. John begins with our need for purification,
for only the pure can commune deeply with the all-pure One. The
two basic liberations from faults and imperfections we have considered
in Chapters 7 (St. Teresa) and 8 and 9 (St. John). As we are freed progressively more and more from obstacles to the divine infusion, we
are slowly transformed in a deepening union with the indwelling Father,
Son and Spirit. When this purification is completed in the second night
of spirit, the transforming union is given. The summit is reached.

THE TYPE OF UNION

How do we humans become one with God? How do we retain our
personal individuality and yet become deiform by participation in the
divine nature itself?[4] What kind of union can this be that on the one
hand is no mere juxtaposition, mixture or hybrid, and yet on the other
does not sink into the impossibility of pantheism?

We may note first what this union is not. While it supposes the natural
inbeing of God, it is much more. The divine, natural omnipresence
sustaining everything that is, all the way from the smallest subatomic
particles to the largest galaxies and the supernal spirits, is necessary
to created beings in the sense that they could not perdure for a moment without the continual divine outpouring of their being and activity. This presence is universal and permanent as long as anything
exists. It is found even in the serious sinner who has rejected and is
completely alienated from his Creator. This simple fact of estrange-
ment and sunderance makes clear that the divine omnipresence is not
a union at all.

Rather, the union entailed in the life of grace is a oneness of likeness,
a likeness of love. It is effected more and more deeply as the human
will is brought into a growing conformity with the divine will. Mutual
love joins persons, and the deeper the love, the more the two wills
become identified, the more they are one. This is why a complete
despoilment of self-centeredness, an entire freedom from serving things
less than God ("you cannot serve God and mammon") is the indispen-

sable condition for close oneness with the Trinity. "To be reborn in the Holy Spirit during this life", says John, "is to become most like God in purity, without any mixture of imperfection."[5] The saint then offers his famous example of the ray of sunlight shining upon a smudged window. To the extent that the glass is stained, it cannot be fully illuminated and transformed by the sunlight. Hence, "the cleaner the window is, the brighter will be its illumination. . . . If the window is totally clean and pure," adds the saint, "the sunlight will so transform and illumine it that to all appearances the window will be identical with the ray of sunlight and shine just as the sun's ray. . . . The window is the ray or light of the sun by participation."[6] It would be difficult to improve upon this example.

The transforming union, the pinnacle of human maturity, occurs when the person is divested of all that is not divine, of all that is creature centered. To put it positively, this culmination happens when one is wholly in love with God. Wholly, not just mostly. "All the things of both God and the soul become one in participant transformation, and the soul appears to be God more than a soul. Indeed, it is God by participation." Yet this is no pantheism, for "truly its being (even though transformed) is naturally as distinct from God's as it was before".[7]

Because this is a union of likeness, it cannot be brought about by created reality, beautiful as the finite universe may be. None of our tastes, feelings, imaginings or ideas can effect this oneness. Only purity and love, poured out by the Spirit into all who are entirely selfless, bring the new creation to pass: "Perfect transformation is impossible without perfect purity."[8] Consummate purity triggers consummate likeness and therefore an entire oneness.

Knowing-union

There are two aspects to this perfect likeness: a new knowing and a new loving. As the very term indicates, infused contemplation includes a divinely given awareness, cognition, enlightenment. Since knowledge is the presence of the object known in the knower, as one perceives more deeply he is "oned" more deeply with what he knows. In the full development of the transformation God communicates "knowings" so sublime and so unusual that John calls them "strange islands". The perceptions of the trinity are now so lofty that they are unlike anything otherwise experienced. The person sees in God "wonderful new things" somewhat like the blessed who "will forever be receiving new surprises and marveling the more", for only to Himself is God neither strange nor new.[9] In the lofty touches we have explained earlier, the attributes of God (love, power, joy, wisdom and so forth) produce in one's deep center a most sublime and delightful knowledge of Him, "the most exalted delight of all the soul here enjoys".[10] This intimate understanding is the person's main delight, even though it is not the final fruition of the beatific vision. She calls it

> a "whistling," because just as the whistling of the breeze pierces deeply into the hearing organ, so this most subtle and delicate knowledge penetrates with wonderful savor into the innermost part of the substance of the soul, and the delight is greater than all others.[11]

Each of the divine attributes, notes our saint, is like a lamp of fire whose light communicates an ecstatic rapture of love and keen delight. Each of the divine perfections — goodness, wisdom, mercy, fortitude — is a lamp that enlightens and transmits love:

> God Himself is for it [the soul] many lamps together, which illumine and impart warmth to it individually, for it has clear knowledge of each, and through this knowledge is inflamed in love. . . . All these lamps are one lamp which, according to its powers and attributes, shines and burns like many lamps.[12]

John considers that this divine manifestation "is the greatest possible in this life".[13] One might think that the story must be finished at this point. Not so. The saint goes on to explain that the person is *within* the divine splendors and is transformed *in* them. Not simply is one enthralled *by* the divine attributes; one is ecstatic within them. Ordinary lamps shed their light around them on the outside, but these lamps enclose the soul in their very splendors, and it is transformed in them. "It is like the air within the flame," says the saint, "enkindled and transformed in the flame, for the flame is nothing but enkindled air."[14] Even though all the divine attributes are utterly one in God, each of them is seen and enjoyed distinctly, and each enlightens the others.[15]

St. John's explanation of the knowing aspect of complete union casts light on the biblical account of our contemplative oneness with God both through faith on earth and in the beatific vision in heaven. We understand better what Jesus meant when He said that eternal life is the very knowing of the Father and the Son[16] and what St. Paul had in mind when he explained to the Corinthians that our final destiny consists in seeing face to face, in knowing just as we are known.[17] We shall be transformed into the divine likeness because we shall know the Lord just as He is,[18] for this cognitive immersion in pure Beauty enthralls and transfigures just as fire ignites and makes to glow any combustible object cast into it.

St. Paul is likewise aware that the contemplative transfiguration of eternity begins in time, for he prays that the Father may give the Ephesians a spirit of wisdom so deep and penetrating that they may be brought to "a full knowledge" of Him.[19] He tells the Colossians that he never fails to pray that the father may bestow on them also a "perfect wisdom" that leads to the "fullest knowledge" of the divine will.[20] This same Father shines in our minds to radiate the light of His own glory, a glory that shines on the face of His incarnate Son.[21] If we did not have the experience and explanation of the contemplative summit described by mystics, we would be hard put to untangle and render intelligible what the revealed word presents to us. Once again we note that John and Teresa say nothing other than what we have in the very sources of revelation. It is in the divine light that we see Light itself.[22]

Loving-union

Infused, transfiguring knowledge is not a sterile insight. With it love is poured into our hearts by the Spirit Who is given to us.[23] Even on the merely natural level we know that there is nothing that unites as genuine love does. In contemplative prayer, knowing and loving are not two discrete, separated realities. We treat them here in sequence for the sake of clarity: our human minds cannot comprehend everything at once. The divine invasion leading to the consummation of the summit is indeed a fusion of unimaginable light and unspeakable love. Hence, John speaks of the frequent experience of an intimate spiritual embrace. This divine clasp or hug (if I may use the common term) can be so wonderfully overwhelming, notes John along with other mystics, that the soul needs an infusion of special strength to endure it.[24] To the uninitiated this sort of language probably seems little more than a pious effusion, but anyone who knows Augustine and Aquinas, Teresa and John, knows that their statements are to be taken at face value. These people have been to the summit, and they speak from experience as well as from revelation. One does not argue successfully against facts.

In an effort to express the inexpressible, St. John of the Cross avails himself both of ordinary literal language and of concrete imagery. He remarks, for example, that "the praises and endearing expressions of love which frequently pass between the two are indescribable".[25] He terms the soul a dove not only because of her purity but also because a dove has "bright and loving eyes", and thus the Bridegroom says that the soul has loving eyes to denote "the loving contemplation by which she looks at God".[26] It is in this spiritual marriage of the summit that "the soul kisses God", a reference to the Song of Songs.[27] From the spousal image John can switch to the maternal: God caresses the soul and like a mother gives the divine breasts to her. So tender is God's affectionate embrace that no human tenderness is comparable to it:

> The tenderness and truth of love by which the immense Father favors and exalts this humble and loving soul reaches such a degree — O wonderful thing, worthy of all our awe and admiration! — that the Father Himself becomes subject to her for her exaltation, as though He were her servant as she His lord. And He is as solicitous in favoring her as he would be if He were her slave and she His god. . . . He is occupied here in favoring and caressing the soul like a mother who ministers to her child and nurses it at her own breasts.[28]

Understandably enough the saint marvels at what he calls the divine "humility and sweetness".[29]

In the transforming union the person is now "all love", and all her actions are love. By this John means that love is not restricted simply to formal times of prayer and to ejaculations scattered through the day. Rather everything — seeing, hearing, tasting, working, resting, playing — triggers love in and through all things. This person is quite literally fulfilling the greatest of all the commandments: she is loving God with her whole heart, soul and mind. "The soul easily extracts the sweetness of love from all the things that happen to her, that is, she loves God in them. Thus everything leads her to love." Whether her daily experiences are delightful or bitter, she finds the Beloved in them and "knows nothing else but love" for Him in each of them.[30]

We have here an adequate explanation of what it means to love God entirely,[31] what it is to be of one spirit with Him,[32] what the remarkable intimacy of the interindwelling means, that is, our dwelling through love in God and His in us.[33] Once again John is careful to rule out a pantheistic understanding of this remarkably close union.[34]

TRAITS AND CONSEQUENCES OF THE UNION

While we usually find tautology and repetition annoying, it is necessary to emphasize the point that the core of the transforming union is union, a profound oneness between God and man. We need to be mindful of this, because all the rest of the message in this chapter follows from this oneness. Once we have appreciated adequately the intimacy of this bondedness, indeed, this wedding, between the human and the divine, we will have no great trouble understanding that what follows is no exaggerated account. We may ask, therefore: What flows from the transforming union? In just what does the transformation consist? What does one experience?

Remarkable delight

Union with beauty brings thrilling elation. While this is true on the sense level (a budding rose, a tasty delicacy, a gorgeous sunset, sublime music), it is more deeply true on the spiritual level of person beauty. It makes sense, therefore, to suppose that a close bonding with unending Beauty would have to issue in a matchless ecstatic joy. The supposition is confirmed by the fact. And the fact we can learn both from God's word and from those who have lived that word to the hilt and thus know of its results through their own direct experience. Over and over the mystics repeat that no literary attempt can portray the delight they find in the loftiest prayer. When the person, says St. John of the Cross, enters deeply into God

> she enjoys all peace, tastes all sweetness, and delights in all delight insofar as this earthly state allows. . . . So little of this is describable that we would never succeed in fully explaining what takes place in the soul that has reached this happy state. . . . This sweetness takes such an inward hold on her that nothing painful can reach her. . . . The delight of this union absorbs the soul within herself and gives her such refreshment that it makes her insensible to the disturbances and troubles mentioned.[35]

Further on the saint remarks that "such is the song of the soul in the transformation that is hers in this life, the delight of which is beyond all exaggeration".[36] Contrary to what most of us would expect, this sparkling exultation never becomes boring, as do pleasures of earth. Never is there wearisomeness, never a jaded satiety. Always the felicity is new and exciting:

> In this state of life so perfect, the soul always walks in festivity, inwardly and outwardly, and it frequently bears on its spiritual tongue a new song of great jubilation in God, a song always new, enfolded in gladness and love. . . . It feels in this state that God is so solicitous in regaling it with precious, delicate, and enhancing words, and in extolling it by various favors, that He has no one else in the world to favor nor anything else to do, that everything is for the soul alone.[37]

This blessedness is well known to biblical writers, and they take it as obviously part and parcel of a serious pursuit of God, a pursuit open to and indeed required of everyone. The psalmist can proclaim that they who meet the Lord are radiant with joy, and when they drink

deeply of Him, they find in their experience how good He is.[38] St.
Peter tells his Christians in what seems to be a baptismal instruction
that there is a joy in God so glorious that it cannot be described,[39] and
Jesus Himself promises a joy, His own joy, not some other, that is complete; that is, nothing is lacking in it.[40] As ever, we find that the sanjuanist teaching is nothing other than an elucidation of what we already
have in the revealed word.

Coaction with God

Every good and perfect gift — without exception — comes from the
Father of lights.[41] No being, no action can possibly exist aside from
the universal Fountain of all that is. Even our acceptance of a grace
requires a grace. As St. Thomas pointed out, the only thing we can
do entirely by ourselves is to say no to God. True as all this is, we
are here involved in one of the most difficult of all philosophical and
theological problems: how God works with human freedom but does
not detract from it in the process. Happily, we need not for our purposes attempt to solve here what centuries of debate have not completely penetrated and clarified. Just as we accept the existence of light
even though physicists have not yet explained how its wave characteristics are compatible with quanta of energy, so we can accept the
present trait of the transforming union, even if we do not see into the
deepest explanatory root of it.

In a manner that transcends divine physical premotion on the natural
level (that is, God's moving anything that moves, as its prime mover),
the indwelling Lord is now so one with the soul that all of its actions
are divine, a mode of expression typical of St. John of the Cross. "In
this state", he notes, "the soul cannot make acts because the Holy Spirit
makes them all and moves it toward them. As a result all the acts of
the soul are divine."[42] It is a characteristic of this spiritual marriage
that "God works in and communicates Himself to her through Himself
alone. . . . It is fitting that God Himself be the guide and means of
reaching Himself."[43] As we have already explained, the union between
the human and the divine is now so close, so intimate, that there are
two principles of one action. Nothing is done without God's innermost coaction.[44] As St. Paul long ago pointed out, he is son of God
who is led by the Spirit of God,[45] and he is most profoundly introduced
into the divine family life who is most penetratingly led by the Holy
Spirit in all he thinks, wills, says and does.

Scholastic theologians spoke of *motus primo primi,* a neat expression
that defies a smooth, accurate translation. These absolutely primal

human inclinations, "firstly first movements", are those that occur in us before our freedom intervenes. They are the fears, joy and desires that spring into being before we intellectually advert to them, and so they are without freedom or responsibility. Some of these primeval motions are worthy; some are not. In the transforming union one is so closely bonded to God that all of this person's first inclinations are directed to the Lord Who originates them. In memory, intellect, will and desire there is no movement contrary to the divine will and goodness. From the first instant and without intellectual advertence, one's spontaneous movements are toward patience in adversity, thanksgiving and praise in prosperity, temperance in delightful occupations, love and chastity in human relations, toward God in everything. One does not even "experience the first motions of sin".[46] Without advertence, and from their first movements, "the intellect, will, and memory go out immediately toward God, and the affections, senses, desires, appetites, hope, joy, and all the energy from the first instant incline toward God, although, as I say, the soul may not advert to the fact that she is working for Him".[47] We find in this teaching a fuller explanation of St. Paul's doctrine that the Holy Spirit brings love, joy, peace, patience, kindness, goodness, trustfulness, gentleness and self-control.[48] The Spirit brings these virtues into operation not simply after we have thought about their need in given situations but, once we have grown to maturity, even before we have noticed their relevance.

Cessation of imperfections

The reader will be struck more than once as we trace out the characteristics of the transforming union that it appears very much like the state of original innocence that theologians speak about. This ought not to be surprising, for it *is* a radical healing, a transformation, a new creation. This pristine freshness and integrity are found in the more or less complete diminution of our human flaws and infirmities. If we may put the matter into John's terminology, the four "passions", that is, the emotions of joy, hope, fear and sorrow, are well under the guidance of reason and thus lose their excessive and disordered tendencies. In place of inner turbulence and overwrought feelings there ensues a calm and abiding serenity even in trying circumstances. One of the most remarkable traits of St. John of the Cross as he suffered persecution and physical beatings in prison was this very inner unshaken serenity and self-composure. When one is anchored deeply in the divine solution to all problems, outer turmoil cannot disturb the inner tranquility. It is a peace that surpasses all understanding.[49]

Together with this self-possession on the emotional level, the summit of prayer brings about a remedy to intellectual wanderings as well. Frequent distractions, daydreaming, idle thoughts and useless cares tend to disappear for the good reason that the contemplative is living a vibrant life of love. People who are enthusiastic, eager, animated and spirited are little subject to the aimless wanderings of the bored and jaded. For this same reason small attachments and selfish clingings are nonexistent: preferring this food or drink to that, seeking more gratification in this activity rather than that, desiring the best for oneself, clinging to one's own preferences. The person is consequently "freed from and protected against all temporal disturbances and changes".[50]

We may make no mistake about the fact that we are dealing here with a lofty degree of perfection, and yet, sublime though it be, it is nothing other than what we find in Scripture. The eye of our mind is to be *always* on the Lord.[51] We are to be holy in *all* we do,[52] to be *perfect* as the heavenly Father is perfect.[53] We are to give up *everything* that does not lead to God,[54] or to put the same idea positively, we are to direct *everything* we do, eating, drinking and all else, to His glory.[55] Our efforts at purity of conscience are to be patterned on the very purity of Christ.[56] The saints find that what they come to experience in the transforming union is nothing other than what they have read and pondered in the divine word. God gives what He commands — provided we allow Him to do it.

Heroic virtue

To appreciate more fully the next facet of the contemplative culmination, we need to reflect on the meaning of heroic virtue. This term does not refer merely to the ordinary fidelity we commend when we say that another is a good and sincere person. Rather, we envision a degree of loving uprightness and moral excellence that, left to our own native resources, we find humanly impossible. It is the living of a Gospel virtue (faith, hope, charity, temperance, fortitude, patience, humility) in a manner surpassing human strength. We may indicate five traits that signal when a virtue is practiced to a heroic degree. The first is that one does what is to be done even in difficult or excruciating circumstances. We love truth heroically not simply when we accept Jesus' and the Church's teaching in ordinarily difficult or unpopular circumstances but even if we must undergo persecution or martyrdom rather than deny it. St. Thomas More unwaveringly loved the papal office, and the sanctity of marriage taught by that office, despite the consequence of literally losing his head in a gruesome death. St. Maria Goretti cherished chastity and gave her life rather than lose her virginity under attack. The next three traits can be grouped together: one acts promptly, easily and joyously. Each of these three qualities needs careful pondering lest we lose their pointedness. The saint does not delay or procrastinate in reacting in a humble manner or in loving an annoying neighbor. The correct response comes readily and easily, as if by second nature. Indeed, heroic virtue is like a second nature, for it is part of the new creation produced by the indwelling Trinity. What needs to be done is done joyously as well, and for the same reason: one is living a new life. To illustrate, one may compare the stoic way in which pagan heroes underwent torture and death and the gladness with which Christian martyrs face their persecutors and the excruciating agonies they suffer. Upon a moment's personal reflection each of us knows that, left to himself, he is entirely incapable of this kind of fidelity. The fifth trait of heroic virtue is habitual constancy. The preceding characteristics (disregarding the degree of difficulty, promptness, ease, joy) are found not simply on an isolated occasion when one may conceivably act with an apparent ease and joy (prompted possibly by pride or a vain defiance) but are customarily observed in whatever situation calls for the virtue in question. This is the kind of sanctity the Church looks for and requires in her canonization processes. It is a result of reaching the summit of union.

St. John of the Cross tells us that in this prayer the soul "experiences in God an awesome power and strength which derives from the intimate bond with God".[57] As a result "a lofty purity and beauty", together with a new strength, flow from the one to the other.[58] This is a flowering of the divinization that the early Greek patristic writers emphasized and that we routinely find in the saints. More than once St. Paul speaks of the power given by the indwelling Spirit, Who makes our inner selves grow strong.[59] The Father Himself has made his incarnate Son our *virtus*, our strength, fortitude and freedom.[60] There is nothing else that Paul himself wants to know and experience but Christ and the power of His Resurrection as he shares in the Lord's suffering and death.[61] It is in and through this divine energy that "the virtues of the soul in this state are now perfect and heroic".[62] Demonic influences, notes St. John of the Cross, are immobilized at this summit of the spiritual life: "When she is united with Him in transformation, they fear her as much as they do Him, and they have not even the courage to look at her. The devil has an extraordinary fear of the perfect soul."[63]

Confirmation in grace

St. John is of the opinion that "this state never occurs without the soul's being confirmed in grace".[64] As we note elsewhere, he differs from St. Teresa, who considers that one must be watchful because mortal sin is possible at any stage in one's life on earth, even in the highest. Given the whole of the sanjuanist analysis of the transforming union, it is difficult to see how he could reach any other conclusion than the one he does reach. Not surprisingly, he argues from the confirmation in grace that this development is the highest state possible in this life.[65]

Innocence of evil

We come to a trait of the summit that could be baffling unless we can identify the conditions that give rise to this characteristic of innocence that renders a person unable to recognize evil. St. John of the Cross discloses that in "the divine union of love" one enjoys a pristine goodness, a probity akin to that of Adam and Eve before the fall. In a context wherein he is describing an immersion in God, the soul being "as though carried away and absorbed in love", such that she is "estranged from all things" and is unable to pay attention to anything worldly because of having passed out of herself to the Beloved, the saint tells us that

> in a way, the soul in this state resembles Adam in the state of innocence, who did not know evil. For she is so innocent that she does not understand evil, nor does she judge anything in a bad light. And she will hear very evil things and see them with her own eyes and be unable to understand that they are so, since she does not have within herself the habit of evil by which to judge them.[66]

In his commentary St. John discusses why and when this "unknowing", as he terms it, takes place. It occurs in the aftermath of, as well as during, a temporary union of the three faculties (that is, during actual union, as distinct from the habitual, permanent union in this state of spiritual marriage), while the soul is "drinking" of the Beloved. "Since the soul is absorbed and imbibed in that drink of love, she cannot advert actually to any other thing." Particular knowledge, including of course the knowledge of evil, is "lost and ignored in that absorption of love". "The drink of highest wisdom makes her forget all worldly things", says John. Consequently, the person is unable to see any other than the Beloved. Not that the person's seeing and hearing (on a sense level) are in any way impeded, but the person simply cannot advert to what is seen and heard and so is "unable to understand" evil things. John explains further: "Since the effect of that act of love [actual union] endures a while, the unknowing also continues, so that the soul cannot advert to anything in particular until the effect of that act of love passes."

From all of this we can conclude that innocence of evil is not continuous in the state of spiritual marriage, and that outside of actual absorption and its aftermath one is again able to recognize evil as such.

Peace and refreshment

The biblical concept of peace was richer than our contemporary idea of an absence of conflict or, even as Augustine put it, the tranquility of order. *Shalom* meant for the Hebrew what today we call prosperity. Augustine was right in seeing peace as a tranquility of things being as they ought to be, but the scriptural concept made explicit the implicit notion of a flourishing animation, a calm but complete spiritual affluence:

> The soul is conscious at this time that the torrent of God's spirit is besieging and taking possession of her so forcibly that all the rivers of the world seem to have flooded in upon her and to be assailing her. She feels that all the actions and passions in which she was formerly occupied are drowned therein. This is not a torment to her, although it is a thing of tremendous force, because these rivers are rivers of peace.[67]

Strong as this language is, it does not go beyond that of St. Paul when he told the Philippians to rejoice in the Lord always and in their lives of prayer to find a peace beyond understanding.[68] This is the peace the Lord wished twice upon His apostles on the evening of His Resurrection,[69] the refreshment that He promised we would find, though laboring and heavily burdened, if we come to Him.[70] It would have to be a prominent trait of the final transformation of those who have given all for the All.

Cessation of inner sufferings

Because we are pilgrims on this earth, from our first cry at birth to our last breath in death we suffer at any stage of prayer growth from the circumstances of human life: weather, weariness, illness, failures and human contradictions. However, as we progress in prayer, we are gradually freed from interior disturbances and sufferings due to sin and imperfection. We recall that the two nights of purification are painful precisely because our selfish clingings are being burned away in the dark fire of contemplative prayer. When this work is finished, there is nothing to be stripped away, nothing to cause inner pain. The per-

son is now purified, and there is consequently no need for further
"working over". The grinding away is finished. Likewise, there are
no distressing longings for the absent Beloved, for the obvious reason
that He is now always experienced as present. He no longer withdraws
as He did in the spiritual espousals.[71] In place of the aching feeling
of emptiness characteristic of the two nights, there is now an abiding
and peaceful exchange of love with the indwelling Father, Son and Spirit.

Symphony of creation

Most of what occurs in the transforming summit is supremely surprising: indeed, eye has not seen or ear heard the likes of it. Yet one
of the teachings of St. John of the Cross that is least understood by
people who have dabbled in his writings is this present trait. Especially
those who have little time for the *nada* doctrine lamentably fail to grasp
the sanjuanist view of created beauty and our rejuvenated return to
it. We are so immersed in our egoism that we take it for granted that
there is no possible enjoyment of natural beauties beyond that which
is commonly experienced. For this reason, one among others, many
people reject John's (and thus the Gospel's) teaching about detachment.
They assume that if they give up their self-centered pursuits, creation
will be lost to them.

They could hardly be more mistaken. It is true that in the fullness
of prayer development God so fills a person with a supreme knowing
and loving of Himself that one is inclined to care little for knowing
mere things for their own sakes. But this does not mean that there is
no delight in created reality. It simply means that exultation in God
far outstrips any other experience. As a matter of fact, the former sheds
a new radiance on the latter. As the saint would put it, infused knowledge perfects habitual natural knowledge, for the latter is joined to
the superior wisdom of God. The person seems now to know created
things more from the new divine light than from "natural habits" of
knowing. "Such," says John, "I believe, will be the case in heaven. The
habits of the acquired knowledge of the just will not be supplanted,
but they will not be of great benefit either, since the just will have more
knowledge through the divine wisdom than through these habits."[72]

It can happen in deeply absorbing prayer that one is so engrossed
in love that she cannot advert to anything particular at that time. This,
notes the saint, is due to the fact that God has made her so consonant
with his own purity and simplicity that she is pure and empty of "all
forms and figures" and is "radiant in simple contemplation".[73]

Still more needs to be said. From the natural point of view we come
to know God from the vestiges of Himself that He has left in the splen-

dors of the visible universe: the blazing red sunset, the snow-covered mountain peaks, the graceful flight of a bird, the breathtakingly magnificent complexity of a single living cell. On a still more exalted level we know Him in the loveliness of the saints—but it remains a knowledge of the infinite through the finite. In the transforming union quite the opposite occurs: we know and appreciate creation through the Creator.

> The soul is conscious of how all creatures, earthly and heavenly, have their life, duration, and strength in Him. . . . Although it is indeed aware that these things are distinct from God, insofar as they have created being, nonetheless that which it understands of God, by His being all these things with infinite eminence, is such that it knows these things better in God's being than in themselves. And here lies the remarkable delight of this awakening: the soul knows creatures through God and not God through creatures.[74]

Remarkable indeed—a truth that merits prayerful pondering.

In this superior knowledge of creation St. John of the Cross was struck by what we might call a symphonic oneness seen as a result of the divine light. Each being gives "voice to what God is in it", and all of them together produce a marvelous harmony: "So creatures will be for the soul a harmonious symphony of sublime music surpassing all concerts and melodies of the world."[75] When we recall the saint's love for music, we can glimpse a little of what he was trying to express. We understand, too, that seeing this harmony in the divine light brings to the person a new fascination beyond anything attainable on the mere natural level.[76] So superior are these infused insights into creation to what was previously known that John considers the latter to be "pure ignorance" when compared with the former, "for where God is unknown nothing is known".[77] Some may view this last remark as hyperbole at best, gross nonsense at worst. Yet no one may intelligently contest it without examining the evidence, or even better, experiencing what John experienced. The saint was well aware of how we judge from what we know and thus how we can be intolerably shortsighted:

> Hence, the wise men of God and the wise men of the world are foolish in the eyes of each other, for the one group finds the wisdom and knowledge of God imperceptible, and the other finds the same of the knowledge of the world. Wherefore the knowledge of the world is ignorance to the knowledge of God, and the knowledge of God is ignorance to the knowledge of the world.[78]

Even though examples limp, especially in a matter of this kind, an illustration may aid us in grasping what John has in mind. When we do not know the author and the purpose of a thing, mere sense data and experience of it are next to useless. In a sense, we know nothing about it. If we were to present to an aboriginal tribe a portable computer without giving any explanation of it, the men and women could handle, touch, shake and visually examine it at great length and yet could reach no knowledge of computers in general or of this one in particular. Because they have no idea of its origin and purposes, they are almost completely ignorant of its actual reality. So also, if we know creation only on a natural level and aside from its divine Author and purpose, we are next to totally in the dark about it. When one reaches the consummation of immersion in trinitarian beauty, everything else is seen as it actually is, and one thrills at what is seen.

All this being so, we cannot be surprised that at the summit of prayer finite beings are no longer stumbling blocks in our path to God. They are what in the divine plan they were designed to be: steps to their Origin. John goes so far as to say that in this union "she feels that all things are God [and] that God is all things for her".[79]

Fullness of joy

While we considered "remarkable joy" above as the first in our list of traits of the transforming union, we did not deal with the aspect of delight that we address at this point. By the expression *fullness of joy* we mean to indicate that the felicity here experienced is such that earthly joys, real though they be, do not add, and in a sense cannot add, to the fundamental and far greater delight in God Himself. Even on the merely human level we sometimes encounter something like this phenomenon when we meet something or someone especially beautiful: incidental pleasures are not noticed. When, for instance, after some years of absence we meet someone especially dear to us, we do not notice the pleasure of drinking a steaming hot cup of coffee as we share those first moments at the airport. St. John's treatment of this aspect of the summit is lucid. Additional joys, he says, do not

> make her aware of less or added abundance, for what she ordinarily enjoys is so great that, like the sea, she neither decreases by the outflowing waters nor increases by the inflowing waters. . . . Even though these joys and accidental sweetnesses are not lacking — ordinarily they are numberless — they do not on this account add anything to the substantial spiritual communications. She already possesses everything that could come to her anew. . . . Hence, every time joyous and happy things are offered to this soul, whether they are exterior or interior and spiritual, she immediately turns to the enjoyment of the riches she already has within herself, and experiences much greater gladness and delight in them than in those new joys.[80]

The saint notes that in this the soul resembles God Himself, Who though He delights in everything He has made, delights far more in Himself, for His own good is infinitely beyond anything created. Thus the incidental joys that occur to one at the summit are so minor in comparison to the matchless delight in God that we may call them nothings. And yet, strange though it may seem, these joys are fresh and new, for "it always seems to her that she receives them anew and also that she has had them before. The reason is that she ever takes pleasure in them anew, since they are her good that is ever new."[81] Once again we find an additional insight into St. Paul's desire that all of us be filled with the Spirit and His gifts.[82]

Continuity

One who lives a serious prayer life notices at the passage of some years that one's love-communion with God is growing not only in depth but also in duration. The first bits of infused contemplation, whether dry or delightful, are both delicate and brief; that is, they are punctured with many distractions. In the transforming union (St. John of the Cross points out what we have already noted in St. Teresa's seventh mansions) there is some sort of continuity to the divine infusion and awareness. What this "some sort" is needs to be explained.

John makes two points that must be taken together, lest they be separately misunderstood. On the one hand he says that an actual and intensely perceived oneness with God cannot be continuous in this life: "A permanent actual union of the faculties in this life is impossible; such a union can only be transient."[83] On the other hand there is a kind of continuity in the divine experience, a "habitual embrace", a "habitual satisfaction and peace".[84] The soul "enjoys in this state an habitual sweetness and tranquillity which is never lost or lacking to her".[85] While it may appear that he is contradicting himself in these passages, a careful reading shows that he is speaking of two aspects of one reality.

John uses four terms to denote what is permanent: *essential, substantial, obscure* and *habitual.* He uses two terms for what is passing and transient: *actual* and *faculties.* The saint is saying that there are a deep-down enjoyment and awareness of God's indwelling that are habitual, that is, practically continuous and pervading all else that goes on in a typical day. Then there are an intense actual knowing and loving that come and go.[86] The images St. John uses to explain what he has in mind bear out this understanding. The flame of love, the Holy Spirit, at times flares up and bathes the soul in glory and thus transforms it in love. These acts of love are most precious, and indeed one of them "is more

meritorious and valuable than all the deeds a person may have performed in his whole life without this transformation". The difference
between the habitual and continual embrace and these actual immersions in living love is "like the difference between the wood that is
on fire and the flame that leaps up from it, for the flame is the effect
of the fire that is present there".[87] John returns to this image when he
speaks of the Holy Spirit mightily absorbing the soul in an intimate
embrace of the Father's delight. "This latter", he says of the habitual
embrace, "resembles the glowing embers, whereas the former is similar
to embers not merely glowing but embers that have become so hot
they shoot forth a living flame."[88]

The saint also illustrates the difference between the habitual and actual perceptions of the indwelling God by likening it to the contrast
between knowing and enjoying a beloved who is asleep in one's presence
and who then awakens. "Although it was experiencing and enjoying
Him, this took place as though with a loved one who is asleep. . . . He
is usually there, in this embrace with His bride, as though asleep in
the substance of the soul. And it is very well aware of Him and ordinarily enjoys Him."[89] The awakenings, which are not continual, occur
within the abiding experience of God's resting and reposing.[90] Kavanaugh
and Rodriguez understand this distinction in the same manner as we
have explained it: "The habitual union of love is the permanent union
formed by the acts and consists of nothing else than the less intense
form of union which the soul lives in its ordinary state after the actual
union is passed."[91]

Because of this trait of the contemplative summit we may speak of
a dual operation occurring within the person. By dual we mean that
one can be cooking a meal, teaching a class or writing a letter and still
experience the deep habitual enjoyment of the Trinity's indwelling. The
latter does not disturb or interfere with the former, at least not as a rule.

This abiding awareness of the Lord present was well known to biblical
men and women. The psalmist takes it for granted that we grow to
a point where our "eyes are always on the Lord".[92] St. Paul exhorts
the Ephesians to sing to the Lord in their hearts always and everywhere,
and he tells the Philippians to rejoice in their God always.[93] What we
find in the transforming union should serve to caution scriptural commentators and spiritual writers not to dilute inspired sayings about continual prayer. They really mean what they say.

Transfiguration, deification, marriage

Actually, this final trait of the summit is far more than a trait. A summation of the whole, it biblically and profoundly expresses the deepest

essence of contemplative culmination, the complete reason for the Incarnation and the redemption. It is the fulfillment of the divine plan for the planet. We men and women were never made simply to be men and women on a natural plane. Because God never thinks prosaic thoughts, never condones lukewarm dilutions, He had in mind nothing less than that we should be deified, that is, transfigured and oned with Him in a union beyond human words. Even though the summit is literally unspeakable, we must do the best we can, presenting the sanjuanist thought first and then noting how Scripture has already said much the same thing in the terminology of divine revelation.

In his *Spiritual Canticle* St. John of the Cross tells us that

> this spiritual marriage is incomparably greater than the spiritual espousal, for it is a total transformation in the Beloved. . . . The soul thereby becomes divine, becomes God through participation, insofar as is possible in this life. . . . There are two natures in one spirit and love. . . . This union resembles the union of the light of a star or candle with the light of the sun, for what then sheds light is not the star or the candle, but the sun, which has absorbed the other lights into its own. . . . The union wrought between the two natures and the communication of the divine to the human in this state is such that even though neither change their being, both appear to be God.[94]

Notice that even though the saint uses bold language to describe this union, he is concerned to avoid any hint of pantheism: "Even though neither change their being, both appear to be God." The union is astonishing, yes, but there is no oriental fusion or loss of personal identity: "We become God through participation", a biblical idea, as we shall note below. The same daring terminology occurs further on when John applies the kiss that is spoken of in the Song of Songs to this final culmination: "This kiss is the union of which we speak, in which the soul is made equal with God through love."[95] It goes without saying that this "equal" is not existential identity but rather an equivalent way of saying that "both appear to be God", so astonishing is the transformation.

The human person has entered profoundly into the inner life of the Trinity, a living of the triune life that is best described by the saint himself:

> By His divine breath-like spiration, the Holy Spirit elevates the soul sublimely and informs her and makes her capable of breathing in the Son and the Son in the Father, which is the Holy Spirit Himself, Who in the Father and the Son breathes out to her in this transformation, in order to unite her to Himself. . . . This kind of spiration of the Holy Spirit . . . is so sublime, delicate, and deep a delight that a mortal tongue

finds it indescribable . . . for the soul united and transformed in God breathes out in God to God the very divine spiration which God — she being transformed in Him — breathes out in Himself to her.[96]

John remarks at this point that he thinks that this was St. Paul's meaning in Galatians 4:6 when he tells us that since we are sons of God, the Father has sent the Spirit of His Son into our hearts, calling to the Father. John likewise understands Jesus' prayer at the Last Supper as referring to this trinitarian transformation, namely, that all of us may be one as the Father is in the Son and the Son in the Father, that we all may be one as the Father and the Son are one, with Jesus in us and the Father in Jesus, that we may be perfect in unity.[97]

The saint maintains that we ought not to consider it impossible that the soul be given this capacity of breathing in God Himself through participation:

> For, granted that God favors her by union with the Most Blessed Trinity, in which she becomes deiform and God through participation, how could it be incredible that she also understand, know, and love — or better that this be done in her — in the Trinity, together with it, as does the Trinity itself! . . . This is transformation in the three Persons in power and wisdom and love, and thus the soul is like God through this transformation.[98]

As we shall note in our next chapter, it is at this very pinnacle of infused prayer that St. John of the Cross cannot contain himself in expressing his conviction that absolutely everyone is called to these heights, that they are the ordinary development of the grace life: "O souls," he proclaims, "created for these grandeurs and called to them! What are you doing? How are you spending your time?"[99] The questions suggest their own answers.

Sacred Scripture, too, speaks of a transformation that is a deification and a marriage with the Lord Himself. In the Old Testament Yahweh makes those who are open to Him exceedingly beautiful . . . famous among the nations for their beauty . . . perfect and queenly . . . and it is a beauty that He alone bestows, for it is His own beauty.[100] They are to be a crown of splendor, His very delight. Like a young man marrying a virgin, so does the Lord wed His people, and as the new husband rejoices in his bride, so does the Lord rejoice in His people.[101] St. Paul tells the Corinthian church that she is a virgin wedded to one husband, Christ.[102] Earlier in the same Letter he had said to the members of this community that they reflect the very splendor of the Lord and are transformed from one glory to another into His very image — a transformation effected by the indwelling Spirit.[103] It would be difficult to find a more accurate, brief description of the contemplative

summit. They and we are to become the very goodness of God[104] and
to live not with our own lives but with the very life of Christ Himself[105] and thereby to become an altogether new creation.[106] All of
this, says Peter, is a participation in the divine nature.[107]

When we consider the greatest of all the commandments not simply
as a goal at which we aim but as a state fulfilled in this life, it is an
ideal summation of the transforming union. To have one's entire interior life, will, mind, heart and strength full of love *is* to be identified
with God. This entire union of wills, human and divine, is, as we have
noted, John's explanation of union by likeness. If we did not have the
mystic's teaching about the loftiest prayer, we would be at a loss to
explain a great deal of Scripture.

SOME COROLLARIES

What a piercing beam of light does to a diamond in the dark, so does
the indwelling Lord do to a soul entirely purified from all selfishness.
Just as one jewel differs from another, so also do those at the contemplative summit vary in the splendors they receive from God. St.
John of the Cross tells us that he often describes "the most that God
communicates", that is, even in the same stage of growth the Lord does
not give everything to everyone. To some He gives more, to others
less; to some in one way, to others in another.[108] Therefore, even in
the seventh mansions one star differs from another in glory.

Our second corollary follows from the first: sublime though the
spiritual marriage is, growth within it is normal. We never reach a point
on earth at which we can say "enough". Just as fire in wood can grow
hotter, with fiery flames shooting out from it, so also can our love
deepen and flare out.[109]

Third, the transforming union is literally ineffable. Because this trait
is frequently mentioned with reference to all the higher states of advanced prayer, we may be content simply to cite one text in which
John makes the point: "So little of this is describable that we would
never succeed in fully explaining what takes place in the soul that has
reached this happy state."[110] If this saint would never succeed, surely
we cannot. We may remark, however, that the New Testament also
declares that the divine favors are beyond human wording.[111] St. Peter
tells his Christians that they have already experienced a joy in the Lord
so deep and glorious that it cannot be described.[112]

Is this loftiest of all possible attainments a temptation to vanity for
those who are led to such heights? Could one possibly be aware of

one's own transfigured beauty without a touch of pride? Surprising
as it may seem, the answer to the first question is negative, to the second affirmative. John is plain on the point when he relates that the
soul "knows that it is pure, rich, full of virtues and prepared for such
a kingdom. God permits it in this state to discern its beauty and . . . it
has no touch of presumption or vanity."[113] How can this be? When
we recall on the one hand that pride is a lie and humility is the truth,
and on the other that a person in this transformed state, this new creation, enjoys a heroic degree of all the virtues, we have the answer to
our question. This individual knows to the roots of his being that by
himself he is nothing but an unworthy sinner and that all the beauty
and goodness that he now possesses are entirely and utterly a divine
gift. Immersed in the divine light of truth concerning himself and all
else ("in your light we see the light", says Psalm 36:9), he is under no
illusion as to how things stand. And what he sees he lives, for this person
is head over heels in love. "He must increase; I must decrease."[114]

Our final corollary: the person in the transforming union is now ready
for heaven and thus for death.[115] The purifications are completed, and
there is an identity of wills, divine and human. All is ready for the Lord's
coming. As a matter of fact, notes John, death itself comes directly not
from sickness or old age but from an impetus of love:

> The death of persons who have reached this state is far different in its
> cause and mode than the death of others, even though it is similar in
> natural circumstances. If the death of other people is caused by sickness
> or old age, the death of these persons is not so induced, in spite of their
> being sick or old; their soul is not wrested from them unless by some
> impetus and encounter of love, far more sublime than previous ones. . . .
> The death of such persons is very gentle and very sweet, sweeter and
> more gentle than was their whole spiritual life on earth. . . . Accordingly,
> David affirmed that the death of the saints is precious in the sight of
> the Lord.[116]

An interesting commentary on this teaching is John's own death. An
eyewitness tells us that at the moment of the saint's passing he was
"muy sereno, hermoso y alegre" (very serene, beautiful and happy). Several
of those present deposed in the canonization process that they had seen
at the point of his death a globe of dazzling light over the bed and resting
on his body.[117]

We may close this chapter with a theological note. Our being filled
with God is, of course, the reason for everything else in the economy
of salvation. Since this chapter is a compact formulation of the indwelling summit, we must be content simply to say that the transforming

union is likewise the purpose of all else in the Church. The Eucharist itself, the Sacrament of all sacraments, is, according to the word of the Lord, aimed at producing eternal life here on earth. Jesus declares that whoever eats His flesh and drinks His Blood *has* eternal life.[118] It is a life that is to be abundant, to the full.[119] The fullness is the transformation; there is no other. In this Mystical Body of Christ we are to find our fulfillment, not something less. Thus all structures in the Church—institutions, priesthood, curias, chancery offices, books and candles and all else—are aimed at producing this abundance of life, this utter immersion in triune splendor, this transforming union.

So also consecrated virginity is directed to undivided attention to the Lord, since "undivided" can signify, when taken seriously, nothing short of a perfect and consummated focusing.[120] It pertains to the hundredfold promised to those who give up marriage and property to pursue the Lord alone.[121] Religious vows have as their primary purpose a deep prayer life and the very fullness of it. This is why canon law insists that "the contemplation of divine things and an assiduous union with God in prayer is the first and principal duty of all religious".[122] This culmination of holiness is not restricted to consecrated celibate men and women alone, of course. It is meant for all. And this is the question we take up next.

CHAPTER ELEVEN

THE UNIVERSAL CALL

We address in this chapter a question of far more importance in explaining our human presence on planet earth than many contemporary theologians ascribe to it. Almost all Christians admit in theory that we are called to be holy by putting on Christ, but the implications of this admission seem to escape most of us. Much of current moral theology is based on minimalistic presuppositions. No one, of course, openly states that it suffices for us to stay out of serious sin, but at the same time infused contemplation and heroic virtue are quite completely bypassed as though not being worthy of mention, much less of the thorough treatment they deserve. Yet Ss. Teresa of Jesus and John of the Cross are emphatic that without a deep rooting in a serious prayer life no one comes close to living the Gospel ideals with completeness.

No serious theologian doubts the universal call to holiness. If in past centuries doubts lingered in individual writers, they have been laid to rest in the now well known chapter 5 of *Lumen gentium* of Vatican II. While the married, religious and sacerdotal paths vary in the efficacy with which they lead to the summit of sanctity (a point also explicitly stated in the council), all men and women in every vocation are called to that summit. This call we assume here, and it is not in question.

What we do now take up is a closely related matter: Is everyone called by God to infused contemplation and to the very fullness of it, the transforming union? Can a person attain to perfect holiness without this kind of prayer? Are there two ways to sanctity, an active, ascetic way and a passive, mystical way? Or is there only one way meant for all, active and ascetic in the beginning, but becoming passive and mystical in full development?

Scripture knows nothing of two ways to God and two differing prayer paths, one for the many, the other for the few. Nor have I found in patristic and medieval literature anything suggesting the two-way theory of recent centuries. This new school of thought claims that most people go to God sufficiently in active, discursive prayer and that they do not need, and ought not to expect, infused contemplation. But another small group of people, an elite, it would seem, are called to the prayer of which Teresa and John say so much, that is, to mystical contemplation. This latecomer theory, the "ordinary" and "extraordinary" ways to holiness theory, we shall not directly consider in this chapter, for our purpose is to present the thought of two saints and how it relates to the Gospel. I may say, however, that this recent view is not only incompatible with clear texts in Vatican II, texts dealing with mystical contemplation, but it is also clearly excluded in many texts by both Carmelites and by the reasons they give.

WHY THIS CHAPTER?

It may be well for us at the outset to answer a question some readers may find lurking at the back of their minds: Why take up this question at all? Is it not sufficient for each of us to live in our state of life as best we can and leave to God just how He is calling us to Himself? Do we actually have to concern ourselves with infused prayer as such? Most of us are not theologians and have not much interest in issues having little application to us. Why this chapter?

These are reasonable questions, and they deserve reasonable answers. We take up the universal call to contemplation because both Teresa and John speak of it repeatedly and strongly. It would be an unpardonable omission to bypass a discussion of what both saints considered to be immensely important even to nontheologians, and not merely for abstract, theological reasons but also for concrete and practical ones.

A second reason for this chapter is that the two-way theory (rejected in advance by both John and Teresa) really implies a two-tiered concept of sanctity itself. There is really no comparison between the holiness we can achieve by our active efforts ("one way") and the holiness given along with infused prayer ("another way"). The first is clearly inferior to the second, and the second simply cannot be achieved in the first. Both Carmelites are perfectly clear about this. Hence, if one holds the two-way theory, he is holding that there are two classes in the Church as regards holiness itself. He is actually, even if unintentionally, implying that there are two kinds of holiness. Because this idea is foreign to Scripture and to the whole of Catholic tradition, the questions it raises are important.

A third reason is that most people, lay, religious and priestly, assume without study that they are not called to advanced prayer. They take it for granted that the prayer of which Ss. Teresa and John write could not be meant for them. They lose sight of the fact that both of these saints are presented by the Church as *universal* Doctors precisely because of their teaching about the lofty reaches of the spiritual life. So deeply engrained among us is the minimalistic view that the majority are surprised to hear it said that the heights of prayer are open also to them. Yet people who really want God are, I find, thrilled at the thought that they too can aspire to fullness.

Our fourth reason is that once we understand the universal call we are more likely to be willing to pay the price to attain its object. Advancing in prayer is not the result of a mere velleity any more than the selfless loving of another human person issues from wishful thinking. Both demand great detachment from self-centeredness and a strenuous carrying of the cross. If we see that the summit is open to us, we find in the vision a fresh impulse to go sell all that we have and buy the pearl of great price.

Finally, the correct answer to the question this chapter raises is required for those who engage in the spiritual direction of others. It goes without saying that we should lead others toward God, not according to our private views but according to divine revelation and the mind of the Church to whom this revelation has been committed. Our two saints are faithful to both.

CLARIFYING THE EXACT QUESTION

Many human disagreements are caused or at least aggravated by a failure to define terms and to clarify what is and what is not at issue. Our present question is no exception. It seems to me that a number of those who reject the universal call to contemplation do not grasp what this contemplation actually is. They seem to assume that there is something striking or flashy about it, something bordering on the esoteric. They appear unaware that the beginnings of infused prayer are so gentle and prosaic that the recipient may not advert to the fact that something new is being received. Anyone who has been led into this incipient contemplation can testify to how ordinary and undramatic it all is. People who love God much might find, on reading about the early stages of infused prayer, that they have experienced, perhaps years earlier, much of what is described. This present chapter is not, therefore, concerned with extraordinary phenomena such as levitation or the stigmata or the perception of fragrances or the seeing of visions.

Furthermore, we are not asking how many persons actually do reach the summit of prayer. This question is what professional theologians call a de facto, or factual, matter. Rather our concern is whether in the nature of things we ought to grow to the summit of prayer life. This the theologians call a de iure question, that is, concerning what ought to be in the nature of things. How many acorns actually become oak trees (not many, obviously) is a factual, de facto matter. Whether a healthy acorn planted in propitious circumstances and receiving normal sunlight and water ought to become an oak is a de iure question. All of us without exception are "called" to avoid idle words, but very few as a matter of fact avoid them entirely, a de facto question. All of us, in the nature of things, are to avoid detraction; few actually avoid it completely. Likewise, all normal human beings are called to infused prayer, a de iure matter. Rather few in the general population do attain it, a de facto matter.

ST. TERESA'S TEACHING

We are now prepared to ask whether the foundress of Carmel taught that all men and women in every vocation should consider a deep prayer life as meant for them. Some commentators, having been impressed by a passage in chapter 17 of the *Way of Perfection,* have concluded in the negative. Unfortunately, and for reasons difficult to fathom, these writers have passed over a multitude of other passages that make it crystal clear that an affirmative response is demanded by the evidence. Before we explore the saint's mind (including the problem text in the *Way*), I should like to make two comments.

It seems likely that many of the proponents of the two-way theory hold their view chiefly because they are impressed by the factual fewness of those who do reach advanced prayer or because they unwittingly assume that this prayer really is somehow extraordinary, after the fashion of visions or locutions. Desirous of consoling the majority of men and women and of offering them some hope of sanctity, they either do not notice or decline to take seriously the numerous statements in both St. Teresa and St. John that contradict their negation. They seem not to grasp that in the orders of both nature and supernature de facto fewness is no argument at all against de iure oughtness. They never, to my knowledge, discuss the principles we have considered above.

Second, the Church could hardly have designated St. Teresa as a universal Doctor if she had not taught the universal call. The saint's principal contribution to our understanding of divine revelation and our living of it is her teaching on advanced prayer and the conditions for attaining it. If only a small elite were called to this infused contemplation, Teresa would be writing only for them, not for the whole body of the faithful. In confirmation of this we have already noted how the liturgy itself speaks of all types and classes of people as "being fed with her heavenly teaching". If the two-way theory were correct, the saint would not be a universal teacher.

First we address the problem text in the *Way*. In a context dealing with the basic necessity of humility, the foundress declares that not all of her nuns are to be contemplatives, that they who are not "strong" should not be discouraged if the Lord tarries long, that they should not give up prayer, even if they do nothing more than say vocal prayers. Carmel is St. Martha's house, she adds, and there is room in it for all kinds of people. Furthermore, Teresa thinks there are many people who can scarcely engage in meditation even after reading. Hence, she encourages such nuns to prepare themselves well for "high contemplation", and if they do not reach it in this life, it is a sign that God is going to give it to them in heaven.[1]

While this passage may appear to negate the universal call to contemplation, there are several reasons that indicate that it does not. Nor need we suppose that St. Teresa contradicts herself when elsewhere she categorically asserts that no one is excluded from the heights. We should first notice that in this very section she urges the "weak ones" to prepare themselves insofar as they can for lofty contemplation, and if they have true detachment and humility, she thinks that God will not fail to grant it to them. This strongly suggests that she is presently speaking of exceptions to the rule, that is, of people who for some human reason experience an impediment. If we say that acorns should become oak trees, we are talking about normal cases, about healthy acorns in propitious circumstances. We do not have in mind abnormalities. So also here: the universal call refers to ordinary, healthy cases, not to exceptions.

This understanding of the saint's thought she herself explicitly affirms further on in chapters 19 and 20 of the *Way*. At the very end of chapter 19 she unequivocally lays it down that "the Lord invites us *all;* and, since He is Truth Itself, we cannot doubt Him. . . . As He said we were *all* to come, without making this condition, I feel sure that *none* will fail to receive this living water unless they cannot keep to the path."[2] At the beginning of the next chapter, adverting to the apparent contradiction between this and what she wrote in chapter 17, she emphatically denies that there are two ways: "He did not say: 'Some must come by this way and others by that.' His mercy is so great that He has forbidden *none* to strive to come and drink of this fountain of life."[3] What began to seem like a difficulty turns out upon examination to be a vigorous affirmation of the universal call.

St. Teresa's mind in this matter is strong and consistent, though she makes allowances for abnormal exceptions. For the sake of clarity I will number each of the ways in which she assumes and states that all are invited to the summit of prayer.

1. For the saint it is a principle that failing to reach the heights of prayer is our fault, not God's. He sets no limits; we do. Speaking of the ascent to perfect love, she declares the problem to be that we do not desire it in any effective way: "The whole fault is ours if we don't soon reach the enjoyment of a dignity so great, for the perfect attainment of this true love of God brings with it every blessing. . . . We do not fully prepare ourselves." Perfect love, for Teresa, is found in the transforming union alone, but we must pay the price of a complete detachment. If we do ready ourselves, she adds that "I believe without a doubt that in a very short time this blessing will be given to us".[4] Writing of ecstatic prayer in her most mature work, she repeats her principle: "I cannot help feeling the pity of it when I see how much we are losing, and all through our own fault. For, true though it is that these are things which the Lord gives to whom He will, He would give them to us all if we loved Him as He loves us."[5] In this passage Teresa explicitly rejects the evasion so many people offer: "God isn't calling me to the heights." She admonishes her readers to understand "how important it is that no fault of yours should hinder the celebration of His Spiritual Marriage with your souls".[6] If we are "very careful" about our prayer life, we will soon find ourselves "gradually reaching the summit of the mountain".[7] Always the explanation for failure to reach the heights is squarely placed on the human level. The divine call is addressed to everyone.

2. St. Teresa's next point is related to the first: God gives infused prayer as soon as we have done our part, as soon as we are ready to receive it. The Lord is so desirous of granting His favors to everyone that He is, as it were, sitting on the edge of His throne, eager to give as soon as we are purified and prepared to receive His gift. The saint makes this point over and over in all of her major works. "The more resolute we are in soul," she says, "the more does Our Lord draw us to Himself and raise us above all petty earthly things and above ourselves, in order to prepare us to receive great favours from Him. . . . His Majesty never wearies of giving."[8] Teresa explicitly and vehemently rejects the idea that God gives lofty favors only to a few: "Reflect that it is indeed certain that God gives Himself in this way to those who give up all for Him. He shows no partiality, He loves everyone. Nobody has any excuse, no matter how miserable he may be, since the Lord so acts with me in bringing me to such a state."[9] She repeats her certitude about this teaching in *Interior Castle*: "It is quite certain that, when we empty ourselves of all that is creature and rid ourselves of it for

the love of God, that same Lord will fill our souls with Himself." We can miss this gift not because the word of Jesus can fail but "because we ourselves fail by not preparing ourselves".[10]

3. St. Teresa was so convinced that "supernatural" prayer is for all that she spontaneously and habitually jotted into her writings remarks that have no other explanation. "God's will is that no bounds should be set to his works", she asserts on one occasion.[11] "Through the goodness of God all may reach this prayer [of quiet]", she declares on another.[12] Speaking of lofty infused prayer, she vehemently cries out to His Majesty, "Either desire, my King, I beseech You, that all to whom I speak become mad from Your love, or do not permit that I speak to anyone!"[13]

4. Sound theology permits that we desire gifts of grace intended by God for everyone, but not that we seek those reserved for the few — the latter being a form of presumption. The foundress considered that we are right in seeking the heights of prayer, and she found nothing presumptuous in this aspiration, provided we are willing to take the necessary means to the end. For her it is an obvious truth that from the great God we should ask great things: "It would be insulting to a great emperor to ask him for a farthing."[14] She expressly states of the differing stages of prayer that they are all to be sought, for they are developments in God's ordinary plan for His people. Speaking of the fourth mansions, the prayer of quiet, Teresa remarks that "you will desire, then, my daughters, to strive to attain this way of prayer, and you will be right to do so".[15] Writing of the spiritual betrothal and ecstatic prayer, she says that "in some ways it is even more necessary that we should wish to receive them".[16] The saint does not conceal her "intention to attract souls to so high a blessing", namely, to ecstatic prayer. We should be mindful that she is referring in the context to all men and women, not just to her nuns.[17] Writing of the transforming union, Teresa is so affected by the sublimity of her subject and its reality that she asks ardently: "My God, since Thou seest how needful it is for us, do Thou inspire Christians to desire to seek it!" Once again she expressly includes all states in life.[18]

5. One might think at this point that there could be no other way in which St. Teresa could teach the universal call. Yet there is: laymen and laywomen are explicitly named and directed toward mystical prayer the same as the saint directs anyone else. Lorenzo, her married brother, became a mystic under his sister's guidance. She likewise names the laity as called to the seventh mansions. This express inclusion occurs when Teresa is describing the exemplary virtues of the faithful laity. "There are many such souls in the world", she remarks. Of their

mode of life she says that "this is certainly a desirable state and there seems no reason why they should be denied entrance into the very last of the mansions; nor will the Lord deny them this if they desire it, for their disposition is such that He will grant them *any* favour".[19] This passage will surprise only those who hold a two-tiered theory of holiness. No less than in three ways does the saint propound the universal call: (a) there is no reason why virtuous married folk should be denied the transforming union, which of course is "the very last of the mansions"; (b) the Lord will not deny this highest prayer, if they are determined to pursue it; and (c) indeed, He will grant to those who are completely generous "any favor". In her diverse expressions St. Teresa is thinking in terms of what we have called de iure, that is, what ought to be in the normal course of things, what God wants, what is given when conditions are fulfilled.

The best of our teresian and sanjuanist scholars do not hesitate in expressing St. Teresa's conviction about the universal call. "There is no doubt whatever", declares E. Allison Peers,

> that she considered mystical experience to be within the reach of all her daughters: we find this conviction enunciated in the nineteenth chapter of the *Way of Perfection* and repeated so frequently in the *Interior Castle* that it is needless to give references. . . . She evidently believes that, generally speaking, infused contemplation is accessible to any Christian who has the resolution to do all that in him lies towards obtaining it.[20]

Kavanaugh and Rodriguez, in their recent introduction to St. Teresa's autobiography, are of the same mind. Speaking of the saint's conviction that His Majesty is reckless, prodigal, lavish and without any seeming limits to the favors of prayer He bestows and that this divine attitude reaches out to every soul, they state that "she is certain that everyone is called to the summit of the mountain where only the glory of God dwells, that God is keeping watch, waiting for the hour to give".[21]

So much for St. Teresa's clear, express and repeated teaching that all men and women are called to an infused immersion in the indwelling Trinity, an immersion that deepens into the transforming union. There remains for us to take account of another kind of evidence that, while indirect, is nonetheless cogent. As she discusses each development in the last four mansions, the saint is at pains to point out how deepening communion brings along with it a greater sanctity, a sanctity not possible to one who lacks the passive purifications that infused prayer itself effects. She makes this point not simply with general statements but also with a great number of specific examples. The idea is part and parcel of the whole teresian corpus: prayer and life interpenetrate. They so influence each other that without infused prayer it is impossible to achieve the holiness to which the Gospel calls everyone.

In the fourth mansions, says Teresa, "the virtues grow incomparably better than in the previous degree of prayer. . . . In arriving here it [the soul] begins soon to lose its craving for earthly things—and little wonder!"[22] One's commitment to prayer becomes robust and enduring . . . servile fear is cast out, and a more mature trusting reverence takes its place . . . one's love of God has much less self-interest . . . and there arises a healthy inclination to solitude with God.[23] What St. Teresa calls an inner dilation, a freedom, takes place within the person, and the former dread of hardships is largely assuaged. Through the gift of growing prayer one gets to know far better the greatness and goodness of God, and hence likewise there springs up a realistic perception of one's own poverty. When the person tastes the divine goodness, "he sees that earthly things are mere refuse; so, little by little, he withdraws from them and in this way becomes more and more his own master". By way of summation the saint points out that one is strengthened in all the virtues and will continue to grow in them unless there is deliberate neglect in giving God everything.[24]

If all this growth results from the beginnings of infused prayer, we rightly expect that still more issues from the prayer of union. In the fifth mansions this continuing transformation is intensified: one is consumed with the desire to praise God . . . would be delighted to die a thousand deaths for Him . . . longs to suffer great trials for the kingdom . . . has vehement desires for penance and solitude . . . becomes so detached from all selfish clingings that one feels a stranger to things of earth . . . enjoys a great conformity to the divine will and experiences a great grief that its Lord is so offended and little esteemed in this world.[25]

That this remarkable transformation continues and intensifies in the sixth and seventh mansions the reader can easily verify by a review of these developments. Anyone who has worked at taking the Gospel seriously knows from experience that extended laboring over the years just cannot produce the sanctity of which we are speaking here. Yet we are all called to perfect holiness, say both the New Testament and Vatican II. The conclusion cannot be evaded: we are all therefore called to the heights of prayer that alone make this heroic virtue possible.

ST. JOHN OF THE CROSS

Whether our two Carmelites ever compared notes on the question we have under discussion I do not know. What is certain is that they were of one mind in their answers. There is even a close similarity in the general pattern they follow. We find one text in each writer that appears to deny the universal call, but it is overwhelmed by an avalanche of other passages that make a final affirmation unmistakable and unhesitating. This similarity in general pattern and in doctrine does not, however, render our consideration of John's teaching superfluous or otiose, for he adds to Teresa's treatment and likewise has his own vigorous ways of thought and expression.

Though the sanjuanist problem passage is not formidable, we should touch upon it lest the reader, when later meeting it, may think we have concealed an unwelcome bit of evidence. In Book One of the *Dark Night* the saint writes of "those who do not walk the road of contemplation". Though God brings them partially into the first night of infused prayer, He does not do it "in order to lead them to the life of the spirit, which is contemplation", for He does not bring to contemplation even half of those who lead a spiritual life. "Why? He best knows."[26] What are we to think of this text? First of all, it is important to note that John is speaking of the factual question, not of what ought to be. The passage therefore is irrelevant to the universal call. Second, as to why God de facto brings only a small number into advanced prayer, John declines to answer here. We shall see, however, that he does give clear explanations elsewhere in his writings. Third, in this passage the saint is speaking of the exceptions: "Because of their weakness they cannot be weaned all at once", he states. Fourth, in this very section he implies the universal call when remarking of the weak ones that "if they are to advance, they will ever enter further into the purgation [which is itself effected by deepening infused prayer]". Hence, we are driven to conclude that John is not at all discussing the de iure question, for he has in mind cases in which something is lacking on the human level. God does not ordinarily prevent us from placing obstacles to His gifts. We may, then, direct our attention to the ways in which St. John of the Cross again and again teaches that all of us are called to the summit of the mountain.

1. We begin with a principle so basic that a thoroughgoing theist cannot logically deny it: the God of revelation gives completely whatever He gives. Being infinitely good, the Lord gives even himself, and that with no limits on His part at all. One who knows something of the self-revealing God cannot imagine His being otherwise. "The Father

of lights [James 1:17]", says John, "is not closefisted but diffuses Himself abundantly, as the sun does its rays, without being a respecter of persons [Acts 10:34], wherever there is room."[27] This imagery is striking: it would be easier for the sun to refuse to shine on one square foot of land while illuminating the next one than for God to refuse to one person what He is ready to give to another. In the context the saint is speaking of the loftiest infused contemplation, and he is saying that the Lord respects no person when He offers this gift. It is available *wherever there is room,* that is, whenever one is purified. The only condition is readiness, "room".

2. The saint's second approach is ubiquitous. In his assumptions, his manner, his mode of reasoning, St. John of the Cross never supposes that what he says is true only of a small elite. On the contrary, he invariably takes it for granted that his teaching is directed to all states of life. The only qualification he makes is that he writes for generous people, only for those who want to love God with their whole heart, mind and will. John therefore habitually expresses his teaching in all-inclusive terms. One example among hundreds: "The love of God in the pure and simple soul is almost continually in act."[28] Actual, continual love is found in the transforming union, and John is stating that wherever there is a "pure and simple soul", a fully prepared man or woman, there is the transforming union. We find no least suggestion that certain pure and simple people are excluded.

3. While the saint states that his main intention (not his only one) in writing the *Ascent* was to address his own friars and nuns, "since they are the ones who asked me to write this work", yet he explicitly avers that his principles apply to everyone who is determined to reach the heights: "Everyone who reads this book will in some way discover the road that he is walking along, and the one he ought to follow if he wants to reach the summit of the mount."[29] It goes without saying that John taught these same principles to the many laymen and laywomen who sought his guidance on an individual basis. Indeed, he expressly says that all these people should desire the spiritual espousals: "Let each soul petition that He [the Holy Spirit] breathe through her garden that the divine fragrance might flow."[30] While we do not ask for the gift of levitation or the stigmata (they are not meant for all), we do well to seek what is in the normal scope of the divine plan, that to which the grace life entitles us, that to which all are called.

4. The fourth way in which St. John of the Cross makes his point relates contemplation to perfect holiness: the latter cannot be had without the former. Indeed, it is no oversimplification to say that the chief reason ordinarily devout people do not become saintly is that they lack

a deep prayer life. There is a vast difference between conventional virtue and heroic holiness, and it is only when God has taken over one's
inner life completely that one passes from the first to the second. Despite
our best and most persevering efforts to eradicate our faults, no one
of us working alone can get rid of them completely. Hence, God must
intervene if we are to become perfect as the heavenly Father is perfect
and to love Him with a whole heart. The Lord effects this full purification by the two passive nights of sense and spirit, both of which are
mystical and contemplative:

> Until a soul is placed by God in the passive purgation of that dark night,
> which we shall soon explain, it cannot purify itself completely from these
> imperfections nor from the others. But a person should insofar as pos-
> sible strive to do his part in purifying and perfecting himself. . . . No
> matter how much an individual does through his own efforts, he can-
> not actively purify himself enough to be disposed in the least degree
> for the divine union of the perfection of love. God must take over and
> purge him in that fire that is dark for him.[31]

This dark fire of contemplation brings about a new authentic self-
knowledge that begets a humility up to now unattainable . . . a new
knowing of the majesty and grandeur of God that discursive prayer
did not yield . . . a limpid understanding of truth . . . a seeing that others
are better than oneself (as St. Paul says we should in Phil 2:3) . . . a new
disinclination to judge others or even to watch anyone else's conduct . . .
a willingness to be taught by others and a desire to obey anyone at
all, even a subordinate . . . a habitual remembrance of God . . . a purification of motivation in one's occupations . . . a gentleness in dealing with God, with oneself and with others . . . a purer love for God
and a keener knowledge of Him . . . a new freedom from the world,
the flesh and the devil along with a quenching of concupiscences.[32]

We do not need much experience in the spiritual life to discover that
active prayer in the human mode does not, and cannot, produce this
level of growth and perfection of love. Because infused prayer is indispensable for attaining this, it must be open to all, meant for all.[33]

5. The sanjuanist organic view of the whole of prayer development
is still another way in which the saint teaches the universal call. For
him, as for St. Teresa, God gives the beginnings of infused communion precisely that we may grow to its fullness. No living seed in nature
is meant to achieve a truncated existence. Acorns are "called" to become
oak trees and tadpoles to become frogs and babies to grow to adulthood.
So also in supernature we are to achieve maturity.[34] If a person remains faithful in response to "lowly favors" from God, "the Lord will

not cease raising him degree by degree until he reaches the divine union and transformation". If we react well to the first morsels of nourishment, God bestows an abundant and much higher quality of food, and thus "if the individual is victorious over the devil in the first degree, he will pass on to the second; and if so in the second, he will go to the third; and likewise through all the seven mansions".[35] This same orientation John sums up when he states that God places people in the state of contemplation "so that by passing through this state they might reach that of the perfect, which is the divine union of the soul with God".[36] In all this we should notice that the saint is speaking of what ought to be, the de iure, the divine intention.

6. Like St. Teresa, St. John of the Cross makes explicit statements to the effect that all of us are called to the summit and should desire it as "the one thing necessary". In two of the most sublime pages in all of literature John writes of a trinitarian prayer so lofty that "a mortal tongue finds it indescribable". Yet he does try to say something of it: "The soul united and transformed in God breathes out in God to God the very divine spiration which God — she being transformed in Him — breathes out in Himself to her." Almost beside himself with the splendor of this consummate communion, John bursts forth with the exclamation, "O souls, created for these grandeurs and called to them! What are you doing? How are you spending your time?"[37] The saint could hardly be more explicit about the call to the pinnacle of prayer. Human beings ("souls") are created for these grandeurs; they are our raison d'être. Moreover, in the very last lines of the *Canticle* John breaks into the prayerful petition that all Christians in every vocation, that is, all who invoke the name of Jesus, may attain the spiritual marriage of earth and its fulfillment in heaven: "May the most sweet Jesus, Bridegroom of faithful souls, be pleased to bring all who invoke His name to this glorious marriage."[38]

7. When he comes to explain why people do not reach the summit de facto, St. John of the Cross, as did St. Teresa, points a finger to the human level, not to the divine intention. When we fail to advance in prayer, he writes, "What is lacking is not that You, O my God, desire to grant us favors again, but that we make use of them for Your service alone and thus oblige You to grant them to us continually."[39] In the saint's view, if we do our part God must give the fullness of prayer; He is "obliged" to give it, so much is it part of His universal plan and will. John does allow that lack of competent spiritual direction can also explain one's failure to grow. While it is true that often people do not advance because they refuse to be purified, it is also true that sometimes they "are without suitable and alert directors who will show them the

way to the summit".[40] What the saint does not allow is the popular explanation that would excuse a lack of progress by arguing that not all are called to the heights. John will have none of this rationalizing:

> Here it ought to be pointed out why there are so few who reach this high state of perfect union with God. It should be known that the reason is not because God wishes that there be only a few of these spirits so elevated; He would rather want all to be perfect, but He finds few vessels that will endure so lofty and sublime a work.[41]

John's mind is Jesus' mind.

THE TRADITION

When our two Carmelites invited everyone to the loftiest contemplation, they were teaching nothing new. No doubt they have brilliantly spelled out the details of what they knew by their immersion in the divine word and by their faithful experience, but actually they were merely affirming the Tradition even while they were developing it. Scripture and the worshipping/teaching Church have been proclaiming the same undiluted message for centuries.

St. Bernard of Clairvaux, that gifted luminary of medieval monasticism, may serve as an example of what I mean. This celebrated mystic and activist, theologian and doctor, took it for granted that every one of us should aspire to the loftiest contemplation. Speaking of a type of prayer surpassing "any others there might be" and standing "at a point where all the others culminate", Bernard declares that

> only a touch of the Spirit can inspire a song like this, and only personal experience can unfold its meaning. Let those who are versed in the mystery revel in it; let all others burn with desire rather to attain to this experience than merely to learn about it.[42]

In another passage Bernard states that absolutely every person, no matter how "enmeshed in vice, ensnared by the allurements of pleasure, a captive in exile . . . fixed in mire . . . distracted by business, afflicted with sorrow . . . and counted with those who go down into hell—every soul, I say, standing thus under condemnation and without hope, has the power to turn and find it can not only breathe the fresh air of the hope of pardon and mercy, but also dare to aspire to the nuptials of the Word."[43] In the context, Bernard is writing of the nuptials of earth, a perfect love for God, an entire immersion in Him. Not surprisingly, he is commenting on what he finds in Scripture.

The Church's liturgical worship and her teaching Tradition are both rooted in the biblical message. While we may not read into this inspired message our own preconceived theories, we may not either neglect or evade its proclamation on the plea that the sacred writers used their own thought patterns and their own terminology. While we do not find in Scripture terms like infused contemplation and mysticism, we surely do find the realities expressed by these modern words. We likewise find that biblical writers consistently take it for granted that there is only one kind of prayer life and development meant for all God's people. The faithful ones of Yahweh in the old dispensation and the members of Christ in the new surely experienced in their prayer something far deeper than a mechanical recitation of words or a discursive reflection on the deeds of the Lord. They experienced a divine intimacy that cannot be produced by human efforts, and this is to say that they received infused prayer.

No biblical writer entertained even a slight inclination toward the idea that the masses of men and women approach God in one way and a small, privileged elite go to Him in another. I cannot think of a single text that makes a distinction on the basis of two tiers of spirituality, two kinds of holiness, two ways of praying—one way superior, the other inferior. What we do find over and over is that deepening prayer is to be the common property of everyone. These biblical men and women found more joy in Yahweh than others could possibly know in their worldliness.[44] They exulted in Him with endless shouts of joy.[45] They rejoiced deeply in their Lord.[46] So profound was their union with God that they delighted in nothing else on earth; their very hearts and flesh pined with love for Him; their joy consisted in nothing other than in being close to Him.[47] Their very flesh tingled with joy in this living God.[48] Even when their prayer was as dark and dry as a desert, they yearned vehemently for Him as their sole salvation.[49] Their pursuit was wholehearted, and they treasured the divine promises in their hearts. The joy they found in the Lord was beyond all wealth, and they were overcome with longing for Him. They clung to Him, contemplated Him all through the night and panted eagerly after Him.[50] Needless to say, one versed in the world of advanced prayer readily recognizes in these outpourings what we now call mystical communion. They are not actively produced sentiments, the results of discursive reflections. Because they occur in the inspired psalter, a book meant for everyone, they are patterns for universal communion with the Lord. Biblical men and women take profound prayer for granted.

This same conviction we find in the New Testament as well. Our prayer is to grow to the point where it becomes continual,[51] a trait that is impossible in discursive or vocal prayers but is found in advanced infused prayer. This communion is a genuine tasting, an experiencing of the Lord Himself.[52] It brings a joy and peace that are continual and beyond understanding or description.[53] Indeed, we are to experience God's power, working in us, and accomplishing infinitely more than we can ask or imagine.[54] The contexts of these pauline passages as well as their wording suggest that the apostle is thinking of a remarkable immersion in God given in this life, not simply one reserved for vision in risen body. Further, he is obviously writing for everyone in the Corinthian and Ephesian communities, most of whom are laypeople. Like all biblical writers, Paul knows nothing of a two-tiered call to holiness.

A brief sketch of the mind of the contemporary Church will fill out our picture of the universal call. Both in her official worship and in her conciliar statements the Church takes it for granted that all the faithful are to possess a profound prayer life that includes advanced contemplation. Over and over in the liturgy we find expressions that can be understood only in terms of a complete maturing in prayer:

> Lord, *fill* our hearts with your love. . . . We pray that in this Eucharist we may find the *fullness* of love and life. . . . *Fill* our hearts with love for you. . . . May the God of infinite goodness *fill* you with joy. . . . Lord, may this lenten observance bring us to the *full* joy of Easter. . . . Lord, *fill* our hearts with your light. . . . *Fill* us with your radiance as you filled the hearts of our fathers. . . . Lord, *fill* us with the power of your love. As we share in the Eucharist, may we come to know *fully* the redemption we have received. . . . *Fill* our minds with your wisdom. . . . *Fill* us with your Spirit. . . . *Fill* us with your gifts.[55]

A hymn for the first week of the psalter in the liturgy of the Hours places on the lips of all the faithful an expression used by the mystics:

> *Laeti bibamus sobriam*
> *ebrietatem Spiritus.*
>
> Let us rejoicingly drink
> the sober inebriation of the Spirit.[56]

If we put together all these liturgical expressions, we find that they make up an ideal definition of infused contemplation, indeed, the very heights of it: a filling with divine love, life, joy, light, power, wisdom and the Holy Spirit Himself. Like God in His revelation, the Church does not speak in fractions. She also knows nothing of a two-tiered spirituality.

We find likewise in the liturgical texts the strong image of burning, an image much favored by the mystics as they attempt to explain the loftiest of infused prayer. In the Liturgy of the Hours, for example, all the faithful are invited to pray for "the spirit of prayer and penance that we may burn [*ardeamus* in the Latin] with the love of God and men".[57] A burning love is infused, not at all the result of discursive reasoning. St John of the Cross therefore describes its beginnings as "enkindlings", and the fullness as fire and flames, both infused. During Mass we prepare for Christ's birth in the Advent liturgy by praying: "May we live as he has taught, ready to welcome him with burning love and faith."[58] The classical hymn the *Stabat Mater* prays:

> *Fac ut ardeat cor meum*
> *In amando Christum Deum.*
>
> Grant that my heart may burn
> In loving Christ our God.[59]

On Pentecost Sunday the Church asks that the fire of the Holy Spirit "burn out all evil from our hearts and make them glow with pure light".[60] These petitions are identical with the sanjuanist doctrine of the infused fire of the Holy Spirit burning away our defects in the mystical nights of advanced contemplation.

Vatican II likewise assumes as obvious that all the faithful are summoned by God to the summit of mystical prayer. This most recent of the councils not only refers to contemplation dozens of times but also applies its message to all the faithful. We may notice four statements in particular. In the *Constitution on Divine Revelation* the council fathers explain how we grow in understanding not only the divine words of revelation but also the very divine realities themselves. This development happens first through contemplation and second through study — and in that order. The text takes it for granted that all are to experience spiritual realities in a mystical manner: "This [growth] happens through the contemplation and study made by believers, who treasure these things in their hearts [cf. Lk 2:19, 51], through the intimate understanding of spiritual things they experience."[61] This language is clearly mystical, and it is indiscriminately applied to everyone in the Church.

Our second passage also is couched in mystical terms that refer to all the faithful:

The liturgy in its turn inspires the faithful to become "of one heart in love" when they have tasted to their full of the paschal mysteries; it prays that "they may grasp by deed what they hold by creed." The renewal

of the Eucharist of the covenant between the Lord and man draws the
faithful into the compelling love of Christ and sets them afire.[62]

"Tasting fully" of the divine mysteries can, of course, refer only to the
summit of prayer, for these are the very words mystics use to speak
of the deepest communion with the Trinity indwelling. The council
fathers are therefore assuming that this normal participation in the
eucharistic liturgy is accessible to everyone. "Grasping by deed" and
being "set afire" are expressions that bespeak a mystical encounter with
God as well.

The Constitution on the Church tells us that priests, all priests, are to
"abound in contemplation", to the joy of God's people.[63] When mystical
theologians use the word contemplation, they normally mean infused
prayer. If they are thinking of something less (like gazing upon a sunset
or a simple reflection on some Gospel truth), they add a qualifying
word such as acquired. Hence, the council fathers are making the point
that each and every priest is to have a profound prayer life, a life of
"abounding" contemplation. If this is true of priests, it is true of everyone
else, for no theologian makes distinctions along vocational lines in the
discussion of the call to mystical prayer.

Our final conciliar text deals with active religious. Concerning contemplation and asceticism in mission territories, Vatican II observes
that "working to plant the Church, and thoroughly enriched with the
treasures of mysticism adorning the Church's religious tradition, religious communities should strive to give expression to these treasures
and to hand them on".[64] Once again there is no least hint that a "thorough mysticism" is the possession of a small elite only. On the contrary, it is assumed that all should have it, all are to be enriched by
it. The new code of canon law takes it for granted that all religious
are called to lofty prayer when it uneqivocally states that "the contemplation of divine things and an assiduous union with God in prayer
is the first and principal duty of all religious".[65] The chief reason for
embracing the three evangelical counsels is not on the horizontal level,
not apostolic activity, not in being relevant to the world. It is being
immersed profoundly in God. Even more: when it comes to the apostolate of active institutes, the first obligation is not work to be done;
it is the witness to sanctity achieved through prayer and penance. "The
apostolate of all religious consists first of all in the testimony of their
consecrated life, which [testimony] they are bound to foster by prayer
and penance."[66] It would be difficult to put the matter more forcefully.
The teaching of Ss. Teresa of Jesus and John of the Cross is, as always,
in complete accord with the inspired word and with the mind of the
Church to whom the word has been committed.

CHAPTER TWELVE

MISCELLANEOUS MATTERS

Our modern mind does not welcome frequent digressions in speech or in writing. A wandering stream of thought rubs our sense of logic and continuity the wrong way. An exception to our preferences seems appropriate in the case of St. Teresa of Jesus, however. Though this woman had not the least formal literary training, she has become probably the most widely read of all writers in the Spanish tongue, regardless of her habit of frequent digressions. Teresa was fully aware of her literary wanderings, and she expressly discussed them. I concur with her view that they were not wasted. If the saint had not strayed often from her immediate subject, we would be much the poorer, for in expounding ideas just as they popped into her mind, she left us a rich legacy of insights about prayer and life that would otherwise have been lost.

Still, her wanderings do create some problems. The chief, perhaps, is that the unwary reader may read Teresa's thoughts on some topic in one passage and then assume her mind is adequately known. Not so. Avoiding this pitfall is in fact one of the main purposes for providing a synthesis by means of this volume. The foundress will sometimes touch upon a given subject in two or perhaps ten different places, and one cannot assume that a partial exposure gives a sufficient grasp of her balanced view.

In this chapter we consider a number of significant prayer questions that do not easily fit into a particular place in the plan of the teresian mansions.

THE HUMANITY OF CHRIST AND ADVANCED PRAYER

For centuries theologians and spiritual writers (for example, Ss. Augustine and Gregory of Nyssa in the patristic age) have uniformly said that in advanced contemplation one leaves aside images, concepts, ideas and words in favor of resting in unintelligible darkness. In this study we also have devoted considerable attention to the *nada* and darkness so stressed by St. John of the Cross and seconded by St. Teresa herself. We must now ask questions of the latter. What then becomes of the humanity of Jesus? Is there no need for the incarnate Word as one grows out of discursive meditation? Does a time come in the spiritual life when one may go to the Father without the Word made flesh?

St. Teresa not only read of this problem in the writers of her day; she felt it in her very person. On the one hand she was personally unable to excite much imagination when it came to prayer. "God didn't give me talent for discursive thought", she says, "or for a profitable use of the imagination. In fact, my imagination is so dull that I never succeeded even to think about and represent in my mind—as hard as I tried—the humanity of the Lord."[1] On the other hand she seems to contradict herself in stating that devotion to the sacred humanity never seemed to impede her contemplation. In the same work, her *Life,* she later observes that "I started again to love the most sacred humanity. Prayer began to take shape as an edifice that now had a foundation. . . . [My confessor] told me . . . that I should always begin prayer with an event from the Passion, but that if afterward the Lord should carry away the spirit I ought not resist Him but let His Majesty bear it away—and not strive to do so myself."[2] If we had only these statements to go by, we might have a problem in reconciling them, but happily we have more.

Teresa expressly adverts to the common teaching regarding this problem. It was said, she notes, that even though infused prayer cannot be acquired, one can help it along by lifting the mind above all created things. These writers strongly urged people to rid themselves of all corporeal images as they advance in prayer, since these images, even when they refer to the humanity of Christ, become impediments to the loftiest contemplation. Alleged to be in support of their view was the statement of Jesus that it was expedient for the apostles for Him to leave them, because if He did not go, the Holy Spirit would not come to them.[3] The saint acknowledged some validity to this line of thought, but she could not and did not accept it as a complete account of the right relationship between imageless prayer and the Incarnation. "This [view of the writers]", she said, "is good, it seems to me, sometimes; but to withdraw completely from Christ or that this divine Body be counted in a balance with our own miseries or with all creation, I cannot endure."[4] She did not wish to contradict these theologians, for they were, in her terminology, both "learned and spiritual", but she found that their advice would have been detrimental to her own progress. "If I should have kept to that practice," she wrote, "I believe I would never have arrived at where I am now because in my opinion the practice is a mistaken one."[5] In *Interior Castle* she remarked that some disagreed with her, but she did not back away from the teaching we find in her autobiography: "Some souls also imagine that they cannot dwell upon the Passion. . . . I cannot conceive what they are thinking of; for, though angelic spirits, freed from everything corporeal, may remain permanently enkindled in love, this is not possible for those of us who live in this mortal body. . . . The last thing we should do is to withdraw of set purpose from our greatest help and blessing, which is the most sacred Humanity of Our Lord Jesus Christ." She tells her readers in no uncertain terms that "I can assure them that they will not enter these last two Mansions [six and seven]" if they set Him aside.[6] For Teresa, therefore, bypassing the sacred humanity is one reason so few get beyond the prayer of union—they are trying to get to the Father without the Son.

How does the saint solve the problem she has posed? Quite simply. It is true that many people cannot meditate with "prolonged reasoning", that is, with detailed reflecting on particular points, but it is not true that they cannot dwell simply on a mystery, especially a mystery of the incarnate Word. She astutely remarks that all of us recall these mysteries to mind, "especially when they are being celebrated by the Catholic Church . . . they are living sparks".[7] The saint is saying that, yes, many of us cannot engage in detailed reasoning even about the sacred humanity and His mysteries, but all of us can begin prayer with a simple recalling of Him—for no one can go to the Father except through Him.[8] Then when the Father "suspends the faculties", we let Him do so gladly. But we do not take the initiative by deliberately setting aside the thought of the Word incarnate.[9]

With this distinction St. Teresa retains and reconciles two truths, that of authentic incarnational theology and that of the experience of advanced prayer. She does this with a skill born not so much of logical analysis as from her solid sense of supernatural reality. She simply cannot see how Jesus' humanity could be an impediment to prayer growth, how it could be anything but a great help and blessing.[10] She goes on to say that except for the seventh mansions (where there may be a rare exception), all through life one must remain at times somewhat active in prayer, that is, "when the fire is not kindled in the will".[11] This "somewhat active" does not mean detailed reasoning, for, in infused contemplation, intellectualizing and deducing can be major obstacles to deepening communion.[12]

Teresa expresses at some length several reasons why one is never to leave the incarnate Word aside even in exalted communion. These we may summarize briefly: (1) Only the proud and stupid would not feel greatly enriched at the foot of the Cross, the source of all blessings. (2) A person lacks humility who wants imageless prayer before

God gives it. (3) Constantly gazing on Jesus in His Passion gives one the example and the strength to "endure all things"—and without generous suffering there is no advancement in prayer. (4) She herself experienced the great benefits of this approach in her own contemplation and life. (5) "The Lord told it [this truth about the place of His sacred humanity] to me." (6) St. Paul himself always had the name of Jesus on his lips and kept Him close to heart—and Paul was a lofty mystic as well as a practical man of action. (7) Contemplative saints have done the same. Teresa mentions explicitly Francis of Assisi, Anthony of Padua, Bernard of Clairvaux and Catherine of Siena. (8) There is an angelism implicit in the opposite approach, for the person who sets aside the sacred humanity "is left floating in the air, as they say; it seems it has no support no matter how much it may think it is full of God. It is an important thing that while we are living and are human we have human support. . . . We are not angels but we have a body. To desire to be angels while we are on earth—and as much on earth as I was—is foolishness."[13]

Teresa concludes that if one thinks himself so spiritual that he is always enjoying a delight at prayer and does not need even a simple active gaze, he is quite mistaken.[14] She summarizes her overall view in one short paragraph:

> This practice of turning aside from corporeal things must be good, certainly, since such spiritual persons advise it. But, in my opinion, the soul should be very advanced because until then it is clear that the Creator must be sought through creatures. Everything depends on the favor the Lord grants to each soul; this is not what I'm concerned with. What I wanted to explain was that the most sacred humanity of Christ must not be counted in a balance with other corporeal things.[15]

"EMPTY" PRAYER

Even though St. Teresa does not use the sanjuanist terminology of the dark night, she knows the reality, and she deals with it in her writings. We shall consider in her own thought patterns what she has to say about prayer in the void, that is, prayer that appears empty, dry, unsatisfying, fruitless. Because most of what the saint has to say on this point supposes generosity in the reader, we shall take it for granted that we are not dealing here with the real emptiness that is born of mediocrity. It should be obvious on a moment's reflection that a person who is deliberately holding back with God cannot be intimate with Him. Even on the merely human level, depth without generosity is impossible.

In the early stages of prayer life (Teresa is writing about the second mansions) one must not even think of "spiritual favors", for that is to build on sand; the edifice will collapse. Rather, what the beginner especially needs to do is to get on with solid virtue and generous suffering, for "it rains manna" later.[16] The divine downpour can occur only when the way is cleared by the unspectacular practice of self-denial and obedience and humility and patience. People who expect fine feelings at prayer with no previous purification do not understand interpersonal intimacy, human or divine. "Oh, humility, humility!" exclaims the saint. "I do not know why I have this temptation, but whenever I hear people making so much of their times of aridity, I cannot help thinking that they are somewhat lacking in it."[17]

Holiness does not consist in delights at prayer but in concretely shown love for God and neighbor.[18] In saying this Teresa is making the same point St. Paul made when he told the Corinthians that no matter what their talents and other gifts may be, if they have no love, they are nothing but cymbals clashing.[19] When God does not give the feelings of devotion even to generous people, they should not be in the least upset but should rather merely conclude that this emotional dimension is not presently necessary. Dryness at prayer is no fault, whereas a lack of determination to live the Gospel generously surely is.[20]

When and for how long may we expect to encounter aridity in contemplative prayer? The saint's answer to this question may come as a surprise. These periods of apparent emptiness occur not only in discursive meditation, not only in the beginnings of infused prayer, but even after one has grown into the advanced stages of the sixth mansions. Periods of desolation can come "during which the soul feels as if it has never known God and never will know Him". The person so afflicted offends God in no deliberate way "and would not do so for anything upon earth, yet this grace is buried so deeply that the soul seems not to feel the smallest spark of any love for God".[21] Despite the clarity of this teaching, almost no one expects to encounter this emptiness once deep union has been previously experienced. Most people do not understand their continuing need for purification, and they therefore conclude that something is gravely amiss. They are especially alarmed when this dryness lasts for a week or two, even though the saint speaks of her period of aridity perduring for about twenty years.[22] She goes so far as to remark that the faithful person is determined to persevere in prayer "even though this dryness may last for his whole life . . . [for] the time will come when the Lord will repay him all at once".[23]

St. Teresa's optimism about empty prayer is not unfounded — the problem occurs for a purpose, and much good can come from it. She writes to her brother, Lorenzo, that "sometimes the ability to pray is taken from us by the mercy of God; and, for many reasons, which I have not time to tell you, I would say that it is almost as great a mercy when He takes it away as when He gives it in abundant measure".[24] A startling statement for those who do not understand the inner workings of deep communion. Though the saint does not relate her reasons in this letter, we can find elsewhere what she probably had in mind. One divine mercy shown in arid prayer is that the Spouse "disregards" our yearnings that they may become deeper still.[25] Because God forces Himself on no one, He gives deepening prayer according as we desire it and are determined so to live that He can give it. Desolation in prayer sharpens the yearning in an earnest person, and this can only be a blessing, for the Lord fills the hungry with good things. So sang the maiden who was given the deepest prayer ever accorded to a human person.

A second reason is that fidelity in the midst of aridity proves that we are seeking God and not merely our own satisfaction. Difficult prayer distinguishes the spiritually mature from the immature.

Third, dryness in devotion offers a vivid experience of our ineptness, our finitude. We learn concretely what we may have thus far understood only in theory, namely, that without the Lord we can do nothing at all. Thus we are grounded in a realistic humility so that later favors will not puff us up.[26]

Fourth, when one remains faithful despite desolation, the theological virtues are deepened, since, being stripped of secondary supports, they are now operating purely from their primary motives. At times of aridity one clings to the Trinity not because other people do, not because it is comforting, not out of mere habit, but because Father, Son and Spirit are purest truth, goodness and love. Since the whole spiritual life revolves around faith, hope and charity, this person is advancing rapidly, even though feelings may be as absent as moisture on desert sand.

Finally, empty prayer is valuable, indeed indispensable, because in it and by it many imperfections are burned away: impatience, worldly inclinations, vanities, laxness. This we have explained in our discussion of the sanjuanist nights of sense and spirit.

What does St. Teresa advise for one in the midst of this desert? To begin with, we should not be worried about the condition and should not fret about it. Nor should we seek a return of consoling prayer. Few follow this advice—mostly, it would seem, because they have great difficulty believing what Teresa and John say about arid prayer. The former goes so far as to say that being unconcerned at this time of desolation is a sign that one has come a long way.[27]

The saint's second bit of advice must be read carefully, lest she be misunderstood. For those who, like herself, cannot meditate discursively, she recommends a judicious use of a book:

> Reading is very helpful for recollection and serves as a necessary substitute — even though little may be read — for anyone who is unable to practice mental prayer. . . . In all those years, except for the time after Communion, I never dared to begin prayer without a book . . . . [Dryness] was always felt when I was without a book. Then my soul was thrown into confusion and my thoughts ran wild. With a book I began to collect them, and my soul was drawn to recollection. And many times just opening the book was enough; at other times I read a little, and at others a great deal, according to the favor the Lord granted me.[28]

The saint is not recommending that we turn contemplative prayer into periods of spiritual reading. She is speaking of times of severe aridity when no contact with God is possible, not even a yearning for Him. She is also careful to follow the Lord's lead: "According to the favor the Lord granted me".

Akin to dryness is a natural restlessness, a being fidgety and ill at ease. This problem did not escape the foundress' attention, and she had some advice for it. Writing to Don Teutonio, who had complained of his restiveness during prayer, she advised him to

> take no notice of that feeling you get of wanting to leave off in the middle of your prayer, but praise the Lord for the desire you have to pray. . . . Try occasionally, when you find yourself oppressed in that way, to go to some place where you can see the sky, and walk up and down a little: doing that will not interfere with your prayer . . . it is essential that the soul be led gently.[29]

DISTRACTIONS

Mental wanderings are perhaps the least understood of problems that occur among people seeking the Lord. Quite universally distractions either during discursive meditation or infused contemplation are interpreted as sure signs that something is amiss, that the person is at fault, that the prayer is worthless. The attitude and advice of our two Carmelites about this problem are poles apart from this general persuasion.

Here we should observe that St. Teresa knew of the matter both from her own firsthand experience and from her direction of others. Her optimistic view did not flow from an ivory tower. The saint observed that some minds are as unruly as horses not yet broken in (the image reflects her girlhood love for horseback riding). They are "never still",

and she feels "very sorry for them". So discouraging is the struggle
with distractions that after a while many people give up through sheer
weariness.[30] The saint frequently mentions her own overactive mind
and the havoc it wreaked in her prayer life. She experienced at times
a great distaste for prayer itself:

> Very often, for some years, I was more anxious that the hour I had deter-
> mined to spend in prayer be over than I was to remain there, and more
> anxious to listen for the striking of the clock than to attend to other
> good things. And I don't know what heavy penance could have come
> to mind that frequently I would not have gladly undertaken rather than
> recollect myself in the practice of prayer. It is certain that so unbearable
> was the force used by the devil, or coming from my wretched habits,
> to prevent me from going to prayer, and so unbearable the sadness I
> felt on entering the oratory, that I had to muster up all my courage (and
> they say I have no small amount of that, and it is observed that God
> has given more me than women usually have, but I have made poor use
> of it) in order to force myself; and in the end the Lord helped me.[31]

The saint's distractions occurred not only in the beginnings of infused prayer but even later when she had advanced a great deal. In
one of her testimonies she tells how

> on the vigil of St. Lawrence, just after receiving Communion, my mental
> faculties were so scattered and distracted I couldn't help myself, and I
> began to envy those who live in deserts and to think that since they
> don't hear or see anything they are free of this wandering of mind. I
> heard: "You are greatly mistaken, daughter; rather, the temptations of
> the devil there are stronger; be patient, for as long as you live, a wander-
> ing mind cannot be avoided."[32]

During the very time that she was receiving raptures, and when writing
a month and a half after her soul was transpierced, St. Teresa speaks
of being distracted after Communion.[33] While most people would expect anything but distractions after experiences so lofty, the saint was
not surprised. As a matter of fact, she notes that infused contemplation is especially subject to mental wanderings, even more than discursive meditation.[34] Because of the multiplicities of images and concepts,
the latter can naturally hold one's attention to some extent, whereas
the very simplicity of imageless, nonconceptual awareness leaves one
especially susceptible to extraneous thoughts. Distractions, therefore,
are not simply to be tolerated but are even expected: they are a necessary
consequence of the woundedness of our human nature as we concretely
experience it.

St. Teresa suffered from a prayer problem that most of us are spared:

tinnitus. While this disease, disturbing noises in one's head, is not rare in our day (several million people in the United States are said to suffer from it), we do not usually find it discussed in books on contemplation. The saint speaks of her affliction in the very course of writing *Interior Castle*. "As I write this," she notes, "the noises in my head are so loud that I am beginning to wonder what is going on in it. . . . My head sounds just as if it were full of brimming rivers . . . and a host of little birds seem to be whistling, not in the ears, but in the upper part of the head." Surprisingly, she adds that "all this physical turmoil is no hindrance either to my prayer or to what I am saying now, but the tranquillity and love in my soul are quite unaffected, and so are its desires and clearness of mind".[35]

Given that Teresa knew well the varying phenomena of the distracted mind, we now ask what advice she gave for all of us who suffer along with her. Her first suggestion is simple: do not fret or worry about distractions. It seems no exaggeration to state that 99 percent of people are anxious, even nettled and irked by the spontaneous wanderings they experience at prayer. A few despair of being able to pray at all. Not Teresa. Throughout her works she consistently takes an optimistic view of the problem. Never does she conclude that even continual distractions render a person hopeless. In her *Life* she emphasizes what she considers "very important", namely, that one ought not to be depressed:

> So I return to the advice—and even if I repeat it many times this doesn't matter—that it is very important that no one be distressed or afflicted over dryness or noisy and distracting thoughts. If a person wishes to gain freedom of spirit and not be always troubled, let him begin by not being frightened by the cross, and he will see how the Lord also helps him carry it and he will gain satisfaction and profit from everything.[36]

Not our customary view of the matter: profit from distractions! To a bishop she writes: "Only today I confessed this fault to Father-Master Fray Domingo, and he told me to take no notice of it. I make the same request of you, for I think the complaint is incurable."[37] In her most mature work the saint rightly puts her finger on the chief reason for the usual pessimistic view: we do not understand our wounded condition, and we expect ourselves to be what we are not. "We suffer terrible trials", she notes, "because we do not understand ourselves; and we worry over what is not bad at all, but good, and think it very wrong." Some people abandon prayer in their discouragement. They do not calmly accept the simple fact that "just as we cannot stop the movement of the heavens, revolving as they do with such speed, so we cannot restrain our thought".[38]

The saint's second suggestion is gentleness, or as the common expression has it, "easy does it". Her reaction to distractions even in the midst of lofty prayer is lighthearted:

> When one of you finds herself in this sublime state of prayer, which, as I have already said, is most markedly supernatural, and the understanding [or, to put it more clearly, the thought] wanders off after the most ridiculous things in the world, she should laugh at it and treat it as the silly thing it is, and remain in her state of quiet.[39]

TENSIONS BETWEEN PRAYER AND WORK

The caption for this section refers to a factual situation, not a theological one. In the nature of things there ought to be neither incompatibility nor conflict between communion with God and the service of neighbor. Like St. Luke in his Gospel and Acts of the Apostles, St. Teresa sees a natural partnership between contemplation and action. For both saints each aspect of human life contributes to the well-being of the other — there ought to be no hint of a clash. A close examination of Luke shows a decided pattern when he writes of prayer and work, a pattern found both in the life of Jesus and in that of His disciples: a person first prays . . . at prayer he receives the Holy Spirit . . . he thus is fitted for fruitful apostolic endeavor. Always this is Luke's order: prayer — Spirit — work (Lk 3:21-23; 4:1-2, 14-15; 6:12-13; Acts 1:14-2:4; 4:31; 6:3-4). One text will serve as an illustration of what we mean by this pattern. When a local Christian community received news of a persecution, Luke remarked that they immediately broke into spontaneous prayer. After summarizing the content of the prayer, he added that "as they prayed, the house where they were assembled rocked; they were all filled with the Holy Spirit and began to proclaim the word of God boldly".[40] If the disciples have their lives ordered properly, Spirit-filled work will flow richly and harmoniously from Spirit-filled communion with God.

St. Teresa is of the same mind. However, the danger is a spotty or partial reading of the saint. We must recall again that Teresa often does not say all she thinks in one place, and one who cites only one text on an issue like the present one will most likely present a caricature of her mind. In this case either prayer or work will seem to be downgraded.

Her first basic principle is that fidelity to work does not hinder communion with God. The one furthers the other. What Luke suggests, Teresa both experienced and taught. In a letter to a religious rector she wrote that

I believe that everything a superior does for the efficient discharge of the duties of his office is so pleasing to God that, when he has occupied himself in that way, He gives him in short time what He would normally give only over long periods of prayer. This, like what I said previously, I also know by experience.[41]

When obedience to one's superior or profit to the neighbor requires it, we must renounce for a time the quiet of prayer. In her graphic manner the saint remarks that "it would be a terrible thing if God were to be telling us [through obedience to a superior] plainly to go about His business in some way and we would not do it but stood looking at Him because that gave us greater pleasure".[42] Even if a superior is thinking only of the community's benefit and not of the individual's welfare, God is disposing and preparing the latter for a growth that Teresa finds "astonishing". There is not only one way in which He benefits us.[43] Solid love is to be found, she says, not "hidden away in corners", but in dealings with others, indeed, "in the midst of occasions of sin".[44]

The saint goes out of her way to insist that she is not here speaking of any kind of work but only of responses to charity and obedience. "If one of these motives is not involved, I do not hesitate to say that solitude is best."[45] She adds that in those who really love God there will always be present the desire for solitude, and in the very course of the work there will be a continual prayerfulness: "We must needs be careful", she writes, "in doing good works, even those of obedience and charity, not to fail to have frequent inward recourse to our God."[46]

An underlying premise explains why work done from charity and obedience furthers prayer and is no hindrance to it: infused contemplation is a pure gift from God and not the automatic result of time or techniques. It flows from faith, hope and love, all given by the Father. The more one conforms his will to the divine will, the deeper are the theological virtues. Teresa is correct, therefore, in her conclusion: "Believe me, it is not length of time spent in prayer that brings a soul benefit: when we spend our time in good works, it is a great help to us and a better and quicker preparation for the enkindling of our love than many hours of meditation."[47]

Yet we must remember that the saint was writing immediately for prayerful women, and she took it for granted that they normally devoted two hours each day to contemplative communion with God. In addition, she presumed that in their solitary work they had their minds and hearts centered on Him insofar as duty permitted. In what we have reported above, Teresa is not speaking about the habitual setting aside of ample time for prayer. She has in mind the exceptions that obedience and charity sometimes place before us. She makes this point explicitly when she observes that prayer time is lent to us and is to be wholly devoted to the Lord: "I say 'wholly', but we must not be considered as taking it back if we should fail to give it Him for a day, or for a few days, because of legitimate occupations or through some indisposition." She adds that her God "is not in the least meticulous; He does not look at trivial details".[48]

St. Teresa well knew that prayer, not work, is primary. Though she did not write a philosophical treatise on the subject, her decisiveness makes clear what she thought. When there was question of professing an ill or disabled novice, an excellent woman, the saint simply wrote to the nuns at Toledo, "I want to have her in my house even if she has to stay in bed all her life long."[49] The intrinsic worth of that novice was, in the foundress' view, far more valuable than the work her illness prevented.

One more item must be added to complete our grasp of the saint's mind: everyone who wishes to reach the transforming union must give up unnecessary cares and occupations. This is true not simply of her enclosed nuns but of any man or woman in any state of life. Speaking in the context of the first mansions about those who are immersed and absorbed in the business and possessions and honors of this world and thus are surrounded by impediments to prayer development, she lays it down that

> everyone who wishes to enter the second Mansions, will be well advised, as far as his state of life permits, to try to put aside all unnecessary affairs and business. For those who hope to reach the principal Mansion, this is so important that unless they begin in this way I do not believe they will ever be able to get there.[50]

DEMONIC INFLUENCES

Faithful as she was to the biblical and Catholic witness to the reality of the personal existence of the lost angels, St. Teresa entertained no cloud of doubt about their influence in human life. Her obedience to revelation was reinforced by her own experiences many times repeated. No one who understands the penetrating intelligence and down-to-earth common sense of this woman will be inclined to dismiss as illusory her vivid, unadorned accounts of satanic encounters. One night, for example, when devils had attacked her, she sprinkled holy water about the room. She then writes that

I saw a great multitude of them go by, as though they were being thrown down a precipice. There are so many times that these cursed creatures torment me, and so little is the fear I now have of them, seeing that they cannot stir unless the Lord allows them, that I would tire your Reverence and tire myself if I told about all these instances. . . . A few times I have seen him in physical form, but many times with no physical form—as for instance in the vision mentioned above in which without seeing any form one knows he is there.[51]

Teresa little fears the demonic not only because Satan cannot exceed the divine permission but also because "whatever these devils do, they cannot, in my opinion, go so far as to inhibit the working of the faculties or to disturb the soul, in the way already described".[52] While demonic influences are entirely possible, we ought not (and the saint does not) to attribute to them our own limitations, selfishness, negligence or blindness.[53]

ASPIRING TO ADVANCED CONTEMPLATION

Because we have already considered the universal call to infused prayer, we will not here repeat the many texts in which both St. Teresa and St. John insist that all men and women in every vocation should hope for and seek the deepest communion with the indwelling Trinity. Our desires for the heights are simply the consistent response to that call. What we do wish to do here is add two corollaries to this aspiration. One is that we ought not to be timorous, fearful midgets regarding the sacrifices needed to grow. Teresa considers that the path to God is a royal road in which the Lord makes everything easy for the person who really loves:

Beyond all natural reason, You make things so possible that You manifest clearly there's no need for anything more than truly to love You and truly to leave all for You, so that You, my Lord, may make everything easy. . . . He who really loves You, my God, walks safely on a broad and royal road. He is far from the precipice. Hardly has he begun to stumble when You, Lord, give him Your hand. One fall is not sufficient for a person to be lost, nor are many, if he loves You and not the things of the world. He journeys in the valley of humility.[54]

Always largehearted, the saint rightly assumes that God Himself is magnanimous, that He does not hold one back from advancing simply because of faults of weakness or partial inadvertance. If one is giving all, he need not worry that at the beginning he does not possess the heroic virtue he reads about in the lives of the saints and sees in a few people far advanced beyond himself. "Let not these souls become anxious", counsels Teresa, "let them hope in the Lord; through their prayer and their doing what they can, His Majesty will bring it about that what they now have in desires they shall possess in deed."[55] Comforting as this is, we should note, however, that for St. Teresa desire does not mean a halfhearted velleity but a sturdy determination. Provided our love is genuine and our will resolute, minor slips are no reason for discouragement. But if we lack determination, we have ample cause to fear an eventual slide into lukewarmness.

THE POSSIBILITY OF MEDIOCRITY AND REGRESSION

In the spiritual life stars can fall from heaven. Magnanimous as St. Teresa is, she is not in the least ambiguous in her warnings that people given to prayer ought not to entertain any illusions about security in grace and continuing progress in contemplative prayer. She said of herself that the hardest trial she had to bear was that she could not know with certainty that she loved God or that her desires were pleasing to Him.[56] While we can have a founded persuasion that we remain in grace, we cannot, short of a revelation, know without the least doubt that we enjoy the divine favor—we work out our salvation with fear and trembling, as St. Paul put it.[57]

The saint, therefore, advised her nuns that no matter how great were the gifts God had given them (and they were indeed great in many cases), they could not be sure of not falling back. For this reason, they were to watch for occasions of sin, and no matter how sublime their contemplation, they were to begin and end every period of prayer with self-examination.[58] Native human weakness remains even after God has given sublime graces. Advanced as she was when she wrote the *Book of Foundations,* Teresa herself could, while under trial, write that

> just as previously everything had seemed easy to me, when I had reflected that it was being done for God's sake, so now temptation began to intensify its hold upon me as if I had never received any favours from Him at all. All I could think of was my own weakness and lack of power.[59]

This saint from Avila is well known for the shrewdness of her insights into human nature, her own and others'. Dealing with this inconstancy of our woundedness, she provides further evidence for her reputation:

Have you never observed this yourselves, sisters? I certainly have: sometimes I think I am extremely detached, and, in fact, when it comes to the test, I am; yet at other times I find I have such attachment to things which the day before I should perhaps have scoffed at that I hardly know myself. At some other time I seem to have so much courage that I should not quail at anything I was asked to do in order to serve God, and, when I am tested, I find that I really can do these things. And then on the next day I discover that I should not have the courage to kill an ant for God's sake if I were to meet any opposition about it. Sometimes it seems not to matter in the least if people complain or speak ill of me, and, when the test comes, I still feel like this—indeed, I even get pleasure from it. And then there come days when a single word distresses me and I long to leave the world altogether, for everything in it seems to weary me. And I am not the only person to be like this, for I have noticed the same thing in many people better than myself, so I know it can happen.[60]

Regression into isolated faults due to weakness is not the only type of reversion possible. A gradual and abiding laxity can creep into a life that began with enthusiasm and generosity, whether in the covenant of marriage or the commitments of priesthood and religious life. For St. Teresa, mediocrity is a deep illness. In this condition of not caring much either about God or about the welfare of one's own soul, the person not only is ill but also enjoys being ill and looks for the illness. Being alive with love, as saints invariably are, Teresa exclaims, "Oh, what a difficult thing I ask You, my true God: that You love someone who doesn't love You, that You open to one who doesn't knock, that You give health to one who likes to be sick and goes about looking for sickness. You say, My Lord, that You come to seek sinners; these, Lord, are real sinners."[61] If the saint seems too hard on the mediocre, one need only read the vigorous condemnations of lukewarmness in Revelation 3:1–6 and 14–22.

Lax people follow their feelings rather than principles, the world rather than the Gospel. They live out their easygoing inclinations with hardly a thought about their merit or demerit. They simply are not concerned about what is more perfect or more pleasing to God.[62] Having their feet in two worlds, they lead an unhappy life, for they cannot find joy in God, and they do not enjoy the world, either.[63] Sometimes the mediocre man or woman exercises an apostolic "zeal", but it lacks fire and effectiveness, of course, and it can be a cover-up for an inner personal poverty.[64] Needless to say, this individual will make no progress in prayer and may end up by dropping a serious Gospel life altogether: choked, as Jesus Himself said, by the cares and pleasures and riches of life and thus hindered from maturing.[65]

ON KEEPING A PRAYER JOURNAL

I have come across only one passage in all Teresa's works in which she mentions what is now popular in many circles, the spiritual life journal. The very manner in which she expresses her opinion of the practice is typical of her personality: clear, concise, definite, no nonsense. Writing to one of her favorite nuns who apparently had broached the question, the saint is blunt:

> It is not only a waste of time; it interferes with the soul's freedom of action; and then, too, it may lead the nuns to imagine all kinds of things. . . . If their experiences are of any substance, they will never forget them; and if they are of a kind that can be forgotten, there is no point in writing them down. It will be sufficient if they tell our Father [Gratian] what they remember of them when they see him. . . . I know what a bad thing it is for them to keep thinking of what they are going to write. . . . Believe me, the best thing for the nuns to do is to praise the Lord Who gives these things, and, as soon as they are over, just let them be.[66]

While we may doubt whether the saint would extend her dismissal to other types of spiritual life journals, it is difficult to rebut successfully her reasons for taking a dim view of the prayer journal. One who has had a deep encounter with God does not need to chronicle it on paper. It is indelible.

SEXUAL FEELINGS AT PRAYER

One of the more surprising and disturbing phenomena that may occur during communion with the Lord is sexual disturbance or arousal. It is "surprising and disturbing" not because the phenomenon is in itself a cause for concern but because most people would never expect that in so holy an occupation there could be sexual repercussions. While they seem not to be common, they do occur. Lorenzo, the saint's married brother who had chosen his sister as spiritual director, had experienced these disturbances, and he asked her for guidance. Her response was typical in its accuracy and decisiveness:

> Pay no attention to those evil feelings which come to you afterwards [after his deep prayer]. I have never suffered from them myself, since God, of His goodness, has always delivered me from such passions, but I think the explanation of them must be that the soul's joy is so keen that it makes itself felt in the body. With God's help it will calm down if you take no notice of it. Several people have discussed this with me.[67]

Even though St. Teresa never had the advantage of studying the philosophy of human nature, her analysis of the phenomenon and her recommended reaction to it are entirely correct. Since the human person is not a cartesian soul dwelling within a body but a single body-soul composite, it is entirely normal that an intense spiritual experience may have bodily repercussions. Blushing from embarrassment and tears of joy or sorrow are other examples of this same basic reality, the profound oneness of the human person. Consequently, to experience sexual stirrings within a completely pure delight in God should be neither a surprise nor a source of worry.

DELIGHT IN PRAYER

Almost everyone considers delight as a valid barometer of progress in contemplative communion with the Lord. Especially do we tend to conclude that, if we are dry and distracted, we are guilty of some fault and are most likely regressing. Since this is not the case, as we have seen above, we may ask what the relevance of delight in prayer may or may not be. St. Teresa draws a sharp distinction between pleasures of earth and those in God. The saint uses language so strong that the worldling is not likely to take her seriously. Yet no one may validly disagree with her without having experienced in prayer what she tasted. Actually, only the saintly may rightly compare pleasures, for no one else has experienced the loftiest, and thus have a standard for discriminating among the lesser. Writing of her own prayer, Teresa remarks that she cannot

> describe what is felt when the Lord gives [me] an understanding of His secrets and grandeurs, the delight that so surpasses all those knowable here on earth; indeed, it rightly makes you abhor the delights of this life, which together are all rubbish. I would find it revolting to have to try to make a comparison between the two delights, even if those of earth were to last forever and those given by the Lord were only a drop of water from the vast overflowing river that is prepared for us.[68]

One would be hard put in trying to express in more vivid language how one reality so far surpasses another. Yet Teresa excels even more. Speaking of an ecstatic union with God, she states that the delight and feeling "are so excessive that if the remembrance of them didn't pass away, all the comparable satisfactions here on earth would ever be nauseating to the soul. As a result, it comes to have little esteem for all the things of the world."[69] The saint's last sentence partially explains why people close to God greatly pity the blindness of the worldling who has no idea of the incomparable enthrallment to be found in union with God.

Teresa likewise distinguishes between the feelings we produce in prayer and the delights given by God. While both are good, the latter are gentle, refreshing, strong, quiet, deeply impressed. The former, as is plainly implied, are not such, and the saint expressly says that they are easily lost "at the first small breeze of persecution".[70] The spiritual feelings we produce arise from "our own nature", whereas the others originate in God. The former are like the satisfaction we derive from numerous human experiences such as acquiring a large property or seeing a dear friend. They may be worthy, but they do not "enlarge the heart" or make one "any the more virtuous".[71]

The saint speaks of differences between degrees or types of spiritual joy both in heaven and on earth, but she does not explain her thought: "These joys of prayer must be like those of heaven. . . . Each one is happy with the place he has, even though there is the greatest difference in heaven between one joy and another. This difference is far more than the difference here below between some spiritual joys and others, which is very great."[72]

About delights in prayer we may add two small bits of teresian advice. First, when a newcomer to the life of prayer begins to receive sense pleasure in it, he ought not to allow himself to be carried away. It comes and it goes, and in any event it is neither perfection nor sanctity.[73] Second, all should realize that, at any time, progress in pursuing God does not consist in enjoying Him more but in doing His will more completely.[74]

CHAPTER THIRTEEN

DISCERNING GROWTH

In most matters of this world we have little difficulty in deciding whether or not we are making progress. A raise in salary is obvious, as indeed so is a cut. Who comes in first, second and third in a foot race is usually clear. The scale tells us precisely whether we are gaining weight or losing it. But in matters of the spirit, gauging our own development is not so plain and simple. This is especially true in the life of contemplative prayer. Almost everyone misjudges what the passive purifications do or do not indicate regarding progress in prayer. It is odd how unreal can be the expectations sincere people entertain as to what their prayer ought to be like or whether they are succeeding in it at all.

As experienced in prayer as he was, St. John of the Cross knew well that "many individuals think they are not praying, when, indeed their prayer is intense. Others place high value on their prayer, while it is little more than nonexistent."[1] Only if we do not reflect on what the saint is saying will we fail to see how strange this situation is: people doing something *intensely* and not even knowing that they are doing it. And there are many in this first group, notes John. Today there are still many. Those in the second group are few, but they do exist: those who are scarcely beginning and yet think they are far advanced. Both mistakes point to one conclusion: most people are unrealistic in their judgments as to whether they are or are not growing in contemplation and consequently in the rest of their spiritual lives as well. They who think the matter simple are probably the most deceived of all.

We turn in this chapter to St. Teresa, for she has scattered throughout her writings the makings of a concise and dependable answer to this problem. We shall synthesize her observations, and, for the sake of clarity, group them under three headings.

A STURDY REALISM

When it comes to the spiritual life, many sincere people assume that good intentions and pious feelings are rather automatic indicators that God has His finger on their enterprise. In recent decades we have heard

countless claims of "listening to the Spirit", as if it were the most obvious thing in the world that one's promptings are truly from the Spirit.
Innocent of the deviance of the human spirit wounded by sin, both
original and actual, they assume with no misgivings that their wishes
and desires and thoughts could really have only one origin, God
Himself. St. Teresa knew better. Repeatedly we find in her works the
acute awareness that an apparently worthwhile experience can have
several possible and diverse causes: divine, merely human, demonic.
She was perceptive in discerning her own spirits, and she by no means
took it for granted that pious ideas originated from God, or that a
disinclination to undertake some task was due to supernatural prudence.
In the latter case she entertained the real possibility that the reluctance
to found a new monastery may have been due to sloth or illness or
old age.[2] So fearful was Teresa that her gifts of lofty prayer may at
times have been illusory that she was able to declare that her other
trials in making the foundations were not "worthy of the least remembrance by comparison".[3] We have here no naïve enthusiast.

The same must be said regarding her visions. Even though through
experience she became expert in noting the traits of authentic communications from God and how genuine visions differ dramatically
from mere imaginations, the saint nonetheless did not assume that her
visions were genuine. Occasionally she would try to doubt them, to
persuade herself that they were not from God. She did not always succeed. Once, on the feast of the Assumption, St. Teresa was given a
vision of our Lady, who appeared to her in extraordinary beauty and
brought to her soul "a state of wonderful glory and happiness" that
left her almost outside herself. Of this experience the saint remarks
that "everything happened in such a way that I could never doubt, no
matter how hard I tried, that the vision was from God".[4] In one of
her accounts written for the inquisitor of Seville in 1576 the saint tells
of how, from the beginning of her religious life, she never thought
about supernatural experiences but only of the Passion of Jesus and
of her own sins. But when visions began to occur "like a lightning flash"
but with no sense characteristics, "she was terrified", and tried desperately to avoid them lest "she be deceived by the devil". To avoid deception, she sought out a number of competent priests for advice, for even
though the fear left her during prayer, she did not want to trust her
own inner persuasions.[5]

St. Teresa was not easily convinced of the supernatural origin of
unusual phenomena even when they occurred in a holy person. She
tells of a Cistercian nun who was becoming famous in her town for
raptures. This nun was virtuous and solid but had become weak through

excessive discipline and fasting. After receiving Communion she would, with genuine devotion, fall to the ground and remain there for eight or nine hours on end. Both she and her companions thought these episodes to be raptures, but Teresa thought otherwise. The saint considered that the nun was wasting her time, "for these fits could not possibly be raptures or anything else but the result of weakness". Hence, Teresa told the nun's director to "forbid her fasting and discipline and provide her with some distraction. She was obedient and did as he said. Soon she became stronger and stopped thinking about raptures."[6] Teresa then gives additional reasons why these experiences were not genuinely ecstatic.

The saint's realism shows itself likewise in her observation that there is a vast difference between thinking holy thoughts and engaging in pious conversations on the one hand and living a virtuous life on the other. "We always have phrases on our lips", she writes, "about wanting nothing, and caring nothing about anything, and we honestly think them to be true, and get so used to repeating them that we come to believe them more and more firmly."[7] We ought not to imagine that we have achieved notable progress simply because we are capable of lofty sentiments. Much better indicators are the signs we shall consider below. But first we should be persuaded that discernment is neither obvious nor easy.

THE DIFFICULTIES OF DISCERNMENT

That our last remark reflects reality may be gathered from the simple fact that the large majority of people assume without question that their inner experiences are sound indicators of progress or decline in prayer. Nor do they usually doubt that their interpretations of these experiences are sound. They assume the matter is clear cut and needs no reflection. Not so St. Teresa. She observed that "people have come to me in great numbers, both men and women, to say nothing of nuns from these houses, and it has been quite clear to me that they often deceive themselves against their will".[8] She includes herself in the strong remark, "O God, what crooked excuses we make and what manifest delusions we harbour!"[9]

Hans Urs von Balthasar has pointed out that "sin obscures sight", and it is for this reason that saints see right through our merely human rationalizations and evaluations. They have been purified sufficiently to penetrate with clear vision both their own former follies and those of the rest of us.

According to St. Teresa we ought not to assume that our impressions at prayer are automatically trustworthy. The saint wanted her nuns to measure their progress far more by the perfection of their obedience than by their felt sentiments in the chapel.

> Do not be troubled because you have no experience of those other kinds of devotion: they are very unreliable. It may be that to some people they come from God, and yet that if they came to you it might be because His Majesty has permitted you to be deceived and deluded by the devil, as He has permitted others.[10]

More sobering still is Teresa's admonition that we do well to entertain a healthy doubt about our very progress in virtue. One day we appear to ourselves invincible, while the next we fall flat on our faces — we are far from what we thought we were.[11] The saint admits that she is not sure herself when her love is spiritual and when it is mingled with merely natural emotions,[12] and she agrees with St. Paul that demonic deceptions are various and many.[13] In her *Book of Foundations* she tells of a woman who reported a vision of our Lady, which Teresa judged on the face of it to have consisted of one or two sensible ideas mingled with a great deal of nonsense. Lest she offend the priest who brought this account to her, the saint avoided a blunt response and instead gave him three guides by which to judge the alleged visions: "I said, therefore, that it would be best for him to wait and see if the prophecies came true, to make enquiries about other effects produced by the vision and find out what kind of life that person was living."[14] Teresa concluded her account with the comment that in the end the priest discovered that the whole matter was foolishness.

SIGNS OF AUTHENTIC PRAYER

Teresian criteria of genuine progress coincide completely with those of the New Testament: "From their fruits you shall know them."[15] The saint's basic principle is solid: "It is by the effects of this prayer and the actions which follow it that the genuineness of the experience must be tested."[16] It is the experience that is tested by the action, not the other way around. Just as Scripture details in many places Jesus' statement "from their fruits you shall know them", so St. Teresa scatters through her written corpus the concrete effects and actions that point to deepening prayer far more accurately than exploring our subjective feelings.

The overall sign is totality, a complete generosity in giving God everything. With this spirit one abhors even a single venial sin; mortal sin is feared "like fire".[17] A lukewarm attitude toward loving one's neighbor, living evangelical poverty or obeying the teaching Church are sure indicators that a person is not advancing in prayer, indeed, is most likely falling back.[18] Concerning obedience as a sign of authenticity, St. Teresa is eloquent:

> Believe me, there is no better way of acquiring this treasure [of loving fire sent from heaven] than to dig and toil in order to get it from this mine of obedience. The more we dig, the more we shall find; and the more we submit to men, and have no other will than that of our superiors, the more completely we shall become masters of our wills and bring them into conformity with the will of God. . . . This is the union which I desire and should like to see in you all: I do not covet for you those delectable kinds of absorption which it is possible to experience and which are given the name of union. They may amount to union if the result of them is what I have described; but if such suspension leaves behind it little obedience, and much self-will, it seems to me that it will be a union with love of self, not with the will of God. May His Majesty grant that I myself may act according to my belief.[19]

The saint mirrors here nothing other than her Master who made obedience to His Church and its leadership the sign of accepting or rejecting the eternal Father Himself.[20] St. Teresa learned this lesson so well that she returns to it in her writings over and over.[21] Obedience is an especially revealing criterion of authenticity for two reasons. On the one hand it ruthlessly empties the humble person of egocentrism. Proud, self-centered people presume to know better than any superior, even those to whom the Holy Spirit has been given to teach and govern in the Church. They are so full of themselves (without, of course, admitting it) that they could not possibly be filled with God. At the same time obedience leaves little room for rationalizing reality to fit our self-will: we either obey this human superior, or we do not. The egocentric individual can often bend a written document to make it mean what he wants it to mean, but he does not easily slide around the Lord's criterion: he who hears you, hears Me; he who rejects you, rejects Me.

A strong desire for God both in the final glory of the beatific vision and through dark faith in solitude on earth is another sign of advancing contemplation. "If anyone advises you to give up your prayer," Teresa says, "take no notice of him. You may be sure he is a false prophet."[22] One of the traits I have repeatedly encountered in men and women who have grown in contemplative prayer is a strong pull toward

healthy solitude. This inclination is not at all toward a neurotic isolation, nor does it arise from a dislike of any kind for human society.
Rather, this solitude is a highly altruistic turning to the supreme Other,
the Other in whom we are united in a deeper way with all our human
sisters and brothers. A moment's reflection makes us realize that a person
profoundly in love desires to be alone with the beloved. So it is in advancing communion with God.

Together with a love for solitude is a desire for suffering with and
for the divine Beloved on His Cross. St. Teresa considers a love for
the Cross as solid and certain evidence that contemplation is not illusory:

> I consider it quite certain that those who attain perfection do not ask
> the Lord to deliver them from trials, temptations, persecutions and con-
> flicts—and that is another sure and striking sign that these favours and
> this contemplation which His Majesty gives them are coming from the
> Spirit of the Lord and are not illusions. For, as I said a little way back,
> perfect souls are in no way repelled by trials, but rather desire them.[23]

One of the specific sufferings comtemplatives seek is humiliation,
the sharing in Jesus' being mocked and treated as a fool in his Passion.
"If they are being led by the Spirit of the Lord, He will grant them
humility, which will lead them to love being despised."[24] The Master
Himself had already said that it is the Father's practice to give His
wisdom to the little ones and to withhold it from the proud and conceited.[25] James proclaimed that God resists the vain but gives boun-
teously to the humble.[26]

A trait allied to humility and indicative of authenticity is openness
to the truth. Genuine people are receptive and docile. They understand
that they are personally fallible, that there is much they need to learn—
especially from an authorized teacher. Vain individuals are quite the
opposite, and this is one reason God leaves them to themselves. Hence,
following the lead of Scripture, St. Teresa proposes docility, teachable-
ness, as a trait of genuine prayer. Egocentrism and the refusal to accept
objective evidence are incompatible with love, the heart of contemplation. Anyone who argues with one's superior or confessor may be sure
that he is on the wrong path, for often it is the path of pride.[27] In contrast, no matter how many fantasies and illusions Satan may attempt
to stir up in humble people, "if they submit to the teaching of the
Church, they need not fear".[28]

Finally, when men and women are strongly and fervently determined
to avoid all sin, they possess "a very clear sign that their contemplation is genuine and that the favours which they receive in prayer are

from God".[29] This criterion Teresa repeats in *Interior Castle* in a similar form: those who endeavor in all possible ways not to offend God and strive always to further the growth of the Church show that they love authentically. Vatican II likewise singles out love for the Church as a sign worthy of special mention. Citing St. Augustine, the council fathers assert that "a man possesses the Holy Spirit to the extent of his love for Christ's Church".[30]

Several general teresian texts bring home to us the solidity of the saint's doctrine on discernment. In a letter to Jerome Gratian she wrote that

> the most potent and acceptable prayer is the prayer that leaves the best effects. . . . I would describe the best effects as those that are followed by actions. . . . If with my prayer there come severe temptations and aridities and tribulations, and these leave me humbler, then I should consider it good prayer. . . . One must not think that a person who is suffering is not praying. He is offering up his suffering, and many a time he is praying much more truly than one who goes away by himself and breaks his head to pieces, and, if he has squeezed out a few tears, thinks that that is prayer.[31]

Writing under obedience and referring to herself in the third person, Teresa had to explain how she advanced in the virtues. This growth calmed her concerns about the authenticity of her prayer, "since it seemed to her that a spirit that left these virtues in her would not be bad. And those with whom she discussed this idea agreed."[32] The same was true of Doña Catalina, for her "humility, obedience and longing to be despised are a clear indication of the genuineness of her desires to serve Our Lord".[33]

When confessors are faced with reports of apparitions, they should, said the foundress, proceed cautiously and "wait for some time to see what results these apparitions produce, and to observe how much humility they leave in the soul and to what extent it is strengthened in virtue". If the experience is of demonic origin, it "will be caught out in a thousand lies".[34]

St. Teresa applies these same principles to distinguishing both in the Church and in the world the true prophets from the false. We are not to believe, she says, everyone who speaks, but only those who model their lives on Christ, that is, those who are humble and unworldly, who "believe firmly in the teaching of our Holy Mother the Roman Church. You may then be quite sure that you are on a very good road."[35]

We reserve for our last text a statement whose closing words are an ideal summation of this entire chapter: "If any one of you receives high favours, let her look within herself and see if they are producing these effects, and, if they are not let her be very fearful, and believe that these consolations are not of God, Who, as I have said, when He visits the soul, always enriches it."[36] Nothing more need be added.

CHAPTER FOURTEEN

LOCUTIONS AND VISIONS

Perhaps the most opportune way to open our discussion of divine communications is to consider the question of whether or not it deserves space in this volume at all. Surely, some people would take the view that in the scientific milieu and widespread literacy of contemporary technological societies, the idea of special divine enlightenments and messages merits at best a patronizing smile, at worst outright ridicule. Even some religiously inclined persons, including a fair percentage of the clergy, give little credence to the proposition that God does communicate with certain common, ordinary individuals. Many people tend to take seriously only what they can see with their own eyes or touch with their own hands. The world of the supernatural — angelic, demonic and divine — does not have much sway in their day-to-day world of business and pleasure and practicalities. They feel that if there is something authentic in the alleged phenomena reported by men and women of advanced prayer, nonetheless they themselves cannot identify with it, for they hear none of these messages and see no visions. Some, of course, flatly deny the very existence of such communications and consequently have no interest in a discussion of what they regard as illusory imaginings of more or less unbalanced enthusiasts.

But there is another group, by no means small in number, who gladly embrace the notion of direct divine communications. Equally citizens of our technological societies and sometimes well educated in their respective secular pursuits, these men and women not only hold to the theoretical possibility that God communes with human beings but also are often enough convinced that He has spoken to them personally or at least that on occasion He sends them an inner light. They readily speak of "listening to the Spirit". Some in this group build their spiritual lives more on alleged apparitions and their own presumed inner illuminations than on the word of the Gospel and the proclamation of the teaching Church.

Within both of these categories, the deniers and the affirmers, there is of course a spectrum of reaction patterns. Among the former we find the small number of atheists who profess no acceptance of anything intangible and also theists who do accept the supernatural but consider it antecedently unlikely (or at least rare) that God would com-

municate with ordinary men and women. Among the affirmers there
are the absurdly credulous who are convinced that they are constantly
privy to divine messages and visions. Others steer clear of these extremes but all the same are not as cautious as they must be in order
to avoid different pitfalls. They are insufficiently sensitive to the dangers
of illuminism, for instance.

While pastoral experience shows that there are not a few men and
women in these two categories, it also indicates that there is a third
large group who are neither sceptical nor credulous. Study and spiritual
direction experiences with people of advanced, authentic prayer make
it clear that the subject of this chapter is much needed by all three classes
of people. Sceptical and overly credulous individuals assume that they
need no instruction. Each is convinced that its position is quite correct
and the other is obviously deluded. They scarcely entertain the idea
that there may be a middle position that is sound and real.

While our purpose in this chapter is not polemical, it may be worthwhile to call attention to the antecedent probability that a loving and
provident God would communicate with the human race He bothered
to create and redeem. Even aside from the data of revelation we would
expect that a love relationship between the divine and the human would
be characterized by a two-way communication. This is not to say that
on the creature's part recognizing the divine is invariably obvious or
easy or free from illusion. But it is possible.

We have no more sound teaching on the question of divine enlightenments and visions than what we find in our two Carmelite saints.
Any unbiased, sober, informed study of their experiences and their
remarkably humble yet brilliant explanations of them shows that God
does indeed communicate with His chosen ones—but not always as
we commonly suppose or expect. His ways are not our ways.

We do not aim here either at arousing or at satisfying mere curiosity about extraordinary phenomena. We discuss them because, first of
all, Scripture takes it for granted that God intervenes in the affairs of
men. The New Testament speaks of both inner enlightenments (locutions) and visions. Jesus promised the apostles that the Advocate, the
Holy Spirit, would come and teach them everything that He Himself
had taught.[1] This Spirit of truth was to speak to them and lead them
to "the complete truth".[2] Jesus explicitly promised this would go on
"forever",[3] and therefore we rightly expect the faithful to be enlightened
from within throughout all the ages. The faithful, of course, are those
who obey the visible teachers in the Church, for they who listen to
these teachers listen to Jesus Himself and to the Father.[4] The Lord speaks
both through a visible community and by His invisible Spirit work-

ing in our hearts, and His communications are heard by the humble and the obedient.

Visions, seen or heard, were likewise taken for granted in the infant, first-century Church. These are so well attested that we shall mention only four found in the New Testament writings. "The angel of the Lord appeared to Joseph" with directions to take the Child and his Mother into Egypt.[5] Cornelius, at the ninth hour, "had a vision in which he distinctly saw the angel of God come into his house", and he received a specific message concerning a course of action to be taken.[6] While Peter was at prayer on the housetop in Jaffa, he saw heaven open with something like a large sheet containing animals and birds being let down. Together with this vision he heard a voice give him instructions.[7] During a hurricane on the Mediterranean Sea St. Paul told the panic-stricken sailors that an angel of the Lord had appeared to him with the message that though the ship would be lost, all lives would be saved. And so it came about.[8]

A further reason for this chapter is that through the centuries it has been well established that locutions and visions have occurred in the lives of numberless saints. Though we are wise not to accept every alleged happening either in the past or in the present, it is close minded and foolish to turn away from sound evidence. No reasonable person can read with an unbiased mind St. Teresa's descriptions of her visions and conclude that they have any explanation except that of divine intervention. This highly intelligent, completely honest, entirely unassuming and down-to-earth woman could not simply be manufacturing what she reports. Her further accounts will cause the reader to agree that her descriptions are far removed from pseudomystical narrations issuing from unbalanced people. Teresa's experiences have nothing in them of fabrication and illusion.

The sanjuanist view that what God did in biblical days He does in our times, too, is borne out in the contemporary Church. Extensive pastoral experience makes it plainly evident that in our day there are cases of divine communications of solid authenticity — and in saying this I am not referring, at least principally, to well-publicized apparition accounts. If a priest does considerable spiritual direction, and if his directees have confidence in his understanding of divine-human intimacy, he will surely hear accounts of experiences that no unbiased individual would discount. Before the conclusion of this chapter it will be made clear that I am not speaking of guillibility. Rather, I am referring to humble, saintly, psychologically sound people who would not dream of sharing their intimacies with the Lord with any but a competent spiritual director. Both St. John of the Cross and St. Teresa of

Jesus are so demanding of evidence when it comes to extraordinary phenonmena that they will surprise many readers, and especially those who pay much attention to special favors. These two saints were neither naïve and credulous nor biased and close minded. They were supremely sensible.

A final reason for this chapter is fully honest reporting. The present volume is an analysis and synthesis of the two saints' teaching and its rootedness in the Gospel. Because locutions get ample attention from both Carmelites, and because visions are dealt with at length by St. Teresa, to bypass them would border on a lack of candor. There is certainly nothing to hide, in any event. St. Teresa, remarking that some revelations and visions are clearly from God, noted that when she wrote her *Book of Foundations* there was not one of her convents in which two or three nuns so favored could not be found. She added that "I know quite well that this does not constitute sanctity, nor is it my intention to praise such nuns as these alone: I say it rather to show that the counsels I wish to give are not purposeless."[9] Nor do they lack purpose in this volume.

OVERALL ATTITUDES

We began this chapter with a discussion of the two extreme views regarding the possibility or likelihood of locutions and visions. Granted that our two saints avoided both extremes, we need still to ask what exactly their outlook was on alleged cases of divine enlightenments. We may summarize their views in four statements.

The first is that divine interventions are normal gifts given whenever God sees fit to give them. They are not rare.

Their second principle may surprise many of those who are happy with the first, and it will perhaps disappoint more than a few others: namely, illusion and deception are not rare, either. St. Teresa told her nuns that they should not suppose "every little imagination" to be a vision. "If it is one, we may be sure the fact will soon become clear", she said. "I have been quite alarmed to find how possible it is for people to think they see what they do not."[10] Neither she nor John were in the least gullible about alleged divine interventions. In their view many think they are "listening to the Spirit", whereas in fact they are hearing nothing other than their own ideas and desires. They baptize their own preferences and somehow convince themselves, and at times others as well, that they enjoy a privileged access to the divine. Illuminism was not dead in the sixteenth century, just as it is by no means dead in the twentieth. In all likelihood it shall be flourishing in the twenty-first as well.

Their third principle is the logical consequence of the first two: the need for objective ecclesial discernment. If God does often work in individual minds and hearts, and if nonetheless many people assign a mistaken value to their own imaginings, we need some nonsubjective perspicacity, the availability of an out-there acumen that can distinguish one from the other. Already toward the end of the first century we find a clear awareness that "there are many false prophets now in the world", that there are competing "spirits" and that there are signs for distinguishing the true from the false.[11] Among the New Testament criteria that are indicators of authenticity are sound doctrine, unpopularity with the world and acceptance of the ecclesial leadership's teaching.[12]

The fourth principle surprises almost everyone when they first hear of it: private divine communications are relatively unimportant. Though this idea runs contrary to what many people take as being of unquestionable importance, the principle has a great deal of intrinsic merit— which we shall consider later. Most people would not even cross the street to witness an unobtrusive act of patience being put into practice, but they will cross an ocean to visit the locale of an alleged apparition. While both Teresa and John appreciated an authentic vision, they were emphatic that a simple act of pure love is of more value. Spiritual directors, says John,

> should explain how one act done in charity is more precious in God's sight than all the visions and communications possible—since they imply neither merit nor demerit—and how many who have not received these experiences are incomparably more advanced than others who have had many.[13]

This is not the only time the saint makes this kind of remark. And it is, of course, completely in accord with St. Paul's teaching in 1 Corinthians 12:30–13:3. Our instinctive reactions run in quite the opposite direction. We rather assume that some extraordinary phenomenon is far more worthy of attention than is a gentle response to an obnoxious person, but the fact remains that the two most important commandments say not a word about private visions and revelations.

All the same, St. Teresa considered that visions are greatly to be prized, even if they are not essential to the life of grace. Nor does she think them to be all that dangerous when they occur in humble, obedient people. Some individuals, she says, "seem to be frightened at the very mention of visions or revelations. I do not know why they think a soul being led in this way by God is on such a dangerous path, nor

what is the source of this alarm." She then comments that few are the
confessors who will not disturb a person who speaks of a vision. "Confessors are really less alarmed", she adds, "when they hear that the devil
is harassing a soul with all kinds of temptations, with a spirit of blas-
phemy or with foolish and unseemly ideas, than they are scandalized
at being told that a person has seen or heard some angel, or has had
a vision of Jesus Christ crucified, Our Lord."[14] The saint herself treasured her visions when she was confident of their authenticity:

> Nonetheless, I was never able to regret having seen these heavenly vi-
> sions, and I would not exchange even one for all the goods and delights
> of the world. I have always considered a vision a great favor from the
> Lord. It seems to me to be a most rich treasure, and the Lord Himself
> assured me of this many times.[15]

It is worth noticing that neither of our two saints makes a clear
line of demarcation between what we now distinguish as ordinary and
extraordinary gifts from God. While they plainly state that the former
but not the latter should be desired and sought (and this of course implies a distinction), they can speak of both types of gift in one breath
and with no need to treat the "extraordinary" as astonishing or somewhat out of line with God's usual dealings with humankind. We shall
see further on how John takes locutions in stride, and we find Teresa
looking upon them as nothing to be surprised at. "There are many people given to prayer who experience them," she observes, "and I would
not have you think you are doing wrong, sisters, whether or no you
give them credence, when they are only for your own benefit, to comfort you or to warn you of your faults."[16] The saint clearly considers
that the seventh mansions are for everyone and thus "ordinary", in our
terminology. Yet, when she discusses this highest development of contemplation, she matter-of-factly says that it begins with an intellectual
vision of the Trinity—what we term "extraordinary".[17]

LOCUTIONS: ST. TERESA

We could at this juncture go in either one of two directions as we consider the question of divine communications: we could attempt to combine Teresa and John into one account or attempt to deal with them
separately. The risk of the first approach is confusion; that of the second, overlapping. Because it seems that it will be easier to minimize
the second risk, we shall discuss them individually while noting the
interrelatedness when that would be helpful.

The word *locution* comes from the Latin *locutio,* a speaking, an ut-
terance. Locutions are messages of diverse types and are received in
differing manners. St. Teresa's division is simple: external, imaginary,
intellectual.[18]

An external locution occurs from outside the person and is heard
with one's bodily ears; one perceives that a human voice is speaking.[19]

The imaginary locution originates within the person, that is, within
his inward sense faculties. The word *imaginary* does not mean here what
it commonly signifies today: unreal, fabricated, illusory. It is simply
an adjective referring to our inner sense capacity, the imagination, which
enables us to recapture various sights, sounds, fragrances and the like
through inner awareness of them. God can work directly within this
faculty.

Intellectual locutions occur in the deepest center of the person and
with no sound, no voice. Yet they have remarkable traits. The intellectual enlightenment far surpasses anything of ordinary human study or
experience. St. Teresa tells us that

> once while with this presence of the three Persons that I carry about
> in my soul, I experienced so much light you couldn't doubt the living
> and true God was there. In this state He gave me understanding of things
> I didn't know how to speak of afterward. Among them was how the
> Person of the Son, and not the others, took flesh.[20]

She writes of another occasion:

> While in prayer one day, I felt my soul to be so deep in God that it didn't
> seem there was a world; but while immersed in Him, understanding
> of that Magnificat verse, *et exultavit spiritus,* was given to me in such a
> way I cannot forget it.[21]

Understandably, most of what the saint has to say about locutions
concerns the intellectual type, and so it is on these that we now concentrate our attention. Notice that as St. Teresa describes these experiences, she is at pains to show how the divine enlightenments are very
different from the ideas our own minds produce. We do not and in
fact cannot originate them.

In the intellectual locution the words received are explicit, much more
clear than those we hear with our bodily ears. One cannot resist listening
to and understanding these words in the same way that one can choose
to "turn off" mere human speech. When the Lord speaks in this manner, the recipient of the message listens whether wishing to or not.
Understanding the words is likewise independent of one's will: when
one wants to understand, one often cannot; when at other times one

does not want to, one is made to understand. It is clear who the teacher is.

When the divinely spoken word deals with something in the future, it always turns out to be true; that is, the message is fulfilled.[22]

In these locutions, one is a receiver; one does not originate. In this divine communication the person's part is simply to listen to the words. There is not the usual composition involved, as there is when, in normal thinking, our intellect goes through a process of formulating integrated ideas. Teresa declares the difference in this case to be great:

> If they are something the intellect fabricates, no matter how subtly it works, a person will know that it is the intellect that is composing something and speaking. The difference is that in the one case the words are composed and in the other they are listened to. The intellect will see that it is not then listening because it is working. And the words it fabricates are as though muffled, fancied, and without the clarity of those that come from God. It is in our power to divert our attention from these words of the intellect, as we do when while speaking we decide to keep quiet; in the case of those words that are from God there is no way of diverting one's attention. . . . It seems to me the difference between the two kinds of locution is the same as that between speaking and listening, no more, nor less.[23]

We want to keep in mind as we go along that the human person cannot bring about what St. Teresa is describing. The content of her explanations together with their lucidity and candor make plain that figments of an unhealthy imagination are not involved in any way. The following traits give further evidence of a divine origin.

God's words, says the saint, unlike ours, do what they say. The words He speaks

> are both words and works. And even though the words may not be devotional ones but words of reproof, they dispose the soul and prepare it from the very beginning, and they touch it, give it light, favor it and bring it quiet. And if the soul suffers dryness, agitation and worry, these are taken away as though by a stroke of the hand since it seems the Lord wants it to understand that He is powerful and that His words are works.[24]

This power of the divine speech is attested in Scripture. As a matter of fact, the unimaginable, infinite power exercised in the moment of creation (which astonished astrophysicists now refer to as the "Big Bang") was, says Genesis, the word of the Lord. When Jesus in the garden on the night before He died was accosted by the soldiers who said they were looking for Jesus the Nazarene, He replied with the simple but overpowering "I am he". The evangelist remarks that on hearing these words, they moved backward and fell to the ground.[25] It was also by His words that the Son raised Lazarus from the dead and cleansed the lepers. By this same power of His word He continues today to enlighten, heal and give life.

In view of this exceedingly effective power of God's word, the next trait of locutions is not surprising: the message is majestic, authoritative, holy. We can do no better than to listen to how Teresa puts it:

> In the words coming from God the experience is as though we were listening to a very holy person or to one who is most learned with great authority, who we know will not lie to us. And even this comparison is a poor one. For these words at times bear with them such majesty that even though one does not call to mind who it is that speaks them, they make one tremble—if they are words of reproof; and if they are words of love, they make one dissolve in love.[26]

Upon a moment's reflection we recognize that our own most vivid imaginations have no authority at all and indeed nothing of an imposing majesty.

Another aspect of the power of the divine locution is seen in the indelible effect it often produces. The very words or at least the substance of the message often cannot be forgotten after the passage of years.

What is taught and learned in a divine enlightenment is rapid. Teresa said that she learned in an instant what would have taken her a month to compose were she left to her own thought processes. In our own day André Frossard describes an instantaneous, unexpected experience of enlightenment he had as an initiating step in his conversion from atheism to theism and the Church. The light he received was not a physical illumination, but rather

> a light of truth, a light that really instructs, that informs as it illuminates, that teaches you more in a moment about the Christian religion than ten volumes of doctrine. And the curious thing is that this wordless instruction is exactly the same as that of the [Catholic] Church. . . . The two things coincide perfectly. The convert discovers America, and the Church's geographers, who have never been there, are at least as familiar with it as he is.[27]

Since locutions can originate from angelic, demonic or saintly sources as well as from the directly divine, we now inquire about whether the recipient can know with certitude whence the message comes. St.

Teresa's responses are nuanced, when we consider all of them. We have here another instance of the danger of dealing only with part of what she says, that is, one or two citations. To ascertain her full mind requires distinctions. First of all, it is healthy to entertain some doubt about what is going on, at least at the beginning and when one is not experienced with the ways of God. Teresa herself often had doubts about what she was hearing—we have already insisted that she was neither naïve nor gullible. The saint declared on one occasion that she was never so sure an experience was from God that she would swear to it.[28] Yet at times, no matter how she might try to believe a favor was from the devil (when her confessor would say so), she could not bring her mind to agree.[29] Even obedience cannot require one to declare that white is black. St. Teresa found that once a person is experienced in these matters, it is easy to know the origin of a locution. Attentiveness and experience enable the recipient to "see the difference very clearly". She adds a comment about words that originate with the Lord:

> They concern matters, as I said, which are very far from one's mind. Such long sentences are said so quickly that much time would have been necessary to compose them, and in no way does it seem to me that we can then fail to know that they are something we do not fabricate ourselves. Thus, there's no reason for me to delay on this matter; rarely it seems can an experienced person be deceived if the person himself does not knowingly want to be deceived.[30]

Clearly we are not dealing here with a naïve enthusiast. Teresa is well aware of the possibility of deception and illusion, and she knows well the difference between authenticity and fantasy, between reality and mirage.

Since few of us would claim to enjoy anything close to St. Teresa's experience of the divine, we naturally enough look to her for some guides, some signs of genuine locutions. How would we lesser ones know whether an enlightenment derives from God or not? The saint answers this question at some length in her *Interior Castle,* and for the sake of clarity we list here in brief form her salient points.[31]

1. The locution bears a "sense of power and authority" both in itself and in its effects. As we have remarked above, God's words are works: His speaking is a doing.

2. The message is in accord with Catholic Faith and morals and therefore with Scripture. The Lord does not contradict Himself: His private enlightenments can never negate His public revelation. Speaking of herself in the third person, Teresa avers that

she ever was and ever is subject to all that the holy Catholic faith holds, and all her prayer and the prayer in the houses she has founded is for the increase in the faith. She used to say that if any of her experiences were to induce her to turn against the Catholic faith or the law of God, she would have no need to go in search of proof, for then she would see it was the devil.[32]

This simple statement of truth lays bare the gulf that yawns between a genuine person such as Teresa and the pitiable self-assurance of the dissenting mind. One cannot improve on Jesus' own formulation: "He who hears you, hears Me."

3. A word from God brings calm and peace.

4. It prompts the recipient to break forth in the praise of the Lord Who has deigned to communicate with one so lowly.

5. The message remains long in the memory; some ideas are indelible and never vanish even after long years.

6. When the locution is concerned with a coming event, the words often bring an unshakable certitude with them that things will come out as they indicate. This is so even when all available external evidence is running in the opposite direction. In St. Teresa's case, for example, she would experience this certitude even though the bishop adamantly refused to give a permission, or her confessor was opposed, or she had no money to carry out a project. She remained secure in her conviction, and the event would prove her to be right.

7. Genuine words from a divine source are clear, not confused as our own ideas often are. St. Raymond of Capua, the spiritual director of St. Catherine of Siena, was about to set off for a journey when he stopped to say the customary Hail Mary before a statue of our Lady. "Suddenly," he relates, "there was a voice, though there was no sound in the air; the words sounded not in my bodily ears but in my mind, and I heard them more clearly than if they had come from the mouth of someone standing only a yard away." These words of comfort and assurance were from Catherine, who had died, and, says Raymond, they "resounded distinctly in my mind".[33] This clarity was a characteristic of the locutions that St. Teresa received.

8. The word often comes unexpectedly, and frequently it is contrary to what one knew, desired or wished. The experience has nothing in common with autosuggestion or wishful thinking.

9. One single word, notes Teresa, can "contain a world of meaning" such as we, left to ourselves, could never rapidly put into human language. Often much more is understood than the words themselves convey, a *sensus plenior,* as Scripture scholars say of the revealed message.

10. An authentic locution brings humility to the recipient. There is little or no inclination to self-exaltation, even when one is aware of the sublimity of the divine gift. Referring to "His Majesty's" often conversing with her, St. Teresa comments that

> these words and gifts make me so extraordinarily embarrassed when I recall what I am (as I have often said, I think, and now sometimes tell my confessor) that more courage is necessary to receive these favors than to undergo the severest trials. When they take place, I am almost completely forgetful of my deeds and am shown that I am wretched.[34]

11. The word spoken by the indwelling Spirit inhibits all other thought and compels attention to it. There is no choice but to listen.

If we may mix our metaphors, we may say that genuine locutions have the divine handwriting all over them. This is why Teresa can remark that when one is experienced (as she surely was), it is easy to know their origin is in God. There is no other explanation.

How ought one to look upon these phenomena either as recipient or as spiritual director? I wish first of all to rule out of our present discussion external "locutions" alleged by mentally unbalanced people. St. Teresa also excluded them, and she offered sage advice as to how we should deal with ill people who imagine that they hear voices. Though the saint is kind, she will tolerate no nonsense:

> Of persons of these two kinds [inner or outer "voices"] no notice should be taken, in my view, even if they say they see or hear or are given to understand things, nor should one upset them by telling them that their experiences come from the devil. One should listen to them as one would to sick persons; and the prioress, or the confessor, or whatever person they confide in, should advise them to pay no heed to the matter, because the service of God does not consist in things like these.[35]

When the enlightenment has the signs we have discussed, one can be confident that it comes from God.[36] This does not mean, however, that if the locution concerns something of importance, one may act upon it without consulting someone both competent and holy.[37]

Further, all of us should be aware (and especially the recipient) that locutions do not render a person any the better for having received them. Profit depends, notes Teresa, on whether or not we use them well. She laconically remarks that Jesus spoke at length with the Pharisees, who were all the worse for the favor.[38]

It is always wise, at least at first, to set locutions aside. Inexperienced people tend to be surprised at this advice, for it appears to them that one should pay attention, perhaps exclusive attention, to something of divine origin. Not so, says Teresa. Even if a message is actually from God, three benefits derive from setting it aside. First, this reaction helps one advance (the saint offers no clear reason why, but John will). Second, it puts the locution to the test — Teresa rightly supposes that they need verification. Third, God favors this reaction, for He increases His communications when people follow this advice.[39]

The recipient ought not to act on what was heard without first consulting a confessor or "a learned man". This is "His Majesty's will", insists Teresa, for He has established the Church to take His place on earth and to speak in His name. So confident is the saint in her Lord that, even if the confessor is obtuse and resistant, the Master will speak to him, "and if such is His pleasure will make him recognize the work of His spirit; if He does not, we have no further obligations".[40] St. Teresa had no time for people who think they have a better plan for the Church than the Lord Himself.

Finally, if there is a clash between the person's experience and the confessor's judgment, it is the latter that is to prevail. While we shall discuss this norm at greater length when we take up St. John of the Cross, we may cite in passing Teresa's reference to her personal policy: "She never did anything based on what she understood in prayer. Rather, if her confessors told her to do the contrary, she did it immediately, and always informed them about everything."[41]

SANJUANIST TERMINOLOGY: SUPERNATURAL KNOWLEDGE AS A WHOLE

We turn our attention now to St. John of the Cross. Before we look into his teaching on locutions, we will sketch his overall view of how human beings get to know God, both naturally and supernaturally. By natural knowledge he meant what we mean today, namely, what we can reach and perceive through unaided reason: God's existence, His power and His wisdom.[42] By supernatural knowledge of the divine he designates those truths or insights whose attainment surpasses native human ability: visions, revelations, locutions, spiritual "feelings".

Speaking of these latter, John places on the lowest (visionary) level divine communications that come through the outer senses: images, words, fragrances, tastes and feelings. Of this type would be the external representations of a saint, including any words spoken. While John considers that God "is wont to perfect" our sense life by these supernatural gifts, when we are ready for them,[43] he also adds that these phenomena can be of demonic origin. Because the Lord usually communicates to the spirit, as the saint puts it, the more exterior the experience, the less certain it is to be of divine origin. In any event, the recipient should never rely on this kind of perception[44] and should realize that nothing of sense can unite one to God, since it bears no proportion to Him.

The next level is the imaginary vision. Imaginary here does not mean fanciful or fictitious. As we have already noted, it refers to our inner capacity to reproduce within ourselves representations of the five outer senses: sights, sounds, smells, touches, tastes. God can work immediately upon these inner powers, and so can the devil. John indicates that visions of this type, that is, visions that occur entirely within the subject, are more frequent than those occurring through the external senses. Like the first group, these also are to be rejected for reasons we shall consider. No harm comes through setting them aside, because they produce their good effects apart from what the recipient does about them; the effects cannot be hindered.[45]

On the highest level of visons comes the intellectual type. These, strictly speaking, are "whatever the intellect receives in a manner resembling sight".[46] Though these usually concern material things (for example, St. Benedict's viewing the whole world spiritually), the absence of the object does not hinder the vision. These can on occasion be of diabolical origin, and John considered that the temptations of Christ in the wilderness may have been by way of spiritual suggestion from the devil.[47] The saint says that even though these visions are far more clear and delicate than corporal ones, they also are to be set aside. They are not God and may not be allowed to interfere with our going to Him in dark faith and according to the public revelation He has given us in Scripture, the Tradition of the Church and her enduring teaching authority.[48]

The second general category of supernatural knowledge is revelation, that is, the disclosure of a new hidden truth, mystery or divine deed: past, present or future.[49] The first type of revelation is the sublime experience of a divine attribute such as omnipotence or goodness or strength, and it produces "incomparable delight".[50] These divine touches are "pure contemplation", and they are received only by one who has reached union with God. They cannot be produced by the devil, nor can he meddle with them. They are not to be set aside, for they pertain to very union with God Himself. So remarkable are these touches of a knowing delight that they "more than compensate for all the trials suffered in life, even though innumerable". They are sometimes given when the recipient is not in the least thinking of them or expecting them. Although they differ in their force, even the weakest of them "is worth more to the soul than numberless other thoughts and ideas about God's creatures and works".[51]

A second type of revelation is a disclosure of truth regarding created things and human events that engenders so deep a conviction that the recipient cannot force himself to deny it. Yet despite this inner persuasion John insists that the person must follow a contrary decision if his spiritual director advises it, for we attain union with God more by faith than by understanding. The saint offers as examples of this kind of revelation Wisdom 7:17-21 and 1 Corinthians 12:8-10. Because diabolical deceit is possible here, and because this type of disclosure is not the path of faith, this experience is to be shared with one's director and then dropped.[52]

Because St. Teresa wrote at length about visions, we shall say no more here, nor shall we discuss John's concept of "spiritual feelings", for he says very little about them that we have not already dealt with elsewhere.[53] However, the subject of our next section merits considerable attention both because of its intrinsic importance and because John's brilliant explanation of it is unique.

LOCUTIONS: ST. JOHN OF THE CROSS

Although the basic sanjuanist concept of locution is the same as the teresian, John adds considerably to her discussion of the subject both by way of analysis of the types and by way of our proper reactions to them. His definition of locutions is simple: words produced in the recipient by divine action. While there are many ways in which God may impress a message in the human mind, the saint reduces them to three classes: successive, formal and substantial.

The first type may be called assisting enlightenments, for they occur when a person is in a prayerful frame of mind and is "attentively absorbed in some consideration". As this individual is thinking about his subject, he proceeds with so much ease and clarity that it seems to him "that another person is interiorly reasoning, answering, and teaching him".[54] What is happening, explains the saint, is that the indwelling Spirit is united with this prayerful person in the truth under consideration, for the Spirit is in every truth:

> While his intellect is thus communing with the divine Spirit by means of that truth, it simultaneously forms interiorly and successively the other truths about its subject, while the Holy Spirit, the Teacher, leads the way and gives light. This is one of the Holy Spirit's methods of teaching.[55]

A prayerful teacher or student or even letter writer may notice that in a difficult matter a sudden surge of ideas flows easily. One did not know what to say or how to put it, and yet at the moment of composition finds an accompanying enlightenment. While this assisting locution in itself contains no deception, there can be error in the conclusions that the recipient may draw from it. The light given is so delicate that it does not fill the intellect completely, and the person remains free to operate in a merely human manner and thus to misunderstand or to misapply the message or to infer erroneously what does not follow. While successive locutions are surely a blessing in themselves when they come from God, yet John was convinced that misapplications are not rare:

> I greatly fear what is happening in these times of ours: if any soul whatever after a bit of meditation has in its recollection one of these locutions, it will immediately baptize all as coming from God and with such a supposition say, "God told me," "God answered me." Yet this is not so, but, as we pointed out, these persons themselves are more often the origin of their locution. . . . They think something extraordinary has occurred and that God has spoken, whereas in reality little more than nothing will have happened, or nothing at all.[56]

One is not to focus attention on these successive locutions for the obvious reason that they are liable to have an uncertain origin, and a great deal of deception and error is possible. If they are indeed from God, the good results will not be lost through turning one's attention in dark faith to public revelation and the teaching of the Church and by applying one's will to the love of God and neighbor.[57] The individual who lives by divine faith is standing on solid ground and is safeguarded from personal or demonic aberrations. The authentic locution is characterized by the usual signs of discerning the Holy Spirit: love, humility, obedience and the pursuit of genuine good.[58] The imagined illuminations of people alienated from the mind of the universal Church derive from anything but a divine source: their own will begets those thoughts that deviate from God's thoughts.

The second type of locution John terms formal. We may also call them ideational enlightenments, for "they are like ideas spoken to the spirit".[59] These words may be implicit or explicit, but they do not come through the senses, nor do they necessarily arise in a prayerful atmosphere. They are supernaturally produced without the human mind contributing to their formation. These words "are received as though one person were speaking to another", and ordinarily they are given to teach or to shed light. When God is the speaker, "this effect is always produced in the soul, for it renders the soul ready to accomplish the command and discerning in understanding it". As an example of this type of communication the saint offers the case of the angel's speaking to Daniel.[60] Because formal locutions do not produce much effect, it is difficult to determine their origin, divine or demonic, by judging just what one experiences within. For this reason the recipient should neither act upon the ideas nor pay any particular attention to them.[61] Rather, one should share the locution with a confessor or some other wise person and then drop it. If no expert adviser is available, then it is best to speak to no one about the matter and pay no further attention to it. Anyone who has dealt much with religious aberrations knows well that St. John of the Cross could not be more correct in his unambiguous advice: "It should be kept in mind that a person must never follow his own opinion, nor do or admit anything told to him through these locutions, without ample advice and counsel from another. For in this matter of locutions strange and subtle deceits will occur."[62]

The third classification is the substantial locution, a kind of dynamic-effective speaking. Coming neither from the human mind nor from demonic deceit but only from the divine Speaker, these words produce what they say in the depths of the soul. They are much superior to the successive and merely formal locutions in that they bring about within the recipient the content of the message itself. Thus, as John explains, if God should say "be good", goodness is immediately imparted. If He should say, "fear not", or "love me", fear is immediately dissipated, or love is given.[63] We have noted elsewhere that for the Hebrews God's word *dabar* was full of power; it did what it said. Such was the word of the original creation; such was the word of Jesus in the working of His miracles. Such is still the case when the Lord wishes to communicate in this manner. There is nothing to fear in regard to this dynamic-effective speaking, for neither the human mind nor demonic intervention can produce the incomparable blessings that these words confer. "As for these locutions," says the saint, "the soul has nothing to do, desire, refrain from desiring, reject or fear. There is nothing to be done, because God never grants them for that purpose, but He bestows them in order to accomplish Himself what they express."[64]

HUMAN REACTIONS TO DIVINE COMMUNICATIONS

At the outset of this chapter we noted that there are two common responses to the suggestion that God communicates His light to or-

dinary men and women. One is to deny the idea outright, or at least
so to minimize its likelihood as to render it innocuous for all practical
purposes. The other is so to embrace enthusiastically and uncritically
every allegation that one is "listening to the Spirit" as to imply that
only a favored few have access to the divine mind. While it is easy
enough to reject in general both of these extremes as clearly mistaken,
it is not always as simple to know how to deal with the allegations
when they do occur in particular cases. The advice given by St. John
of the Cross may surprise the unwary, but informed experience in
spiritual direction soon shows its wisdom. We will touch here some
of his main guidelines.

We turn our attention first to imaginative visions and other communications that may come through the external senses: visions of saints,
pleasant fragrances, words perceived through the sense of hearing.[65]
Even though these may issue from God Himself, John insists that they
must be set aside and renounced. The recipient does share them with
a trustworthy, informed guide, but once that is done he turns his attention to God and to his duties of state. The saint offers two reasons
for this mode of behavior. One is that God produces what He wishes
in the soul through these experiences without the individual's being
able to impede the divine intent. Only sin or possessiveness can hinder
what God plans to do through these communications. The second
reason is that by setting aside these experiences, the person is freed
from false ones and from preoccupation with them. "Such an effort
[spent in determining the true origin]", says John, "is profitless, a waste
of time, a hindrance to the soul, an occasion of many imperfections
as well as spiritual stagnancy, since the individual is not then employed
with the more important things" involved in serving God and neighbor.[66] As far as John is concerned, it is the soul's imperfection that is
the occasion for God's dealing with it in these manners. If it were highly
perfect and capable of more spiritual gifts, God would not feed it with
the crumbs of forms, figures and particular knowledge.[67] The last few
words reflect John's terminology and are expressive of his vigorous
thought. To put the matter positively, what the receipient should do
is to

> fasten the eyes of his soul only upon the valuable spirituality they cause,
> and endeavor to preserve it by putting into practice and properly doing
> whatever is for the service of God, and pay no attention to those repre-
> sentations, nor desire any sensible gratification. By this attitude a per-
> son takes from these apprehensions only what God wants him to take,
> that is, the spirit of devotion, since God gives them for no other prin-
> cipal reason.[68]

Not content with this general guidance, John goes on to specify the harms that come upon people and spiritual directors who pay undue attention to visions and locutions. The recipients slowly lose humility in that they believe themselves prominent in God's eyes. They begin to wonder if others receive such favors, and, if they do, whether they are authentic or not. The overly credulous are likely to become attached to their "communications" far more than to public revelation as it is received in the Church. Instead of deepening their life of faith and love by complete self-emptying, they cling to their visions and enlightenments, and they fail "to soar to the heights of dark faith".[69]

Then there is the likelihood that they will, wittingly or not, shape their communications to their own thoughts, desires and preferences. While divine light is sure and solid in itself, God offers no infallible assurance that ordinary people will understand, interpret and apply correctly what they have received.[70] John shows with examples from both the Old and New Testaments how even Abraham, and also the disciples on the road to Emmaus, together with others in Israel, misunderstood divine revelations and promises, "for God's spiritual meaning is difficult to understand and different from our literal interpretation".[71] When the Lord gives messages, notes the saint, He "always refers to the more important and profitable meaning, whereas man will refer them to a less important sense".[72] John's conclusion is sobering: "Evidently, then, even though the words and revelations be from God, we cannot find assurance in them, since in our understanding of them we can easily be deluded, and extremely so."[73] If the history of religions teaches us anything, it is that this sanjuanist caution is entirely correct. The thousands of sects that have sprung up in twenty centuries of Christianity alone are eloquent, even if tragic, witnesses to the vagaries, whimsies and oddities presented to the world in the name of private enlightenments. And history is not able to record the numberless private extravaganzas and blind alleys into which men and women have been and still are led when they depart from the solidity of the Spirit-indwelt Church to pursue their own personal persuasions.

What, then, is one to do who has reason to think he has been favored with a locution or vision? John's answer is entirely biblical and ecclesial, even if it is not popular in dissenting quarters. We may recall New Testament advice regarding discerning true prophets from false ones. They must be tested that we may know who is of God and who is not. Those who are authentic will have the sound doctrine the Church proclaims, while the others will not. Those led by the Spirit will be unpopular with the world, while the others will be applauded and sought after. They who are of God listen to and accept the teaching of the leaders in the Church; the false prophets reject that teaching.[74] St. John of the Cross offers the same basic answer. If one thinks he has an enlightenment, let him submit it to the judgment of one of the Church's approved priests[75] and then abide by his decision. "We must be guided humanly and visibly in all by the law of Christ the man and that of His Church and of His ministers. . . . Any departure from this road is not only curiosity, but extraordinary boldness."[76] The saint offers no opening to illuminism and to the arrogance of people who are persuaded that they have a mission from heaven to correct the teaching of the Church guaranteed by Jesus Himself. John rightly states that throughout salvation history God gave His teaching not to everyone "but only to the priests and prophets from whom the common people were to learn the law and doctrine".[77] He notes, too, that when the Lord actually does send His inner light to a person, He also gives an accompanying inclination to manifest that light to an officer in the Church:

> God is so content that the rule and direction of many be through other men, and that a person be governed by natural reason, that He definitely does not want us to bestow entire credence upon His supernatural communications, nor be confirmed in their strength and security until they pass through this human channel of the mouth of man. As often as He reveals something to a person, He confers upon his soul a kind of inclination to manifest this to the appropriate person.[78]

This recourse to the visible Church has been the uniform practice of the saints. St. Paul himself, notes John, who had an immediate and direct mission from the risen Lord, nonetheless "could not resist going and conferring about it with St. Peter and the Apostles".[79]

A further sanjuanist note: God does not usually communicate to a person what can be attained by ordinary human means of study or counsel: "He is ever desirous that man insofar as possible take advantage of his own reasoning powers. All matters must be regulated by reason save those of faith, which though not contrary to reason transcends it."[80] Again John leaves no room for the extravagances to which illuminists in every century are prone. If we live according to the incarnational nature of the Church, with the visible and invisible elements working closely together and neither excluding the other, both individual intimacy with God and the public good of the whole people are secured. Eroding and destructive aberrations cannot grow in this kind of climate.

A final principle: "Whatever is received through supernatural means [in whatever manner] should immediately be told clearly, integrally, and simply to one's spiritual director."[81] Even though there may seem to be no need to share the communication if one simply sets it aside, St. John maintains that it is to be relayed to the spiritual director. He offers three reasons. One is that the light, strength and security of many divine enlightenments are not entirely confirmed in the recipient until he has shared them with one whom God Himself has "destined to be spiritual judge" in the Church with the "power to bind, loose, approve and reprove". John points out that this reason is established in the New Testament and is verified every day through experience. By this submission to the visible element in the Church and thus through obedience to Christ Himself, "the communications are then seemingly imparted anew".[82] A second reason is that the soul ordinarily needs instruction as to how to continue along the dark path of faith and complete denudation from everything that is not God. The third reason is "humility, submission, and mortification". Because the communications may seem trivial or because the recipient may fear the director's reaction, there may well be reluctance to share them, but by doing so the person grows in humility and simplicity.[83]

On his part the spiritual director or confessor should by no means

> show severity, displeasure, or scorn in dealing with these souls. . . . Since God is leading them by this means, there is no reason for opposing it, nor becoming frightened or scandalized over it; the director should instead be kind and peaceful. He should give these souls encouragement and the opportunity of speaking about their experience, and, if necessary, oblige them to do so.[84]

What may well have appeared at the outset as unmanageable incompatibilities (objective ecclesial doctrine and subjective individual enlightenments), leading to hopeless confusion and contradiction, can now be seen to form a harmonious whole. From the theological point of view the sanjuanist and teresian teaching is nothing other than a concrete application of the incarnational nature of the divine economy of salvation. God does indeed operate invisibly in the human person, but He also carries out His plan through a hierarchical community.[85] Crucial to this divine plan is the stipulation that the latter is to test the former, not vice versa.[86] John and Teresa are completely in accord with the revealed word.

VISIONS: ST. TERESA

It is said of Edith Stein that when she had finished reading St. Teresa's autobiography she closed the book and exclaimed with conviction: "This is the truth." Before long, this brilliant woman entered the Catholic

Church. Though I tend to be more than a little wary of commonly
alleged supernatural phenomena among so many of our contemporaries,
my reaction to St. Teresa's account of her visions is identical to that
of Edith Stein: these are authentic, true . . . they could not be imagined
or made up . . . no one could manufacture what this woman describes.
I cannot think of a more reliable guide to our present question of visions. Apparently St. John of the Cross was of the same mind: Madre
Teresa had written so well on the subject that he felt no need to add
to the literature, and so he did not.

St. Teresa's division of visions into three types is routine and does
not require special attention.[87] She distinguishes corporeal, imaginative
and intellectual visions. The first are seen with bodily eyes, and they
are the least perfect. The saint states several times that she never received
this type of communication.[88]

"Imaginative", the name for the second type of vision, does not refer
to autosuggestion, for these are not fabricated by the person. They
originate from another source and are perceived by the inner senses.
These communications have sense traits and are far superior to visions
seen with the bodily eyes.

Most perfect of all visions are the intellectual. They are immaterial,
spiritual and without the traits of sense; as the name indicates, they
are seen by the intellect alone.

St. Teresa's explanations of imaginary visions are most persuasive.
To appreciate that such is the case, the reader may simply compare,
as we go along, each of the descriptive traits she gives with the prod-
ucts of his own imagination. The two are entirely different, the one
irreducible to the other in any dimension. The better to illustrate this,
we may consider one of her visions of Christ. It is, she says, rapid,
like a flash of lightning, and the brilliance of it is such that one cannot
keep on gazing. When one can look long, it is probably not a vision
at all but only an imagination produced by one's own self.[89] We are,
of course, already way beyond what we can ourselves bring about,
for no one can innerly produce a light so like the sun's brilliance that
it cannot be gazed upon.

Moreover, says Teresa, the image is alive; one does not see it as
though it were a painting, "a dead image".[90] Remarking that she has
seen many well-done works of art, the saint concludes that "it is foolish
to think that an earthly drawing can look anything like a vision; it does
so no more nor less than a living person resembles his portrait. No
matter how good the portrait may have turned out, it can't look so
natural that in the end it isn't recognized as a dead thing. But let us
leave this example aside; it applies well here and is very exact."[91]

Third, the vision is awesome: "The sight is the loveliest and most delightful imaginable", and it far exceeds what one could conjure up. Even if one "strove to imagine it for a thousand years", he could not do so, she says,

> because it so far exceeds all that our imagination and understanding can compass, its presence is of such exceeding majesty that it fills the soul with a great terror. It is unnecessary to ask here how, without being told, the soul knows Who it is, for He reveals Himself quite clearly as the Lord of Heaven and earth. This the kings of the earth never do.[92]

With feminine acuity for detail Teresa adds that we would never know an earthly ruler to be a king unless he had a retinue or splendid robes and insignia of office. As a mere man he is no more impressive than a tramp on the street. Not so with the Lord of the universe: He is awesome of Himself and needs no artificial props. She comments on the effects His eyes alone produced on her:

> I can tell you truly that, wicked as I am, I have never feared the torments of hell, for they seem nothing by comparison with the thought of the wrath which the damned will see in the Lord's eyes — those eyes so lovely and tender and benign. I do not think my heart could bear to see that; and I have felt like this all my life. How much more will anyone fear this to whom He has thus revealed Himself, and given such a consciousness of His presence as will produce unconsciousness.[93]

Teresa's last comment introduces our next trait: the awesomeness of this experience almost always produces ecstasy.[94] It is in the rapture that the vision mercifully disappears, because the soul would not be able to endure it for long. The saint explains the overwhelming effect of the divine disclosure:

> I say that this vision has such tremendous power when the Lord desires to show the soul a great part of His grandeur and majesty that it would be impossible for any subject to endure it unless the Lord should want to help it very supernaturally by placing it in rapture and ecstasy since in the enjoyment of that divine presence the vision of it is lost.[95]

Autosuggestion is likewise ruled out, in that the vision is unexpected and appears suddenly in its wholeness: it could not be made up piece by piece by one's imagination. Indeed, not only does what is given appear with immediate completeness; the underlying idea itself has also never before so much as passed through the recipient's mind.[96]

A genuine vision of divine origin brings with it a complete certitude as to its authenticity. Yet, because she was so obedient, St. Teresa did have second thoughts later on if her confessor opposed her conviction.[97]

The extraordinary richness of the vision both in its content and in the results it produces in the recipient can be accounted for only by the Lord Who gives it. Referring to the splendor of the risen Lord in His glorified body, Teresa reflects: "If I should have spent many years trying to imagine how to depict something so beautiful, I couldn't have, nor would I have known how to; it surpasses everything imaginable here on earth, even in just its whiteness and splendor."[98] The saint explicitly discusses the question of whether a vision from God could be the product of one's imagination. Her judgment is that this is

> the most impossible of impossible things; it is utter nonsense to think so, for the beauty and the whiteness of one hand alone is completely beyond our imagination. It's impossible to see in a moment, without thinking or ever having thought about them, things represented that in a long time could not have been put together by the imagination, because they go far beyond, as I said, what we can comprehend here on earth.[99]

The transformative results of the vision, both physical and spiritual, likewise point to God as the sole explanation of its origin. Not only did St. Teresa sometimes find that bodily health was a consequence of her experience, but much more importantly, she was struck by the transformation of her inner person. She considered that her sudden change for the better was unanswerable proof that God Himself produced her vision. To make this point vivid she fashioned a charming parable.

> I told them [some very holy persons] that if they were to tell me that a person whom I knew very well and with whom I had just finished speaking were not that person, but that I had imagined it, I would without doubt, as they knew, believe what they said rather than what I had seen. But if this person were to leave me some jewels, and they were left in my hands as tokens of great love, I would not believe what they said, even though I desired, because I hadn't had any jewels before and was poor, whereas now I found that I was rich. I was able to show them these jewels because all who knew me saw clearly that my soul was changed, and my confessor told me so. The difference in all things was very great: it was not feigned, but all could see it very clearly.[100]

The final trait of an authentic imaginary vision is that everything in the experience is beyond human control. It all happens exactly as the Lord wishes: there is no inducing or stopping it. Desire to see or not to see has no effect. If the recipient even tries to focus on some specific aspect of the vision, it simply ceases. God is in entire control.

In the vision we are dealing with there is no possibility of fashioning it ourselves, but we must look at what the Lord desires to show us, when He desires, and as He desires. There is no taking it away or inducing it, nor, however much we try, is there any way of doing either; nor when we desire is there a way to see it or to stop seeing it. If we want to look at some particular thing, the vision of Christ ceases.[101]

St. Teresa tells of a vision of "His Majesty" in which she wished to discover the color of His eyes and His height, so that she could be able to describe these characteristics. She remarks that she could not find out what she wanted to know, and as a matter of fact through this effort she lost the vision entirely.[102] "This", she concludes, "is the case in all visions without exception: our effort can neither do nor undo anything when it comes to seeing more or seeing less."[103]

Though intellectual visions are more perfect than the imaginary ones, St. Teresa does not say as much about them, no doubt because not as much needs to be said. However, she does describe in some detail an intellectual vision of Christ that bore with it "wonderful blessings". On the feast of St. Peter she was at prayer when she became aware of Jesus at her side, even though she saw nothing with her bodily eyes. Up to this moment she had been completely unaware that there could be a vision of this type, and, until He reassured her, she was greatly frightened. She was more sure that He was at her side in some per-during way than if she had seen Him with her bodily eyes, and yet she could not explain how she knew this or how He was present. More than a little concerned as to what this all meant, she went to consult her confessor.

> He asked me in what form I saw him. I answered that I didn't see Him. He asked how I knew that it was Christ. I answered that I didn't know how, but that I couldn't help knowing that He was beside me, that I saw and felt Him clearly, that my recollection of soul was greater, and that I was very continuously in the prayer of quiet, that the effects were much different from those I usually experienced, and that it was very clear.[104]

Teresa tried as best she could to explain herself with comparisons, but she concluded that no comparison would do, that there is really no way she could get across to others what she experienced. There is nothing of sense, but at the same time there is no darkness, either. "The vision", she said, "is represented through knowledge given to the soul that is clearer than sunlight . . . a light, without your seeing light, il-lumines the intellect."[105] Unlike the imaginary vision, which is short in duration, the intellectual one can "last for many days — sometimes for more than a year".[106]

The saint observes that intellectual and imaginary visions almost always occur together. This is not surprising, for it fits the human mode of understanding: insight together with image. Teresa tells us that

> this is the way they occur: with the eyes of the soul we see the excellence, beauty, and glory of the most holy humanity; and through the intellectual vision, which was mentioned, we are given an understanding of how God is powerful, that He can do all things, that He commands all and governs all, and that His love permeates all things.[107]

Because authentic visions do not leave the recipient unchanged, Teresa was aware of the enriching results of having Jesus at her side. Her love for Him grew in its tenderness, and she was given special insight into the divine nature. A deeper humility together with a great purity of conscience accompanied still more profound yearnings to give herself totally to her Lord's service. Hence, she comments that if a person with this gift falls into any fault, it "pierces his very vitals". The vivid awareness of Jesus at one's side makes one "sensitive to everything".[108] We can observe in our merely human experiences dim reflections of these consequences, for if we are in the close presence of a dearly loved friend, we are more sensitive to what is happening to both of us. We grow in love and a desire to give to the other.

Are visions necessary? Happily for most of us, the answer is no. St. Teresa leaves her readers under no illusions about the matter. Of themselves visions bring no merit to the recipients, but they who do receive these favors lie under a heavier obligation to serve. There are, adds the foundress, many saintly people who never experience a single vision, while others receive these gifts and are not saintly. Yet while it is true that divine visions can be of the greatest help in growing to a lofty perfection, one who has attained advanced virtue through hard work has gained more merit.[109] It follows, therefore, that visions are not a secure basis for judging one's position in the spiritual life. "Let none of you imagine", the saint admonishes her nuns, "that because a sister has had such experiences, she is any better than the rest; the Lord leads each of us as He sees we have need. . . . Sometimes it is the weakest whom God leads by this road."[110] Like the Church in her canonization processes, we are to judge our advancement not by visions or other extraordinary phenomena but by the perfection with which we live the Gospel: humility, obedience, love, patience, chastity, honesty, kindliness and all else.

How ought the recipient of a vision react to it? And what line of judgment should spiritual directors follow when directees report experiences of this type? St. Teresa's practice and advice were solid and down to earth. True to her no-nonsense character, she was by no means credulous regarding visions, for she entertained the lively conviction that they could easily arise from imagination or demonic activity.[111] In one of her letters to Jerome Gratian she writes about a particular priest that

> he is extremely sceptical about revelations. . . . I have always been attracted by people I knew to have ideas of this kind, supposing that, if I was under a delusion, they would show me where I was wrong better than others. As I no longer have such fears, I am not so anxious about this.[112]

We may recall, too, what the saint had written in her *Foundations*: "It is essential that we should not at once suppose every little imagining of ours to be a vision; if it is one, we may be sure that the fact will soon become clear." Well aware of the propensity of some people toward the unusual, she added that "I have been quite alarmed to find how possible it is for people to think they see what they do not".[113]

Both St. Teresa and St. John insisted that the recipients of any unusual communication should share the experience with their confessor or spiritual director — or some wise individual, should the former be lacking.[114] And one should not act upon a vision before clearing the matter and getting advice from the confessor.[115] The reasons for these norms are the same as those we have already considered when we discussed locutions.

Moreover, we ought not to desire visions. St. Teresa felt strongly about this matter: "I will only warn you", she tells her nuns, "that, when you learn or hear that God is granting souls these graces, you must never beseech or desire Him to lead you along this road."[116] She proceeds to list no less than six reasons for her strict admonition.

The first is that asking for extraordinary gifts shows a lack of humility. We do not in the least deserve visions, and the Lord will not grant them, at least ordinarily, to those who lack this virtue. The second reason is the high likelihood that people who want this sort of thing, who like to dabble in unusual experiences, will be deceived and misled. They are in great danger "because the devil has only to see a door left slightly ajar to enter and play a thousand tricks on us".[117] Her next reason shows that St. Teresa did not need modern psychology to alert her to the fact that the wish is easily father to the thought. "When a person has a great desire for something, he persuades himself that he is seeing or hearing what he desires, just as those who go about desiring something all day think so much about it that after a time they begin to dream it." The fourth reason is presumption: we simply do not know the best way to God for ourselves; this we must leave to Him Who does know. Fifth, the trials suffered by the recipients of extraordinary gifts are heavy and of many kinds. Who of us knows whether he is able to bear them successfully? And last, she cautions, "You may well find that the very thing from which you had expected gain will bring you loss, just as Saul only lost by becoming king."[118] These reasons would be hard to rebut.

CHAPTER FIFTEEN

FRIENDSHIP

Few people would spontaneously connect the name of Teresa of Avila with a comprehensive teaching on human relationships. Her fame rightly derives from her masterly explanations of advanced communion with the indwelling Trinity, not from her insights into friendship. Yet a careful investigation into all of her writings, letters included, yields abundant materials from which one can construct an impressive doctrine on close human relationships. As is the case with almost everything written by the saint, we find these ingredients of friendship in no single place. They must be gathered from the four winds of her published thoughts and then woven together in a thematic and logical manner.

It is best to consider St. Teresa's personal friendships first of all and only then what she has to say about those of other people. Her life and her words are mutual commentaries. We need them both.

ST. TERESA'S FRIENDSHIPS

Friendship is envisioned here as being not merely casual acquaintances but also interpersonal relationships of considerable depth. St. Teresa felt and expressed a special fondness for certain men and women in all states of life. To a layman she writes: "May the Lord preserve you many years, and permit me to enjoy your friendship, for indeed I love you in the Lord." To the same individual she remarks about the children of another couple: "I send remembrances to our little angels."[1] Writing of a laywoman, Doña Juana Dantisco, Teresa states that "I have been delighted to have her: every day I love her more", and she refers to this woman as "the angel".[2] Referring to another laywoman, Señora Doña Maria, the saint declares that "whenever I am away from her, I realize how dearly I love her".[3] She entertains a special affection for certain among the clergy, especially her confessors and directors. At a time of considerable suffering she is able to say of her "good Father", Jerome Gratian, that

I became afflicted in seeing I was without him, since I had no one to
whom I could have recourse in this tribulation. It seemed to me I was
living in great loneliness, and this loneliness increased when I saw that
there was no one now but him who might give me comfort and that
he had to be absent most of the time, which was a great torment to me.[4]

One who does not understand the saints may well have a problem
here: How can this woman, who found so much delight and fulfillment
in her deep communion with unending Beauty, desire and experience
comfort in mere human beings? One answer to this question lies in
contemporary experience: men and women today who are gifted by
God with lofty contemplation still do need and appreciate the understanding and caring of a competent spiritual director or other spiritual
friend. But the best answer is Jesus Himself. He Who enjoyed unspeakable closeness to His Father[5] nonetheless desired the companionship
and support of His disciples in His own agony.[6] Teresa is in good company. When she hears from one of her nuns of the goodness of the
bishop of Avila, she writes to him that "as it is such news as I wish
to hear, I can endure the long time I have to spend without a glimpse
of your writing".[7]

While St. Teresa did love deeply, she could not entertain a special
affection indiscriminately. She could be close only to those she called
"spiritual persons". After the Lord told her one day that He did not
want her to converse with men but with angels, she explains that indeed such became a pattern for her life:

These words have been fulfilled, for I have never again been able to tie
myself to any friendship or to find consolation in or bear particular love
for any other persons than those I understand love Him and strive to
serve Him; nor is it in my power to do so, nor does it matter whether
they are friends or relatives. If I'm not aware that the person seeks to
love and serve God or to speak about prayer, it is a painful cross for
me to deal with him.[8]

People who have never loved deeply may find it difficult to identify
with Teresa's inability to be close to worldly individuals who may
nonetheless have naturally attractive traits. But for a person profoundly
in love, anything unrelated to the beloved is a burden. Only the mediocre need further explanation. We may not forget that before she was
anything else St. Teresa was a woman head over heels in love with
God. She had experienced the very best; anything less was insipid, if
pursued for itself. We can catch a glimpse of this trait even on a natural
level. One who appreciates Beethoven or Shakespeare or Michelangelo
has little taste for rock music or comic books. We have discussed

elsewhere in these pages the awesome experiences of God that St. Teresa had enjoyed. What would be surprising, indeed, even suspect, would be to find that this same woman could find anything delightful sought aside from Him. Then, too, she, like all the saints, took seriously Jesus' saying that we are to avoid idle words[9] and Paul's admonition to the Ephesians that we are to sing to the Lord in our hearts always and everywhere.[10] There is no room in the divine plan for useless gossip. One who loves another has far more important things to do.

MOTIVATION

There is no doubt that the saint's fondness for and closeness to special people was the divine in them, and she gives us some insights into how she translated this into practice. St. Teresa tells us explicitly that she conceived a special love for those who were generous with God and detached from the world, those whom in her own terminology she called "spiritual people".[11] Her great affection for Father Jerome Gratian was due mainly to his showing "such perfection that he astounds me".[12] While Teresa was human enough to be attracted to intelligence, cheerfulness, wittiness and comeliness, these traits were secondary. We might say that for her a person's degree of immersion in God was the degree of her love for that person. She tells us that when a priest gave her help in coming closer to God, she almost automatically conceived a special love for him. Of one of her guides she writes: "I loved one of them very much because my soul owed him an infinite debt and he was very holy; I felt it infinitely when I saw that he didn't understand me; he strongly desired that I might advance and that the Lord might give me light."[13] So immersed were her friendships in God she considered a friend's growing closer to God as a real proof of love for herself. "I beg your Reverence", she wrote to a priest, "that we may all be mad for love of Him who for love of us was called mad. Since your Reverence says that you love me, prove it to me by preparing yourself so that God may grant you this favor."[14]

St. Teresa looked upon friendship as a source of mutual aid in our pilgrimage to the fatherland—a concept that nicely integrates our propensity toward human intimacy with our even deeper need for God. To four of her trusted friends the saint extended this invitation:

> I should like the five of us who at present love each other in Christ to make a kind of pact that since others in these times gather together in secret against His Majesty to prepare wicked deeds and heresies, we

might seek to gather together some time to free each other from illusion and to speak about how we might mend our ways and please God
more since no one knows himself as well as others who observe him
if they do so with love and concern for his progress. I say we should
gather in secret because this kind of talk is no longer in fashion. Even
preachers are composing their sermons so as not to displease.[15]

DIVINE ALTRUISM

St. Teresa could suffer nothing willingly imperfect in her friendships.
She wrote to a priest that "when conscience enters into anything, friendship does not weigh with me, for I owe more to God than to anyone".[16]
As an application of this principle the saint held that visits ought not
to interfere with one's need for prayerful solitude, and as much as she
loved her brother Lorenzo (for whom, we recall, she was spiritual director), she found that he came too often to see her. Although she realized
his excess was well intentioned, she nonetheless would politely suggest that he leave. "He goes like an angel", she commented. "It is not
that I do not love him dearly, for I do; only I should like to be more
alone."[17]

While Teresa had too large a mind to be troubled by petty scruples,
she did not allow her magnanimity to degenerate into laxity. She wished
that her visits with friends would include no idle words, no mere gossip.
To one of her correspondents she writes that "to see each other for
a short period is very tiring: the whole time goes in visits, and we chatter
so much that we lose our sleep; and we might even have slipped into
idle words through our longing to talk to each other".[18] Although the
saint recognized the need human beings have to comfort one another
and to be comforted, yet for her the amount of time spent in visits
or in writing letters is to be determined not by mere pleasure but by
honest necessity. In the canonization process one of her nuns said of
Teresa that

> she taught us detachment from all things saying that those who were
> not detached from visible things could not enjoy the invisible ones nor
> would they reach high contemplation. . . . Even her affection for her
> superior or confessor she feared, striving not to be with them nor writing
> to them more than she need, for she was most careful to avoid her own
> pleasure.[19]

St. Teresa's friendships were fully compatible with her dedication
to the virginal life. By this I mean that not only were they entirely

pure and chaste; they were also nonpossessive, nonexclusive. It is right and proper, even necessary, that wife and husband love each other possessively and exclusively, but the consecrated celibate loves universally. While this love is warm, deep, individual, it is neither limited to nor focused on one alone. St. Teresa was never upset or displeased when she noticed that someone else also loved her dear friend, and she herself loved deeply a goodly number of men and women. She told Gratian, for example, "I enjoyed seeing Fray Juan de Jesus. Whenever I observe what a great affection he has for your Reverence, it makes me the more attached to him."[20] And she revealed to one of her nuns that she loved her even more when she saw how she loved Gratian and was concerned about him.[21]

EXPRESSED WARMTH

As is typical of those saints whose correspondence I have read, St. Teresa made it plain that feeling affection and showing it can be holy and proper. So loving was she in manner that before people got to know her well, some of them were apprehensive about her expression of warmth. But when they got to know better her authenticity and unquestioned chastity, their initial misgivings evaporated like mist under the sun. The world cannot understand how intimate love can be totally pure. In their lives the saints show that it is not only possible but normal.

> Since I believe that my confessors stand so truly in the place of God, I think they are the ones for whom I feel the most benevolence. Since I am always very fond of those who guide my soul and since I felt secure, I showed them that I liked them. They, as God-fearing servants of the Lord, were afraid lest in any way I would become attached and bound to this love, even though in a holy way, and they showed me their displeasure. This happened after I became so subject to obeying them, for before that I didn't experience this love. I laughed to myself to see how mistaken they were, although I didn't always express so clearly how little attached I was to anyone. But I assured them; and as they got to know me better they realized what I owed to the Lord, for these suspicions they had about me always came at the beginning of our acquaintance.[22]

Since this saintly, tender love is not well understood, even though we find it in Jesus Himself, it may serve our purpose to illustrate the freedom with which Teresa expressed her affection. To Brianda de San José she writes:

I am very anxious to know if you are well. . . . For love of Our Lord, do try to write me soon. . . . It will be very cruel of you if you fail to write; even if you cannot send me a long letter, just let me know how you are. . . . May His Majesty preserve you to me and give me enough patience to last me all this time I am having to endure without seeing your writing.[23]

She lovingly teased Maria de Jesus: "If I could, I would write to you so often that I should not let you sleep."[24] To Maria de San José she declares that "I don't know why it is, but, in spite of all the annoyance your Reverence causes me, I cannot help loving you dearly, and all [my displeasure] passes in a moment."[25] In an earlier letter to the same nun Teresa partially explains her great affection for Maria:

All the nuns were amazed to find how clever you are, and are very, very grateful to you, and so am I, for it is quite clear how much you love me from the way you give me pleasure in everything. I have known that all the time — and I can assure you that the love on my side is even greater, for I am amazed at my affection for you. You must not imagine I love anyone more than you, for not all the nuns appeal so much to my nature.[26]

This letter alone vaporizes the idea that nuns or saints are starchy people.

So confident is St. Teresa in the goodness of her affection that she is not at all reluctant to express it to men as well as to women. To the priest Ambrosio Mariano she writes that "I have only to see you ill or in trouble to realize how deep is my love for you in the Lord".[27] She tells Gratian: "You write like an angel."[28] And she declares in another letter, "Oh, how much lonelier my soul gets each day when I am so far from your Paternity."[29] Perhaps the most surprising (to those who do not know Teresa well) expression of her affection occurs in a letter to this same priest. In it the saint is referring to herself under the code name of Laurencia:

I have been wondering which of the two your Paternity loves better — Señora Doña Juana [Gratian's mother], who, I reflected, has a husband and her other children to love her, or poor Laurencia, who has no one else in the world but you, her Father. May it please God to preserve him to her. Amen.[30]

I cannot imagine those few lines being penned by anyone else in the history of letter writing other than the Carmelite foundress. Nor could I conceive the following sentence flowing from any other heart but hers: "I have only one consolation: freedom from fear . . . that the friars would attack this Holy of Holies of mine." To this statement E. Allison

Peers appends a footnote: "i.e., P. Gratian himself [the original has the Latin phrase *sancta sanctorum,* which is currently used in Spanish to denote anything precious, without distinction of gender]".[31] Marcelle Auclair is quite correct in her characterization of Teresa's extraordinary capacity to love on a human level. Speaking of the saint's love for Bishop Alvaro de Mendoza, who had given her constant support, Auclair comments that "she gave him her affection till he died, as she alone knew how to give it — an affection that was the most reverent, most tender and most exacting in the world".[32]

RECEPTIVITY TO HUMAN LOVE

One might suppose that a person who had the awesome experiences of God and the most profound delights in Him that we have described in other chapters of this volume would care little or nothing for the satisfactions mere human beings can afford. Yet it is typical both of canonized saints and of deeply prayerful contemporaries that they are profoundly appreciative of human understanding and love. The surprise that some may initially experience at this fact dissolves when one reflects that it is actually a simple concretization of another fact, namely, that Jesus proclaimed the first and second of the commandments to be inseparable. A burning love for God does imply and bring about a disappearance of self-centered clingings and egoisms, but it does not destroy the reciprocity of interpersonal human love. On the contrary, divine love intensifies human love. Reality, another name for sanctity, is an integrated whole: everything fits with and reinforces everything else. Truth is indeed symphonic.

St. Teresa takes all of this theory for granted. In her unaffected realism she openly declares that her friends comfort, rejoice and strengthen her. At the end of a two-page letter to a laywoman the saint admits: "It is such a comfort to me to talk to your Ladyship that I had not realized how much I had written."[33] To one of her nuns the saint writes: "God forgive you, for I assure you your letters make me happier than you would think possible."[34] To her favorite Maria: "I was delighted to get your letter and I should be more so still if I could see you. . . . I think we should be very close to each other. There are few women with whom I should like to discuss so many things, for talking to you gives me real pleasure."[35] In a letter to Gratian Teresa exclaims, "Oh Jesus, how wonderful it is when two souls understand each other! They never lack anything to say and never grow weary [of saying it]."[36] In another message she makes known that "if anything could give me

any pleasure, it would be to see Paul [her code name for Gratian]".[37]
And she tells him in still another missive to "be sure you do not fail
to write to me—and a long letter, too—for you know what a comfort
to me your letters are".[38]

LOYALTY TO FRIENDS

Anyone who has much experience of human life knows how fragile
friendships can be. A person who has expressed an explicit and great
love for another will, only too often, eventually set the other aside.
I do not refer here to separation resulting from conflict (though that,
too, is due to human fault) but to the termination of friendships where
there has been no shadow of offense. One seems simply to tire of the
other—which, of course, raises the question of how much genuine love
there was in the first place. A mere need-based closeness is not love-
based closeness and is likely to last only as long as the need lasts.

Like genuine love, genuine friendship is eternal. And so it is with
the saints. Their loves are not based, at least not primarily, on their
own needs being satisfied by the other. Like anyone who loves deeply
and authentically, St. Teresa was fiercely loyal to her friends. She can
say to Gratian that "it is of no importance about Fray Antonio, but
if, when he casts reflections upon me, he also casts them on my Paul,
I can't bear it. What he says about me doesn't matter in the least."[39]
In another letter, remarking how her knowledge that a dear one is
suffering is a sore trial to her, Teresa steadfastly says: "I have the saintly
Paul with me and no one can make me break my promise to that saint."[40]
She herself tells him that "the love I have for you in the Lord . . . produces a natural weakness in me and makes me very resentful that
everybody should not realize what they owe to you, and how you have
laboured, and I am unable to stand hearing a word against you".[41] Who
would not treasure a friendship with this woman?

A NOTE

A further point needs to be made: not only is saintliness compatible
with tender human love; it also brings it about. It is not accidental that
Teresa of the transforming union is the same Teresa of fiercely loyal
and tenderly warm human relationships. The former is the mainspring
of the latter. The fact that divine love produces human love we know
from experience with people of advanced prayer; the explanation for

this we know from theology. There is only one virtue of charity, and by it we love God, ourselves and our neighbor. As we grow in loving God, the result of advancing prayer depth, we must be growing in loving ourselves and our brothers and sisters. The various loves cannot be separated.[42] Another way of putting the matter is to say that contemplation brings about a sensitivity to beauty, any and all beauty, created and uncreated. This is why a reflective person sees far more beauty in a tulip than a superficial one sees. Scripture has it that God "put his own light into their hearts to show them the magnificence of his works".[43] As a person grows in prayer, he puts on the mind of God more and more, and thus he sees others as "precious . . . God's beloved . . . sacred temples . . . transformed from one glory to another".[44] Seeing more beauty in sister and brother, we are more disposed to love them.

FRIENDSHIPS AMONG OTHERS

When we come to consider what St. Teresa said to others about friendships, we run into an apparent contradiction with what we have already seen of her thought. In her customary way, she does not consider this subject completely in any one place. Contained in her many scattered remarks are two streams of texts, one posing a problem for the other. On the one hand she seems to rule out special friendships, at least among her own nuns. In her constitutions[45] she disallows embraces, touching of face or hands and special relationships in the community.[46] Nor does she conclude from her showing affection for Gratian that such is permissible to all the nuns. One may object, "if shown warmth is proper for one nun, it is proper for any of them, all else being equal". Apparently, the saint did not think all else was equal, as she explains at some length in a letter to Gratian himself.

> For many reasons it is permissible for me to feel great affection for you and to show it in the dealings we have together. But it is not permissible for all the other nuns to do so. . . . I say and do things which are allowable in me because of my age and because I know whom I am dealing with. . . . Do me the kindness, as I have begged you, of not reading in public the letters I write you. . . . Just as I should not like anyone to overhear my conversation with God or to disturb me when I am alone with Him, so it is with Paul.[47]

This explanation invites comment. Teresa's expression "all the other nuns" suggests that she would consider shown affection proper if and when the circumstances for them were as they are for her. Further, the saint does not, of course, praise her own sanctity, but she must have been aware of her utterly pure intentions and lofty chastity, and she knows that not all enjoy a similar freedom from temptations against this virtue. Nor may we forget the holiness of Jerome Gratian—Teresa did know with whom she was dealing.

However, while what we have just considered seems to dissuade the nuns from special friendships, we have other texts that not only permit but also commend, and highly commend, what she calls spiritual friendships. Teresa considered it "a great evil" to be friendless amidst the dangers this world poses for those seeking God earnestly. We need one another, as she explains in a lengthy passage, only part of which we cite here.

> For this reason I would counsel those who practice prayer to seek, at least in the beginning, friendship and association with other persons having this same interest. . . . Since friends are sought out for conversations and human attachments, even though these latter may not be good, so as to relax and better enjoy telling about vain pleasures, I don't know why it is not permitted that a person beginning truly to love and to serve God talk with some others about his joys and trials, which all who practice prayer undergo. . . . I believe that he who discusses these joys and trials for the sake of this friendship with God will benefit himself and those who hear him, and he will come away instructed; even without understanding how he will have instructed his friends. . . . Since this spiritual friendship is so extremely important for souls not yet fortified in virtue—since they have so many opponents and friends to incite them to evil—I don't know how to urge it enough. . . . It is necessary for those who serve Him to become shields for one another that they might advance. . . . It is a kind of humility not to trust in oneself but to believe that through those with whom one converses God will help and increase charity while it is being shared. And there are a thousand graces I would not dare speak of if I did not have powerful experience of the benefit that comes from this sharing.[48]

The saint was keenly convinced that she herself desperately needed this kind of friendship and sharing: "Of myself," she acknowledged, "I know and say that if the Lord had not revealed this truth to me and given me the means by which I could ordinarily talk with persons who practiced prayer, I, falling and rising, would have ended by throwing myself straight into hell."[49]

Good as this kind of friendship is in itself, it is also subject to human abuse. Sensitive to this possibility, Teresa worried at times about whether there was something less than perfect in the comfort and consolation she experienced from sharing with those she loved. She tells us of the answer to this concern, which she received from the Lord Himself:

> The Lord told me that if a sick person who was in danger of death thought a doctor was curing him, that sick person wouldn't be virtuous if he failed to thank and love the doctor; that if it hadn't been for these persons what would I have done; that conversation with good persons is not harmful, but that my words should always be well weighed and holy, and that I shouldn't fail to converse with them; that doing so is beneficial rather than harmful. This consoled me greatly because sometimes, since conversing with them seemed to me to be an attachment, I didn't want to talk to them at all.[50]

St. Bernard, too, was of the same mind as the Lord, and in point of fact the great Cistercian found in what the Lord Himself taught publicly in the Gospel the same instruction that was taught to Teresa privately. Writing long before the foundress' day, and speaking of the bride-soul much in pursuit of the Beloved, Bernard comments that

> while she and those companions are conversing together, the Bridegroom on whom the conversation centers, suddenly appears, for he loves to draw near to those who speak about him. It is his way. For example he proved himself a pleasant and affable companion to the two men who conversed together as they went to Emmaus. This is no more than what he has promised in the Gospel: "Where two or three meet in my name, I shall be there with them."[51]

As was invariably the case, St. Teresa's personal experience with the Lord she so loved was in entire accord with sound biblical study and theology. She saw a spiritual friend as a way of having God and of possessing Him still more deeply. While it is perfectly true that there are few friends of the type the saint had in mind, when that rare person is found, one should make every effort to further the relationship. In her mind this friend cannot be loved too much.

> When you make the acquaintance of any such person, sisters, the Mother Prioress should employ every possible effort to keep you in touch with them. Love such persons as much as you like. There can be very few of them, but none the less it is the Lord's will that their goodness should be known. When one of you is striving after perfection, she will at once be told that she has no need to know such people—that it is enough for her to have God. But to get to know God's friends is a very good way of "having" Him; as I have discovered by experience, it is most helpful.[52]

HARMFUL RELATIONSHIPS

Experience and reflection make it clear to any honest, thoughtful individual that not every interhuman closeness is of the saintly variety. We need, therefore, to turn our attention to what the saint had to say about harmful relationships. Teresa had known firsthand "extremely vain friendships", and she constantly regretted those of her early life.[53] Perhaps the chief bane of closeness among otherwise good people is idle chatter, even "holy" idle chatter, and of this fault the saint had ample experience as a young nun. She could not bring herself to countenance it among her own sisters. She writes to Gratian toward the very end of her life:

> Oh my Father, how troublesome Julian [of Avila, an easygoing priest in his later years] is getting! There is no way of forbidding Mariana [a nun] to see him every day if she wants to. . . . Everything they say is quite holy, but God deliver me from confessors of long standing! . . . Holy though their conversations may be, I cannot allow the thing to go on.[54]

Within a community itself a whole series of troubles can arise from a harmful friendship existing between the superior and another. Since each of us can readily imagine what these troubles may be, there is no need to detail them. St. Teresa was so aware of this possible aberration that she singled it out for explicit mention to those who were commissioned to make canonical visitations to her convents. The visitator, she wrote, must find out if the prioress is showing any favoritism, doing more for one nun than for the others or showing undue attention and preference. The saint understood, for she mentions it, that a superior can have reason to consult often the more discreet and intelligent members of the community, and this Teresa does not fault.[55] Rationalization of a supposed need to consult can, however, lead to much waste of time and to legitimate complaints of favoritism.

The foundress mentions a number of ills that can occur in a community when two members indulge in a selfish friendship. They are harms that lax people do not even recognize for what they are; indeed, they are sometimes defensive of sillinesses that are obvious to everyone but themselves. While the saint writes of these at some length, for our purposes a summary of her main ideas will suffice. She is of the opinion that these faults are more common among women than among men. One harm is that the two friends pay disproportionately more attention to each other than they do to the rest of the community, and thus their love for God also weakens and cools, for He, too, gets less attention. St. Paul's admonition that equal kindness should be shown to all is simply not observed,[56] and factions are likely to develop. When one's friend suffers from supposed or actual offenses by others, resentment builds up along with the consequent risk of strife and lack of peace. The two will probably conceive the desire to give gifts to each other and to spend valuable time in vain gossiping. "The puerilities are innumerable", Teresa concludes.[57]

It goes without saying that egocentric relationships occupy the mind with almost anything but God, and this involves another transgression of Scripture, which bids us to keep our minds on the Lord always.[58] To lesser people this may appear to be no great fault, but when Teresa looked back at her early days, she considered that it did her inestimable harm. When she found that others liked her, and she in turn found them attractive, her memory slowly became fixed on them, even though she had no intention of offending her Lord. "This was something so harmful it was leading my soul seriously astray", she comments. "After I beheld the extraordinary beauty of the Lord, I didn't see anyone who in comparison with Him seemed to attract me or occupy my thoughts."[59] In other words, the saint saw the gravity of this defect only after she had fallen deeply in love. Goodness brings insight.

TRAITS OF HOLY FRIENDSHIP

We turn now to the other side of the coin. As we consider what a genuine closeness to others is like, we should note how completely theocentric Teresa's human love was. And not only that. It is precisely because all was immersed in God that her friendships enjoyed the security of tenderness, patience, durability and permanence. Even a modicum of experience with others makes evident how fragile many relationships turn out to be. Not rarely do supposedly close friends lose interest in each other after the passage of a few years. There may have been no conflicts, no ugly words, no unkindnesses, and yet there is a gradual drifting apart; their friendship slowly evaporates. The most likely explanation of this phenomenon is that it is no match for the love of which Teresa speaks and probably never was anything more than a need relationship. When the need is satisfied elsewhere, the closeness ceases.

A genuine friend, according to the teresian mind, experiences an intense longing that the other party be immersed in God. This trait shows both that the relationship is informed by the divine and that their closeness is not a mere need satisfaction. It is not accidental that the quality of St. Teresa's love for other men and women is as rare as was the depth of her prayer life.

I've experienced this for some years: as soon as I see a person who greatly
pleases me, with longings I sometimes cannot bear, I want to see him
give himself totally to God. And although I desire that all serve God,
the longings come with very great impulses in the case of these persons
I like; so I beg the Lord very much on their behalf. With the religious
I'm speaking of, it so happened to me.[60]

Because divine and human loves grow or disappear together, it is
not likely that beginners in the spiritual life will be capable of deep
friendship, even though many of them are convinced that they are. This
naïveté is not unlike that of people who interpret their felt emotions
at prayer to be lofty contemplation.

The second trait of a holy friendship may come as a surprise to those
who know only of need relationships: true friends correct each other
when such is necessary. They realize that Gospel admonition is an act
of love, nothing less.[61] To illustrate this point, one deeply rooted in
the Scriptures, I have singled out the man and the woman for whom
St. Teresa had the greatest affection. She does not in the least hesitate
to admonish them. In one of her letters to Jerome Gratian she complained that he had added too many extra obligations to the nuns' keeping of their rule.[62] She was, of course, only carrying out the divine
practice described in Revelation 3:19: "Those whom I love I rebuke and
chastize." To Maria de San José the saint wrote that "I love you tenderly. . . . The more I love people, the less I can bear their having any
faults. I know that is silly, because one learns by making mistakes."[63]
She explains her mind more fully in another letter to the same Maria:

> When I really love anyone, I am so anxious she should not go astray
> that I become unbearable . . . true friendship does not express itself in
> covering up things . . . bad though you are, I wish I had a few more
> like you . . . what silly things you said in that letter, just to get your
> own way![64]

In a playful manner Teresa could say to the same nun: "God grant that
you are telling the truth: I should be delighted if you were, but you
are a fox, and I expect there is a subterfuge about it somewhere."[65]
That she could write these things to her dearest friends without any
fear of losing their affection suggests that the saint had a strong confidence in their permanent love, and they in hers. Only too often in
lesser friendships, what was thought to be a deep and lasting bond turns
into a hurt withdrawal as soon as one party suggests a fault in the other.
And yet Scripture has it that the person who rejects correction is foolish
and arrogant, while the one who welcomes reproof is wise and hum-

ble. The latter loves his friend more, not less, for the favor shown him.[66] Once again, we see that St. Teresa's teaching and practice coincide perfectly with the revealed message.

DISCERNING GENUINE FRIENDSHIP

There are probably few aspects of living the Gospel in which beginners are more prone to err than in this question of friendships. Not rarely, neophytes are convinced that they have a true friend, that theirs is a deep, indeed, undying love, that nothing could possibly separate them, that their relationship is compatible both with love for others in their life and with a growing love for God Himself. Occasionally they are right; often they are wrong. How then do we discern saintly friendships from their counterfeits?

First of all, the attraction is not based primarily upon bodily beauty or merely natural qualities. True enough, notes Teresa, God gives physical comeliness, and we ought to praise Him for it, but we do not dwell on it more than momentarily — it is just a shadow.[67] Rather, the love is rooted in deeper, permanent qualities. Second, the friends find that they cannot really be interested in anything unless it has to do with God,[68] and therefore any affection that does not benefit their souls wearies them.[69] If this trait seems too demanding and even unreasonable, we must recall that saints are men and women completely in love with God. No one who knows this happiness will have any difficulty with Teresa's logic. Third, the closeness found among authentic friends is selfless. Each party is anxious for the welfare of the other, and it is the eternal well-being of the beloved one that is foremost:

> This, as I have said, is love without any degree whatsoever of self-interest; all that this soul wishes and desires is to see the soul it loves enriched with blessings from Heaven. This is love, quite unlike our ill-starred earthly affections — to say nothing of illicit affections, from which may God keep us free.[70]

The fourth trait we have already touched upon: genuine friends welcome being admonished if they stray or commit faults.[71] Fifth, their closeness is permanent, because it is not based on physical characteristics that change with illness and age. Rather, says Teresa, one "digs" (the very word she uses) to find eternally lovable beauty in the other, and if one digs deeply, gold will be found within the mine of the beloved.[72] Last, the saint observes that authentic friendship can be known only by experience: "What it is to love the Creator and what to love the creature must be discovered by experience, for it is a very different matter from merely thinking about it and believing it."[73]

In one of his letters, C. S. Lewis insightfully integrates human and divine loves:

> When I have learnt to love God better than my earthly dearest, I shall love my earthly dearest better than I do now. In so far as I learn to love my earthly dearest at the expense of God and instead of God, I shall be moving toward the state in which I shall not love my earthly dearest at all. When first things are put first, second things are not suppressed but increased.[74]

THE DESIRE FOR HUMAN LOVE

Whether it is right and completely consonant with the Gospel to seek to be loved by others obviously depends on whether what is sought is what we have been discussing in this chapter. St. Teresa tells us that she had pondered this question carefully and came to the conclusion that seeking affection is "sheer blindness" unless "it relates to persons who can lead us to do good so that we may gain blessings in perfection".[75] People who are entirely intent on holiness of life, she adds, laugh at their earlier concerns as to whether their affection for others was being returned or not. Observing that, however pure our affection is, it is understandable and natural for us to wish it to be returned, the saint cautions that at the same time we ought to have the good sense to realize how insubstantial this return is, "like a thing of straw, as light as air and easily carried away by the wind". But does this realism imply that such people love and delight exclusively in God? No, says Teresa, "they will love others much more than they did, with a more genuine love, with greater passion [vehemence is what she means] and with a love which brings more profit; that, in a word, is what love really is". These people are much more pleased to give love than to receive it.[76]

St. Teresa accepted human love, appreciated it and even liked to hear that she was loved. She wrote to Maria de San José that "the only thing that worries me is about my brother, who misses me dreadfully". She takes it as perfectly normal that Lorenzo would love her much.[77] When the same Maria tells the saint of her love, Teresa, with no inhibition, answers that "it is a joy to me to hear you say so".[78] Toward the very end of her life the foundress explains in a charming passage that our desire for a return of love is nothing other than imitating the Lord Himself:

> It was a great comfort to me to get your letter, not that that is anything new, for your letters rest me as much as other people's letters weary me. I assure you that, if you love me dearly, I for my part return your love, and like you to tell me of yours. How unmistakable a trait of our nature is this wish for our love to be returned! Yet it cannot be wrong, for Our Lord wishes it too. . . . Let us be like Him, even in a thing like this.[79]

MARKS OF AFFECTION

It is abundantly evident that the New Testament, in giving the example of the Lord Himself, takes for granted that Christians are to express their love visibly and tangibly. The father receives back his prodigal son with an embrace and a tender kiss. Jesus embraces children before He blesses them, and He weeps at the tomb of Lazarus, His friend. The apostles admonish the faithful to greet one another with a holy kiss. It would be surprising indeed if the saints were to teach or act otherwise. When in her constitutions St. Teresa forbade the nuns to touch or embrace one another, she must have had in mind unacceptable hand holding and similar inordinate displays of childish fondness. Surely she was not objecting to suitable sisterly affection being shown, if her own behavior is any indicator. She does say that they are to avoid extravagant terms of endearment such as should be reserved for God alone: "My life! . . . my soul! . . . my good!"[80] This really is only common sense. Yet she does not rule out an emotional element in the nuns' love for one another. In the context where she declares that having good friends is a way of having God Himself, she comments that "at first [love] may be mingled with emotion, but this, as a rule, will do no harm. It is sometimes good and necessary for us to show emotion in our love, and also to feel it, and to be distressed by some of our sisters' trials and weaknesses."[81] The entire God-centeredness of Teresa's life shows itself here, as it does in her thoughts about expressions of endearment for members of one's natural family: the nuns are to avoid foolishness and to seek only the genuine benefit of those they love:

> Neither with your relatives nor with anyone else must you use such phrases as "If you love me," or "Don't you love me?" unless you have in view some noble end and the profit of the person with whom you

are speaking. It may be necessary, in order to get a relative—a brother
or some such person—to listen to the truth and accept it, to prepare him
for it by using such phrases and showing him signs of love, which are
always pleasing to sense. He may possibly be more affected, and influ-
enced, by one kind word, as such phrases are called, than by a great
deal which you might say about God, and then there would be plenty
of opportunities for you to talk to him about God afterwards. I do not
forbid such phrases, therefore, provided you use them in order to bring
someone profit.[82]

As for embraces, we find that she considered this expression of sincere
love to be normal both for herself and for the nuns, but she wanted
nothing excessively demonstrative. Interestingly, we have apparently
conflicting attitudes described in one and the same deposition of Maria
de San José:

> The Mother had so much gratitude for the smallest service done for her
> by anyone that she would turn round thanking them and caressing them
> for it. . . . [Then about five hundred words later in the same testimony]
> When this witness saw her leave this house in Valladolid, she did not
> permit the nuns who came to her to make any demonstration of affec-
> tion, which, she said, was effeminate, and she would in no wise consent
> to her nuns appearing to be effeminate in any way. That day she con-
> sented to everything and embraced affectionately each one of them.[83]

However we understand the saint's reactions in this deposition, it is
clear from other evidences that she entertained no rigid opposition to
shown affection. In a letter to one of her nuns, which she wrote toward
the end of her life, she asked the nun to "give a warm embrace to my
Casilda [just professed]—I only wish I could give it her myself".[84]
And to her favorite Maria she stated warmly: "Though I have always
loved you dearly, I love you so much more now that it amazes me,
and so I long to see you and embrace you again and again."[85]

It is not difficult to show in detail that St. Teresa's concept of friendship is in total accord with what we find in the Scriptures. It is also
of one piece with the familiar relationships we find in the lives of other
saints. It is part of heroic holiness. As the New Testament puts it, a
genuine love for others not only does not happen, it cannot happen,
until we have accepted divine revelation (become "obedient to the
truth"), been stripped of our selfishness ("purified your souls") and been
born anew "from the everlasting word of the living and eternal God".[86]

CHAPTER SIXTEEN

SPIRITUAL DIRECTION

In recent years we have seen in the Church a number of extraordinary developments associated with the renewal of ecclesial and religious life. Some of these have been beneficial, and some have not. Among the latter must be counted the widespread trend whereby men and women with meager training have been assuming the guidance of others in their spiritual lives. Veteran directors are likely to have encountered the endless variety and complexity of problems and questions that arise in the concrete circumstances of the human pursuit of the divine. Naïve neophytes seem to suppose that taking a few courses in Scripture, theology and psychology amply qualifies a person as an adept tutor in the life of prayer and equips one to deal with the vast ramifications that can arise. In other fields, such as medicine or law, amateurism is not tolerated for a moment, and laws are framed to prevent and to punish incompetence. Yet, in the matter of guiding immortal souls, the barest background preparation is presented and popularly accepted as normal, indeed, even advocated as being a healthy approach.

Deplorable as incompetent spiritual direction is, one can be sympathetic with what is probably its chief motivating cause: a dire lack of reliable guides for those intent on a serious prayer life. The proliferation of unequipped directors is meant to provide a remedy for the shortage. In my lecture and retreat work, at home and abroad alike, I meet everywhere the persisting question: "Where can I find a priest who really understands contemplative prayer? There is none I know of in our area." It is all too apparent that a six-year program in philosophy, Scripture, theology, canon law and pastoral practice does not of itself automatically ensure that a priest has the necessary competence to do this work. Surely, then, a small sampling of coursework cannot be an adequate and responsible preparation for work that spans several disciplines and that supposes at least some familiarity with mental problems and counseling techniques. The state would prosecute as criminal a person who took a smattering of courses in biology and anatomy and then attempted to perform triple-bypass surgery. In the Church there are no existing plans or procedures designed to discover and weed out incompetent spiritual directors. Almost anyone who is of a mind to can venture the guidance not of mortal bodies but of immortal souls, and he can do so without having to meet any standards whatsoever and without any certification being required. Moreover, very few people seem alarmed by this.

Needless to say, such was not the mind of our two Carmelite masters. St. Teresa insisted that she and her nuns be guided only by "learned men". By this she meant those well versed in Scripture, theology and the practice of advanced prayer. She and John would have been appalled by the nonchalance of our contemporary views and practices and our disregard for the disastrous consequences that can come of them, since the good of souls is at stake. Their quite different expectations of spiritual direction will now be considered.

ST. JOHN OF THE CROSS

The sanjuanist concept of direction is thoroughly Christological and ecclesial. The chief guide and mover of souls is the Holy Spirit, for they alone are sons and daughters of the Father who are led by the Spirit Who is sent by the Son. While the human spiritual director (ordinarily a priest) is important, his role is only instrumental. He is not primarily a teacher of abstract norms, for they presumably are taught in the classroom or from the pulpit. He endeavors to adapt universal and unchanging truths to this particular person with these particular needs and this individual capacity. He does teach, when that is necessary, but that is not his main function. Few people easily understand how doctrine and general principles apply to their concrete circumstances and needs. It is the duty of the director to aid in these practical applications.

The instrumentality of the human guide working along with the Holy Spirit is evidenced in three ways. The first is that he helps to dispose the soul for the divine action by showing concretely how one attains denudation of spirit, that is, how to remove all obstacles, even the smallest and the most subtle. What this means specifically is clearly detailed throughout the *Ascent of Mount Carmel*. To the extent that the directee is rid of all selfish clingings, the divine director is freed to do the rest.

Second, the human director verifies from the outside what the indwelling teacher is working from within. In God's name the former authenticates the validity and quality of the person's life and prayer.

Third, the human guide explains the specifics of how one lives by faith, by the divine word and not merely by secondary supports (human approval from others in one's milieu, for example). Upon a moment's reflection we can readily see why a scant preparation will not fit a man or woman to be a competent instrument of the Holy Spirit. To teach another how to achieve nudity of spirit and, in the teaching, to escape both exaggeration and dilution is no simple task. The proper ability to authenticate an individual's life and prayer requires an extensive background in Scripture, in doctrinal, moral and mystical theology and in the lives and teachings of the saints. Showing another how to live by the divine word rather than by worldly wisdom requires this same extensive knowledge — knowledge gained by growing in sanctity as well as by study.

John's first principle, that is, the instrumentality of the human director, is completed by the second: spiritual direction is completely incarnational and ecclesial. It is an activity that happens in, from and for the Church of Christ. The director is not simply a wise adviser who operates solely on the basis of his own competence. He is a missioned person, one sent by the Church, who in turn has been sent by Christ, Who was sent by the Father. "As the Father has sent me, so I send you."[1] Therefore, the sanjuanist director is speaking in the name of God because he is functioning in the name of the Church sent by the incarnate Son.

Neither John nor Teresa raises the question of a nonordained person, without a canonical mission, regularly advising others in the spiritual life and serving in a quasi-public capacity (not, therefore, merely as two friends privately chatting). However, St. Teresa herself was spiritual director for her married brother and for at least one bishop. She and other saints like Catherine of Siena were, because of their high degree of intelligence, profound experience of God and knowledge of sound doctrine, in a class by themselves. The official Church does not prevent nonordained men and women of this caliber from engaging in spiritual direction. In fact, I know religious women who are so well instructed in theology, so sharp in mind and of sound judgment, so advanced in solid virtue and enjoying infused prayer that I would not hesitate to recommend them as guides to others. These ought not to be confused with the ill-equipped people previously mentioned.

Would this uncanonical spiritual direction be incarnational and ecclesial? A helpful distinction used in sacramental theology is that of ordinary and extraordinary ministers. In suggesting this latter distinction as possibly applicable to nonordained spiritual directors, I am thinking only of men and women who completely identify with the Ecclesia, accept her teaching fully and are living profoundly her in-Spirited life. They have talents and gifts, natural and supernatural, for the work of guiding others that many ordained priests do not claim for themselves. They represent the true mind and practice of the Church far more perfectly than do dissenting clergy. Consequently, there is a realistic basis for regarding their role in the guidance of souls along paths of prayer as a participation in the Church's mission to lead all to "taste and see how good the Lord is".

This ecclesial approach to spiritual direction excludes definitively the religious bane of the ages, the illuminist who heeds only his own imagined inner light and will be guided by no other person. John notes that Jesus promised to be not with the individual alone, but where two or three are gathered in His name, and he concludes that God does not want anyone to believe inner communications thought to be of divine origin but rather to accept only those that are confirmed by the Church and her ministers.[2] The saint applies to the spiritual director the binding and loosing power of the Church herself as we find it in Matthew 18:18.[3] His conclusion is firm:

> We must be guided humanly and visibly in all by the law of Christ the man and that of His Church and of His ministers. . . . Any departure from this road is not only curiosity, but extraordinary boldness. One should disbelieve anything coming in a supernatural way, and believe only the teaching of Christ the man, as I say, and of His ministers who are men.[4]

It goes without saying that when John credits so great an authority to the ministers of the Church, he has in mind only those who are in complete accord with the episcopal and petrine offices.

This ecclesiality of spiritual direction is simply one aspect of the law of providence by which men are saved by other men, and those progressing toward higher sanctity are to be led by others. We have in both Old and New Testaments many examples of this providential disposition by which God deals with His people through selected individuals: Abraham, Moses, the prophets, the apostles and most of all Mary. A pointed case is found in the Acts of the Apostles when Saul on the road to Damascus is suddenly confronted by the risen Lord Himself. We would have expected that Jesus would have told the future apostle in detail what he was to do, but as a matter of fact Paul was given only one direction: go to my representative for guidance — "Get up now and go into the city, and you will be told what you have to do."[5] In the spiritual life God ordinarily does not lead people to Himself with inner visions and messages, but when He does even then He wills that the message be confirmed by the visible authorities of the Church He established.

From this incarnational/ecclesial nature of spiritual direction we infer that it involves an intimate act of faith and thus fits entirely within the Gospel and sanjuanist insistence that we attain union with the Trinity in this life, not according to our own natural lights but through the word of God communicated to us as He has chosen to communicate it. There can be no transforming union except through faith, hope and charity. The indwelling Spirit does enlighten from within,[6] but this must always be confirmed from without.[7] The incarnational economy of salvation is not an angelism.

St. John of the Cross did not consider spiritual direction to be optional. While he did not determine in his writings to what extent one needs specific, individualized guidance, he did make it clear that a person without a master is like a single burning coal—he grows colder rather than hotter.[8] Or, to use another image, he is like a blind man who takes the wrong road.[9] We are poor judges in our own case, and so we need a faithful and objective other who may stand in the Lord's place and serve both as a prod and as a source of light.

Like the Church herself, John leaves the choice of the director to the individual. It is the latter who, for weal or for woe, makes the judgment of suitability, that is, the judgment that this priest is intelligent, of good judgment, himself given to a serious prayer life and faithful to the mind of the Church. In a more general sense the local bishop decides on the minimal aptitude of a priest for ministry when he gives him diocesan faculties, but this grant does not assure a competency for guiding people in advancing prayer. In fact, in conversations with priests many readily admit that they do not know enough to advise people in such matters. In seeking direction, therefore, a careful choice must be made. In this regard St. John candidly cautions: "It is very important that a person, desiring to advance in recollection and perfection, take care into whose hands he entrusts himself, for the disciple will become like the master, and as is the father so will be the son."[10]

This of course raises the question as to the specific qualities one should look for in a spiritual director. St. John's response is concise: "Besides being learned and discreet, a director should have experience."[11] By learning the saint means theological competence together with a genuine understanding of the spiritual life and mystical prayer. By discretion he envisions good, solid judgment, that is, a sound knowledge of practical human psychology together with the ability to apply general principles accurately to concrete cases. By experience he means especially one's own growth in advancing prayer. Regarding this last qualification John asserts that "although the foundation for guiding the soul to spirit is knowledge and discretion, the director will not succeed in leading the soul onward in it, when God bestows it, nor will he even understand it, if he has no experience of what true and pure spirit is".[12]

We should, I think, note the words "*no* experience". It seems that the saint does not require that a competent guide be within or close to the transforming union but that he should at least be receiving infused prayer of some sort. If one does not know firsthand the fourth mansions, he is not likely to understand the last three except perhaps in a verbal manner.

This leads us to the mistakes inept directors tend to make. Gentle John has hard words for pastoral incompetence. While never diluting the truth, the saint is invariably calm, benign and compassionate with wayward human nature. But when it comes to those who bungle the divine artistry in holy men and women, John does not hide his exasperation. The first defect he points out is the failure to understand or recognize genuine growth in prayer, which in turn leads to blundering advice. "Many spiritual directors cause great harm", says the saint, when they instruct advanced souls "in other baser ways, serviceable only to beginners, which they themselves have used or read of somewhere. Knowing no more than what pertains to beginners—and please God they would even know this much—they do not wish to permit souls to pass beyond these beginnings and these discursive and imaginative ways", though these are keeping them from progressing on that way along which God is now leading them.[13] Writing on this subject at some length, the saint warms up to his denunciation:

> How often is God anointing a contemplative with some very delicate unguent of loving knowledge, serene, peaceful, solitary, and far withdrawn from the senses . . . when a spiritual director will happen along who, like a blacksmith, knows no more than how to hammer and pound with the faculties . . . . The director's whole concern should not be to accommodate souls to his own method and condition, but he should observe the road along which God is leading them, and if he does not recognize it, he should leave them alone and not bother them.[14]

Furthermore, he declares, "these directors do not know what spirit is. They do a great injury to God and show disrespect toward Him by intruding with a rough hand where He is working."[15]

Nor is John yet finished. We began this section by wondering at the contemporary and widespread view that men and women may assume the direction of immortal souls with the thinnest of theological/professional backgrounds. They may mean well, but that does not excuse the consequent extensive damage that most likely is the result. John's additional comments could hardly be more to the point:

> Perhaps in their zeal these directors err with good will because they do not know any better. Nor for this reason, however, should they be ex-

cused for the counsels they give rashly, without first understanding the road and spirit a person may be following, and for rudely meddling in something they do not understand, instead of leaving the matter to one who does understand. It is no light matter or fault to cause a person to lose inestimable good and sometimes to do him veritable harm through temerarious counsel.

Thus he who recklessly errs will not escape a punishment corresponding to the harm he caused, for he was obliged, as is everyone, to perform the duties of his office well and not be mistaken. The affairs of God must be handled with great tact and with open eyes, especially in so vital and sublime a matter as is that of these souls, where there is at stake almost an infinite gain in being right and almost an infinite loss in being wrong.[16]

The second mistake of inept directors is by no means unknown or uncommon in our contemporary scene: the misinterpretation of ordinary human sufferings as cases of the dark nights. It probably is not an exaggeration to say that this error is widespread among sincere people, and, if it is widespread, this is likely enough due to the fact that they have had their trials interpreted in this fashion by retreat masters or by confessors. A wife may be having a stormy time with her wayward husband, or a nun may be suffering from illness or from some community problem, or a husband may have been deserted by his neurotic wife. The advice given in cases like these only too often is something like the following: "This is indeed a severe trial, but God is testing you. There are many wrongs in life that we can neither correct nor control, but if we suffer them well, we gain great merit. These are the dark nights that all of us must go through." The first two sentences have value, no doubt (even though God's "testing" may be no more than His permission of evil for greater good), but the third sentence is simply a false depiction of the dark nights that the soul undergoes. When St. John of the Cross speaks of the dark nights, he is dealing with mystical contemplation, not with trials deriving from human ignorance, illness and sin. A particularly pernicious example of this ineptitude is the interpretation of a clinical depression as "the dark night". John is aware of this mistake, even though he uses a different term, *melancholia,* to describe the mental problem.[17] A director (or conversely, a psychiatrist) who confuses these very different conditions shows a lack of understanding of one or the other of them. Needless to say, the misdiagnosis can have unfortunate effects for the directee who takes it seriously.

The third fault is to cling to one's directee and to hinder him or her from seeking another's help when such is necessary. John was of the opinion that ordinarily one director is not adequate for all a person's needs, and yet he does not favor a plurality of guides. How may we reconcile what appear to be two mutually incompatible views? On the one hand he perceives rightly that not everyone knows all that can happen in the spiritual journey, nor is everyone so perfect in prayer as to know every state of the interior life that can occur: "Not everyone capable of hewing the wood knows how to carve the statue." Even a modest amount of experience in aiding people advanced in prayer soon makes it clear that while all follow the general outlines of growth described so well in St. Teresa's mansions, yet there are numberless differences in detail as to how God communicates Himself. "God", says John, "leads each one along different paths so that hardly one spirit will be found like another in even half its methods of procedure." Mistaken, therefore, is that director who so holds on to his directees that he is unhappy should he learn that they have consulted someone else. John goes so far as to liken this possessiveness to the jealous quarrelsomeness one finds among husbands and wives.[18] On the other hand it is wrong for directees to have two or three habitual guides. Once a person is blessed to have a sound director, support should be found "wholly and entirely" in this individual, "for not to do so would amount to no longer wanting a director. And when one director is sufficient and suitable, all the others are useless or a hindrance."[19] Multiple consultations can also waste time of both parties and can beget no little confusion.

St. John saves for the fourth fault perhaps his most scorching label: a lax guide advising laxity is, he says, "pestiferous". What happens in this case is that while God is anointing beginners with holy desires aimed at renouncing the world and leading godly lives, these directors by their merely human reflections and rationalizations place obstacles in the way of progress. Lacking devotion themselves and "fully clothed in worldliness, since they do not enter by the narrow gate of life, these directors do not let others enter either". The saint applies to them the searing words of woe Jesus aimed at those who have taken away the key of knowledge so that they neither enter nor allow others to enter.[20] They are obstacles at the gate of heaven, and they will be punished.[21]

So much for the more common faults. John's final observation is concerned with what is to follow competent guidance: action. True to his whole bent of mind and life, true also to his Lord's admonition about idle words, the saint insists that the time of talking is to be followed by the time of silence and action. There are, in our fallen world, only too many individuals and communities that speak much and do little.

They seem to feel that by spending long hours in discussions and meetings, they are somehow changing either themselves or the world for the better. An insightful comic cartoon captured the reality quite simply. The lead character is gleefully announcing a brilliant scheme to three others: "I know . . . let's form a committee! That way we can give the appearance of doing something without having to do anything." There are individuals who can talk on and on in spiritual direction but remain stuck in the same rut session after session. They seem not to be aware that the reason can be traced to a lack of real effort toward progress in the nitty-gritty of everyday life. To his favorite nuns at Beas, St. John explained that he did not write at a given time because he thought that enough had already been said and written:

> What is wanting, if anything is wanting, is not writing or speaking — rather these usually superabound — but silence and work. . . . Once a person knows what has been told him for his benefit, he no longer needs to hear or speak, but to put it into practice, silently and carefully and in humility and charity and contempt of self.[22]

Needless to say, this observation aptly applies to reading also, the present work included.

ST. TERESA OF AVILA

Teresian thoughts on spiritual direction are typically tossed to the four winds of her writings. What is fragmentary and incomplete in the isolated passages makes a coherent whole in synthesis. Taking the sanjuanist theological underpinnings for granted, this woman was concerned with the practicalities, and among these the first are the necessity and advisability of spiritual direction. Accepting fully the biblical idea that "he who trusts in himself is a fool",[23] Teresa held that we ought not to have confidence in our own subjective experiences; rather, we should get an objective assessment of them. Despite her extraordinary knowledge of infused prayer and its accompanying gifts, she could state that she did not trust herself in anything. Instead, "I have always consulted others," she says, "even though I find it difficult."[24] What she did in her own life she advised for others, namely, that experiences at prayer should be shared with the confessor "very plainly and candidly".[25] The saint took it for granted that the confessor was to be competent. That being the case, she considered that he could provide light for the penitent's growth: "Do all you can to discuss these graces and favours with someone who can give you light and have no secrets from him."[26] Even though she did not render explicit the incarnational/ecclesial bases for her view, quite clearly Teresa understood the confessor to be more than a mere human guide. Like John, she considered him to be speaking in the name of the Lord, Who sends him by means of the missioning Church.

We may ask of the teresian texts what specific benefits the saint saw in this ecclesial guidance. In her autobiography she explains that as infused prayer grows, one can be perplexed about the advisability of giving up the human, discursive manner and about whether the new, infused, simple awareness is really prayer. When the infusion is strong, a sensible person, aware of the possibility of self-deception and of imagining a mere emotion to be an experience of God, rightly begins to be anxious. Of herself, Teresa writes: "Since I saw that my fear was increasing — because the prayer was increasing — it seemed to me there was in the prayer either some great good or some terrible evil. I understood well that I was already experiencing something supernatural because sometimes I was unable to resist; to have it whenever I wanted was out of the question."[27] If one as wise as Teresa in the ways of God could be concerned about authenticity, the lesser of us are well advised to seek competent counsel.

A second benefit flows from the first: as one is freed from the danger of illusion and from one's subjective perplexities, there arises the inner calm so helpful to contemplative growth.[28] People who can share their prayer experiences with a competent guide find a great peace in being assured that all is well. They are then able to let go and allow the indwelling Lord to give abundantly and without obstacles deriving from human fears and hesitations.

A further benefit pertains particularly to those living the enclosed life of the cloister, whose opportunities to speak to others are less frequent in both number and extent. Knowing this well from her own experience, the foundress recognized that "for the nuns to be disciplined in external matters and have no one to help them interiorly is a great trial".

Finally, remarked the saint, everyone in a monastery (and, we might add, in the world as well), the prioress included, can be preserved from "flagrant errors" by a competent confessor. After admonishing the nuns that they "must always consult persons of learning", she addresses a word to prioresses:

> If superiors wish to do their work well, it is very necessary for them to have learned men as their confessors; otherwise, though believing themselves to be acting in a holy way, they will commit many flagrant errors; they should also see that their nuns have learned men as confessors.[29]

It is worth noting that St. Teresa's dependence on consultation was by no means an impediment to her having a mind of her own or to her vigorous sense of initiative. Genuine people have no problem in combining perfect obedience and docility with a magnanimous spirit and inner freedom. However, at the same time she exercised a great deal of discrimination as to whom she would consult. Her wide experience made it clear to her that not everyone is fit to guide others in the ways of the spirit. While she found that sincere, competent theologians had what she termed a certain instinct to guide them in advising others, she also spoke of "timid, half-learned men whose shortcomings have cost me very dear".[30] The saint explained what she meant with an example. After affirming that "a truly learned man has never misguided me", she went on to speak of halfhearted confessors:

> Those others certainly could not have wanted to mislead me, but they didn't know any better. I thought that they really knew and that I was obliged to no more than to believe them, especially since what they told me was liberal and permissive. If it had been rigid, I am so wretched that I would have sought out others. What was venial sin they said was no sin at all, and what was serious mortal sin they said was venial. This did me so much harm that it should not surprise anyone that I speak of it here in order to warn others against so great an evil.[31]

This woman who had so tremendous a respect for the priesthood was not in the least hesitant to warn against incompetent clergy. Observing that the first step in a serious spiritual life is freedom from venial sins and even imperfections, she states: "You might suppose that any confessor would know this, but you would be wrong."[32] Not everyone, therefore, is acceptable as a spiritual leader. St. Bernard, in a letter to his young cousin, expressed the same opinion: "Believe not every spirit. Be at peace with many, but let one in a thousand be your counselor."

Supposing, then, that one has found a guide competent in some areas of the spiritual life, it does not necessarily follow that he will be suitable in every area. Teresa further elaborates that a director ought not to discuss matters of which he is ignorant. If he lacks experience of advanced prayer, he may be acceptable if he is "learned", but then he should limit himself to advising in matters accessible to reason and Scripture. "As for the rest," advises the saint, "he shouldn't kill himself for thinking he understands what he doesn't, or suppress the spirit; for now, in respect to the spirit, another greater Lord governs them [the directees]; they are not without a Superior."[33] One can almost guess what Teresa would say to those in our day who take a few courses and then launch into teaching others.

One who has followed the saint's thoughts thus far is likely to wonder

what exactly the specific qualities are that she expects in spiritual directors for anyone pursuing a serious prayer life. Although some of these
qualities are intimated above, more needs to be said, for Teresa is precise
about the matter. At the head of her list of expectations are spiritual
depth and intellectual soundness. Regarding the first she stresses that
she wants "spiritual" men, unworldly and "disillusioned with the things
of the world", men who are obedient to their own superiors. Writing
to the superior general about two of her favorite priests (and defend-
ing them before him), she straightforwardly states that "you may be
quite sure that, if I found they [Mariano and Gratian] were disobedient, I would neither see them nor listen to them any more".[34] Her
reasoning is, of course, rooted in the Gospel: they listen to the Lord
who listen to His representatives, and they reject the Lord who reject
those He sends to teach and govern. Hence, a disobedient director,
not having the mind of Jesus, will be guiding others according to his
own worldly view of things.

Spiritual depth includes also the practice of advancing prayer. St.
Teresa says that even the prayer of quiet is "completely obscure" to
those who know of it only from their reading.[35] The ideal guide is
the individual who knows contemplation from the inside, who has a
feel for the reality because of direct experience. In a similar manner,
the person who has never loved unselfishly and deeply may be able
to repeat worded definitions, but he cannot understand fully the advanced directee. Mere verbal information is no substitute for what we
might call tasted insight. However, true as this is, it does not mean
that those devoid of infused contemplation can be of no help at all,
for "if they are virtuous even though they may not experience spiritual
things, they will benefit me", Teresa concludes.[36] In the context she
was speaking of competent theologians who may be able to help in
matters related to prayer, even if they do not enjoy much connatural
understanding of prayer itself. They should, of course, confine their
advice to their own fields of competence.

St. Teresa laid great store on sound theological "learning" in those
who advised her and her nuns: "My opinion has always been and will
be that every Christian strive to speak if he can with someone who
has gone through studies; and the more learned the person the better.
Those who walk the path of prayer have a greater need for this counsel;
and the more spiritual they are, the greater their need."[37] A strong statement, no doubt. It reflects a position that excludes with no least am-
biguity the plague of illuminism, the idea that one needs no guide, not
even a teaching Church. The saint went on to explain what she herself
had found:

I have consulted many learned men because for some years now, on account of a greater necessity, I have sought them out more; and I've always been a friend of men of learning. For though some don't have experience, they don't despise the Spirit nor do they ignore it, because in Sacred Scripture, which they study, they always find the truth of the good spirit. I hold that the devil will not deceive with illusions the person of prayer who consults learned men, unless this person wants to be deceived.[38]

The third quality of the director is that he should be neither credulous nor incredulous; that is, he should not indiscriminately accept that every alleged phenomenon is from God, nor should he in an a priori manner assume that almost never does God deal directly with the individual person. As we have said, at one extreme are people who believe that any idea they conceive and find appealing must be the result of "listening to the Spirit", and at the other extreme are those who think that God infuses nothing but unperceived grace. The soundness of Teresa's judgment is apparent in the following passage. Speaking of herself in the third person, she fears that her many supernatural "favors" might be attributed to "women's fancy".

She went to the extreme of not submitting herself to the judgment of any person whom she thought believed that everything was from God, for she feared that then the devil would deceive both him and her. She discussed her soul more willingly with anyone whom she saw was more fearful. Although it also caused her grief to deal with those who completely despised these experiences — they did so to try her — for some of them seemed to her to be very much from God. And she did not want them to give definite condemnation of the experiences simply because they didn't see any reason for them. Nor did she want them to act as though everything were from God, for she understood very well that there could be some deception.[39]

The prudent director, when given an account of extraordinary phenomena, approaches it with a calm, open mind. He realizes both that such things do occur and that there can be illusions about them. He also knows how to distinguish the first from the second.

Fourth, St. Teresa preferred that the spiritual guide not be cast in the same mold as the directee. The latter ought not to seek out someone who will surely agree with a course already decided upon.[40] Self-serving and foolish as this procedure is, we ought not to think it uncommon. Dissenters from the Church's teaching rarely seek advice from one who accepts it. They who live a tenuous prayer life and indulge in comfort and luxury seldom consult a guide who is given to contemplation and the asceticism that is companion to it. And there are

directees who remain with a solid guide until the day comes when the
director's counsel contradicts what they intend to do. They then quietly
drop from contact and go their own way, telling themselves that they
are, after all, "seeking light".

The fifth trait St. Teresa wanted in a guide was a sympathetic understanding. While she by no means desired or expected him to agree with
her every thought, she did wish him to have some feel for the individual
as such, an understanding of individual differences and a genuine care
for the directee. She told the Dominican Bañez that "a priest must be
more than a confessor to me now. The soul's desire can only be assuaged
by some other soul which understands it."[41]

Finally, the saint was healthily cosmopolitan in her choices. Directors did not have to be members of her own Order. She did not suffer
from the parochialism of religious who feel they must not be exposed
to retreat masters and guides from outside their own institute. Being
the ecclesial woman that she was, Teresa looked for quality and competence, and it mattered little to her whether the priest was diocesan
or Franciscan or Jesuit or Dominican or Carmelite. She knew well that
the Church is far larger than any Order, and she wanted to profit from
a breadth of vision. Unquestionably, she loved her own Carmelite family,
yet, large minded as she was, the foundress saw clearly that "His Majesty" could not be wholly reflected by any one Order or even a number
of them.

It is noteworthy that St. Teresa did not recommend in her works
how frequently or regularly one should consult the director. Not making this specification was wise, because people vary in their needs not
only among themselves but also at different times in their lives.

What, according to St. Teresa, are the duties of a spiritual guide?
Supposing competency and therefore continuing study, we may answer
this question with a few brief guidelines. The director is to keep con-
fidences even of things discussed ouside of confession but within the
counseling situation.[42] He should limit his activity to what he understands and leave alone what he does not.[43] He should not expect of
beginners what only the advanced can do; that is, he should not push
them beyond their present readiness and strength.[44] Ideally, he joins
a discerning wisdom to gentleness in dealing with those who imagine
they have visions but do not. The saint counsels that the director should
listen to these people as to sick persons, for such they are. However,
he should not upset them by attributing their ideas to a demonic origin
or by analyzing their sufferings as clinical depressions, for these diag-
noses will just lead them to affirm all the more their ill-founded per-

suasions. What the director should do, above all, is to advise these people that the genuine service of God does not consist in extraordinary experiences and that they should pay no heed to them.[45] This advice coincides with that of St. John of the Cross.

It may be well for the sake of completeness to add here a negative duty that Teresa does not mention but that she would surely second were she asked. The spiritual director does not attempt to govern a household, be it convent, family or parish. His responsibility is to the inner life and conscience of his directee, not to the external ordering of a community. It follows from this that the prioress of a convent (or a husband or wife, or the pastor of a parish) need not follow the advice a penitent says a confessor or director has given for the latter's spiritual life. This is so for several reasons. The director has no jurisdiction over the external running of a community, and consequently the person in charge need not place any particular weight on what he may have said. Further, his knowledge of the community in question is incomplete in that he has heard only one side of the matter. Then, too, it is possible that his penitent may have misunderstood wholly or partially what he had to say.

What are the duties of the directee? Though St. Teresa mentions only two, they are powerful in their simplicity. While many people take the first one for granted, there is reason to think that they make careless decisions in regard to it, decisions they probably avoid in the choice of a medical doctor or a lawyer. The directee needs to make a judgment of suitability regarding the person chosen as a guide to God. Teresa herself evaluated the competence of her guides, and she approached only those who measured up to her criteria.[46] The second duty of the directee is obedience. Given Teresa's premises, one cannot argue with her conclusion. Faithful, competent priests speak in the name of the Lord Who sent them, and once we are satisfied with this fidelity and adequacy, obedience is the only justifiable course to follow. The saint is well known for her absolute refusal to follow an interior light or locution until she had the approval of her confessor, and if the latter said no, she would obey him rather than her vision.[47] She took her principles not only from sound theology but also from the Lord's private communications to her.

> The safest thing, as the Lord told me, is to make known to my confessor the whole state of my soul and the favors God grants me, that he be learned, and that I obey him. The Lord has often told me this. It is what I do, and without doing so I would have no peace. . . . As

often as the Lord commanded something of me in prayer and my confessor told me to do otherwise, the Lord returned and told me to obey my confessor; afterward His Majesty would change the confessor's mind, and he would agree with the Lord's command.[48]

God takes care of those who are diligently obedient to the Church He Himself has founded. They will not go astray, for they are following His own providential plan.

CHAPTER SEVENTEEN

LIBERATING COMPLETION

Introduced into ever increasing intimacy with the indwelling Trinity, the mystic is identified with the expansive and the universal, but the mere activist is restricted in focus, constrained by the limiting and the particular. The former is, therefore, opened out and freed for everything, while the latter is hemmed in by the bounds of preoccupation with space and time. Success in business or politics or science or education provides money and at times some small semblance of notoriety, but never does it issue in the transforming enthrallment reserved to the fullness of contemplative prayer. The work of the activist cannot ultimately satisfy, and while amusements may provide momentary thrills, they inevitably leave an undefined vacuum: "Is that all there is?" Anything less than everything is simply not sufficient. The mystical experience, in contrast, imparts a lasting impression that "this is *it;* this is the Enough", although the possession here below is but a foretaste. This tasting of the All is the biblical "one thing", the better part that cannot be taken away, the fire within that cannot be extinguished, the dark immersion of time that dissolves in the emerging brightness of eternal day.

The deepest prayer rests the heart and satisfies every human yearning,[1] being as it is a freeing communion with triune Beauty, Light and Love. Refreshed by contact with the Infinite, the human person returns to the finite order with an ineffably greater appreciation and delight: "God our Father, may we love you in all things and above all things, and reach the joy you have prepared for us beyond all imagining."[2]

Knowing the divine Artist in immediate intimacy, the mystic finds in the exquisiteness of a rose what the mere naturalist misses: the created artifact gives a glimpse of the divine glory and splendor. Even more important to this liberation is the fact that the mystic knows with certainty that in whatever form goodness and beauty are discovered — in a tulip or a peanut or a human face — they can be experienced without limitations only in the Father of lights from Whom every good and perfect gift proceeds.[3]

Human completion can happen only through an encounter with beauty and love. No matter how skilled one may be in business or medicine or science or law or athletics, if the mind does not thrill in truth, and if the heart is not intertwined in an eternal embrace, there can be no realistic fulfillment. In the sanjuanist formulation, "outside of God everything is narrow".[4] The simple fact is that all else is finite. The unending yearnings of the human spirit are satisfied by nothing that can be measured, seen, heard or touched. To focus selfishly on anything in the created order is to be restricted and thus to fall that far short of full freedom. The plumber and the physicist, the nurse and the teacher, the farmer and the politician find themselves fully only when, along with making the most of their natural skills and gifts, they become permeated with the divine life in its limitless abundance.

Men and women who can exult in the view of a snowcapped mountain or the enjoyment of a symphonic performance have a vague idea of the point we are making. Veiled as these experiences are, they nonetheless suggest why the human spirit is rested by nothing in the created order. Because a splendid panorama, a beautiful face and a musical masterpiece strike a spark of yearning for an undefined more, they also serve to indicate that the finite realm is meant only as a stepping-stone and reminder of the infinite. The mystic sees this and, more importantly, lives it.

MYOPIA

Being plunged into the triune life is the ultimate cure for the fragmentary visions afflicting all ideologies. Heralds of the various "isms" have their kernels of truth, but by lacking the perspective of the large picture, they reach mistaken and sometimes bizarre conclusions. Narrow materialism, impervious illuminism, feverish activism, radical feminism and egoistic hedonism are all shortsighted and short-circuited. When these ideologies have their own way, that is, when they are permitted to pursue their incomplete insights to their untrammeled conclusions, they issue in tyranny. It is in proceeding down these myopic dead ends that individuals and societies come to their dissolution. The name of this problem is not popular: sin.

The majority of people often do not see in realistic proportion the sundry elements that constitute their daily round. Small things loom large, and large things are ignored. Most human quarrels center on petty differences and faults. Gossiping is usually concerned with trivialities. The nonmystic is imprisoned in pettiness. In the penetrating light of eternity the pursuit of fleeting fame and monetary fortune, together with all the pleasures they can buy, is readily seen as myopic and fast fading: as Scripture puts it, a puff of wind. Immersed as they were in the divine center that has no boundaries, Ss. Teresa and John shattered the strictures of finitude even as they went about the business of living as we all must do.

FROM SUFFERING INTO FREEDOM

One way to illustrate this wholeness born in the divine sea is to reflect on the sanjuanist attitude toward suffering, an attitude shared, of course, by St. Teresa. For the worldly person pain can be a prison, tending as it does to focus attention on oneself to the almost total exclusion of others. Even religiously inclined people can be so riveted by their sufferings that they express little or no concern about the interests and needs of their own families and friends. For example, I have received letters from individuals in pain that express no least interest in anything communicated in my last letter to them—all revolves around their hurting.

Being Other-centered, the mystic's view of the human situation is quite the opposite of this egocentrism. Piercing pain, which in others fastens attention on the self, prompts St. Paul to rejoice in his privilege of suffering for the Colossians.[5] The apostle discounts his frightful beatings, imprisonments, stoning, shipwreck and hunger as of very small account, for they open to him the weight of eternal glory, which is out of all proportion to them.[6] While mystics suffer as much as anyone else, and often far more, they do not see it as a problem as others do. Their prayerful union with the crucified risen One bestows a liberating insight into the wisdom of the Cross. They understand that in suffering we enjoy a divine power, for God is close to the burdened and the broken.[7] St. John of the Cross declares that God ordains adversities "for the everlasting joy of the elect".[8]

What makes deliverance from the egocentric prison of pain possible? Suffering with Jesus on his Cross brings joy, says John, because He so immensely loves us that He "cannot long endure the sufferings of His beloved without response to them".[9] Throughout the sanjuanist corpus we find the underlying conviction that God loves each of us so intensely that He cannot tolerate delay in coming to the aid of one totally given to Himself. On the other hand, our love makes the burdens we carry light—as the Master Himself has promised.[10] Why the saints rejoice in their pains, whether casual or crushing, John explains in two sentences that invite a great deal of prayerful pondering:

It is not God's will that a man be disturbed by anything, or suffer trials, for if he suffers trials in the adversities of the world it is because of his weakness in virtue. The perfect man rejoices in what afflicts the imperfect man.[11]

The contemplative is so identified with the crucified risen One that he triumphs over anything and everything. Even crushing misfortunes cannot hold this person bound. As is invariably the case, the sanjuanist thought is seconded in Scripture. St. Paul declares to the Romans that through trials we triumph by the loving power of Him who loves us. Nothing at all, not life or death, neither angel nor prince, nothing present or future, nothing in the finite order can separate us from the love of God that has become visible in Christ Jesus.[12] Mystics know this through their acceptance of the revealed word, but they know it also in their experience of transforming prayer.

One of the most mysterious of all sanjuanist statements is his assertion that from purest suffering a purest joy arises via a purest knowledge. Piercing pain embraced with love for the Crucified plunges one into the thicket of divine wisdom. From this knowing, which comes "from deeper within", emerges a purest joy.[13] Paradoxical as this thought is, it forms one piece with St. Paul's idea that for those who love God, everything works together for good.[14] The joy of the mystic is more intense because the purification that has made it possible is more thorough; consequently, the union with purest Joy is deeper.[15]

We have here part of the explanation of why saints desire to suffer and counsel others to do the same. We ought not to flee from trials, says St. John of the Cross; rather, we should esteem them, for few people merit to be brought to perfection through suffering.[16] When there is a choice and all else is equal, we are to be inclined to favor the more difficult and the more demanding course of action.[17] To the faithful soul John advocates a love for trials "as a small way to please your Spouse, Who did not hesitate to die for you".[18] What to the worldling is unmitigated disaster is to the mystic a royal road to liberty. "Suffering for God is better than working miracles."[19] We cannot improve upon the divine plan: Resurrection through crucifixion.

APOSTOLIC POWER

Even a cursory review of ecclesiastical history makes evident that the greatest doers through the centuries have been the saints. The momentous apostolic accomplishments of Augustine, Gregory the Great, Thomas, Bonaventure, Catherine of Siena, Francis Xavier, Teresa, John and Philip Neri (to mention only a few) have had repercussions down to the present day. While sincere but lesser men and women make moderate headway in their apostolic endeavors, it is the saintly who ignite fires. A young woman in her late teens told me of a nun who impressed her mightily: "She's a woman almost visibly on fire with love; talking to her is like holding the straw of my soul close to a fire." This is the fire the Lord Himself came to cast upon the earth. It is the fire flaming forth from the furnace of mystical communion.

At this moment, in one's deepest center, the Father is begetting His Word Whom He never began to beget and shall never cease begetting. At this moment the Father and the Son are breathing forth Their common Bond, the Spirit Kiss, Whom They never began to spirate and shall never cease spirating. Which is to say that at this moment the Trinity's inner life is going on in the indwelling presence. Theologians point out that all apostolate in the Church originates from the inner trinitarian processions. The Son's being sent into the world through the Incarnation is as a continuation of the eternal begetting of the Son by the Father. The mission of the Holy Spirit on Pentecost is as a continuation of the eternal spiration of Father and Son. When Jesus sends the apostles into the world, He emphasizes the essential connection between their being sent forth and Himself having been sent: "As the Father sent me, so I send you."[20] The hierarchical Church, sent by the Son, in turn sends priests to carry on this work by the conferring of ordination and the granting of faculties to them. She sends religious congregations into their various apostolates by the approbation of their consecrated life and of the particular constitutions and founding charisms that guide their institutes and by their being part of local diocesan families as well.

Hence both the external projects of the Church of Christ and the inner love dynamo that energizes them receive their origin from the Fire within. It is not surprising that the two patrons of the universal missionary endeavors of the Church are mystics: St. Francis Xavier and St. Thérèse of Lisieux. One traveled across the globe from west to east; the other never left her cloister. Both, however, enjoyed lofty contemplative prayer. It is exemplars such as these who move the world and show the way to transformation to those of us who wish to be transformed.

RENEWAL OF THEOLOGY

One of the most commonly admitted, frequently lamented and rarely corrected defects in current moral theology is its dire lack of a contemplative/mystical dimension. It is not accidental that at the same time we have not a few ethicists claiming that the New Testament does not add any significant precepts to those known to natural reason. We have been at pains throughout this volume to show that the teresian and sanjuanist teaching is "pure Gospel", to use the phrase of Pius XI. To test the claim to which we have just referred, one need only read side by side any humanist ethicist and either Teresa or John. The latter obviously present numerous concrete modes of action that the former does not dream of, much less discuss or promote. Moral theology unfortunately tends in our day to be minimalistic and myopic. It does not envisage what mystics have fixed their sights upon, and as an inevitable consequence its teaching is necessarily truncated and often enough indistinguishable from that to which a non-Christian adheres.

The separation of moral theology from doctrinal, and both of them from mystical, indicates that something is fundamentally awry. It is true, of course, that one cannot be a specialist in everything, but the fact remains that few theologians make any real effort to consider and introduce mystical reality into their discussions of human acts . . . of the basic principles of morality . . . of achieving heroic holiness (who even mentions, let alone advocates, practice of heroic virtue?) . . . of the correlation of all these to infused contemplation and the transforming union.

A single example of this glaring omission will suffice to illustrate the point. One of the unspoken premises in the loose sexual morality so widely countenanced both in the general population and in certain ethical circles is the idea that almost nothing may be allowed to interfere with easy access to erotic pleasures. Masturbation is viewed as a needed and harmless release from "tension". Homosexual activity is acceptable because the alternative would deprive homosexuals of a crucial dimension of life's promises. Artificial contraception has to be licit because husband and wife should have an unconstrained right to genital relations when they have a mind to have them.

Nowhere in this mind set is a trace of the exalted truth that men and women are made for delights that even on earth immeasurably outstrip the erotic. This exciting reality just does not surface at all in 99 percent of articles and books on sexual morality, but it can be discovered anew if we apply the themes prominent in this volume to questions of sexuality: freedom from selfish clingings . . . doing all for the glory of God (really) . . . passive purifications from all egocentrism . . . unspeakable enthrallment in ecstatic prayer . . . centering one's life on what eye has not seen or ear heard. Viewed from a holistic standpoint, sexuality retains its significance, but it is kept in its proper place. Once it ceases to be seen as the end of human life, it loses much of its tyrannizing impulse, an impulse to which the world, the flesh and the devil would give free rein.

The ethicist, who knows from experience what a deep immersion in the indwelling Trinity bestows on mind and heart and being, is equipped to impart a refreshingly exact, intrinsically true moral theology worthy of the human person. Being holistic and comprehensive, it can answer our needs in all their dimensions. The same must be said of the exegete and the systematic theologian. A knowledge of philology and archeology and ancient history is not a knowledge of divine realities. Mere technicians are helpless in explaining many of the biblical texts we have noted in this volume, and the candid among them admit it. Only to those in profound communion with the Holy Spirit Who inspired the sacred pages are opened the inexhaustible riches of the word in its deepest meanings.

Because goodness bestows insight, the contemplative person is bound to see human nature and the many problems that beset us in our woundedness not only in the light of unaided reason (which St. Paul said is foolishness to God) but also in the light of an intellect transformed in divine love and truth. It is safe to say that until many more theologians and exegetes are deeply prayerful men and women, we will not have a comprehensive renewal in the sacred sciences. Hans Urs von Balthasar was surely on target when he so often and so eloquently pleaded that theologians pay far more attention to the saints. There is no doubt that his own monumental contributions were due partially to the fact that he did just that.

A LIVING WORD OF GOD

While some saints write books of theology, all saints are books of theology: the living word enfleshed. Saints Teresa and John are Doctors of the Church because they lived and sang of the deepest immersions of the human spirit in the divine Fire. They are the Church's mystics par excellence. They are unparalleled torchbearers of the Fire within. This is why the liturgy prays that all of us may be "fed with St. Teresa's heavenly doctrine" and that men and women in every vocation "imitate John always". Pope John Paul II, celebrating in Avila the four-hundredth anniversary of the foundress' death, declared that she "became a living word of God",[21] and later on the same day at her tomb the Pontiff addressed her in prayer: "You are a messenger of Christ. You are the universal word of the experience of God."[22]

The universal word of the experience of God. That is the very essence of this volume. We have tried to summarize what really cannot be summarized—it really cannot be spoken. The Fire within is literally ineffable, but, aside from the inspired word, there is none who has come closer than our two saints in telling us what it is like.

THE WEDDING

Contemplative depth and existential boredom are incompatible. We cannot drink deeply of divine reality without becoming irrepressible enthusiasts. St. John of the Cross marvels at the splendor of creation, and St. Francis of Assisi dances during his homily before the papal court because the mystics overflow with divine fullness. The psalmist proclaims that his very heart and flesh sing for joy in the living God.[23] Like Jesus, Who is never alone because the Father is always with Him,[24] so the mature contemplative enjoys the abiding presence that alone stills the restless human heart.

The divine plan is a story, a love story, a stranger-than-fiction story. St. John of the Cross sings that God created the world to be a splendid palace for the bride. And the bride's destiny?

> I will hold her in My arms
> And she will burn with Your love.[25]

In this incomparable love story the Author does not impose details of the unfolding plot. Instead, He allows everyone on life's stage freely to work out what shall happen and how it shall happen. It is His ultimate plan, however, that the climax of the plot is to be a spectacular and eternal marriage celebration in the kingdom. All are invited, but He forces no one to come and take part in this "happy ending" that is the best of beginnings. Unlike the prosaic weddings of this world, this one brings about a transformation of the bride into the Beloved. This love union has its inception in the here and now and continues forever after for all who are fittingly dressed in the wedding garment of grace given them by the divine Bridegroom.[26]

NOTES

CHAPTER ONE

[1] Jn 17:23.

[2] Eph 3:19.

[3] See these expressions in LG, no. 41; AG, no. 18; DV, no. 8; Canon 663.

[4] Unfortunately the current English translation changes and dilutes the original Latin of these prayers for October 15 and December 14.

[5] Louis Bouyer, *Introduction to Spirituality* (Paris: Desclee, 1961; Collegeville, MN, 1961), p. 303.

[6] Deidre Macken, "The Baby Boomers Turn 40", *The Age* (Melbourne, Australia) Feb. 1, 1986, pt. 2, p. 2.

[7] 1 Pet 1:8; Jn 15:11; 16:22.

[8] Lk 14:33.

[9] Phil 4:4.

[10] 2 Cor 6:10.

[11] Mt 7:13-14.

[12] Hans Urs von Balthasar, *The Glory of the Lord,* vol. 3 (San Francisco: Ignatius Press, 1986), p. 146.

[13] When I say that Buddhist awareness is impersonal and agnostic, I am making no judgment as to what an individual Buddhist may or may not attain in his exercises. One can hope that he is touched by grace and reaches out to the one God. Rather, I am reporting here what Buddhist writers themselves say of their contemplation.

[14] Bouyer, p. 5.

[15] Ibid., p. 301.

[16] Lk 10:38-42.

[17] Acts 6:3-4.

[18] Ps 34:5.

[19] Vatican Council II, *Sacrosanctum Concilium,* no. 2. Unless stated otherwise, citations from Vatican Council II are taken from the Abbott translation.

[20] Lk 12:49.

[21] Heb 1:1-3.

[22] 2 Cor 3:18.

[23] 1 Cor 2:9.

[24] Eph 3:19.

[25] Max Zerwick, *The Epistle to the Ephesians* (New York: Herder and Herder, 1969), p. 94.

[26] Ibid., p. 96. Zerwick is more than a technician, for he sees the limitations of philological analysis.

CHAPTER TWO

[1] Mt 7:13-14.

[2] 1 Cor 2:9.

[3] *Testimony* 58, no. 16, p. 353.

[4] *Life,* chaps. 3 and 4, pp. 38–45.

[5] Ibid., chap. 5, nos. 7–8, p. 49.

[6] Ibid., chap. 7, no. 11, p. 60. See also Marcelle Auclair, *Teresa of Avila* (New York: Doubleday, Image edition, 1961), pp. 73–74, for a more detailed description of one of these frightful illnesses.

[7] Letter 57, p. 144.

[8] E. Allison Peers tells us that Ana reports this "from their own mouths". See his introduction to the *Book of Foundations,* vol. 3, p. xii.

[9] Auclair, p. 77.

[10] Letter 19, p. 75.

[11] *Complete Works,* vol. 3, p. xi.

[12] Auclair, p. 26.

[13] Ibid.

[14] Ibid., p. 185.

[15] *Depositions,* p. 15.

[16] Ibid., pp. 30, 216.

[17] Ibid., pp. 68–69.

[18] Ibid., p. 96. See also *Life,* chap. 3, no. 7, p. 40; and *Testimony* 1, no. 7, p. 312.

[19] *Way,* chap. 20, p. 149; Kavanaugh and Rodriguez edition (hereafter KR), no. 6, p. 117.

[20] Auclair, p. 208.

[21] Ibid., p. 401.

[22] The saint strikes this writer as one of the most normal human beings he has ever read about—and her contemporaries from all accounts seem to support this judgment.

[23] Letter 269 to Jerome Gratian, p. 638.

[24] Letter 239 to Gratian, p. 585.

[25] Letter 126, pp., 326–27.

[26] IC, mans. 4, chap. 3, pp. 92–93; KR, no. 11, p. 333.

[27] Letter 57 to Don Antonio Gaytan, p. 144.

[28] Letter 60 to Maria Bautista, p. 150.

[29] Letter 400, p. 909.

[30] Letter 19 to Lorenzo, p. 74.

[31] E. Allison Peers cites these terms of the foundress; *Letters,* p. 13.

[32] Letter 6 to Doña Luisa de la Cerda, p. 48.

[33] Letter 10, p. 52.

[34] Letter 99 to Maria de San Josè, pp. 252–53.

[35] Letter 100, p. 255.

[36] *Life,* chap. 3, no. 5, p. 40.

[37] Ibid., chap. 4, no. 2, p. 41.

[38] *Foundations,* chap. 31, p. 188; KR, no. 12, p. 291.

[39] Auclair, p. 23.

[40] Letter 23, p. 81.

[41] *Way,* chap. 22, pp. 156–57; KR, no. 1, p. 122.

[42] *Foundations,* chap. 28, p. 162; KR, no. 37, p. 264.

[43] Letter 71 to Don Alvara de Mendoza, p. 174; and Letter 423 to Gratian, p. 945.

[44] *Life,* chap. 40, no. 8, p. 280.

[45] Letter 185 to Maria de San José, p. 469.

[46] IC, mans. 4, chap. 2, p. 81; KR, no. 2, p. 323.

[47] *Life,* chap. 34, no. 8, p. 230; 1 Cor 6:17.

[48] *Life,* chap. 38, nos. 9 and 11, p. 260.

49 Ibid., chap. 38, no. 2, pp. 257–58.

50 Ibid., chap. 40, no. 1, p. 277.

51 IC, mans. 6, chap. 5, pp. 157–58; KR, nos. 1–3, pp. 386–87.

52 *Life*, chap. 29, nos. 13–14, pp. 193–94.

53 Ibid., no. 14, p. 194.

54 *Depositions*, p. 111.

55 Ibid., p. 133. See also the witness of Maria de Nacimiento, ibid., p. 151. Others report the same phenomenon.

56 Deposition of Julian of Avila, ibid., pp. 59 and 61.

57 *Soliloquy* 6, no. 1, p. 379.

58 *Life*, chap. 40, no. 10, pp. 280–81.

59 Ibid., p. 281. See also *Life*, chap. 33, no. 3, p. 221; chap. 34, no. 10, p. 230.

60 Letter 30 to Doña Maria de Mendoza, p. 92.

61 *Life*, chap. 35, no. 2, p. 235; chap. 35, no. 12, p. 239.

62 Ibid., chap 19, no. 8, p. 125; Letter 231 to Gratian, pp. 566–69.

63 See, for example, Ana de la Encarnacion, *Depositions*, p. 12; and Maria Bautista, ibid., p. 135.

64 *Depositions*, Ana of Jesus, p. 91.

65 Cited by Peers in his introduction to *Interior Castle*, p. 9. For more examples of this expressed distaste see IC, mans. 1, chap. 2, p. 36; KR, no. 7, p. 290; *Foundations*, chap. 27, p. 148; KR, no. 22, p. 250.

66 *Life*, chap. 40, no. 24, p. 284.

67 Lk 10:16; Gal 2:1–2, 6.

68 See an example of this in the deposition of Isabel de la Cruz, *Depositions*, p. 17.

69 *Foundations*, chap. 28, p. 155; KR, no. 19, p. 257.

70 IC, mans. 6, chap. 6, p. 164; KR, no. 2, p. 392.

71 *Foundations*, chap. 27, p. 145; KR, no. 15, pp. 246–47.

72 *Testimony* 58, no. 14, p. 352.

73 Vatican Council II, *Sacrosanctum Concilium*, no. 2.

74 *Life*, chap. 7, no. 14, p. 61.

75 Mt 12:36.

76 Letter 231, p. 567.

77 See Eph 2:10.

78 *Life*, chap. 39, no. 17, p. 273.

79 *Way*, Prologue, p. 34; KR, no. 2, p. 39.

80 *Testimony* 59, nos. 19 and 25, pp. 360 and 361.

81 Deposition in Peer's introduction to IC, p. 18.

82 *Life*, Epilogue, no. 2, p. 286.

83 *Life*, chap. 14, no. 8., p. 100; see also chap. 16, no. 4, p. 110.

84 IC, Prologue, p. 24; KR, no. 3, p. 282.

85 Teresa of Jesus, the saint's niece, *Depositions*, p. 38.

86 *Optatam totius*, no. 9.

87 See, for example, our Chapter 4, "Creation and Meditation".

88 Romances 3 and 4, *Creation*, KR, pp. 726–27.

89 E. Allison Peers, *Spirit of Flame* (New York: Morehouse-Gorham, 1945), p. 110.

90 KR, *Complete Works of St. John of the Cross*, p. 709.

91 *Spirit of Flame*, p. 136.

92 Ibid., p. 138.

93 Ibid., p. 139.

94 Letter 6, p. 687.

[95] Ibid., p. 688.

[96] Letter 7, p. 688.

[97] Letter 8, p. 689.

[98] Crisogono of Jesus, O.C.D., *The Life of St. John of the Cross* (New York: Harper and Brothers, 1958), p. 268.

[99] *Spirit of Flame*, pp. 111–12.

[100] *Sayings of Light and Love,* nos. 27 and 28, p. 669.

[101] *Maxims,* no. 3, p. 674.

[102] *Dark Night of the Soul* (hereafter DN), bk. 1, chap. 1, no. 2, p. 298.

[103] Crisogono, p. 75.

[104] See Crisogono, pp. 103–5, and Bruno of Jesus and Mary, O.C.D., *St. John of the Cross* (New York: Sheed and Ward, 1932), pp. 169–70.

[105] Crisogono, p. 128.

[106] Ibid., p. 239.

[107] Bruno, pp. 347–48.

[108] Letter 261, p. 625.

[109] Letter 240, p. 496.

CHAPTER THREE

[1] Ps 34:5, 8; Jn 14:15–17; Phil 4:4.

[2] SC, no. 10; DV, no. 8; AG, no. 18.

[3] See *Ascent of Mt. Carmel* (hereafter A), bk. 2, chap. 24, no. 9, p. 192; *Spiritual Canticle* (hereafter SC), st. 40, no. 6, p. 565.

[4] IC, mans. 4, chap. 3, pp. 85–86; KR, nos. 2–3, pp. 327–28.

[5] IC, mans. 4, chap. 3, pp. 85–86; KR, no. 3, p. 328.

[6] IC, mans. 4, chap. 3, p. 89; KR, no. 6, p. 330.

[7] *Life,* chap. 12, no. 5, p. 87.

[8] *Living Flame of Love* (hereafter F), st. 2, no. 22, p. 603.

[9] Cited in Omer Englebert, *St. Francis of Assisi* (Ann Arbor: Servant Books, 1979), p. 27.

[10] F, Prologue, no. 1, p. 577; st. 2, no. 21, p. 602.

[11] IC, mans. 6, chap. 2, p. 134; KR, no. 1, p. 367.

[12] IC, mans. 6, chap. 2, p. 135; KR, no. 3, pp. 367–68.

[13] IC, mans. 6, chap. 2, p. 137; KR, no. 7, p. 369.

[14] IC, mans. 6, chap. 4, pp. 150–51; KR, no. 6, p. 380.

[15] SC, st. 26, no. 8, p. 513.

[16] Ibid., st. 25, no. 8, p. 508.

[17] F, st. 1, no. 27, p. 590.

[18] SC, st. 14–15, no. 2, p. 463.

[19] F, st. 2, no. 21, p. 603.

[20] A, bk. 2, chap. 26, no. 3, p. 194.

[21] Ibid., no. 5, p. 195.

[22] Ibid., nos. 7–8, p. 195.

[23] Ibid., no. 9, p. 195.

[24] DN, bk. 2, chap. 13, no. 2, p. 357.

[25] Ibid., bk. 2, chap. 24, no. 3, p. 387.

[26] SC, st. 1, nos 17–22, pp. 422–24.

27 F, st. 1, no. 8, p. 582.

28 Ibid., st. 2, nos. 9-10, pp. 598-99.

29 Lk 12:49.

30 F, st. 2, no. 11, p. 599.

31 Ibid., no. 7, p. 597.

CHAPTER FOUR

1 SC, st. 4, p. 432.

2 SC, st. 4, no. 1, p. 432.

3 Ibid., nos. 2-4, pp. 432-33.

4 See Wis 13:1-9 and Rom 1:19-20.

5 SC, st. 5, p. 434.

6 Ibid., no. 3, pp. 434-35.

7 Ibid., st. 6, p. 436.

8 Ibid., nos. 2-4, p. 436.

9 Ibid., no. 6, p. 437.

10 Ibid., no. 7, p. 437.

11 Ibid., st. 7, p. 437.

12 Ibid., no. 1, p. 438.

13 Ibid., no. 4, pp. 438-39.

14 A, bk. 2, chap. 12, nos. 2-3, p. 137.

15 Ibid., no. 5, p. 138.

16 F, st. 3, no. 32, p. 621.

17 A, bk. 3, chap. 15, no. 2, p. 236.

18 Ibid., p. 237.

19 A, bk. 2, chap. 12, nos. 5-6, pp. 138-39.

20 See SC, st. 11, no. 5, p. 450.

21 A, bk. 2, chap. 8, nos. 2-3, p. 126.

22 Ibid.

23 Ibid., bk. 2, chap. 16, no. 7, pp. 151-52

24 Karol Wojtyla, *Faith According to St. John of the Cross* (San Francisco: Ignatius Press), p. 62.

25 A, bk. 2, chap. 3, no. 1, p. 110.

26 1 Jn 3:2.

27 1 Cor 13:12.

28 Jn 17:3.

29 A, bk. 2, chap. 24, no. 4, p. 190.

30 Ibid., chap. 1, no. 1, p. 107.

31 SC, st. 12, no. 1, p. 453.

32 Rom 10:17.

33 A, bk. 2, chap. 3, no. 3, p. 111.

34 Ibid., no 4, p. 111.

35 Ibid., chap. 4, nos. 4-5, p. 114.

36 Ibid., no. 6, p. 114.

37 Ibid., nos. 2-3, pp. 112-13.

38 Gal 1:6-9.

³⁹ Is 55:8-9.
⁴⁰ A, bk. 2, chap. 6, nos. 1-4, pp. 119-20.

CHAPTER FIVE

¹ *Life,* chap. 8, no. 5, p. 67.
² Ibid., chap. 10, no. 1, p. 74.
³ *Way,* chap. 28, pp. 183-84; KR, no. 2, pp. 140-41.
⁴ *Way,* chap. 27, p. 179; KR, no. 1, p. 137.
⁵ *Life,* chap. 27, no. 4, p. 175.
⁶ Ibid., chap. 23, no. 5, p. 153.
⁷ Ibid., chap. 39, no. 23, p. 275.
⁸ Ibid., chap. 24, no. 2, p. 159.
⁹ IC, mans. 6, chap. 2, p. 135; KR, no. 2, p. 367.
¹⁰ IC, mans. 6, chap. 2, p. 138; KR, no. 8, p. 370.
¹¹ IC, mans. 5, chap. 2, p. 104; KR, no. 1, p. 341.
¹² IC, mans. 5, chap. 2, p. 109; KR, no. 12, p. 346.
¹³ *Life,* chap. 24, nos. 7-8, p. 161.
¹⁴ See *Testimony* 1, no. 13, pp. 313-14.
¹⁵ See *Testimony* 59, no. 7, p. 356; *Testimony* 1, no. 15, p. 314; *Life,* chap. 18, no. 14, p. 121; chap. 12, no. 6, p. 88; chap. 29, nos. 8-12, pp. 191-93.
¹⁶ Lest the reader be distracted by a multitude of footnotes in these few paragraphs, I shall include them all in one reference when we have completed the saint's descriptions.
¹⁷ Mt 7:20.
¹⁸ Gal 5:22; cf. also 1 Cor 13:4-7.
¹⁹ A, bk. 2, chaps. 12-15, p. 139-49; DN, bk. 1, no. 1, and chaps. 10, 11, pp. 297 and 316-20; chaps. 1, 5, 8-13, 17, pp. 329-71; SC, st. 39, no. 12, p. 561.
²⁰ Ps 84:2.
²¹ Ps 46:10.
²² Mt 6:7.
²³ Mk 6:46-48; Lk 6:12.
²⁴ Ps 34:5.
²⁵ Ps 34:8.
²⁶ 1 Pet 1:8.
²⁷ Phil 3:10.
²⁸ 2 Th 3:7; Phil 3:17.
²⁹ Ps 27:4.
³⁰ Ps 25:15.
³¹ Ps 16:8.
³² Ps 73:25.
³³ Ps 46:10.
³⁴ Ps 11:7.
³⁵ Ps 119:55.
³⁶ Ps 119:130.
³⁷ Lk 2:19, 51.
³⁸ Lk 10:39.
³⁹ Col 1:9.
⁴⁰ See Chapter 10 on the transforming union.

⁴¹ Even if one follows the interpretation of this book as dealing with an ideal human marriage, it becomes an ideal vehicle for celebrating the marriage of Yahweh with his people, the marriage of Christ with his Church.

⁴² Rom 5:5.
⁴³ Ps 73:25–26, 28.
⁴⁴ Ps 16:8, 9, 11.
⁴⁵ Phil 4:4, 7.
⁴⁶ Col 1:11.
⁴⁷ Ps 63:1–2.
⁴⁸ Ps 119:10, 20, 81, 131, 174.
⁴⁹ Is 26:9.
⁵⁰ 2 Pet 1:4.
⁵¹ Lk 2:19, 51.
⁵² Mk 1:35; 6:46–48; Lk 5:16; 6:12 et al.
⁵³ Acts 1:14.
⁵⁴ Acts 2:4; cf. 4:31.
⁵⁵ Ps 73:25; Phil 3:8.
⁵⁶ Ps 119:159.
⁵⁷ Ps 36:8–9.
⁵⁸ Eph 5:18; 3:19.

CHAPTER SIX

¹ Jn 10:10.
² Eph 3:19.
³ *Sacramentary of the Roman Rite*, October 15. Unfortunately the new English translation rewrites the original Latin text; only partially is it a translation. I have translated from the Latin.
⁴ *Way*, chap. 19, p. 144; KR, no. 14, p. 113.
⁵ Ibid.
⁶ Ibid.
⁷ *Life*, chap. 14, no. 7, p. 99; emphasis added.
⁸ *Way*, chap. 22, p. 158; KR, no. 3, pp. 122–23.
⁹ *Life*, chap. 20, no. 16, p. 134.
¹⁰ Lk 9:23.
¹¹ Mt 7:13–14.
¹² 1 Cor 2:9.
¹³ *Way*, chap. 25, p. 170; KR, no. 1, p. 131.
¹⁴ Vatican Council II, *Constitution on the Liturgy*, no. 10.
¹⁵ IC, mans. 4, chap. 1, p. 32; KR, no. 7, p. 286.
¹⁶ *Way*, chap. 31, p. 209; KR, no. 12, p. 159.
¹⁷ *Way*, chap. 26, p. 173; KR, no. 1, p. 133.
¹⁸ *Way*, chap. 26, p. 174; KR, no. 3, pp. 133–34.
¹⁹ *Way*, chap. 26, p. 177; KR, no. 9, p. 136.
²⁰ Jn 14:6.
²¹ *Way*, chap. 28, p. 183; KR, no. 1, p. 140.
²² *Way*, chap. 28, p. 185; KR, no. 5, pp. 141–42.
²³ *Way*, chap. 28, p. 184; KR, no. 3, p. 141.
²⁴ Ibid.

[25] *Way,* chap. 28, p. 187; KR, no. 8, p. 143.

[26] *Life,* chap. 11, no. 7, p. 81.

[27] IC, mans. 1, chap. 1, p. 28; KR, no. 1, p. 283.

[28] IC, mans. 1, chap. 1, pp. 33–34; KR, no. 1, p. 288.

[29] IC, mans. 1, chap. 1, p. 37; KR, no. 8, p. 291. See also *Way,* chap. 28, pp. 187–88; KR, no. 9, pp. 143–44.

[30] *Depositions,* p. 70.

[31] Rev 21:3, 9–11, 23.

[32] IC, mans. 5, chap. 2, pp. 106–7; KR, no. 7, p. 344.

[33] IC, mans. 6, chap. 4, p. 150; KR, no. 4, p. 380.

[34] IC, mans. 1, chap. 2, pp. 40–41; KR, nos. 12–14, pp. 293–94.

[35] Lk 8:14.

[36] IC, mans. 1, chap. 2, p. 41; KR, no. 14, p. 294.

[37] 1 Jn 2:15–17.

[38] Titus 2:12.

[39] IC, mans. 5, chap. 1, pp. 104–5; KR, no. 2, p. 342.

[40] *Way,* chap. 21, p. 151; KR, no. 3, p. 118.

[41] IC, mans. 4, chap. 1, p. 76; KR, no. 7, p. 319.

[42] Letter 57 to Don Antonio.

[43] The traits may be found in IC, mans. 2 — there is only one chapter in this mansion — pp. 47–51; KR, nos. 2–7, pp. 298–301.

[44] The following items come from the same mansions 2; pp. 49–53; KR, nos. 6–11, pp. 300–303.

[45] Mt 7:21.

[46] Phil 3:12–14.

[47] Jn 10:7.

[48] IC, mans. 3, chap. 1, p. 59; KR, no. 5, p. 306.

[49] Ibid.

[50] IC, mans. 3, chap. 2, p. 66; KR, no. 9, p. 313.

[51] IC, mans. 3, chap. 2, p. 67; KR, no. 9, p. 313.

[52] IC, mans. 4, chap. 1, p. 73; KR, no. 2, p. 317.

[53] *Way,* chap. 28, p. 185; KR, nos. 4–5, pp. 141–42.

[54] IC, mans. 4, chap. 3, p. 94; KR, no. 14, p. 334.

[55] IC, mans. 4, chap. 2, p. 81; KR, nos. 3–4, pp. 323–24.

[56] *Life,* chap. 12, no. 5, p. 87.

[57] IC, mans. 4, chap. 3, pp. 85–87; KR, nos. 1–3, pp. 327–29. See also *Testimony* 59, no. 3, p. 355.

[58] IC, mans. 4, chap. 3, p. 90; KR, no. 8, p. 331.

[59] *Testimony* 59, no. 4, pp. 355–56.

[60] *Way,* chap. 31, p. 207; KR, no. 10, p. 157.

[61] *Life,* chap. 14, no. 2, p. 97.

[62] Ibid., chap. 15, no. 1, p. 102.

[63] *Way,* chap. 31, p. 201; KR, no. 3, p. 154.

[64] *Way,* chap. 31, p. 203; KR, no. 4, pp. 154–55.

[65] *Way,* chap. 31, p. 203; KR, no. 5, p. 155.

[66] *Life,* chap. 14, no. 4, p. 98.

[67] Ibid., chap. 15, no. 1, p. 102; chap. 14, no. 6, p. 99; *Way,* chap. 31, p. 201; KR, no. 3, p. 154.

[68] *Way,* chap. 31, p. 202; KR, no. 3, p. 154. The desert Fathers regarded such tears as usual for all at certain stages of prayer and to be desired.

[69] *Life,* chap. 14, no. 5; chap. 15, no. 14, pp. 98, 108.

[70] IC, mans. 4, chap. 3, pp. 90–91; KR, no. 9, pp. 331–32.

[71] Rom 5:5.

[72] 1 Cor 13:4–7.

[73] Gal 5:22.

[74] Our answers to this practical question illustrate why much better formation in prayer is a condition for any extensive and deep renewal in the Church. Before all else revitalization requires an inner transformation and intimacy with the indwelling Trinity. Structural changes are secondary at best. The faithful need to be instructed not only in what contemplative and liturgical prayers are but also in how one goes about growing in them. If the clergy and religious are not themselves knowledgeable and prayerful, there is small chance that any notable revival will happen in and through our parishes.

[75] *Way,* chap. 31, p. 204; KR, no. 6, p. 155.

[76] *Life,* chap. 15, no. 4, p. 103.

[77] *Way,* chap. 31, pp. 205–6; KR, no. 9, pp. 156–57.

[78] IC, mans. 4, chap. 3, p. 87; KR, nos. 3–4, pp. 328–29.

[79] IC, mans. 4, chap. 3, p. 88; KR, no. 5, pp. 329–30.

[80] IC, mans. 4, chap. 3, p. 89; KR, no. 6, p. 330.

[81] *Life,* chap. 15, no. 9, p. 105.

[82] *Way,* chap. 31, p. 204; KR, no. 7, p. 156.

[83] *Life,* chap. 15, no. 6, p. 104.

[84] *Way,* chap. 31, p. 209; KR, no. 12, p. 159.

[85] *Way,* chap. 30, p. 198; KR, no. 7, p. 152.

[86] *Way,* chap. 30, p. 199; KR, no. 7, p. 152.

[87] *Way,* chap. 31, p. 209; KR, no. 12, p. 159.

[88] *Way,* chap. 31, pp. 205, 207; KR, nos. 8 and 10, pp. 156 and 158. See also *Life,* chap. 15, no. 6, p. 104.

[89] IC, mans. 4, chap. 3, p. 91; KR, no. 10, p. 332.

[90] *Way,* chap. 31, p. 208; KR, nos. 11–12, pp. 158–59.

[91] Lk 8:14.

[92] Col 3:1–2.

[93] Lk 14:33.

[94] *Way,* chap. 31, p. 204; KR, no. 7, p. 156.

[95] Mk 1:35; 6:46–48; Lk 5:16; 6:12.

[96] *Life,* chap. 16, no. 2–3, p. 109. See also chap. 17, no. 3, p. 113.

[97] IC, mans. 5, chap. 1, p. 99; KR, no. 5, p. 337.

[98] *Life,* chap. 16, nos. 1–4, pp. 109–10.

[99] Ibid., chap. 17, no. 2, p. 112; IC, mans. 5, chap. 1, p. 97; KR, no. 4, p. 336.

[100] IC, mans. 7, chap. 1, p. 209; KR, no. 5, pp. 429–30.

[101] *Testimony* 59, no. 6, p. 356.

[102] IC, mans. 5, chap. 2, p. 106; KR, no. 7, p. 343. For this same remark see *Testimony* 59, no. 6, p. 356.

[103] IC, mans. 5, chap. 1, pp. 101–2; KR, nos. 9–11, pp. 339–40.

[104] *Testimony* 59, no. 7, p. 356.

[105] *Life,* chap. 20, no. 1, p. 129. See also chap. 18, no. 7, p. 118–19.

[106] IC, mans. 5, chap. 4, p. 118–19; KR, no. 3, p. 354.

[107] 2 Cor 3:18.

[108] Heb 11:13–16.

[109] IC, mans. 5, chap. 2, pp. 106–9; KR, nos. 7–11, pp. 343–46.

[110] *Life,* chap. 20, no. 18, p. 134–35. See also *Testimony* 1, no. 2, p. 311; *Testimony* 59, no. 7, p. 356; IC, mans. 6, chap. 4, p. 155; KR, no. 13, p. 384.

[111] *Life,* chap. 18, no. 14, p. 121.

[112] IC, mans. 6, chap. 4, p. 150; KR, no. 4, p. 380.

[113] IC, mans. 6, chap. 5, p. 162; KR, no. 11, p. 390.

[114] *Life,* chap. 18, no. 12, p. 120; no. 13, pp. 120-21; IC, mans. 6, chap. 4, p. 155; KR, no. 13, p. 384.

[115] *Life,* chap. 39, no. 23, p. 275.

[116] Ibid., chap. 20, no. 19, p. 135.

[117] Ibid., no. 4, p. 130.

[118] *Book of Foundations,* chap. 6, p. 26; KR, no. 1, p. 124.

[119] IC, mans. 6, chap. 6, p. 163; KR, no. 1, p. 391.

[120] Letter 163; p. 409.

[121] *Testimony* 1, no. 2, p. 311.

[122] See *Foundations,* chap. 6, p. 29; KR, no. 1, p. 124.

[123] *Life,* chap. 39, no. 23, p. 275.

[124] Ibid., chap. 20, no. 11, p. 133.

[125] IC, mans. 6, chap. 6, p. 169; KR, no. 13, p. 396.

[126] IC, mans. 6, chap. 5, p. 157; KR, no. 1, p. 386.

[127] IC, mans. 6, chap. 5, pp. 160-61; KR, nos. 7-9, pp. 388-89.

[128] *Testimony* 59, nos. 13-15, pp. 358-59.

[129] Ibid., no. 16, p. 359.

[130] Ibid., nos. 17-18, p. 359.

[131] IC, mans. 6, chap. 11, pp. 197-200; KR, nos. 2-6, pp. 422-24.

[132] *Testimony* 1, no. 3, p. 311.

[133] IC, mans. 5, chap. 4, p. 120; KR, no. 5, p. 355.

[134] IC, mans. 6, chap. 4, p. 153; KR, no. 9, p. 382.

[135] IC, mans. 7, chap. 2, pp. 213-14; KR, no. 3, pp. 433-34.

[136] IC, mans. 7, chap. 2, pp. 213-14; KR, no. 4, p. 434.

[137] *Life,* chap. 20, no. 7, p. 131.

[138] Ibid., no. 21, p. 136. See also chap. 18, no. 11, p. 120.

[139] Ibid., nos. 22-23, pp. 136-37.

[140] IC, mans. 6, chap. 6, p. 164; KR, no. 3, p. 392.

[141] *Life,* chap. 20, nos. 28-29, pp. 138-39.

[142] *Depositions,* pp. 60-61.

[143] IC, mans. 7, chap. 1, pp. 209-10; KR, no. 6, p. 430.

[144] IC, mans. 7, chap. 2, p. 213; KR, no. 2, p. 433.

[145] IC, mans. 7, chap. 2, pp. 214-15; KR, no. 4, p. 434.

[146] 1 Cor 6:17.

[147] Gal 2:20.

[148] IC, mans. 7, chap. 2, p. 215; KR, no. 5, pp. 434-35.

[149] IC, mans. 7, chap. 4, p. 226; KR, no. 1, p. 444.

[150] IC, mans. 6, chap. 1, p. 127; KR, no. 2, p. 360; *Testimony* 65, no. 9, p. 365; *Testimony* 14, p. 327; IC, mans. 7, chap. 1; KR, no. 7, p. 430.

[151] IC, mans. 7, chap. 1, p. 211; KR, nos. 9-10, p. 431; IC, mans. 7, chap. 2, p. 214; KR, no. 3 p. 434.

[152] IC, mans. 4, chap. 1, p. 73; KR, no. 3, p. 317.

[153] IC, mans. 7, chap. 1, p. 211; KR, no. 10, p. 431.

[154] *Life,* chap. 17, no. 4, pp. 113-14.

[155] Lk 10:27; Mt 5:48; Jn 17:23.

[156] 2 Cor 3:18.

[157] IC, mans. 7, chaps. 3 and 4, pp. 219-26; KR, pp. 438-50.

[158] *Depositions,* p. 65.

[159] IC, mans. 7, chap. 4, pp. 229-30; KR, no. 10, p. 447.

160 IC, mans. 7, chap. 2, p. 218; KR, nos. 10-11, pp. 437-38.

161 IC, mans. 7, chap. 2, p. 217; KR, no. 9, p. 436. See also *Life,* chap. 31, no. 19, p. 210. It seems that 1 Jn 5:18 supports John of the Cross' stance: "God protects the one begotten by him, and so the evil one cannot touch him." Also, if one is "inseparably one" with God in spiritual marriage—as Teresa herself puts it—how, then, can one be separated and fall away?

162 Mt 7:13-14.

163 Lk 9:23.

164 Lk 10:16.

165 Heb 13:17.

166 Jn 13:34-35.

167 Mt 25:31-46; James 2:14-17.

168 Eph 4:32.

169 Rom 12:3-21; 1 Pet 5:14.

170 James 3.

171 Jn 17:23; 1 Cor 1:10f.; 1 Tim 1:3, 10; 4:6; 6:3-5; 2 Tim 4:1-5; Titus 1:9; 2:1.

172 Lk 14:7-11; Phil 2:3; Lk 18:9-14.

173 Lk 9:48.

174 Jn 13:14-15.

175 Lk 14:33.

176 Titus 2:12.

177 1 Cor 10:31.

178 Ps 1:2.

179 Jos 1:8.

180 Ps 27:4.

181 Ps 25:15.

182 Ps 34:5.

183 Ps 34:8; 1 Pet 2:3.

184 Ps 46:10.

185 Lk 2:19, 51.

186 Lk 10:39.

187 Ps 36:8-9.

188 Ps 84:2.

189 Dt 6:4-5; Lk 10:27.

190 Eph 1:4.

191 Eph 5:19-20.

192 Eph 3:19.

193 Phil 1:10-11.

194 2 Cor 3:18.

195 1 Cor 2:9.

CHAPTER SEVEN

1 Is 55:8-9.

2 See in our last chapter what St. Teresa says in the first three mansions.

3 IC, mans. 3, chap. 1, p. 51; KR, no. 8, p. 301.

4 *Way,* chap. 16, pp. 117-18; KR, nos. 3-4, pp. 94-95.

5 *Foundations,* chap. 4, p. 17; KR, no. 6, p. 115. The KR rendition does not make this point as clearly as does the Peers.

[6] *Way,* chap. 33, p. 218; KR, no. 1, p. 165.

[7] IC, mans. 5, chap. 1, p. 97; KR, no. 3, p. 336.

[8] Ibid.

[9] *Life,* chap. 39, no. 6, pp. 269–70.

[10] IC, mans. 3, chap. 2, pp. 65–66; KR, nos. 7–8, pp. 311–12.

[11] Mt 7:13–14.

[12] Mk 4:18–20.

[13] *Foundations,* chap. 2, p. 7; KR, no. 7, p. 105.

[14] *Way,* chap. 32, p. 213; KR, no. 7, p. 162.

[15] *Life,* chap. 22, no. 17, p. 151.

[16] Ibid., chap. 39, no. 9, p. 270.

[17] IC, mans. 3, chap. 2, p. 69; KR, no. 12, p. 315.

[18] IC, mans. 5, chap. 4, p. 121; KR, no. 8, p. 357.

[19] *Way,* chap. 7, p. 77; KR, no. 6, p. 68.

[20] IC, mans. 5, chap. 4, p. 122; KR, no. 9, p. 357.

[21] *Foundations,* chap. 12, p. 58; KR, nos. 1–2, pp. 156–57.

[22] *Way,* chap. 21, p. 150; KR, no. 2, pp. 117–18.

[23] Lk 8:14.

[24] Rev 3:2–3.

[25] Rev 3:14f.

[26] 2 Cor 1:19–20; 5:14.

[27] *Way,* chap. 4, p. 53; KR, no. 4, p. 54.

[28] *Way,* chap. 17, p. 123; KR, no. 1, p. 98.

[29] *Life,* chap. 22, no. 11, pp. 148–49. For another text in this same vein see ibid., chap. 38, no. 17, p. 262.

[30] IC, mans. 7, chap. 4, p. 229; KR, no. 8, pp. 446–47.

[31] IC, mans. 1, chap. 2, p. 38; KR, no. 9, p. 292. One may see also mans. 3, chap. 2, p. 66; mans. 4, chap. 2, pp. 83–85; mans. 5, chap. 1, p. 103; KR, no. 8, p. 312; nos. 9–10, pp. 326–27; no. 13, p. 341.

[32] *Way,* chap. 14, p. 109; KR, no. 2, p. 89.

[33] *Foundations,* chap. 2, p. 7; KR, no. 7, p. 105.

[34] *Testimony* 1, no. 16, p. 314.

[35] *Life,* chap. 10, no. 4, p. 75.

[36] Ibid., no. 6, p. 76.

[37] *Testimony* 3, no. 2, p. 320.

[38] 1 Pet 5:5.

[39] Mt 18:1–4.

[40] Lk 10:21.

[41] *Way,* chap. 17, p. 124; KR, no. 1, p. 99; IC, mans. 7, chap. 4, p. 229; KR, no. 8, p. 447.

[42] Maxim 49, p. 258.

[43] Lk 10:16; cf. also 1 Jn 4:1, 6.

[44] Acts 20:28.

[45] *Foundations,* chap. 5, p. 23; KR, nos. 10–11, pp. 120–21.

[46] *Foundations,* chap. 5, p. 24; KR, no. 12, p. 121.

[47] *Way,* chap. 36, pp. 238–41; KR, nos. 3–7, pp. 178–80.

[48] *Life,* chap. 31, no. 21, p. 211.

[49] Ibid., no. 22, p. 211.

[50] Ibid., chap. 31, no. 12, p. 207.

[51] *Way,* chap. 36, p. 237; KR, no. 2, p. 178.

[52] Ibid., chap. 15, p. 111; KR, no. 1, pp. 90–91.

[53] *Way,* chap. 15, p. 112; KR, no. 1, p. 91.

54 *Way,* chap. 15, pp. 111–15; KR, nos. 1–7, pp. 91–93.

55 *Foundations,* chap. 31, p. 203; KR, no. 46, p. 305.

56 *Soliloquy* 2, no. 1, p. 375.

57 IC, mans. 1, chap. 2, p. 41; KR, no. 14, p. 294.

58 Lk 8:14.

59 *Way,* chap. 4, p. 56; KR, no. 9, p. 56.

60 *Way,* chap. 28, p. 188; KR, no. 11, p. 144.

61 *Life,* chap. 8, no. 6, p. 68.

62 1 Th 4:11.

63 St. John of the Cross, *Counsels to a Religious on How to Reach Perfection,* no. 2, p. 662.

64 IC, mans. 3, chap. 2, p. 69; KR, no. 13, p. 315.

65 *Life,* chap. 23, no. 15, pp. 157–58.

66 Ps 25:15; Eph 5:18–20.

67 *Life,* chap. 13, no. 10, p. 92.

68 Ibid., chap. 7, no. 5, p. 58.

69 Mt 12:36.

70 *Constitutions,* no. 18; KR, vol. 3, p. 324.

71 *Constitutions,* no. 20, p. 324.

72 Lk 24:26.

73 Rom 6:3–5.

74 *Life,* chap. 19, no. 3, p. 123.

75 *Way,* chap. 32, p. 215; KR, no. 6, p. 162.

76 *Counsels to a Religious on How to Reach Perfection,* no. 3, p. 663.

77 *Way,* chap. 13, pp. 103–4; KR, nos. 1–2, pp. 85–86.

78 *Way,* chap. 32, p. 215; KR, no. 11, p. 164.

79 Col 1:11.

80 *Way,* chap. 32, p. 213; KR, no. 7, p. 162.

81 Lk 8:14.

82 *Foundations,* chap. 5, pp. 25–26; KR, nos. 15–16, p. 123.

83 *Foundations,* chap. 5, p. 26; KR, no. 17, p. 123.

84 *Way,* chap. 32, pp. 212–13; KR, no. 5, pp. 161–62.

85 *Life,* chap. 9, no. 9, p. 74.

86 *Testimony* 1, no. 9, p. 313.

87 *Way,* chap. 16, p. 122; KR, no. 12, p. 98.

88 IC, mans. 5, chap. 4, p. 121; KR, no. 8, p. 357.

89 IC, mans. 5, chap. 3, p. 117; KR, no. 12, p. 353.

90 *Way,* chap. 7, pp. 80–81; KR, nos. 10–11, pp. 70–71.

91 *Way,* chap. 4, p. 57; KR, no. 10, p. 56.

92 Mt 5:23–24.

93 Auclair, p. 185.

CHAPTER EIGHT

1 Mt 7:13–14.

2 2 Tim 4:1–4.

3 A, bk. 1, chap. 3, nos. 1–2, p. 76.

4 Ibid., no. 4, p. 77.

5 Ibid.

6 Ibid.

[7] Ibid., chap. 11, no. 2, p. 96.

[8] Ibid., no. 3, p. 96. For further examples of John's concept of attachment, see A, bk. 1, chap. 1, no. 1, p. 73; chap. 6, no. 1, p. 84; chap. 9, no. 3, p. 92; chap. 12, no. 6, p. 101; SC, sts. 20–21, nos. 7–8, pp. 490–91.

[9] 1 Cor 10:31.

[10] 2 Cor 3:18.

[11] 2 Pet 1:3–4.

[12] A, bk. 2, chap. 5, pp. 115–18.

[13] 1 Jn 3:3.

[14] Ps 40:12.

[15] Ps 38:10.

[16] Ps 6:7.

[17] 1 Cor 2:14.

[18] A, bk. 1, chap. 8, no. 4, p. 90.

[19] Mt 5:8.

[20] A, bk. 1, chap. 5, no. 3, p. 82; bk. 3, chap. 29, no. 2, p. 266.

[21] Ibid., bk. 1, chap. 5, no. 4, p. 82.

[22] Ibid., bk. 1, chap. 5, nos. 7–8, p. 84.

[23] Ibid., bk. 3, chap. 16, no. 2, p. 238.

[24] Ibid., chap. 19, no. 10, p. 246.

[25] Phil 4:4.

[26] A, bk. 1, chap. 9, no. 1, pp. 91–92.

[27] Ibid., chap. 4, no. 3, p. 78.

[28] Ibid., no. 4, p. 79.

[29] Ibid., chap. 6, no. 3, p. 85.

[30] Ibid., chap. 10, no. 1, p. 94.

[31] Ibid., nos. 1–4, pp. 94–95.

[32] 1 Kings 3:10.

[33] Mt 5:8.

[34] Col 3:1–2.

[35] 2 Pet 2:19.

[36] Mt 7:13–14.

[37] Lk 14:33.

[38] Mk 8:34–37.

[39] Jn 12:24.

[40] A, bk. 2, chap. 7, nos. 4–5, p. 122.

[41] Ibid.

[42] Ibid., no. 6, p. 123.

[43] Ibid., nos. 8–12, pp. 124–25.

[44] Ibid., bk. 1, chap. 13, no. 3, p. 102.

[45] Jn 4:34.

[46] A, bk. 1, chap. 13, no. 4, p. 102.

[47] Ibid., no. 6, pp. 102–3.

[48] Titus 2:12.

[49] A, bk. 1, chap. 13, nos. 6–7, pp. 102–3.

[50] Ibid., no. 11, pp. 103–4.

[51] 1 Cor 2:9.

[52] Mt 5:8.

[53] Titus 2:12.

[54] DN, bk. 2, chap. 19, no. 2, p. 374.

[55] Lk 16:10.

[56] A, bk. 3, chap. 20, no. 1, p. 246.

[57] Letter 20, p. 700.

[58] 1 Tim 6:7–8.

[59] A, bk. 3, chap. 2, no. 14, p. 218.

[60] Ibid., chap. 16, no. 5, p. 238.

[61] Ibid., chap. 21, no. 2, p. 249.

[62] SC, st. 3, nos. 1–2, p. 428.

[63] 1 Cor 10:31.

[64] A, bk. 3, chap. 24, no. 4, p. 255.

[65] Ibid., no. 5, p. 255.

[66] Ibid., no. 6, p. 256.

[67] Poem, *Glosa a lo Divino*, sts. 3, 5, 6, 9, pp. 735–37.

[68] A, bk. 3, chap. 20, no. 4, p. 248. See also Letters 14, 16 and 20; pp. 696, 697, 700.

[69] A, bk. 3, chap. 26, no. 6, p. 259.

[70] 2 Cor 4:17–18; A, bk. 3, chap. 26, no. 8, p. 260.

[71] See Letters 14, 16 and 20, pp. 696, 697, 700.

[72] Letter to Dom Bede Griffiths, O.S.B., Apr. 23, 1951, in *Letters of C. S. Lewis*, p. 228.

[73] St. Augustine, *The Lord's Sermon on the Mount*, bk. 2, chap. 17, no. 56. Translated by John J. Jepson, S.S., in *Ancient Christian Writers*, no. 5 (Westminster, Md.: Newman Press, 1956), p. 142.

[74] Ibid., chap. 13, no. 44, p. 132.

[75] Raymond of Capua, *The Life of Catherine of Siena*, trans. by Conleth Kearns, O.P. (Wilmington: Michael Glazier, Inc., 1980), p. 334.

[76] *Rule of 1221* in *St. Francis of Assisi: Omnibus of Sources* (Chicago: Franciscan Herald Press, 1972), p. 48.

[77] *Admonitions*, no. 16; ibid., pp. 83–84.

[78] St. Bonaventure, *Soul's Journey into God*, chaps. 2 and 3 in *The Classics of Western Spirituality* (New York: Paulist Press, 1978).

[79] Ibid., chap. 7.

[80] *Life of St. Francis*, in ibid., chap. 10, no. 1.

[81] St. Paul of the Cross, *Mystical Death*, trans. by Silvan Rouse, C.P. (private printing, n.d.), pp. 11–13.

[82] Francis Talbot, *Saint among Savages* (New York: Doubleday, Image edition), p. 74.

[83] *Life*, chap. 40, no. 3, p. 278.

[84] *Way*, chap. 12, p. 98; KR, no. 1, p. 82.

[85] Titus 2:12.

[86] 1 Cor 10:31.

[87] *Life*, chap. 40, no. 4, p. 278.

[88] *Way*, chap. 13, p. 107; KR, no. 6, p. 87.

[89] *Life*, chap. 11, no. 3, p. 79.

[90] Ibid., chap. 35, no. 12, p. 239.

[91] IC, mans. 3, chap. 2, p. 62; KR, no. 1, p. 309.

[92] *Way*, chap. 28, p. 189; KR, no. 12, p. 145.

[93] *Life*, chap. 18, no. 4, p. 118.

[94] Ibid., chap. 23, no. 5, p. 153.

[95] IC, mans. 5, chap. 4, p. 119; KR, no. 4, p. 355.

[96] *Way*, chap. 31, p. 208; KR, no. 11, p. 158.

[97] *Foundations*, chap. 4, p. 17; KR, no. 5, p. 115.

[98] *Way*, chap. 2, p. 41; KR, no. 5, p. 45.

[99] 2 Cor 6:10.

[100] *Way*, chap. 28, p. 187; KR, no. 8, p. 143.

[101] *Life,* chap. 21, no. 6, p. 141.

[102] 2 Cor 4:18.

[103] *Way,* chap. 10, pp. 88–89; KR, no. 2, p. 76.

[104] Ibid.

[105] *Way,* chap. 28, p. 186; KR, no. 6, p. 142.

[106] 1 Cor 10:31.

[107] *Way,* chap. 9, p. 86; KR, no. 3, p. 74.

[108] *Way,* chap. 9, pp. 84–87; KR, nos. 1–5, pp. 73–75.

[109] *Way,* chap. 4, p. 52; KR, no. 2, p. 53.

[110] *Life,* chap. 7, no. 17, pp. 62–63.

[111] 1 Jn 2:15–17.

[112] IC, mans. 2, chap. 1, p. 49; KR, no. 4, p. 299.

[113] *Way,* chap. 13, p. 108; KR, no. 7, p. 88.

[114] *Foundations,* chap. 12, p. 60; KR, no. 7, p. 159.

[115] *Life,* chap. 11, no. 12, p. 83.

[116] Mt 7:13–14.

[117] *Life,* chap. 13, no. 6, p. 90.

[118] *Testimony* 2, no. 3, p. 318.

[119] IC, mans. 3, chap. 2, p. 64; KR, no. 4, p. 310.

[120] Lk 8:14.

[121] Mt 19:23–24.

[122] *Way,* chap. 2, p. 42; KR, no. 6, p. 45.

[123] *Way,* chap. 34, pp. 224–25; KR, no. 2, p. 169. The KR translation of this is very different.

[124] Lk 14:33.

[125] Col 3:1–2.

[126] 1 Cor 10:31.

[127] 2 Cor 6:10.

[128] Eph 4:22–23.

[129] 2 Pet 2:19.

[130] 1 Jn 3:3.

[131] Rom 6:3–5.

[132] 1 Tim 6:7–8.

[133] Titus 2:12.

[134] Lk 9:23.

CHAPTER NINE

[1] Eph 4:22.

[2] DN, bk. 1, chap. 8, no. 1, p. 311.

[3] Ibid., bk. 2, chap. 3, no. 1, p. 333.

[4] It is significant that while a contemporary Carmelite places "trials coming from exterior agents" under the second night of spirit, he offers neither text nor reference from St. John of the Cross to support his inclusion. The reason, of course, is that exterior agents do not produce the dark contemplative fire that John tells us does cause the passive purifications. P. Marie-Eugene, *I Am a Daughter of the Church* (Westminster, Md.: Newman Press, 1979), pp. 327–34.

[5] Is 45:15.

[6] 1 Tim 6:16.

[7] I Cor 13:12.

[8] DN, bk. 2, chap. 16, no. 10, p. 366.

[9] Ibid., chap. 13, no. 10, p. 360.

[10] F, st. 1, nos. 19, 23, pp. 586, 588.

[11] DN, bk. 1, chap. 3, no. 3, p. 303. See also bk. 1, chap. 1, no. 5, p. 75; chap. 7, no. 5, p. 311; bk. 2, chap. 2, no. 4, p. 332.

[12] Ibid., bk. 1, chap. 11, no. 2, p. 319.

[13] Ibid., chap. 9, no. 1, p. 313.

[14] Ibid., chap. 10, nos. 1–2, pp. 316–17.

[15] Ibid., chap. 14, nos. 1–4, p. 328.

[16] Ibid., chap. 8, no. 4, pp. 312–13. See also F, st. 3, no. 32, p. 622.

[17] DN, bk. 1, chap. 11, no. 4, p. 320.

[18] Ibid., chap. 9, no. 2, p. 313.

[19] Ibid., no. 3, pp. 313–14.

[20] Ibid., no. 6, p. 315.

[21] Cited in Luigi Borriello, O.C.D., *Spiritual Doctrine of Blessed Elizabeth of the Trinity* (Staten Island, N.Y.: Alba House, 1986), p. 59.

[22] DN, bk. 1, chap. 9, no. 7, p. 315.

[23] Ibid.

[24] Ibid., no. 8, p. 315.

[25] Eph 4:22.

[26] Phil 2:3.

[27] DN, bk. 1, chap. 13 *in toto,* pp. 321–27.

[28] Ibid., no. 14, p. 327.

[29] A, Prologue, no. 6, p. 72.

[30] DN, bk. 1, chap. 10, no. 4, p. 317.

[31] Ibid.

[32] Ibid., no. 5, p. 318.

[33] Ibid., bk. 2, chap. 2, nos. 1–4, pp. 331–32; chap. 3, no. 3, p. 333.

[34] Ibid., chap. 1, no. 1, pp. 329–30.

[35] What follows is a summary of John's thought as expressed in DN, bk. 2, chaps. 3–8, pp. 332–45.

[36] Ps 54:16.

[37] DN, bk. 2, chap. 6, no. 6, pp. 339–40.

[38] Ibid., chap. 7, no. 3, p. 341.

[39] Ibid., chap. 6, no. 6, p. 339.

[40] Ibid., chap. 7, nos. 4–6, pp. 342–43.

[41] F, st. 1, no. 24, p. 589. See also st. 2, no. 25, p. 604, and DN, bk. 2, chap. 7, no. 3, p. 342.

[42] DN, bk. 2, chap. 11, nos. 1–2, p. 353.

[43] Ibid., chap. 7, no. 3, p. 341.

[44] Ibid., chap. 10, no. 6, p. 351.

[45] Letter 19 to Doña Juana de Pedraza, Oct. 12, 1589, p. 699.

[46] She said comparatively little, probably because she was well aware of the thoroughness of John's teaching.

[47] *Life,* chap. 30, no. 16, p. 201.

[48] Ibid.

[49] Ibid., no. 12, p. 199.

[50] Ibid.

[51] Ibid.

[52] Ibid., chap. 20, nos. 9–11, pp. 131–32.

[53] Ibid., nos. 11, 13, 15, pp. 133, 134.
[54] Ibid., no. 16, p. 134.
[55] Ibid., chap. 11, nos. 14–17, pp. 84–85.
[56] Ibid., chap. 37, no. 7, p. 255.
[57] Prov 3:12.
[58] Dt 8:2, 5.
[59] Wis 11:9–10.
[60] Wis 12:22.
[61] 2 Macc 6:12–14.
[62] Wis 6:14–16.
[63] 1 Cor 11:32.
[64] Malachi 3:1–3.
[65] Jn 15:2.
[66] 2 Cor 3:18.

CHAPTER TEN

[1] Eph 3:19–20.
[2] 2 Cor 5:17.
[3] 2 Cor 3:18.
[4] 2 Pet 1:4.
[5] A, bk. 2, chap. 5, no. 5, p. 117.
[6] Ibid., no. 6, p. 117.
[7] Ibid., no. 7, p. 117.
[8] Ibid., no. 8, p. 118.
[9] SC, sts. 14–15, no. 8, p. 465.
[10] Ibid., no. 12, p. 467.
[11] Ibid., no. 14, p. 468.
[12] F, st. 3, no. 3, p. 611.
[13] Ibid.
[14] Ibid., no. 9, p. 614.
[15] Ibid., no. 17, p. 617.
[16] Jn 17:3.
[17] 1 Cor 13:12.
[18] 1 Jn 3:2.
[19] Eph 1:17.
[20] Col 1:9; see also 3:16.
[21] 2 Cor 4:6.
[22] Ps 36:9.
[23] Rom 5:5.
[24] SC, st. 22, nos. 5–6, p. 498.
[25] Ibid., st. 34, no. 1, p. 540.
[26] Ibid., no. 3, p. 541.
[27] Ibid., st. 22, no. 7, p. 499.
[28] Ibid., st. 27, no. 1, p. 517.
[29] Ibid.
[30] Ibid., st. 27, no. 8, pp. 519–20.
[31] Lk 10:27.
[32] 1 Cor 6:17.

[33] 1 Jn 4:16.

[34] See F, st. 2, no. 34, p. 608.

[35] SC, st. 20–21, nos. 15–16, p. 494.

[36] Ibid., st. 39, no. 10, p. 560. See also st. 14–15, nos. 11–12, p. 472.

[37] F, st. 2, no. 36, p. 609.

[38] Ps 34:5, 8.

[39] 1 Pet 1:8.

[40] Jn 15:11.

[41] James 1:17.

[42] F, st. 1, no. 4, p. 580.

[43] SC, st. 35, no. 6, pp. 544–45.

[44] Ibid., st. 37, no. 6, p. 551.

[45] Rom 8:14.

[46] SC, st. 27, no. 7, p. 519.

[47] Ibid., st. 28, no. 5, p. 521. See also Maxim 50, p. 678.

[48] Gal 5:25.

[49] Phil 4:7.

[50] All these traits are found in SC, st. 20–21, no. 4, p. 489; st. 26, nos. 15, 18, pp. 515, 516; st. 39, no. 8, p. 560.

[51] Ps 25:15.

[52] 1 Pet 15–16.

[53] Mt 5:48.

[54] Titus 2:12.

[55] 1 Cor 10:31.

[56] 1 Jn 3:3.

[57] SC, st. 14–15, no. 4, pp. 463–64.

[58] Ibid., sts. 20–21, nos. 1–2, pp. 487–88.

[59] Eph 3:16.

[60] 1 Cor 1:30.

[61] Phil 3:10.

[62] SC, st. 24, no. 3, p. 502.

[63] Ibid., no. 4, p. 503.

[64] Ibid., st. 22, no. 3, p. 497.

[65] Ibid.

[66] Ibid., st. 26, nos. 11, 13, 14, 17, pp. 512–15. See also DN, bk. 2, chap. 24, no. 2, p. 387.

[67] SC, st. 14–15, no. 9, p. 465. See also no. 4, p. 464; no. 13, p. 467; and F, st. 1, no. 3, p. 580.

[68] Phil 4:4–7.

[69] Jn 20:19–21.

[70] Mt 11:28–30.

[71] SC, sts. 14–15, nos. 2, 30, pp. 463, 474.

[72] Ibid., st. 26, no. 16, p. 515.

[73] Ibid.

[74] F, st. 4, no. 5, pp. 644–45.

[75] SC, st. 14–15, no. 25, p. 472.

[76] Ibid., st. 39, no. 11, p. 561.

[77] Ibid., st. 26, no. 13, pp. 513–14.

[78] Ibid.

[79] Ibid., sts. 14–15, no. 5, p. 464. See also st. 40, no. 2, p. 564; and F, st. 2, no. 34, p. 608.

[80] SC, sts. 20–21, nos. 11–12, pp. 492–93.

[81] Ibid., no. 13, p. 493.

[82] Eph 3:19.

[83] A, bk. 2, chap. 5, no. 2, p. 115.

[84] SC, sts. 20–21, no. 14, p. 493; st. 24, no. 6, p. 503.

[85] Ibid., st. 24, no. 5, p. 503.

[86] We may leave aside here the unusual case of some who are "very habitually" moved by God in what they do, and who therefore are not usually operating in a merely human manner. Almost no one, says John, is always so divinely moved. A, bk. 3, chap. 2, no. 16, p. 219.

[87] F, st. 1, no. 3, p. 580.

[88] Ibid., no. 16, p. 585.

[89] Ibid., st. 4, nos. 14–15, pp. 648–49.

[90] Ibid. See also SC, st. 24, no. 6, p. 504; st. 26, no. 11, p. 513.

[91] *Complete Works,* introduction to *Living Flame of Love,* p. 572.

[92] Ps 25:15.

[93] Eph 5:18–20; Phil 4:4.

[94] SC, st. 22, nos. 3–4, p. 497.

[95] Ibid., st. 24, no. 5, p. 503.

[96] Ibid., st. 39, no. 3, p. 558.

[97] Ibid., no. 5, pp. 558–59; Jn 17:20–24.

[98] SC, st. 39, no. 4, p. 558.

[99] Ibid., no. 7, p. 559.

[100] Ezek 16:13–14.

[101] Is 62:2–5.

[102] 2 Cor 11:2.

[103] 2 Cor 3:18.

[104] 2 Cor 5:21.

[105] Gal 2:20.

[106] Gal 6:15.

[107] 2 Pet 1:4.

[108] SC, sts. 14–15, no. 2, p. 463.

[109] F, Prologue, no. 3, p. 578.

[110] SC, sts. 20–21, no. 15, p. 494.

[111] 1 Cor 2:9.

[112] 1 Pet 1:8.

[113] F, st. 1, no. 31, p. 592.

[114] Jn 3:30.

[115] SC, st. 39, no. 8, p. 560.

[116] F, st. 1, no. 30, pp. 591–92.

[117] Bruno, pp. 354, 356.

[118] Jn 6:54–56.

[119] Jn 10:10.

[120] 1 Cor 7:32–35.

[121] Lk 18:29–30.

[122] Canon 663.

CHAPTER ELEVEN

[1] *Way,* chap. 17, pp. 123–27; KR, nos. 1–7, pp. 98–101.

[2] *Way,* chap. 19, p. 145; emphasis added; KR, no. 15, p. 113.

[3] *Way,* chap. 20, p. 145; emphasis added; KR, no. 1, p. 114.

[4] *Life,* chap. 11, nos. 1–2, p. 79; emphasis added.

[5] IC, mans. 6, chap. 4, p. 154; emphasis added; KR, no. 12, p. 383.

[6] IC, mans. 7, chap. 1, p. 207; KR, no. 2, p. 428.

[7] *Way,* chap. 12, p. 99; emphasis added; KR, no. 3, p. 82. See also chap. 25, p. 172; KR, no. 4, p. 132; *Life,* chap. 13, no. 6, p. 90; chap. 15, no. 2, p. 102; chap. 22, no. 13, p. 150; chap. 22, no. 15, p. 150; chap. 8, no. 9, p. 69.

[8] *Way,* chap. 32, p. 216; KR, no. 12, p. 164.

[9] *Life,* chap. 27, no. 12, p. 178.

[10] IC, mans. 7, chap. 2, pp. 216, 217; KR, nos. 7, 8, pp. 435, 436. See also *Way,* chap. 16, p. 121; chap. 28, p. 189; chap. 29, p. 191; KR, no. 9, pp. 96–97; no. 12, p. 145; nos. 2–3, p. 146; *Life,* chap. 8, no. 5, p. 67; chap. 11, no. 8, p. 81; chap. 16, no. 6, p. 111; chap. 19, no. 7, p. 125; chap. 21, no. 9, p. 142; IC, mans. 4, chap. 2, pp. 84–85; mans. 5, chap. 1, p. 97; KR, no. 10, pp. 326–27; nos. 2–3, pp. 335–36.

[11] IC, mans. 1, chap. 1, p. 31; KR, no. 4, p. 285.

[12] *Life,* chap. 15, no. 7, p. 105.

[13] Ibid., chap. 6, no. 4, p. 110; emphasis added.

[14] *Way,* chap. 42, p. 277; KR omits this sentence.

[15] IC, mans. 4, chap. 2, p. 83; KR, no. 8, p. 325.

[16] IC, mans. 5, chap. 4, p. 121; KR, no. 6, p. 356.

[17] *Life,* chap. 18, no. 8, p. 119.

[18] IC, mans. 7, chap. 3, p. 224; KR, no. 13, pp. 442–43.

[19] IC, mans. 3, chap. 1, p. 59; emphasis added; KR, no. 5, p. 306.

[20] Introduction to *Interior Castle,* p. 14.

[21] Ibid., p. 24.

[22] *Life,* chap. 14, no. 5, p. 98.

[23] Ibid., chap. 15, no. 14, p. 108.

[24] IC, mans. 4, chap. 3, pp. 90–91; KR, no. 9, pp. 331–32.

[25] IC, mans. 5, chap. 2, pp. 106–9; KR, nos. 7–11, pp. 344–46.

[26] DN, bk. 1, chap. 9, no. 9, p. 316.

[27] F, st. 1, no. 15, pp. 584–85.

[28] *Sayings of Light and Love,* no. 51, p. 671.

[29] A, Prologue, nos. 9 and 7, pp. 72–73.

[30] SC, st. 17, no. 9, p. 481.

[31] DN, bk. 1, chap. 3, no. 3, p. 303.

[32] Ibid., chaps. 12 and 13, pp. 321–27. Still more striking is the necessity of the second purification of the spirit. Our faults have deep roots that the first infused prayer cannot eradicate, and so we need the advanced fire of the second mystical night, a night in which the deepest roots of our defects are literally burned away. This night slowly brings one to an "impassioned and intense love . . . a spiritual inflaming." Ibid., bk. 2, chap. 11, nos. 1–3, p. 353.

[33] See also ibid., chap. 2, no. 4, p. 332; F, st. 1, no. 22, p. 588; no. 25, p. 589.

[34] Lk 8:14.

[35] A, bk. 2, chap. 11, no. 9, p. 135.

[36] DN, bk. 1, chap. 1, no. 1, p. 298.

[37] SC, st. 39, no. 7, p. 559.

[38] Ibid., st. 40, no. 7, p. 565.

[39] DN, bk. 2, chap. 19, no. 4, p. 375.

[40] A, Prologue, no. 3, p. 70.

[41] F, st. 2, no. 27, p. 604; emphasis added.

[42] Sermon I, *On the Song of Songs* (Kalamazoo, Mich.: Cistercian Publications, 1981), vol. I, p. 6.

[43] Sermon 83, in ibid., vol. 4, pp. 180–81.

[44] Ps 4:7.

[45] Ps 5:11.

[46] Pss 9:3; 16:9.

[47] Ps 73:25–28.

[48] Ps 84:2.

[49] Ps 63:1.

[50] Ps 119 passim.

[51] Lk 18:1; Eph 5:18–20; 1 Th 5:17.

[52] 1 Pet 2:3.

[53] Jn 16:22; Phil 4:4, 7; 1 Pet 1:8.

[54] Eph 3:20.

[55] *The Sacramentary* (New York: Catholic Book Publishing Co., 1985): fourth Sunday of Lent, opening prayer; Holy Thursday, evening Mass of the Lord's Supper, opening prayer; twenty-second Sunday in Ordinary Time, opening prayer; Christmas Midnight Mass, Solemn Blessing; Saturday, third week of Lent, opening prayer; Friday before Epiphany, opening prayer; Wednesday after Epiphany, opening prayer; Friday, third week of Lent, prayer after Communion; Monday, first week of Lent, opening prayer; second Sunday in Ordinary Time, prayer after Communion; sixteenth Sunday in Ordinary Time, opening prayer.

[56] Monday at morning prayer.

[57] Lent, Monday of the second week.

[58] *The Sacramentary*, Friday, second week of Advent, opening prayer.

[59] St. II.

[60] *The Sacramentary*, Pentecost, Solemn Blessing.

[61] *Dei Verbum*, no. 8.

[62] *Sacrosanctum Concilium*, no. 10.

[63] *Lumen gentium*, no. 41.

[64] *Ad gentes*, no. 18.

[65] Canon 663, no. 1; translated by present author.

[66] Canon 673.

CHAPTER TWELVE

[1] *Life,* chap. 4, no. 7, p. 44.

[2] Ibid., chap. 24, nos. 2, 3, pp. 159 and 160.

[3] Jn 16:7.

[4] *Life,* chap. 22, no. 1, p. 144.

[5] Ibid., chap. 22, no. 2, p. 145.

[6] IC, mans. 6, chap. 7, p. 172; KR, no. 6, pp. 399–400.

[7] IC, mans. 6, chap. 7, p. 175; KR, nos. 10–11, pp. 401–2.

[8] Jn 14:6.

[9] *Life,* chap. 22, no. 9, p. 147.

[10] Ibid., no. 4, p. 145.

[11] IC, mans. 6, chap. 7, p. 174; KR, no. 9, p. 401.

[12] IC, mans. 6, chap. 7, p. 176; KR, no. 12, p. 403.

[13] *Life,* chap. 22, nos. 1–10, pp. 144–48.

[14] See IC, mans. 6, chap. 7, p. 177; KR, nos. 13–14, pp. 403–4.

[15] *Life,* chap. 22, no. 8, p. 147.

[16] IC, mans. 2, chap. 1, p. 50; KR, no. 7, pp. 300–301.

[17] IC, mans. 3, chap. 1, p. 60; KR, no. 7, p. 307.

[18] IC, mans. 3, chap. 2, p. 67; KR, no. 10, p. 313.

[19] 1 Cor 13:1–3.

[20] *Life,* chap. 11, nos. 14–15, p. 84.

[21] IC, mans. 6, chap. 1, pp. 131–32; KR, nos. 8, 11, pp. 363, 364–65.

[22] In *Life,* chap. 4, nos. 8–9, pp. 44–45, she writes of experiencing a "great dryness" for eighteen years, whereas in *Testimony* 58, no. 2, p. 349, she speaks of it being twenty-two years.

[23] Ibid., chap. 11, no. 10, p. 82.

[24] Letter 158, p. 394.

[25] IC, mans. 6, chap. 1, p. 126; KR, no. 1, p. 359.

[26] *Life,* chap. 11, no. 10, p. 83.

[27] Ibid., no. 13, p. 83; also chap. 22, no. 10, p. 148.

[28] Ibid., chap. 5, nos. 8–9, pp. 44–45.

[29] Letter 59, pp. 147–48.

[30] *Way,* chap. 19, p. 135; KR, no. 2, p. 107.

[31] *Life,* chap. 8, no. 7, p. 68.

[32] *Testimony* 39, no. 1, p. 341.

[33] *Testimony* 13, no. 1, p. 326.

[34] *Life,* chap. 9, no. 5, p. 71.

[35] IC, mans. 4, chap. 1, pp. 77–78, KR, no. 10, pp. 320–21.

[36] *Life,* chap. 11, no. 17, p. 85.

[37] Letter 381 to Don Sancho Davila, p. 869.

[38] IC, mans. 4, chap. 1, p. 77; KR, no. 9, p. 320.

[39] *Way,* chap. 31, p. 207; KR, no. 10, pp. 157–58.

[40] Acts 4:31.

[41] Letter 234 to P. Gonzalo Davila, S.J., p. 579.

[42] *Foundations,* chap. 5, pp. 20–21; KR, nos. 3–5, pp. 117–18.

[43] *Foundations,* chap. 5, pp. 20–21; KR, no. 6, p. 119.

[44] *Foundations,* chap. 5, p. 25; KR, no. 15, p. 122.

[45] Ibid.

[46] *Foundations,* chap. 5, p. 26; KR, no. 17, p. 123.

[47] Ibid.

[48] *Way,* chap. 23, p. 163; KR, no. 3, p. 126.

[49] Letter 215, p. 530.

[50] IC, mans. 1, chap. 2, p. 41; KR, no. 14, p. 294.

[51] *Life,* chap. 31, nos. 9–10, p. 206.

[52] IC, mans. 6, chap. 1, p. 133; KR, no. 14, p. 366.

[53] See St. Paul, Eph 4:18, 22–24, 29, 31, and many other texts.

[54] *Life,* chap. 35, nos. 13–14, pp. 239–40.

[55] Ibid., chap. 31, no. 18, p. 210.

[56] *Way,* chap. 42, p. 276; KR, no. 2, p. 202.

[57] Phil 2:12.

[58] *Way,* chap. 39, pp. 258–59; KR, nos. 4–5, pp. 190–91.

[59] *Foundations,* chap. 3, p. 12; KR, no. 11, p. 110.

[60] *Way,* chap. 38, p. 252; KR, nos. 6–7, pp. 186–87.

[61] *Soliloquy* 8, no. 3, p. 380.

[62] *Way*, chap. 15, p. 113; KR omits this passage found in Peers.

[63] *Life*, chap. 8, no. 2, p. 66.

[64] Ibid., chap. 7, no. 13, p. 61.

[65] Lk 8:14.

[66] Letter 223 to Maria de San José, pp. 544–45.

[67] Letter 163, p. 411.

[68] *Life*, chap. 27, no. 12, p. 178.

[69] *Testimony* 59, no. 8, p. 357.

[70] *Life*, chap. 25, no. 11, p. 165.

[71] IC, mans. 4, chap. 1, pp. 73–75; KR, nos. 4–6, pp. 317–19.

[72] *Life*, chap. 10, no. 3, p. 75.

[73] *Foundations*, chap. 6, p. 27; KR, nos. 2–3, pp. 124–25.

[74] *Testimony* 15, p. 328.

CHAPTER THIRTEEN

[1] A, Prologue, no. 6, p. 72.

[2] *Foundations*, chap. 31, p. 185; KR, no. 4, pp. 287–88.

[3] *Foundations*, chap. 3, pp. 12–13; KR, no. 11, p. 110.

[4] *Life*, chap. 33, no. 15, p. 226.

[5] *Testimony* 58, nos. 2–5, pp. 349–50.

[6] *Foundations*, chap. 6, pp. 31–32; KR, no. 14, pp. 129–30.

[7] *Way*, chap. 38, p. 255. The KR edition does not include this section of chapter 38.

[8] *Foundations*, chap. 4, p. 16; KR, no. 2, p. 114.

[9] *Foundations*, chap. 4, p. 18; KR, no. 7, p. 115.

[10] *Way*, chap. 18, p. 133; KR, no. 9, p. 105.

[11] *Way*, chap. 38, p. 252; KR, no. 6, p. 187.

[12] *Way*, chap. 6, p. 68; KR, no. 2, p. 62.

[13] IC, mans. 1, chap. 2, p. 42; KR, no. 15, p. 295. See Gal. 1:6–9.

[14] *Foundations*, chap. 8, p. 43; KR, no. 7, p. 142.

[15] Mt 7:20.

[16] IC, mans. 4, chap. 2, p. 83; KR, no. 8, p. 325.

[17] *Way*, chap. 41, p. 268; KR, no. 1, pp. 196–97.

[18] See *Way*, chap. 40, p. 262; KR, no. 3, pp. 192–93.

[19] *Foundations*, chap. 5, pp. 24–25; KR, no. 13, pp. 121–22.

[20] Lk 10:16.

[21] See *Foundations*, chap. 4, p. 16; KR, no. 2, pp. 113–14; *Way*, chap. 39, p. 258; KR, no. 3, p. 190; chap. 18, pp. 131–32; KR, nos. 7–8, pp. 104–5. In this last passage Teresa declares that she is absolutely certain that no one will ever succeed in the contemplative life, or indeed in the active life, for that matter, who does not obey.

[22] *Way*, chap. 42, p. 278; KR, no. 4, p. 203.

[23] *Way*, chap. 38, p. 249; KR, no. 1, p. 185. See also *Way*, chap. 36, p. 242; KR, no. 8, pp. 180–81.

[24] *Foundations*, chap. 8, p. 44; KR, no. 9, p. 143.

[25] Lk 10:21.

[26] James 4:6.

[27] *Foundations,* chap. 6, pp. 34, 35; KR, nos. 21–22, pp. 132, 133. St. Teresa was not thinking of the abnormal situation where the superior dissents from the Church's teaching or discipline. Disagreement then may be mandatory.

[28] *Way,* chap. 40, p. 263; KR, no. 4, p. 193.

[29] *Way,* chap. 42, p. 276; KR, no. 3, p. 202.

[30] OT, no. 9.

[31] Letter 122, pp. 316–17.

[32] *Testimony* 58, no. 14, pp. 352–53.

[33] *Foundations,* chap. 22, p. 114; KR, no. 20, p. 215.

[34] IC, mans. 6, chap. 9, pp. 188–89; KR, no. 11, p. 414. See also mans. 4, chap. 3, pp. 90–92; KR, no. 9, pp. 331–32; and no. 10, p. 333.

[35] *Way,* chap. 21, p. 155; KR, no. 10, p. 121.

[36] *Way,* chap. 36, p. 244; KR, no. 13, p. 182.

CHAPTER FOURTEEN

[1] Jn 14:26.

[2] Jn 16:13.

[3] Jn 14:15–17.

[4] Lk 10:16.

[5] Mt 2:13.

[6] Acts 10:3f.

[7] Acts 10:9f.

[8] Acts 27:23.

[9] *Foundations,* chap. 4, p. 18; KR, no. 8, p. 116.

[10] *Foundations,* chap. 8, p. 43; KR, no. 6, p. 141.

[11] 1 Jn 4:1f.

[12] 1 Jn 4:2–6. The whole biblical teaching on authentic discernment may be found in my *Authenticity: A Biblical Theology of Discernment* (Denville, N.J.: Dimension Books, Inc., 1977). Subjective experiences are evaluated by and subjected to objective office: "He who hears you, hears me", and not otherwise.

[13] A, bk. 2, chap. 22, no. 19, p. 187.

[14] *Foundations,* chap. 8, pp. 40–41; KR, no. 1, p. 139.

[15] *Life,* chap. 29, no. 4, p. 190. See also *Testimony* 65, p. 364. In this last reference she makes the explicit point that it is the authentic vision that is to be valued, not a mere illusion.

[16] IC, mans. 6, chap. 3, p. 140; KR, no. 4, p. 37.

[17] IC, mans. 7, chap. 1, p. 209; KR, no. 6, p. 430.

[18] See IC, mans. 6, chap. 3, p. 139; KR, no. 1, pp. 370–71.

[19] Emotionally disturbed people who report "voices" should not be easily believed. What St. Teresa advised about them we will consider further on.

[20] *Testimony* 51, p. 345.

[21] *Testimony* 56, p. 348. The Latin words mean "and (my) spirit rejoices".

[22] *Life,* chap. 34, no. 18, p. 234.

[23] Ibid., chap. 25, no. 3, pp. 162–63.

[24] Ibid., p. 163. The saint returns to this idea a number of times: *Life,* chap. 25, no. 18, pp. 168–69; chap. 26, no. 2, p. 171; chap. 38, no. 16, p. 261; *Foundations,* chap. 28, p. 154; KR, no. 16, p. 256; IC, mans. 7, chap. 2, p. 216; KR, no. 7, p. 435.

[25] Jn 18:4–6.

[26] *Life,* chap. 25, no. 6, p. 164.

[27] André Frossard, *Be Not Afraid* (New York: St. Martin's Press, 1984), p. 49. Frossard adds to this passage that "this is a strong argument, so it seems to me, for the truth of Christian teaching. I am sorry that it has been so infrequently employed."

[28] *Testimony* 58, no. 11, p. 352.

[29] *Testimony* 1, no. 26, p. 317.

[30] *Life,* chap. 25, no. 6, p. 164.

[31] Unless we indicate otherwise all references here come from IC, mans. 6, chap. 3, pp. 140–47; KR, nos. 4–18, pp. 351–52.

[32] *Testimony* 58, no. 10, pp. 351–52.

[33] Raymond of Capua, *Life of St. Catherine of Siena,* p. 337.

[34] *Life,* chap. 39, no. 21, p. 274.

[35] IC, mans. 6, chap. 3, pp. 139–40; KR, no. 2, p. 371.

[36] IC, mans. 6, chap. 3, p. 144.

[37] Ibid.

[38] IC, mans. 6, chap. 3, p. 140; KR, no. 4, p. 372.

[39] IC, mans. 6, chap. 3, p. 140; KR, no. 3, p. 371.

[40] IC, mans. 6, chap. 3, p. 144; KR, no. 11, p. 375; *Life,* chap. 25, no. 14, p. 167.

[41] *Testimony* 58, no. 11, p. 352.

[42] See Wis 13:1–9; Rom 1:19–20.

[43] A, bk. 2, chap. 17, no. 4, p. 156.

[44] Ibid., chap. 11, nos. 5–9, pp. 133–35.

[45] Ibid., chap. 17, nos. 7–9, pp. 158–59.

[46] Ibid., chap. 23, no. 3, p. 188.

[47] Mt 4:1–10.

[48] A, bk. 2, chaps. 23–24, pp. 187–92.

[49] Ibid., chap. 25, no. 1, p. 193.

[50] Ibid., chap. 26, nos. 3–5, pp. 194–95.

[51] Ibid., nos. 7–9.

[52] Ibid., nos. 11–18, pp. 196–99.

[53] Ibid., chap. 32, pp. 211–13.

[54] Ibid., chap. 29, no. 1, p. 203.

[55] Ibid., p. 204.

[56] Ibid., nos. 4–5, pp. 204–5.

[57] Ibid., no. 7, p. 205.

[58] Ibid., no. 11, pp. 206–7. See also Gal 5:22.

[59] A, bk. 2, chap. 30, no. 2, p. 208.

[60] Dan 9:22; A, bk. 2, chap. 30, nos. 1–3, p. 208.

[61] Like Teresa, John allows no room for illuminism. History, past and present, bears out the soundness of his judgment.

[62] A, bk. 2, chap. 30, no. 6, p. 209.

[63] Ibid., chap. 31, no. 1, p. 210.

[64] Ibid., no. 2, p. 210.

[65] The reader will observe that these guidelines extend beyond mere locutions. This will enable us to avoid repetition when we consider visions, for the norms are similar, often identical.

[66] A, bk. 2, chap. 17, no. 7, p. 158.

[67] Ibid., nos. 8–9, p. 159.

[68] Ibid., no. 9, p. 159.

69 Ibid., chap. 18, no. 2, p. 160.

70 Ibid., nos. 8–9, pp. 162–163.

71 Ibid., chap. 19, nos. 1–14, pp. 163–69; citation in no. 7, p. 165.

72 Ibid., no. 12, p. 168.

73 Ibid., no. 10, p. 167.

74 1 Jn 4:1–6.

75 The saint assumes, of course, that he is a priest faithful to the Gospel and therefore to the mind of the Church.

76 A, bk. 2, chap. 22, no. 7, p. 181.

77 Ibid., no. 8, p. 182.

78 Ibid., no. 9, p. 182.

79 Ibid., no. 12, p. 184; Gal 2:2.

80 A, bk. 2, chap. 22, no. 13, p. 184.

81 Ibid., no. 16, p. 185.

82 Ibid., no. 16, p. 186.

83 Ibid., nos. 17–18, p. 186.

84 Ibid., no. 19, pp. 186–87.

85 See, among other texts, Jn 14:26; and 2 Cor 4:6 on the one hand, and Mt 28:18–20 and Acts 20:28 on the other.

86 1 Jn 4:1–6.

87 For these types see *Life*, chap. 28, no. 4, p. 182.

88 Ibid. See also *Testimony* 58, no. 15, p. 353, and no. 2, p. 349; *Life*, chap. 30, no. 4, p. 196.

89 IC, mans. 6, chap. 9, pp. 185–87; KR, nos. 3–8, pp. 411–13.

90 Ibid.

91 *Life*, chap. 28, no. 7, p. 184.

92 IC, mans. 6, chap. 9, p. 186; KR, no. 5, p. 412.

93 KR, no. 7, pp. 412–13.

94 Ibid., no. 4, p. 412.

95 *Life*, chap. 28, no. 9, p. 185.

96 IC, mans. 6, chap. 9, p. 188; KR, no. 10, p. 413.

97 IC, mans. 6, chap. 9, p. 188; KR, no. 10, p. 414.

98 *Life*, chap. 28, no. 4, pp. 182–83.

99 Ibid., no. 11, p. 186.

100 Ibid., no. 13, pp. 186–87.

101 Ibid., chap. 29, no. 1, p. 189.

102 Ibid., no. 2, p. 189.

103 Ibid., no. 3, p. 189.

104 Ibid., chap. 27, no. 3, p. 174.

105 Ibid., p. 175.

106 IC, mans. 6, chap. 8, p. 179; KR, no. 3, p. 406.

107 *Life*, chap. 28, no. 9, p. 185. On occasion St. Teresa mentions or describes other visions, e.g., of Mary, *Testimony* 43, p. 343; of "my Eliseus", *Testimony* 39, pp. 341–42. Other visions include Ss. Dominic and Peter Alcantara.

108 IC, mans. 6, chap. 8, pp. 181–82; KR, no. 4, p. 407.

109 IC, mans. 6, chap. 9, p. 192; KR, no. 16, p. 417.

110 IC, mans. 6, chap. 8, p. 184; KR, no. 10, p. 410.

111 See *Life*, chap. 39, no. 24, p. 276.

112 Letter 382 to Jerome Gratian, p. 873.

113 *Foundations*, chap. 8, p. 43; KR, no. 6, p. 141.

114 *Life*, chap. 38, no. 1, p. 257.

[115] *Foundations,* chap. 8, p. 42; KR, no. 5, p. 141.
[116] IC, mans. 6, chap. 9, p. 190; KR, no. 14, p. 416.
[117] IC, mans. 6, chap. 9, p. 191; KR, no. 15, p. 416.
[118] Ibid.

CHAPTER FIFTEEN

[1] Letter 24 to Don Alonso Ramirez, p. 83.
[2] Letter 228 to Jerome Gratian, p. 559.
[3] Letter 280 to Maria Bautista, p. 665.
[4] *Testimony* 53, no. 1, p. 347.
[5] Jn 16:32.
[6] Mt 26:36–46.
[7] Letter 52 to Don Alvaro de Mendoza, p. 132.
[8] *Life,* chap. 24, no. 6, p. 161.
[9] Mt 12:36.
[10] Eph 5:19–20.
[11] See *Testimony* 1, no. 14, p. 314; *Foundations,* chap. 30, p. 180; KR, no. 6, p. 282.
[12] Letter 210 to Don Teutonio de Braganza, p. 513.
[13] *Life,* chap. 28, no. 17, p. 188.
[14] Ibid., chap. 16, no. 6, p. 111.
[15] Ibid., no. 7, p. 111.
[16] Letter 121 to P. Ambrosio Mariano, p. 308.
[17] Letter 93 to Maria Bautista, pp. 232–33; see also Letter 107, p. 272.
[18] Letter 64 to Maria Bautista, p. 157; see also Letter 162 to Maria de San José, p. 405.
[19] *Depositions,* Ana of Jesus, p. 93.
[20] Letter 367 to Gratian, p. 842.
[21] Letter 95 to Brianda de San José, p. 241.
[22] *Life,* chap. 37, no. 5, p. 253.
[23] Letter 95, pp. 241, 244.
[24] Letter 308, p. 724.
[25] Letter 307, p. 718.
[26] Letter 233, p. 573. For further examples see Letter 53 to her niece, pp. 136–37; and Letter 72 to Inez of Jesus, p. 175.
[27] Letter 161, p. 401.
[28] Letter 216, p. 533.
[29] Letter 278 to Gratian, p. 661.
[30] Letter 111, p. 275.
[31] Letter 366 to Gratian, p. 839.
[32] Auclair, p. 148.
[33] Letter 30 to Doña Maria de Mendoza, p. 93.
[34] Letter 365 to Ana de San Augustin, p. 837.
[35] Letter 159 to Maria de San José, p. 397. Peers remarks that the last clause could be translated "you are one after my own heart—*es a mi gusto*".
[36] Letter 146, p. 368.
[37] Letter 305, p. 716.

[38] Letter 356, p. 827. For other examples in this same vein see Letter 354 to Doña Ana Enriquez, p. 823; Letter 220 to Don Luis de Cepeda, p. 540; Letter 223 to Maria de San José, p. 544; Letter 128 to Gratian, p. 331; Letter 366 to Gratian, p. 841.

[39] Letter 231, p. 568.

[40] Letter 239, p. 587.

[41] Letter 350 to Gratian, p. 811.

[42] 1 Jn 4:20.

[43] Sir 17:7-8.

[44] Is 43:4; Rom 1:7; 1 Cor 3:16-17; 2 Cor 3:18.

[45] Peers edition, p. 227; KR, no. 28, p. 328.

[46] Our response to this difficulty may be brief at this point, for we shall consider the question more fully below. We may note at the moment that in view of her own behavior it seems that she is ruling out effeminacy and cliques and what we might call foolish handholding.

[47] Letter 135, pp. 345-46.

[48] *Life*, chap. 7, nos. 20-22, pp. 64-65.

[49] Ibid. See also *Testimony* 12, no. 4, p. 326.

[50] *Life*, chap. 40, no. 19, p. 282.

[51] Sermon 9 *On the Song of Songs*, no. 4; Kilian Walsh, O.C.S.O., trans., *The Works of Bernard of Clairvaux*, (Kalamazoo, Mich.: Cistercian Publications, 1981), vol. 2, p. 56.

[52] *Way*, chap. 7, p. 76; KR, no. 4, p. 67.

[53] *Life*, chap. 38, no. 16, p. 261.

[54] Letter 382, pp. 874-75.

[55] *Visitation*, p. 244; KR, no. 19, p. 343.

[56] Rom 12:16.

[57] *Way*, chap. 4, pp. 54-56; KR, nos. 5-9, pp. 54-56.

[58] Ps 25:15.

[59] *Life*, chap. 37, no. 4, pp. 252-53.

[60] Ibid., chap. 34, no. 7, p. 230.

[61] See Mt 18:15; Col 3:16.

[62] Letter 232, pp. 571-72.

[63] Letter 309, p. 727.

[64] Letter 302, pp. 704, 707.

[65] Letter 162 to Maria de San José, p. 404.

[66] Prov 9:7-9.

[67] *Way*, chap. 6, p. 69; KR, no. 4, p. 63.

[68] *Way*, chap. 6, p. 70; KR, no. 6, p. 63-64.

[69] *Way*, chap. 6, p. 69; KR, no. 5, p. 63.

[70] *Way*, chap. 7, p. 73; KR, no. 1, p. 65.

[71] *Way*, chap. 7, p. 75; KR, no. 4, p. 67.

[72] *Way*, chap. 6, p. 71; KR, no. 8, p. 64.

[73] *Way*, chap. 6, p. 68; KR, no. 3, p. 62.

[74] "Letter to a Lady", Nov. 8, 1952, in W. H. Lewis, ed., *Letters of C. S. Lewis*, p. 248.

[75] *Way*, chap. 6, p. 70; KR, no. 5, p. 63.

[76] *Way*, chap. 6, pp. 70-71; KR, no. 7, p. 64.

[77] Letter 107, p. 271.

[78] Letter 118 to Maria de San José, p. 301.

[79] Letter 385 to Maria de San José, p. 878.

[80] *Way*, chap. 7, pp. 78-79; KR, no. 8, p. 70.

[81] *Way,* chap. 7, p. 76; KR, no. 5, p. 67.

[82] *Way,* chap. 20, p. 148; KR, no. 4, p. 115.

[83] *Depositions,* Maria de San José, pp. 82–84.

[84] Letter 165 to Maria Bautista, p. 417.

[85] Letter 284 to Maria de San José, p. 674.

[86] 1 Pet 1:22.

CHAPTER SIXTEEN

[1] Jn 20:21.

[2] A, bk. 2, chap. 22, no. 11, p. 183.

[3] Ibid., no. 16, pp. 185–86.

[4] Ibid., no. 7, p. 181.

[5] Acts 9:6.

[6] Jn 16:13.

[7] Lk 10:16; Acts 20:28.

[8] *Sayings of Light and Love,* no. 7, p. 667.

[9] Ibid., no. 11; see also nos. 8, 9, 13, p. 667.

[10] F, st. 3, no. 30, p. 621. The common and severe problem of finding a suitable spiritual director oftentimes admits of no easy solution. What is one to do? We can only answer: pray earnestly and search diligently for a competent, prayer-centered guide. Better to be without a director, however, than to settle for one who lacks the essential qualities. When a proper guide is not available, recourse to carefully selected, spiritually sound reading may supply the need—to some extent, at least.

[11] Ibid.

[12] Ibid.

[13] Ibid., no. 31, p. 621.

[14] Ibid., nos. 43, 46, pp. 626, 627.

[15] Ibid., no. 54, p. 631.

[16] Ibid., no. 56, p. 632.

[17] A, Prologue, no. 4, p. 71.

[18] F, st. 3, nos. 57–61, pp. 632–33.

[19] Letter 10 to Doña Juana de Pedraza, p. 691.

[20] F, st. 3, no. 62, pp. 633–34; Lk 11:52.

[21] Ibid.

[22] Letter 7; p. 688.

[23] Prov 28:26.

[24] *Testimony* 3, no. 13, p. 322.

[25] IC, mans. 6, chap. 9, p. 189; KR, no. 12, pp. 414–15.

[26] *Way,* chap. 39, p. 259; KR, nos. 4–5, p. 190.

[27] *Life,* chap. 23, no. 5, p. 153.

[28] *Testimony* 3, no. 13, p. 322.

[29] *Foundations,* chap. 19, p. 92; KR, no. 1, p. 192.

[30] IC, mans. 5, chap. 1, pp. 100–101; KR, nos. 7–8, pp. 338–39.

[31] *Life,* chap. 5, no. 3, pp. 46–47.

[32] Way, chap. 5, p. 63; KR, no. 3, p. 59.

[33] *Life,* chap. 34, no. 11, pp. 231–32.

[34] Letter 74 to Rubeo, pp. 178–80.

[35] IC, mans. 4, chap. 1, pp. 72–73; KR, no. 2, p. 316. See also IC, mans. 6, chap. 8, p. 183; KR, no. 8, p. 409.

[36] *Life,* chap. 13, no. 19, p. 95.

[37] Ibid., no. 17, p. 95.

[38] Ibid., no. 18, p. 95.

[39] *Testimony* 58, no. 13, p. 352.

[40] IC, mans. 3, chap. 2, p. 68; KR, no. 12, p. 314.

[41] Letter 65, p. 161.

[42] *Life,* chap. 23, no. 13, pp. 156–57.

[43] Ibid., chap. 34, no. 11, p. 231.

[44] Ibid., chap. 23, nos. 8–10, pp. 154–55.

[45] IC, mans. 6, chap. 3, pp. 139–40; KR, no. 2, p. 371.

[46] *Foundations,* chap. 30, p. 178; KR, no. 1, p. 280.

[47] See one case among many, *Foundations,* chap. 17, p. 80; KR, no. 3, p. 180.

[48] *Life,* chap. 26, nos. 3 and 5, pp. 171, 172.

CHAPTER SEVENTEEN

[1] Ps 62:1,5 and 37:4.

[2] *Sacramentary,* twentieth week of ordinary time.

[3] James 1:17.

[4] Letter 12, p. 694.

[5] Col 1:24.

[6] 2 Cor 4:17; cf. 11:23–28.

[7] See *Sayings of Light and Love,* no. 4, p. 667.

[8] Ibid., no. 61, p. 672.

[9] DN, bk. 2, chap. 19, no. 4, p. 375.

[10] Mt 11:30.

[11] *Sayings of Light and Love,* no. 54, p. 671.

[12] Rom 8:37–39.

[13] SC, st. 36, no. 12, p. 549.

[14] Rom 8:28.

[15] See DN, bk. 2, chap. 10, no. 8, p. 352.

[16] F, st. 2, no. 30, p. 606.

[17] *Sayings of Light and Love,* no. 14, p. 667.

[18] Maxims, no. 15, p. 675.

[19] Ibid., no. 13, p. 682.

[20] Jn 20:21.

[21] *L'Osservatore Romano,* Nov. 29, 1982, p. 3.

[22] Ibid., p. 5.

[23] Ps 84:2.

[24] Jn 16:32.

[25] Romance *On Creation,* Romance 4, st. 2; Romance 3, st. 5; p. 727.

[26] Mt 22:1–14.

INDEX

Abandonment by God: impression of, in night of spirit, 169, 171–172

Absorption in God, 68–69, 94; not permanent in this life, 106; as experienced by St. Teresa, 23. *See also* Union, prayer of

Action and contemplation: harmony between, in a well ordered life, 226; mutual benefit, 226; primacy of contemplation in, 228; in St. Luke, 226; tensions between, in actual life, 226; teresian principles concerning, 226–228; unnecessary cares to be given up, 228

Activity: in advanced contemplation, 217–220; in infused prayer, cessation of, 91; and receptivity, 91

Affection: marks of, 287–288; St. Teresa's love, 275–277; and Scripture, 287; warm love in holy friendship, 275–277

Angelic transfixion, 24–25, 46–47. *See also* Wounds of love

Angelism: in advanced prayer, 217–220; incompatible with ecclesial character of spiritual direction, 293

Apostolic power, derives from contemplative depth, 308–309

Apparitions, 236; testing of, 241

Appetites: habitual, 135; meaning of in St. John of the Cross, 132. *See also* Attachments

Aridity in prayer: advice concerning, 221, 222–223; benefits from, 221–222; found within sixth mansions, 99; long duration of, 221; according to St. Teresa, 220–223. *See also* Dark nights; Distractions; Dryness of prayer; Emptiness in prayer; "Empty" prayer

Asceticism, 156–157; joy in, 138–139, 148, 154; in New Testament, 6–7; in prayer life, 113. *See also* Attachments; Dark nights; Delight in God; Detachment; Joy; Purification; Virtues

Atmosphere for contemplative prayer: immersion in the divine milieu, 122. *See also* Solitude

Attachment: definitions of, 136; destructive of joy, 138–139; diminishes the person, 139; drain on psychic energy, 140, 152; harms flowing from, 136–140, 152; impediments to prayer, 80, 93, 138; like a cataract in the mind's eye, 137; multiplies desires, 139–140; prevents transformation into divine beauty, 139; and slavery to things, 140, 156; source of related faults, 137; weakens practice of virtue, 140, 145; what it is, 133–136; what it is not, 133. *See also* Detachment

Augustine, St., 43, 164; commentaries on Scripture, 11; on detachment, 149; and imageless prayer, 217; and love for Church as sign of authenticity, 241; on nature of peace, 187; on proper love for creation, 147

Authenticity of locutions and visions, signs of, 252–254, 258. *See also* Spiritual direction; Spiritual directors

Balthasar, Hans Urs von: on detachment, 7; on theology needing influence of saints, 311

Baptism of the Spirit, 43

Beatific vision, 54, 103; longings for, results of touches, 46, 47; a transfiguration, 104. *See also* Trinitarian life

Beginners: advice for, in first mansions, 81–83; advice for, in second mansions, 84; attracted to both God and world in second mansions, 83; worldliness of, in first mansions, 81

Bernard, St.: commentaries on Scripture, 11; on fewness of good spiritual-directors, 299; and indwelling presence, 58; on need for spiritual friendship, 281; on the universal call to contemplation, 212

Betrothal, spiritual. *See* Spiritual betrothal

Biblical exegesis: and patristic commentaries, 11; on questions of deep prayer, 11–12

Bonaventure, St.: on seeking God, true delight, in all delights, 149; on selfless use of creation, 149

Books: use of in advanced prayer, 222–223

Buddhist contemplation, 57; vastly different from Christic, 7. *See also* Zen contemplation